The Sovereign Debt Investor

The Sovereign Debt Investor

An Essential Guide to Returns, Defaults, and Government Bond Investing

LUPIN RAHMAN

WILEY

Published by John Wiley & Sons, Inc., Hoboken, New Jersey.

For general information on our other products and services or for technical support, please contact our Customer Care Department within the United States at (800) 762-2974, outside the United States at (317) 572-3993 or fax (317) 572-4002.

Wiley also publishes its books in a variety of electronic formats. Some content that appears in print may not be available in electronic formats. For more information about Wiley products, visit our web site at www.wiley.com.

Library of Congress Cataloging-in-Publication Data has been applied for:

Print ISBN: 9781394250530
ePDF ISBN: 9781394250547
epub ISBN: 9781394250554

Cover Design: Wiley
Cover Image: © monsitj/Getty Images
Printed and bound by CPI Group (UK) Ltd, Croydon, CR0 4YY

C9781394250530_230626

For Mum and Dad

Contents

Introduction

SOVEREIGN DEBT is the cornerstone of modern financial markets and is one of the most actively traded and widely held asset classes. Sovereign debt instruments enable governments to raise finance, corporates to hedge interest and credit risk, and institutional investors like pension funds and sovereign wealth funds to invest in safe and liquid assets. They are the building blocks of numerous investment strategies, and as such, can not be ignored.

From sacred loans by the Temple of Apollo in Delos to the trillion-dollar bond markets of today, sovereign finance has evolved through centuries of financial experimentation. What began as religious and royal borrowing evolved into medieval monarch loans, the rise of syndicated lending, and the advent of publicly traded government securities in the 20th century. Modern sovereign bond markets took shape after the 1980s Latin American debt crisis and the Brady Plan, which transformed commercial bank loans into tradable bonds. This laid the foundation for the emerging market asset class and the analytical frameworks that now define sovereign credit risk.

Crises in the 1990s and early 2000s—involving Mexico, Russia, Argentina, and Brazil—exposed new risks of investing in emerging markets. From 2008 onward, the global financial crisis and Eurozone turmoil showed that advanced economies were not immune, with stress in Italy and Spain and defaults in Greece and Cyprus. These shocks forced a reassessment of sovereign default risks, even in high-income monetary unions. Rising debt burdens in the US and China added fresh concerns about the resilience of the world's largest economies and the stability of global sovereign debt markets.

Today, we are entering a new dimension in sovereign debt investing characterized by high debt levels, mounting fiscal stress, and a fragmented geopolitical landscape. At the same time, technological advances and rising international capital flows have made the sovereign bond market more global, interconnected, and complex than ever before.

These developments are reshaping the parameters for sovereign debt investing. Traditional distinctions between developed and emerging market debt are being blurred. Investors can no longer rely solely on credit ratings or income classifications to define risk and investment strategies. As sovereign credit risks rise in advanced economies, they are beginning to exhibit characteristics previously associated with emerging markets. Meanwhile, as emerging economies develop, their markets are increasingly exhibiting characteristics typically observed in developed markets.

Investors must therefore adopt a more nuanced and comprehensive investment framework that draws on a complete set of tools to navigate sovereign bond markets effectively. These include traditional analysis such as macroeconomics, credit assessments, and bond math, as well as detailed legal reviews of bond contracts, restructuring precedents, and geopolitical risk evaluations.

This book offers a structured guide to sovereign debt investing from the perspective of institutional portfolio managers. Unlike standard approaches that treat developed and emerging markets separately, it takes a comprehensive approach to assessing sovereign risk. It integrates traditional financial and macroeconomic analysis commonly applied to advanced economy financial markets, with detailed assessments of legal enforceability, policy credibility, and credit and default risk typically used in emerging market investing.

Emphasis is placed on foundational elements such as the various types of bonds and derivative instruments, sovereign credit analysis, legal documentation, and portfolio construction, along with guidelines for navigating sovereign defaults and debt restructurings. Real-world examples drawn from market experience bring theoretical concepts to life. Contemporary developments, including sustainable investing and digital innovations, are also addressed to ensure relevance and applicability in today's investment climate.

Whether you are an asset allocator, portfolio manager, fixed-income strategist, or policymaker, this book aims to be a practical and authoritative resource for navigating the complexities and opportunities of sovereign debt markets. It has been a privilege to share this knowledge. I trust this book will serve as a valuable resource for your continued professional growth and success in the dynamic field of sovereign bond investing.

PART ONE

The Investible Universe

CHAPTER ONE

The Strategic Case for Sovereign Debt

THE SOVEREIGN debt market is one of the oldest and most important parts of the global financial markets. Its significance comes from the unique role that government bonds play in these markets and investment portfolios. This includes being the risk-free rate, providing liquidity, generating income, and aiding in risk diversification.

As a benchmark, government bonds provide a reference point for the interest rates at which corporations and other entities in the economy can borrow. King among them, US government bonds or *US Treasuries* are considered global *risk-free* instruments because of their creditworthiness, liquidity, and capital preservation features.

In investment portfolios, sovereign bonds provide income generation, risk management, and diversification benefits, making them a staple for balanced and resilient investment strategies. The relatively longer tenor of government debt ensures its suitability for portfolios with long-term liabilities, such as pension funds or insurance accounts. The liquidity of government bonds offers investors an attractive option for managing cash and liquidity needs, making them an essential part of fixed-income portfolios.

Despite these benefits, lending to a government carries unique risks that distinguish it from corporate lending. Sovereigns possess significant power as debtors, which limits the enforceability of contracts. The absence of a formal bankruptcy framework complicates sovereign restructurings, necessitating coordination and consent among creditors.

Investing in sovereign debt, therefore, presents distinct challenges that investors do not face in other markets. This necessitates a thoughtful approach that brings together traditional fixed-income strategies with analysis of macroeconomic, political, geopolitical, and legal factors to navigate the complex world of sovereign bond investments successfully.

This chapter presents the strategic rationale for sovereign debt, highlighting the unique role of government bonds in global investment portfolios. It evaluates the risk and return profiles of sovereign investments and explores the distinct aspects of lending to governments. The analysis concludes with an overview of the key stakeholders who hold sovereign bonds within the financial ecosystem.

1.1 ROLE IN GLOBAL FINANCIAL MARKETS

Government securities represent the largest component of global financial markets. As of the end of 2023, total government bonds and derivatives totaled $687 trillion out of a worldwide market of $1088 trillion.[1] This compares favorably with global equities at $175 trillion, currency markets at $118 trillion, and international credit at $81 trillion. Government debt can be further divided into sovereign bonds with $70 trillion outstanding and derivatives linked to sovereign debt totaling $617 trillion outstanding (see Figure 1.1).

The size of the sovereign debt market means it cannot be ignored. Even so, the case for government debt goes beyond a matter of scale. United States government bonds, known as US Treasuries, are the cornerstone of modern financial markets. They are regarded as the global *risk-free* rate due to their credit quality, liquidity, and capital preservation characteristics.[2] These attributes stem from US Treasuries being backed by the full faith and credit of the United States economy, resulting in an extremely low probability of default. As the risk-free rate, US Treasuries serve as a barometer for the performance of global financial markets, including various components of the equity and fixed-income markets.

The US yield curve also establishes a benchmark for sovereigns, corporations, agencies, and other issuers. This determines the interest rates at which different actors can borrow from commercial creditors. The difference, or *spread*, between the rate at which an

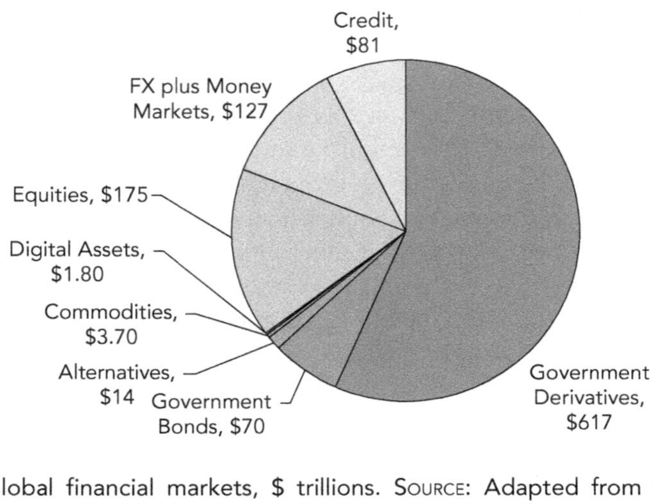

FIGURE 1.1 Global financial markets, $ trillions. Source: Adapted from London Stock Exchange Group (2024).

issuer can borrow and the rate on US Treasuries offers a measure of the relative riskiness of the investment. In other words, it represents the compensation the issuer must pay the lender to hold its debt instead of the risk-free rate.

For example, if 10-year US Treasuries have a yield of 4.5% and a US corporate 10-year bond has a yield of 5%, investors would need to be compensated with an additional 50 basis points above US Treasuries to hold that corporate's debt. The comparison also applies across sovereigns. If Brazilian 10-year government bonds yield 6.5%, investors would need an additional 200 basis points above US Treasuries to hold Brazilian government debt.

In each country's financial markets, government bonds are benchmark instruments in relation to other parts of their domestic capital structure. For instance, German Bunds in the euro area, Gilts in the United Kingdom, and NTNs (National Treasury Notes) in Brazil hold this benchmark status in their respective markets.

Other issuers in these markets, such as corporates or municipalities, are priced off these benchmark instruments.[3] For instance, in Brazil, a Brazilian corporation issuing a 10-year bond may need to offer a yield of 7.5%, which is a spread of 100 basis points over 10-year Brazilian government bonds yielding 6.5%.

These risk-free and benchmark attributes of sovereign debt mean that even if an investor chooses to invest in another asset class—whether it's a different fixed-income sector, equities, commodities, or currencies—sovereign debt markets cannot be overlooked.

1.2 ROLE IN INVESTMENT PORTFOLIOS

Sovereign bonds provide additional advantages in investment portfolios. These include income generation, capital preservation and appreciation, diversification benefits, risk management and hedging, and liquidity provision. These qualities mean they play a unique role in the strategic allocation of large institutional investment funds.

Sovereign bonds offer a consistent income stream through regular interest (coupon) payments, making them appealing for income-focused investors. Their relatively superior credit quality compared to other segments of the capital structure ensures that the principal value of a government bond is returned to the investor in full at maturity. This characteristic of capital preservation can be particularly attractive to risk-averse investors.[4]

Sovereign bonds also offer the potential for capital appreciation, allowing investors to benefit from increases in bond prices on the secondary market to generate additional returns (also called total return investment strategies).

Regulators often recommend government bonds for capital adequacy or provisioning purposes in the banking sector. This underlying demand reinforces their stability, with returns on high-quality sovereign bonds typically displaying lower volatility and a low correlation with equities and other fixed-income securities (see Figure 1.2). Incorporating sovereign debt into an investment strategy can, therefore, help reduce a portfolio's overall volatility, diversifying the sources of risk.

Asset Class	UST	Global DM Govt	US IG	Euro IG	US HY	EM Sovereign Credit	EM Corporate Credit	EM Local Bonds Unhedged	EM Local Bonds Hedged	EM FX board	EM Equities	US Equities	Commo-dities
UST	1.00	0.70	0.58	0.34	−0.15	0.26	0.19	0.12	0.43	0.01	−0.16	−0.21	−0.26
Global DM Govt		1.00	0.64	0.80	0.19	0.49	0.40	0.52	0.54	0.50	0.26	0.13	0.12
US IG			1.00	0.54	0.58	0.78	0.76	0.56	0.66	0.42	0.41	0.36	0.15
Euro IG				1.00	0.41	0.59	0.54	0.70	0.52	0.75	0.53	0.41	0.36
US HY					1.00	0.78	0.79	0.64	0.46	0.60	0.71	0.73	0.50
EM Sovereign Credit						1.00	0.92	0.80	0.74	0.68	0.66	0.58	0.39
EM Corporate Credit							1.00	0.72	0.65	0.65	0.66	0.57	0.42
EM Local Bonds Unhedged								1.00	0.79	0.93	0.79	0.59	0.46
EM Local Bonds Hedged									1.00	0.59	0.50	0.35	0.07
EM FX board										1.00	0.82	0.61	0.56
EM Equities											1.00	0.74	0.58
US Equities												1.00	0.47
Commodities													1.00

FIGURE 1.2 Cross asset correlations. SOURCE: Adapted from J.P. Morgan Local Markets Guide (2022).

The diversification of risk from sovereign bonds can be enhanced by including bonds from various countries. The sovereign debt asset class ranges from highly rated, risk-free securities like US Treasuries and German Bunds to emerging markets such as Mexico and Hungary, and frontier markets like Zambia and Sri Lanka. The variety of countries enables investors to diversify returns across various economies, political systems, and geopolitical themes.

As the more liquid component of fixed-income markets, government debt is usually traded without high transaction costs and can be executed in larger volumes compared to other issuers. This feature makes government bonds, particularly those issued by major economies, an integral part of liquidity management in portfolios. Cash in corporate credit and equity funds is generally invested in short-dated sovereign instruments. This is another attribute of sovereign debt that makes it relevant for portfolios beyond sovereign debt fixed-income mandates.

High-quality sovereign bonds can act as a macroeconomic hedge against riskier parts of an investment portfolio, offering a *flight-to-quality* asset during times of economic uncertainty or market volatility. They can serve as a hedge against economic slowdowns when government bonds increase in value due to expectations of lower inflation and a decline in interest rates. This contrasts with investing in growth-oriented sectors of the economy, which may experience a slowdown or decline in profit depending on the business cycle.

Some government bonds can protect against inflation. For instance, US Treasury Inflation-Protected Securities (TIPS) adjust their principal value by inflation, helping investors maintain their purchasing power over time. Government bonds can also serve as a vehicle for tax-efficient investing, such as through bonds with non-taxable coupons, like US municipal bonds.

1.3 ROLE IN STRATEGIC ASSET ALLOCATION

Sovereign bonds play a crucial role in strategic asset allocation. Bonds from stable economies with risk-free status are essential components of insurance accounts, sovereign wealth funds, and foreign exchange reserve portfolios, where capital preservation is paramount. As a long-duration asset, they can also be utilized to match long-term liabilities, such as pension or social security payments. These institutional asset owners are significant components of the global financial ecosystem and global savings.

Sovereign bonds are a cornerstone of traditional 60:40 investment strategies, which allocate 60% of the portfolio to equities and 40% to fixed income, thereby striking a balance between growth and stability. Developed market government bonds provide capital preservation, liquidity, and hedging benefits due to their low default risk and low or negative correlation with equities during crises. Their reliable income streams and strong performance during risk-off periods have historically helped offset equity volatility, particularly during recessions or market shocks.

Meanwhile, emerging market bonds enhance yield and diversification, increasing returns but also bringing currency and credit risks. These considerations have led strategic allocators to gradually increase the share of emerging markets (EM) while maintaining the overall sovereign allocation in 60:40 strategies relatively stable.

1.4 IMPACT BEYOND FINANCIAL RETURNS

The benefits and use of sovereign debt go beyond financial outcomes. Sovereign instruments can help investors achieve non-financial objectives, such as sustainable investment goals. Those seeking to promote decarbonization or other environmental and social goals may consider financing governments that are leaders in these practices. Governments, in turn, are motivated to pursue these objectives if their financing is tied to them.

Sovereign debt can also be used to demonstrate national support by its diaspora. For instance, Lebanon has a long history of sovereign bond purchases by Lebanese living abroad. Government bonds can also serve as a means to channel worker remittance flows, as seen in Sri Lanka, which issues debt securities for this purpose.

So far, we have discussed the vital role that sovereign debt plays in investment portfolios and global financial markets. Yet, the strategic case for understanding sovereign debt markets goes even beyond this. As voters and taxpayers, citizens should be aware of government budgets and borrowing, since they will ultimately be repaying this debt. Pensioners and insurance policyholders who rely on payouts during tough times should understand how their funds are being invested and what returns they can expect. Sovereign debt investing is therefore not an obscure, theoretical topic reserved only for investment banks and financial experts but a topic that has far-reaching practical implications for all citizens.

1.5 RISK AND RETURN CHARACTERISTICS

A key question for any investor is whether investing in sovereigns is worthwhile and what the risk and return characteristics of sovereign bonds are.

Historically, sovereign bonds have offered investors competitive *real* returns with relatively low volatility (see Figure 1.3). In recent decades, annual *nominal* returns have

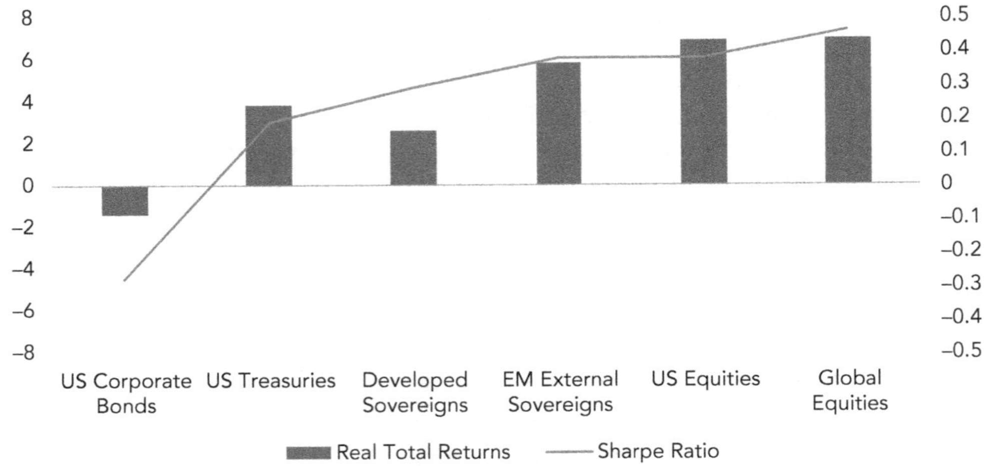

FIGURE 1.3 Risk and return over 200 years. SOURCE: Adapted from Meyer, J., Reinhart, C.M., and Trebesch, C. (2022).

averaged around 5% for developed market sovereigns and about 6–8% for emerging markets. This is in comparison to returns of approximately 6% for US investment-grade corporate bonds and about 11% from US equity markets.[5]

Sovereign bond returns appear even more favorable when considering the volatility of returns. Risk-adjusted returns, as measured by the Sharpe ratio, average between 0.2 and 0.3 for developed market sovereigns. This compares to a Sharpe ratio of 0.4 for emerging market sovereigns and the US equities.[6]

Another factor influencing returns is the risk of default and the potential recovery following a default. Sovereign defaults are quite rare, with an annual default rate between 2% and 4%.[7] In the event of a sovereign default, the median creditor loss has been between 40% and 50%, which is 15–20% lower than for corporate debt. Importantly, sovereign debt investors generally recoup their pre-crisis investments within five years after default, and in 25% of cases recover their losses in less than one year.[8]

The correlation between the returns on government bonds and other riskier financial assets highlights the benefits of sovereign debt in portfolios. Looking back to Figure 1.2, we see that since 2003, the correlation of developed market government bonds with US equities has generally been negative, suggesting that sovereign bonds serve as a risk-off asset hedge. This flight-to-quality phenomenon has the potential to increase the stability and resiliency of portfolio returns and may reduce the potential losses that investors could face in crisis periods.[9]

PRO TIP: *Understand the roles sovereign securities play in your portfolio (e.g., income generation, diversification, liquidity, liability matching) and examine its historical performance in this function.*

1.6 DISTINCT ASPECTS OF LENDING TO GOVERNMENTS

Lending to a government involves unique risks for an investor that go beyond the traditional factors associated with fixed-income investing. Sovereigns are uniquely powerful as debtors. Sovereign immunity in international law provides substantial protection for government assets held abroad. Consequently, the attachment of assets held abroad is extremely difficult, even for aggressive investors with judgments on debt issued under international law.

Sovereigns also exercise considerable autonomy within their geographic and legislative boundaries, which can make the domestic enforcement of contracts and the attachment of assets hard. They retain the authority to shape the legal and regulatory framework governing their domestic debt capital markets and to change the rules affecting onshore investors at will. While such actions can carry costs—deterring future investment, triggering macroeconomic spillovers, and provoking political repercussions—they remain a powerful tool for governments facing a crisis.

Sovereigns can tax and can bring forward future income to service current debt, providing them with greater flexibility to avoid default compared to other issuers. Unlike corporations, which focus on financial goals and profit maximization for shareholders, sovereigns pursue multiple objectives, making *their willingness to repay* debt a crucial factor in fulfilling debt service obligations.

At the same time, government policy choices shape the direction of a country's macroeconomic policy and can be altered at discretion. Monetary policy, the exchange rate regime, and capital control regulations significantly affect inflation and currency outcomes, which in turn impact investor returns. The optionality of sovereigns to change course complicates sovereign credit assessment, as a weakening credit can shift gears and swiftly improve, while a strong one can just as easily deteriorate.

As a lender of last resort for the economy, the sovereign balance sheet bears the ultimate burden of crises within its jurisdiction, whether in the banking, corporate, or household sector. Investments in government debt can therefore be affected by the actions of other actors without direct linkages to the sovereign, introducing an additional layer of analysis for sovereign credit risk assessment.

Unlike corporations, government debt restructurings are not subject to bankruptcy proceedings, making the division of assets complicated and requiring intense negotiations. Investors cannot compel sovereigns to liquidate assets to fulfill debt repayments. Moreover, investors are at an informational disadvantage in restructuring discussions, as sovereigns have better insight into their ability to repay and a broader overview of their assets and liabilities. The participation of official creditors adds further complexity because commercial investors do not operate within the same geopolitical framework as official entities.

Counterbalancing some of these risks is the fact that sovereign entities cannot be dissolved, unlike corporations, which can restart under a new incorporation. This permanence of sovereigns means that governments have an incentive to play the long game and cooperate with investors.

Historically, sovereigns have been reluctant to default, with many countries imposing significant hardship on their citizens and exhausting policy options before defaulting on their debts. This reluctance has stemmed from several factors, including the fear of triggering a macroeconomic crisis, losing financial market access, and facing permanently higher borrowing costs.

Another distinguishing factor of lending to sovereigns is that external balance sheets often support governments. Countries in crisis have access to funds from the International Monetary Fund (IMF) and can receive backing from friendly governments through bilateral lines of credit. Contagion risks, along with geopolitical and strategic considerations, drive this support, which can be significant. A case in point is the IMF's large-scale bailouts of Eurozone economies from 2010 to 2012, which were primarily motivated by concerns about contagion in Europe and the global economy.

Taking these factors together, investing in sovereign debt presents unique aspects that investors do not encounter in other markets. This makes successful investment in sovereign debt a nuanced endeavor that requires distinct investment techniques, valuation models, risk management strategies, and restructuring frameworks.

1.7 OWNERSHIP OF SOVEREIGN DEBT

Understanding who owns sovereign debt provides essential context for sovereign debt investors. The nature of a government's creditors has implications for bond pricing, market liquidity, volatility, and the sensitivity of debt to global and domestic factors. In extreme cases, where the sovereign is restructuring debt, knowing the complete list of creditors and their rank in the seniority structure is crucial for debt negotiations.

Given the varied role of sovereign debt in global financial markets and investment portfolios, there is a broad-based ownership of government securities.[10] Resident (or onshore) holders include domestic banks, non-financial institutions like pension or insurance funds, mutual funds, retail investors, and the central bank. Non-resident (or offshore) holders include foreign banks, mutual and hedge funds, foreign central banks, sovereign wealth funds, and other overseas institutional investors.

In both advanced and emerging markets, the majority of sovereign bonds are held by domestic banks and non-bank institutions like pension funds and insurance companies. Domestic banks hold government bonds to meet liquidity, regulatory, and capital requirements. Pension funds and insurance companies invest in government bonds because of their safety, predictability, and long duration, which match their long-term liabilities. A country's central bank may also hold government debt securities to implement monetary policy and achieve policy-related goals.

Other resident holders of government debt include investment vehicles like mutual funds. These allocate resources to government bonds due to liquidity needs and the superior credit rating of the sovereign compared to corporate issuers. Other holders include domestic retail investors who may perceive government debt as a safe savings instrument, often with tax advantages.

Non-resident holders of a country's debt include foreign banks, global investment funds, foreign central banks, sovereign wealth funds, and other foreign institutional investors. Their motivations include risk diversification, asset allocation, and market opportunities centered on relative value and risk-adjusted returns. Sovereign wealth funds and foreign central banks typically prioritize capital preservation and diversification, often allocating funds to highly rated government bonds.

In the past two decades, there have been several noteworthy trends in the ownership of sovereign debt securities. First, there has been an increase in the proportion of foreign official holdings in advanced economies as foreign central banks and sovereign wealth funds have increased their exposure. Second, central banks in developed economies increased their exposure to sovereign debt following the Great Financial Crisis of 2008 as a result of unconventional monetary policies.

Third, there has been a rise in foreign ownership of local currency emerging market debt in countries like Mexico, Brazil, and South Africa. These markets have grown in terms of their institutional framework, ease of access, liquidity, and policy-making credibility, attracting foreign mutual and hedge fund flows. Against these trends, the foreign bank and non-bank share of sovereign holdings has been relatively stable.

Beyond ownership, another relevant consideration is identifying the marginal buyer of debt. This is useful for predicting the market impact of shocks or assessing demand for new bond issues. Investment funds tend to be the key drivers of marginal foreign demand for debt in both advanced and emerging markets. Meanwhile, domestic demand tends to be driven by pension and insurance funds. Other domestic players are context-specific, such as the significant role of money market funds in the US or local hedge funds in Brazil.

1.8 SUMMARY

This chapter examined the strategic case for investing in sovereign debt. It highlighted the size of the market and the central role these instruments play in global finance. Sovereign bonds serve as benchmarks and contribute to income generation, capital preservation, risk diversification, hedging, and liquidity provision in investment portfolios.

The discussion highlighted that the historical returns and risk characteristics of sovereign debt compare favorably with other asset classes. The review also covered the unique aspects of lending to governments, emphasizing points that are especially important for investors. The chapter concluded with a detailed look at sovereign bond ownership, outlining the roles of domestic and foreign investors, central banks, and other institutional participants.

Next, we turn to the instruments investors can use to get exposure to sovereign debt, starting with bonds and loans in Chapter 2 and then moving on to financial derivatives in Chapter 3.

NOTES

1. London Stock Exchange Group, *The Size of Global Markets.*
2. The term *risk-free* is a concept that refers to relative credit/default risk, as government bonds have other embedded risks, including interest rate risk, volatility risk, and liquidity risk, among others.
3. Some corporate issuers can issue at yields below that of the government. For instance, multinationals may be domiciled in a given country but have revenues and production bases across the world.
4. Government default, where less than the principal is repaid, is comparatively infrequent, with the total loss on the initial investment generally well below 100%.
5. See J.P. Morgan, *Local Markets Guide* for returns since 2003, Damodaran, *Database on Historical Returns* for returns for US markets, and Meyer, Reinhart, and Trebesch, "Sovereign Bonds Since Waterloo" for bond-level returns.
6. Meyer, Reinhart, and Trebesch, "Sovereign Bonds Since Waterloo."
7. Tomz and Wright, "Empirical Research on Sovereign Debt," and Brauer, Martin, and Paja, *Emerging Market Sovereign Defaults Primer*.
8. Meyer, Reinhart, and Trebesch, "Sovereign Bonds Since Waterloo."
9. There is an extensive literature on the equity-bond correlation over time and across countries. See Boucher and Tokpavi, "Stocks and Bonds" for an overview. The general finding is that although the stock–bond returns correlation is generally positive, the relationship may turn negative in periods of turbulence.
10. See Fang, Hardy, and Lewis, Who Holds Sovereign Debt. Arslanalp and Tsuda, *Tracking Global Demand,* collect a quarterly, cross-country database of sovereign debt holdings.

REFERENCES

Arslanalp, Serkan, and Takahiro Tsuda. *Tracking Global Demand for Emerging Market Sovereign Debt.* IMF Working Paper WP/14/39. Washington, DC: International Monetary Fund, 2014.

Boucher, Christophe, and Sessi Tokpavi. "Stocks and Bonds: Flight-to-Safety Forever?" *Journal of International Money and Finance* 95 (2019): 27–43.

Brauer, Jane, Lucas Martin, and Merveille Paja. *Emerging Market Sovereign Defaults Primer – A Survival Guide.* GEMs FI Strategy Viewpoint. Bank of America Global Research, 2022.

Damodaran, Aswath. *Database on Historical Returns on Stocks, Bonds, Bills & Real Estate – United States.* 2024. https://pages.stern.nyu.edu/~adamodar/New_Home_Page/data.html (accessed 29 July 2025).

Fang, Xiang, Brian Hardy, and Kelly L. Lewis. *Who Holds Sovereign Debt and Why It Matters.* BIS Working Paper No. 1099. Basel: Bank for International Settlements, 2023.

J.P. Morgan. *EM Local Markets Guide.* 13th ed. J.P. Morgan Emerging Markets Research, 2022.

London Stock Exchange Group. *The Size of Global Markets 2024 in Charts.* LSEG Data and Analytics, 2023. https://www.lseg.com (accessed 29 July 2025).

Meyer, Josefin, Carmen M. Reinhart, and Christoph Trebesch. "Sovereign Bonds Since Waterloo." *The Quarterly Journal of Economics* 137, no. 3 (August 2022): 1615–1680.

Tomz, Michael, and Mark L. J. Wright, "Empirical Research on Sovereign Debt and Default." *Annual Review of Economics* I5 (2013): 247–272.

CHAPTER TWO

Instruments: Government Bonds and Loans

INVESTORS SEEKING exposure to sovereign debt can access a variety of instruments. These include cash securities such as government bonds and syndicated loans, as well as more complex derivatives like credit default swaps and interest rate swaps. Other options include sovereign bond funds managed by professional portfolio managers. Each approach offers a unique risk-return profile, liquidity feature, and structural characteristic, fulfilling different functions in an investment portfolio.

This chapter outlines the main types of investible cash instruments in today's sovereign debt market. Government bonds are a primary channel for investors to gain exposure to sovereign risk. Issued by sovereign entities, these debt securities come in a range of legal and financial forms. Commercial government loans offer another route for obtaining sovereign risk exposure. These are syndicated among banks, asset owners, and asset managers and can be held privately or traded publicly.

Beyond cash bonds and loans, synthetic instruments also provide sovereign risk exposure. Credit default swaps allow investors to take directional views on sovereign creditworthiness, hedge existing positions, and capitalize on relative value opportunities. Interest rate derivatives offer tools to manage interest rate risk, speculate on future movements, and express views on yield curve changes. These derivative instruments are discussed in greater detail in Chapter 3.

Finally, pooled investment vehicles that invest in individual government securities offer diversified access to sovereign risk. Options such as government bond funds and exchange-traded funds (ETFs) vary in structure, liquidity, and risk profile and are managed by professional fund managers with regulatory oversight. These vehicles enable investors to gain exposure to a diverse range of sovereign issuers; a topic explored further in Chapter 10.

2.1 THE SOVEREIGN ISSUER

Before examining sovereign debt instruments, it is important to define the sovereign issuer. Sovereign debt encompasses the total liabilities of a government and its related entities. The borrower may be the central government, the general government (which includes both the central government and subnational governments), or the broader public sector, which consists of the general government, public corporations, and the central bank (see Figure 2.1).

Identifying the specific issuer of sovereign debt is essential for investors to assess creditworthiness and the overall debt burden. The United States illustrates this point: at the end of 2024, total public debt outstanding was nearly $29 trillion, but including intergovernmental debt raised the figure to about $36 trillion.[1]

The Ministry of Finance is typically the issuing authority for the central government. In countries with extensive state-owned enterprises (SOEs), such as China and Russia, bonds may also be issued by quasi-sovereign entities. Likewise, in countries with large state governments, like India and Brazil, state and provincial issuers may be active in the market. By convention, the central bank is considered separate from the general government but may also issue its own debt securities.

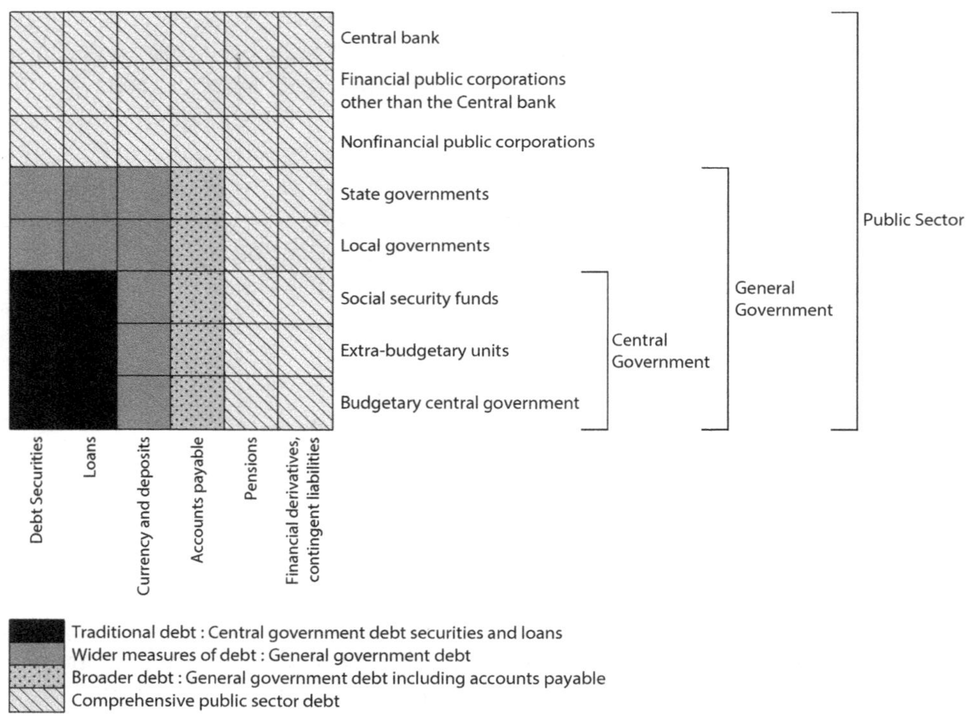

FIGURE 2.1 Sovereign issuers by sector and instrument. SOURCE: Arslanalp, S. et al., 2022/ Oxford University Press.

Understanding the scope of the sovereign issuer and the nature of its liabilities is essential to make fair cross-country comparisons. Without this context, investors risk underestimating debt in countries with large unfunded pension obligations or overestimating debt in those that include SOE or state liabilities in government totals.

With this foundation in place, we can now turn to government bonds, the principal instruments sovereign issuers use to raise capital.

2.2 GOVERNMENT BONDS ACROSS THE WORLD

Bonds are one of the main ways investors get exposure to sovereign risk. At its core, a bond represents a promise: in exchange for capital, the sovereign issuer agrees to make a defined series of interest payments and to repay the principal (the amount borrowed) at maturity. This promise can be extended to different creditors and structured in a variety of ways. As a result, government bonds can be classified by the characteristics of the issuer, the type of security, the key financial features, and their contractual terms.

Each country's bond market has its own terminology, conventions, and issuance process. In the United States, government bonds are known as Treasuries. In the Eurozone, Germany issues Bunds, France issues OATs, and Italy issues BTPs. In the United Kingdom and many Commonwealth countries, government bonds are called Gilts. Japan issues JGBs, Mexico issues Bonos, and in China, they are referred to as China Government Bonds (CGBs).

In developed markets, sovereign bonds are typically issued in the national currency—US dollars for Treasuries; euros for Bunds, OATs, and BTPs; and pounds sterling for Gilts. In emerging markets, issuance occurs in both local and foreign currencies. These bonds trade actively across borders and are held by a wide range of domestic and international investors.

The following sections of this chapter examine the defining features of government bonds in greater detail. This includes the different types of bonds, maturity, currency of issue, Eurobonds, legal provisions, collateralization, and the use of proceeds.

2.3 TYPES OF GOVERNMENT BONDS

Government bonds can be classified into different types according to the financial features that define their structure and risk profile. A *bullet bond* is one where the principal outstanding is paid at maturity, in contrast to a *sinking bond* (or *sinker*), where payment occurs over several years throughout the life of the bond. A *fixed-rate* bond pays the same interest at specified intervals, whereas a *floating-rate* bond features payments that are adjustable and change in response to specific conditions. Hybrid bonds include *step-up* or *step-down* bonds, where the coupon changes at specified maturities or in response to the issuer's actions or inactions.

The most common type of government bond is a fixed coupon bullet bond, a security with defined interest payments and principal paid at maturity. T-bills and short-dated instruments are often floating instruments since the interest rate is linked to a short-term rate, such as monetary policy or the overnight rate, which changes over time.

Sinkers and adjustable coupon sovereign bonds are less common. The former can feature in lending for large-scale investment projects or to high-yielding countries where repaying all outstanding principal in a given year may be deemed too risky. Bonds with adjustable coupons are typically associated with restructured bonds, where the sovereign enhances its repayment capacity over time. They also appear in sustainability-linked instruments, where the issuer must fulfill specified goals, such as reducing carbon emissions, to trigger lower coupon payments.

In some markets, sovereigns issue *inflation-linked* bonds, with both coupon and principal payments indexed to inflation. These bonds offer real returns to investors by adjusting the returns of nominal bonds according to the country's selected inflation index. Other types of macro-indexed bonds include *GDP-linked* and *commodity-linked* bonds, whose payments are linked to GDP or commodity production.

PRO TIP: *For each country in your portfolio, list the types of bonds, identify the most traded instruments, and document any unique financial features.*

2.4 GOVERNMENT BONDS BY MATURITY

Government bonds are issued across a wide range of maturities, from short-term instruments to multi-decade obligations, with each segment serving distinct financing and investment objectives. Debt securities with maturities of less than one year are called bills (Treasury or central bank bills) and are typically used for short-term budget financing or as money market instruments. Securities with maturities greater than 1 year are referred to as bonds, categorized into short-term (1–5 years), medium-term (10 years), and long-term maturities (30 years or more).[2] Some countries, including Austria, Mexico, and Peru, have even issued 100-year or century bonds. Bonds are used for both current budgetary expenditures and capital financing.

The market convention is to consider government bonds with 5-, 10-, and 30-year maturities as benchmark securities. The term benchmark refers to bond issuances that are large enough to be included in standard bond indices. These typically correspond to $500 million to $1 billion in issuance, depending on index inclusion rules.

Portfolio managers invest in various maturities of bonds based on their objectives and investment outlook. For example, short-dated Treasury bills may be used to manage cash reserves. They may also take exposure to bonds in the two- to five-year maturity range to reflect their views on future interest rate movements or growth expectations. Investors with long-term liabilities may choose to invest in 30-year or longer instruments. Emerging market investors may focus on 5–10 year maturities for their liquidity. Meanwhile, in high credit risk countries, investors often favor short-maturity bonds, as they potentially offer greater visibility regarding repayment capacity.

2.5 CURRENCY OF ISSUE

Sovereign bonds can be issued in domestic or foreign currencies. Almost all sovereigns can issue debt instruments denominated in their own currency, referred to as *local or domestic currency* bonds. The appeal of local currency issuance lies in the fact that the sovereign (through the Ministry of Finance and the central bank) can influence the exchange rate, set the policy interest rate, and, in extreme cases, print money to service debt.

In advanced economies and emerging markets with strong macroeconomic and policy frameworks, local bond markets are generally well-developed and liquid. Investor confidence that the government will maintain the real value of its obligations enables borrowing at market interest rates in the domestic currency. By contrast, many frontier and low-income countries face what is termed "original sin," which is the inability to borrow from international investors in local currency.[3] This compels them to issue debt in foreign currencies, most commonly the US dollar.[4]

These *foreign, external, or hard currency* bonds are generally priced off the US Treasury curve or the sovereign debt curve of the relevant borrowing currency (e.g., Bunds for euro-denominated issuance). They allow the issuer to access a larger and more diverse investor base that can extend credit at longer maturities at lower interest rates than domestic investors. The main disadvantage is that the country then needs to generate foreign currency to service the bond payments, which leaves investors exposed to credit and default risks.

2.6 EUROBONDS

Eurobonds are a specific type of external bond issued in a foreign currency and sold outside the issuing country. They can be denominated in US dollars, euros, pounds sterling, or yen, among others. For example, Eurodollar bonds pay interest and principal in US dollars and are issued and sold outside the United States; Euroyen bonds are denominated in yen and sold outside Japan.

Note that Eurobonds are not synonymous with *euro-denominated* bonds and are not limited to issuance in the European market. In fact, the vast majority of Eurobonds are dollar-denominated. Their naming convention originates from the time when dollar-denominated bonds were issued to tap into dollar savings in Europe.

Eurobonds are bearer bonds, which means they are owned by whoever holds them rather than a registered owner. They typically pay annual coupons and are exempt from withholding taxes on interest payments. Most are available in electronic form, traded primarily over-the-counter (OTC), with some also transacted on exchanges.

Often issued by a consortium of international banks, Eurobonds are commonly structured as RegS securities.[5] A RegS offer refers to a bond issued in the Eurobond market for international investors, usually cleared through Euroclear and Clearstream. These securities do not require SEC registration and may only be purchased in the secondary market by US investors after they have been *seasoned*, i.e., on the market for at least 40 days.

To broaden access to US institutional investors, issuers commonly pair a RegS offering with a 144A tranche. The 144A offering is a private placement available in the United States for US investors, typically cleared through the Depository Trust and Clearing Corporation (DTCC).

Other types of external bonds include Yankee bonds, which are US dollar–denominated bonds issued by foreign entities and primarily traded in the United States domestic market. They are registered securities with the SEC, pay interest semiannually, and are syndicated via US bankers. Higher-rated sovereigns or supranational agencies typically issue Yankee bonds.

Similar to Yankee bonds, other markets feature securities issued by foreign entities in the local currency and regulated domestically. Examples include the Bulldog market in the UK, where non-UK issuers sell British pound–denominated bonds in the United Kingdom, and the Samurai market, where non-Japanese issuers sell yen-denominated bonds in Japan. These markets are smaller than the Eurobond or Yankee bond markets.

2.7 LEGAL FEATURES

Bonds can also be classified based on their place of issuance, governing law, and other legal features. *Local law bonds* are issued within the domestic market of the issuing country and are governed by that nation's laws, rules, and regulations. They are usually denominated in the country's own currency, although some governments also issue them in foreign currencies. It is important not to confuse local law bonds with local currency bonds, as these two classifications cover different aspects of a bond.

External or foreign law bonds are issued outside the domestic market, typically in foreign currencies. They are governed by the legal jurisdiction under which they are issued, such as New York or English law. Likewise, they should not be confused with foreign currency bonds, even though many such bonds are governed by external law.

A third category is global bonds, which are sold simultaneously in both the foreign and domestic markets of the issuer. They can be issued in the issuer's local currency (most commonly) or a foreign currency, and are designed to appeal to both domestic and international investors. Global bonds must comply with the regulatory requirements of the issuer's home country as well as with the regulations applicable in the international markets where they are sold.

The governing law and legal jurisdiction are important because they determine how disputes between creditors and issuers are resolved. This is especially relevant for investors' rights and their ability to recover funds in the event of default. In the case of domestic law, investors may be at a disadvantage, as a government with a substantial legislative majority can revise domestic laws to their advantage. See Chapter 7 for further details.

2.8 COLLATERALIZATION

Sovereign bonds are generally issued as senior unsecured instruments. This means that they are not backed by specific collateral or assets, and repayment relies on the overall health of the issuer. As senior debt, they are positioned higher in the capital structure than subordinated debt, meaning they have priority for repayment.

Some government bonds are secured by collateral, with repayment backed by financial or physical assets. These assets can include foreign currency reserves, gold, fiscal revenues, commodity earnings, or shares of corporate entities. This type of debt security is less common than senior unsecured debt and may be issued if the country is struggling to issue in the market or has recently restructured its debt.

Closely related are instruments whose interest or principal payments are insured or guaranteed by development or multilateral organizations. Brady Bonds were the prototype, but there are recent examples. The World Bank guaranteed Ghana's 2030 Eurobond for up to $400 million of debt payments. Similarly, the US Development Finance Corporation (DFC) insured Ecuador's 2023 Galápagos Islands deal against political risk.

A unique type of financial instrument is the *sukuk bond*, in which holders have ownership of a tangible asset instead of a debt obligation as in conventional bonds. Several predominantly Muslim countries issue sukuks. They are structured so that holders receive a share of the profits generated by the underlying asset, rather than earning interest, which is forbidden in Islamic finance. They represent a small but growing subset of the government bond universe.

2.9 USE OF PROCEEDS

Most sovereign bonds are *general-purpose* bonds where the use of proceeds is defined in broad terms. They may be applied to cover budgetary needs or other activities, without specifying particular expenditures or earmarking of their use. This contrasts with *use-of-proceeds* (UoP) bonds, where the allocation of funds is clearly defined and often ring-fenced for specific projects.

With the growth of sustainable investing, governments are increasingly issuing UoP bonds, which earmark spending for specific green or social projects. A related instrument is *sustainability-linked bonds*, which are general-purpose bonds but where spending is connected to sustainability outcomes or key performance indicators (KPIs).

For example, Germany's inaugural green bond, issued in 2020, specified a ring-fenced use of proceeds for transportation, international cooperation, research, energy and industry, agriculture, and forestry. Meanwhile, Chile's sustainability-linked bond issued in 2022 outlined a general use of proceeds while committing to reducing greenhouse gas emissions and increasing renewable energy generation. We discuss these and other instruments used in sustainable investing in further detail in Chapter 19.

2.10 GOVERNMENT LOANS

Beyond bonds, other cash instruments can also provide exposure to sovereign credit risk, including loans and government guarantees. Commercial government loans are a niche option, typically syndicated among a select group of investors such as banks, asset owners, and large institutional managers. They occupy a middle ground between private lending and public markets, offering specialized opportunities just outside the mainstream of sovereign bond investing.

Unlike bonds, which have standardized terms for all investors, commercial loans can be tailored to meet the specific needs and objectives of both the borrower and lender. Customization may include the tenor, currency, interest rate, repayment schedule, callability, covenants, and other conditions. Disclosure requirements are also lower than for publicly traded securities. Such flexibility requires bespoke documentation and in-depth negotiation, adding complexity to their assessment. Commercial loans typically have shorter maturities than bonds, often seven years or less. They are largely illiquid and are usually held to maturity.

Historically, loans were the primary source of financing for sovereigns. The 1970s marked the peak of syndicated lending in the post–World War II era, as developing countries borrowed heavily from commercial banks in the United States and Europe. After the Latin American debt crisis, many of these loans were restructured into bonds, paving the way for modern, securitized, sovereign bond markets.

Today, commercial loans are a small fraction of the sovereign debt market. They are most often used by high-yield issuers that require rapid access to funding or face limited financial depth in their domestic markets. Some governments may use this type of financing if they are unable to meet the disclosure standards of the public bond market. On the investor side, large asset managers may participate in these loans to gain higher yields and negotiate favorable contract terms. Access to opportunities not available in public markets may also enhance diversification and portfolio returns relative to benchmarks.

2.11 GOVERNMENT GUARANTEES

Government guarantees are commitments made by a sovereign to take responsibility for a borrower's debt obligation if the borrower defaults. These guarantees can be explicitly stated in debt contracts or seen as implicit, existing without a legal basis but with an expectation of a government bailout.

Government guarantees can apply to a variety of instruments. These include issuances by state and local governments, state-owned enterprises, strategic companies (such as utilities, insurance companies, or large employers), and national champions (like national airlines). These serve as an alternative to the standard expression of sovereign risk through government bonds.

As guarantees reduce the relative credit risk of the instrument, investors may be able to reap an excess premium compared to simple government bonds. That said, investors should be mindful of the fine print and whether the guarantee is explicit or implicit. Also relevant are the triggers for enforcing the guarantee, including whether they are automatic or available only after litigation and a legal judgment is received. Guaranteed bonds that are *pari passu* (or treated similarly) with other government debt are generally preferable, as the sovereign will have a greater incentive to comply with the guarantee to avoid triggering default across all its liabilities.

Documentation for government guarantees is often not publicly available, which makes them complicated for investors to assess. In these cases, a prudent assessment of the scope and reliability of the government backstop is essential before considering it a substitute for sovereign risk.

2.12 SUMMARY

This chapter examined the full spectrum of sovereign cash instruments, beginning with the definition of the sovereign issuer. It reviewed how government bonds differ across countries and explored their classification by financial feature, maturity, currency, and governing law. It also covered Eurobonds, collateralization, and the use-of-proceeds, showing how these features shape the instrument's risk characteristics.

Syndicated government loans and government guarantees were reviewed next. While smaller in scale, these instruments serve important niches and often involve bespoke terms, distinguishing them from standardized public bond issues. Together, these topics highlighted the diversity of structures and legal frameworks that shape sovereign debt markets.

This foundation sets the stage for Chapter 3, which turns to financial derivatives linked to sovereign debt. These instruments allow investors to manage, transfer, or speculate on sovereign credit and interest rate risk without directly holding the underlying bonds, adding another dimension to the sovereign debt landscape.

NOTES

1. https://fiscaldata.treasury.gov
2. In the US, maturities between 1 and 10 years are referred to as Treasury notes, and those over 10 years as Treasury bonds.
3. See Eichengreen, Hausmann, and Panizza, "The Pain of Original Sin."
4. Some countries also borrow in euros, the British pound, the Japanese yen, and the Swiss franc, although these are less common.
5. The term RegS refers to Regulation S, a series of rules that clarify the position of the US Securities and Exchange Commission (SEC) that securities offered and sold outside the US don't need to be registered with the SEC.

REFERENCES

Arslanalp, Serkan, Wolfgang Bergthaler, Philip Stokoe, and Alexander F. Tieman. "Concepts, Definitions and Composition." In *Sovereign Debt: A Guide for Economists and Practitioners*, edited by S. Ali Abbas, Alex Pienkowski, and Kenneth Rogoff, Chapter 2. Oxford: Oxford University Press, 2022.

Eichengreen, Barry, Ricardo Hausmann, and Ugo Panizza. "The Pain of Original Sin." In *Other People's Money: Debt Denomination and Financial Instability in Emerging-Market Economies*, 13–47. Chicago: University of Chicago Press, 2005.

CHAPTER THREE

Financial Derivatives Linked to Sovereign Risk

THE GROWTH of financial derivatives since the mid-1990s has created a variety of financial instruments that investors can use to gain exposure to and hedge against sovereign risk. These financial contracts derive their value from the performance of an underlying sovereign asset or sovereign bond, focusing on specific types of risk.

This chapter examines the main types of derivatives used in sovereign bond investing and explores their application within sovereign bond portfolios. They can be categorized into those linked to sovereign credit exposures (such as credit default swaps), interest rates (such as interest rate swaps), and currency risk (such as currency forwards).

As with other financial instruments, derivatives expose the portfolio to various risks that require monitoring. These include counterparty risk (the risk that the other party does not fulfill their obligations), liquidity risk (the risk that the derivative cannot be easily unwound or sold at a reasonable price), legal and regulatory considerations, and potential costs associated with margin requirements.

3.1 CREDIT DEFAULT SWAPS

Sovereign credit default swaps (CDS) and their composite indices (CDX indices) are credit derivative instruments associated with sovereign credit risk.

A CDS is a contract between two parties in which the seller of the CDS *(the seller of protection)* agrees to compensate the buyer of the CDS *(the buyer of protection)*, in the event of a default or credit event over a specified period. The buyer of protection pays a fixed coupon every quarter to the seller for the duration of the contract or until a default event occurs.

Simply put, a CDS contract can be viewed as an insurance policy for the credit risk associated with a bond. The buyer of protection pays the seller an insurance premium for the assurance of compensation if a trigger event occurs during the policy's lifetime. Meanwhile, the seller earns the premium for providing this guarantee.

A standard CDS contract specifies the underlying reference entity (the sovereign debt instrument whose credit is the focus of the contract), the notional size of the agreement, maturity, fixed coupon rate, and upfront payment. It also includes a list of deliverable obligations (the bonds or instruments the seller of protection can use as compensation), a definition of what constitutes a credit event, and the effective date from which the protection is provided.

The reference entity of a sovereign CDS is generally a government bond or loan, with the CDS contract paying out if the government defaults or fails to meet obligations related to the instrument. If this happens before the maturity date of the contract, the seller of protection transfers the agreed payment to the buyer of protection. If the CDS contract is not triggered, it expires without further payment from the seller of protection.

CDS contracts are a crucial tool for portfolio managers. Similar to cash bonds, they can be utilized to express a view on the credit of a sovereign entity. By selling CDS protection on sovereign credit, portfolio managers add credit risk and can earn a premium akin to the coupon paid on a bond. Conversely, by buying CDS protection on the credit, the portfolio manager can reduce credit exposure, much like selling cash bonds.

The use of CDS enables the portfolio manager to further *short* the benchmark exposure by scaling the buy CDS exposure to exceed the benchmark weight. Additionally, they can be utilized to add leverage to a portfolio since CDS contracts are unfunded.

Note that a CDS contract replicates only the credit exposure of the cash bond, not the interest rate exposure. To replicate both credit and interest rate risk from cash exposures, the portfolio manager can pair a CDS position with a US Treasury bond or interest rate derivative (discussed later in this chapter). This approach allows for tailored views to be implemented, including the type of risk to be added or hedged, as well as the tenor and scaling of the position.

CDS markets provide valuable information to traders about the valuation of sovereign risk. A key indicator is the basis between the cash bond and CDS spread. A *positive* basis indicates that the cash bond spread is wider than the CDS spread, while a *negative* basis indicates the opposite.

The cash-CDS basis can arise from differences in liquidity or market technical factors such as variations in funding costs, debt management operations, or the supply of new bond issues. It may also stem from contractual differences, such as maturity and coupon. In some instances, the cash-CDS basis may reflect credit views; for example, investors might buy CDS protection as default concerns increase, or there may be high demand for sovereign CDS to hedge risky corporate exposures.

Emerging markets are the predominant reference entities in the sovereign CDS market. Countries like Brazil, China, and Turkey represent a significant portion of the notional outstanding. CDS on high-credit-risk countries like Argentina also trade, and they can be particularly liquid when the issuer is close to (or in) default.

Historically, derivatives on developed market sovereigns have concentrated more on interest rate risk and less on credit risk. However, during the Eurozone crisis, CDS on the peripheral European sovereigns (Greece, Portugal, Spain, Italy, and Ireland) started to trade, reflecting increased sovereign credit risks (see Figure 3.1).

Today, the focus in developed economies is less on credit default risk and more on the risk of technical disruptions to payments. For example, in May 2023, one-year US CDS spreads widened to highs of +156 bps from +18 bps in January 2023 due to concerns about the US government hitting the debt ceiling.[1]

CDS contract terms are standardized via International Swaps and Derivatives Association (ISDA) contracts. This facilitates netting, clearing, unwinds, rolls, novations, and compressions.[2] Contracts can also be bespoke and tailored to meet investors' objectives, including non-standard maturities, triggers, and deliverables. Details of CDS exposures, including the notional amounts outstanding by maturity and contract, as well as the associated cash bond exposures, are available on the Depository Trust & Clearing Corporation (DTCC) website.

CDS is traded over-the-counter, with the standard maturity being the five-year or the *on-the-run* contract. One-year and ten-year contracts also trade for some names, but tenors outside of the five-year point tend to be significantly less liquid. To avoid illiquid exposures, holders can roll CDS contracts from older contracts into the latest five-year on-the-run contract semi-annually. While investors can own the old contract, it becomes increasingly illiquid and, therefore, harder to price, trade, and exit. Not rolling into the on-the-run contract should be viewed as holding the instrument to expiry.

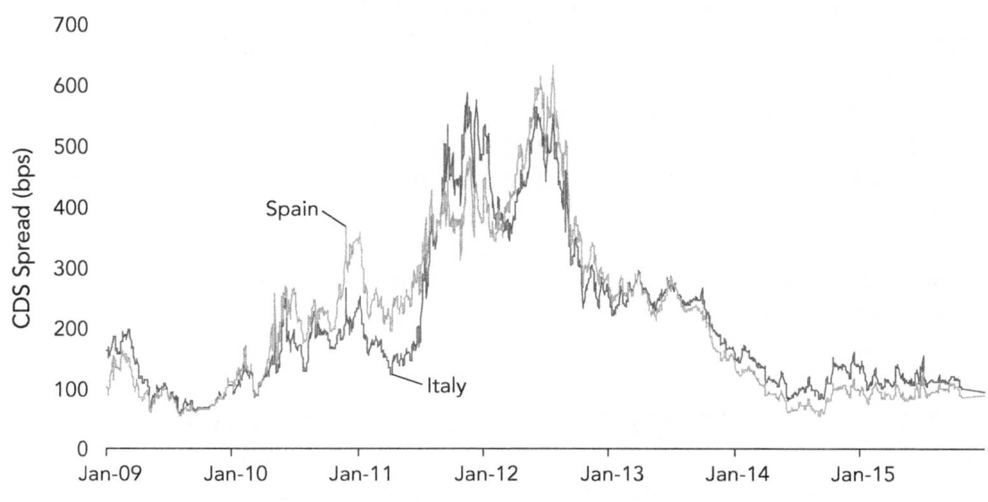

FIGURE 3.1 Italy and Spain five-year CDS. Source: Bloomberg Finance L.P.

3.2 CDX INDICES

CDX indices are composites of individual sovereign CDS and provide investors with synthetic credit exposure to a collection of credits. There are numerous applications for CDS indices due to their tradability, liquidity, and lower transaction costs.

As an index product with standardized terms and well-established legal documentation, CDX indices can be traded more easily than a basket of cash bonds or single-name CDS. They are cost-efficient with low transaction costs and allow investors to gain exposure to a range of credit exposures through a single trade. Given this, the liquidity and notional outstanding of CDX indices are generally greater than those of cash bonds and single-name CDS.

These characteristics make them highly useful for portfolio managers looking to adjust their portfolio's risk relative to an index or asset class. For instance, if a portfolio manager has a positive outlook on the sovereign asset class, they can boost the credit exposure (or beta) of the portfolio with a single trade using CDX instead of buying individual cash bonds. Conversely, if they need to lower the credit beta, the manager can quickly cut exposure via CDX, enabling traders to reduce cash exposures more gradually.

There are several sovereign CDX indices, with CDX.EM the most widely traded.[3] It includes a selection of emerging market countries, such as Brazil, Mexico, and South Africa, among others (see Table 3.1). The index provides the same default and credit exposure as the weighted single names and, like single-name CDS, can be leveraged and shorted. The weights of each country and the entry or exit of countries from the index are determined by the ISDA Committee. Markit handles the index maintenance and administration.

CDX.EM standard contracts are rolled every six months in March and September. The five-year contract is considered the on-the-run tenor with the highest liquidity. Similar to single-name CDS, older contracts can be held, but their liquidity significantly diminishes after the roll date into the latest contract.

The index trades based on price and benefits from electronic straight-through processing via Swap Execution Facilities (SEFs) and trading within a Clearing House framework. Third parties, such as IHS Markit, provide transaction processing and valuation services.[4]

PRO TIP: *Roll derivatives exposures to on-the-run securities to maintain risk exposures and avoid illiquid or hard-to-trade positions in the portfolio.*

3.3 CREDIT EVENTS IN CDS AND CDX CONTRACTS

Credit events, as determined by the ISDA Determinations Committee, trigger the CDS contract.[5] The result is a payout, or settlement, from the seller of protection to the buyer of protection.

TABLE 3.1 CDX.EM Select Constituents and Single-Name CDS Transaction Data

Reference Entity	CDX.EM.40 Index Weight (%)	Average Daily Notional (USD Equivalent)	Total No. of Clearing Dealers	Average Number Trades/Day
Federative Republic of Brazil	9	275,000,000	10	37
Republic of Turkey	9	250,000,000	10	43
People's Republic of China	9	225,000,000	8	22
United Mexican States	9	225,000,000	8	36
Republic of South Africa	9	300,000,000	9	49
Republic of Indonesia	9	200,000,000	9	27
Republic of Colombia	6	125,000,000	8	19
Kingdom of Saudi Arabia	4	5,000,000	9	1
Malaysia	3	75,000,000	8	10
Republic of Peru	3	75,000,000	7	8
State of Qatar	2	75,000,000	8	10
Arab Republic of Egypt	2	22,500,000	11	8
Argentine Republic	2	7,500,000	7	5
Dominican Republic	2	5,000,000	4	1
Federal Republic of Nigeria	2	5,000,000	8	2
CDX.EM.37		25,000,000	2	0
CDX.EM.38		25,000,000	4	1
CDX.EM.39		175,000,000	7	8
CDX.EM.40		1,500,000,000	8	133

Transaction Data September 23 to December 22, 2023.
Source: Adapted from IHS Markit, DTCC.

CDS auctions are a standardized process used to determine the settlement price for CDS contracts following a credit event. The auctions are designed to provide an efficient and transparent method for settling CDS contracts in size, avoiding the need for each contract holder to individually sell or buy the underlying bonds to realize their credit protection. The auction process emerged due to the complexity of CDS contracts and the size of CDS notional amounts compared to outstanding bonds.

A typical CDS auction consists of the following steps:[6]

- *Credit event determination:* A credit event is officially declared by ISDA, which triggers the auction process.
- *Auction announcement:* This includes details about the auction, such as the date and the specific obligations of the reference entity that will be involved.
- *Dealer participation:* Major dealers submit initial bids and offers for the bonds of the reference entity. This initial market-making phase establishes a preliminary price

range for the auction. They also submit requests for physical settlement to buy or sell bonds at the final price.
- *Limit orders:* Market participants, including CDS protection buyers and sellers, submit limit orders that indicate the prices at which they are willing to buy or sell the bonds of the reference entity.
- *Determination of final price:* The auction administrator calculates the final price based on the submitted bids, offers, and limit orders, seeking to match buy orders in a way that clears the market. This final price is used to settle CDS contracts, with protection sellers paying protection buyers the difference between the final price and the par value of the bonds, multiplied by the notional amount of the CDS contracts.

The sovereign CDS auction following Greece's default in 2012 highlights the importance of the ISDA Determinations Committee. In the initial phase of the restructuring, the Committee did not declare a credit event. This decision was later reversed when Greece changed local legislation and employed collective action clauses to bind all investors into the restructuring. The auction ultimately settled with a recovery rate on Greek bonds of 21.5 cents, meaning the compensation owed to buyers of CDS protection was 78.5 cents. Approximately $2.9 billion in net notional contracts was settled.[7]

After a credit event occurs, a new version of the CDX index is published. It assigns a 0% weight to the constituent entity, and the notional amount of the index is reduced by the weight of that entity in the index. For example, consider a default in an index with 100 equally weighted names and an outstanding notional of $10 million. The new version of the index will include 99 names and have a revised notional of $9.9 million instead of $10 million. This version of the index will remain in effect from the date of the credit event determination until the day after the auction date.[8]

Information on ISDA deliberations, CDS auctions and their outcomes, as well as index and single-name roll information can be found on the websites of the following organizations:

- Markit: CDS data, credit events, auction results, and background material.
- DTCC: Data on outstanding volumes and trading activity of credit derivatives.
- ISDA: Requests and outcomes from the Deliberation Committee, and information regarding credit events.
- Credit Fixings: Information on auctions conducted by ISDA.
- BIS: Data on OTC Financial Derivatives.

3.4 INTEREST RATE DERIVATIVES

Exposure to government bonds inherently includes exposure to interest rate and yield curve movements. To manage and hedge these risks, as well as speculate on future movements, investors use interest rate derivatives. These are financial contracts whose value is derived from specified interest rates or interest rate instruments. In this section, we review

TABLE 3.2 Uses of Interest Rate Derivatives

Interest Rate Derivative	Uses	Advantages	Disadvantages
Interest Rate Swaps	Duration management, yield curve trades, hedging local rates	Customizable, duration flexibility	OTC complexity, counterparty risk
Futures	Duration management, yield curve trades, tactical trading	Liquid, low cost, fast execution	Basis risk, standardized instruments
Options	Tail risk hedges	Tail hedge, volatility exposure	Expensive, less liquid, complex
FRAs	Hedging local currency rates, tactical trading	Short-term rates trades	Short tenor

some of the main instruments used by sovereign debt investors and discuss some common applications (see Table 3.2).

Using interest rate derivatives instead of buying or selling cash government bonds has advantages similar to those discussed for CDS and CDX instruments. These advantages include ease of trading, liquidity, the ability to match maturities or contract dates, as well as to hedge and leverage the portfolio.

Each country's financial market has its own rules, regulations, market structures, and conventions regarding the use of derivatives. These contribute to the diversity and availability of instruments for the portfolio manager.[9]

PRO TIP: *List the main derivatives traded in each country and review their trading and market access protocols.*

3.5 INTEREST RATE SWAPS

Interest rate swaps are financial derivatives that enable two parties to exchange interest rate payments based on a predetermined principal amount. The swap exchanges a fixed interest rate for a floating interest rate, or vice versa.

Interest rate swaps can be utilized to hedge against the risk of interest rate fluctuations that could negatively impact the value of portfolio holdings or to speculate on the direction of interest rate changes. For example, a portfolio manager worried about rising interest rates can *pay swaps*, which reduces the interest rate exposure in the portfolio. Similarly, if they believe interest rates will fall, they can *receive swaps* to increase the rate exposure in the account.

Interest rate swaps are highly customizable and traded over-the-counter. They can effectively manage duration at the portfolio level, implement yield curve strategies, and isolate interest rate risk from specific countries. They are also helpful in hedging non-USD or local rate exposures across multiple countries. Used widely by investors, corporate

Treasuries, and speculators, interest rate swaps are one of the largest traded instruments in global financial markets.

As such, the swap rates are closely watched as a leading indicator of fixed-income market conditions and, in some countries, are considered the benchmark rate for pricing and valuation. The *swap spread* is the difference between the fixed rate of an interest rate swap and the yield on a government bond of the same maturity. It reflects factors such as relative funding costs, liquidity conditions, credit risk perceptions, and the supply-demand balance for government bonds versus swaps. While usually positive due to the perceived safety of government bonds over the bank credit underpinning swaps, swap spreads can turn negative amid heavy sovereign issuance, dealer balance sheet pressures, or strong demand for fixed-rate swaps.

3.6 FUTURES

Interest rate futures are financial derivatives that enable investors to hedge against or speculate on changes in interest rates. They are based on a notional principal amount and are settled in cash. The underlying asset is typically a government bond or a collection of bonds. The futures contract specifies the interest rate that will be paid on the notional principal amount upon the contract's expiration.

Interest rate futures are exchange-traded and standardized, contributing to their liquidity and low transaction costs. Standard contracts include US Treasury futures (for example, the 10-year contract), as well as Eurodollar futures and SOFR (Secured Overnight Funding Rate) futures in the US.

Interest rate futures enable portfolio managers to hedge against rising interest rates. For example, a portfolio manager can sell 10-year US Treasury futures to decrease duration and safeguard their portfolio from a decline in bond prices. Alternatively, they can purchase US Treasury futures if rates are anticipated to drop (and bond prices are expected to rise). They can also be utilized to implement yield curve strategies such as flatteners or steepeners.

Given their standardized format, there can often be basis risk and imperfect matching with the portfolio's underlying cash position. Margin requirements and potential slippage during periods of volatility are additional factors to consider.

3.7 OPTIONS

Interest rate options are financial derivatives that grant the buyer the right, but not the obligation, to purchase or sell a specified amount of an underlying asset at a predetermined price on or before a specified date. The underlying asset is typically a bond, currency, or index. Interest rate options are used to hedge against interest rate risk, speculate on interest rate movements, and create synthetic positions.

Options provide a way to manage asymmetric risks with greater flexibility (but also increased complexity). They require the payment of a premium but can offer significant leverage and control over large interest rate exposures for a relatively small initial investment.

A *call option* gives the buyer the right, but not the obligation, to purchase an asset at a specified *strike price* within the *expiration date*. A *put option* gives the buyer the right, but not the obligation, to sell an asset at a predetermined *strike price* within the expiration date.

Options are frequently utilized as hedges against the tail risks associated with significant changes in interest rates. For instance, a portfolio manager can purchase swaptions (options on interest rate swaps) to safeguard against a sharp increase in US Treasury yields resulting from unexpected inflation. Investors can also use options to capitalize on volatility in interest rates without having a directional view of the underlying interest rate movement. Strategies like straddles (buying both a call and a put option) can be profitable if significant movements occur.

Options tend to be less liquid than interest rate swaps or futures and are not typically transacted in less developed or frontier sovereign bond markets. Together with other volatility-based instruments, options add layers of complexity to the portfolio, including model risk, sensitivity to implied volatility, and time decay.

3.8 FORWARD RATE AGREEMENTS (FRAs)

Interest rate forwards are OTC contracts that enable two parties to agree on a fixed interest rate for a loan or deposit at a future date. The rate is set at the time of the agreement and is unaffected by market fluctuations.

FRAs allow investors to lock in interest rates on borrowing or lending for a future period, which can help manage the interest rate risk associated with anticipated cash flows. They are often used in local currency portfolios to hedge against short-term interest rate movements, such as central bank policy changes. As a result, they are beneficial for short-term tactical trades and managing event-driven interest rate movements.

3.9 CASE STUDY: MEXICO'S BOND AND DERIVATIVES MARKET

Table 3.3 lists the bond and derivative instruments available to investors seeking exposure to Mexico. Mexican government debt is issued by the Mexican Treasury, officially known as the Secretaría de Hacienda y Crédito Público, or the Hacienda. They issue hard currency Eurobonds of varying maturities, denominated in dollars, euros, and yen. Peso-denominated securities are issued through regular auctions. Cetes are bills with maturities of less than one year, mbonos are bonds with maturities exceeding one year, and udibonos are inflation-linked bonds.

Derivatives linked to Mexican government debt include CDS, interest rate swaps, and cross-currency swaps. FX spot, forwards, and options can be traded to take a position on the currency. Note that each market has its own trading conventions and specific infrastructure.

The cash bond and derivatives instruments available in Mexico highlight its market development and depth within the emerging market universe. Other large emerging

TABLE 3.3 Mexico's Bond and Derivatives Instruments

Bonds	BBG Ticker	Description	Conventions
Eurobonds	MEX Govt	Maturities: various USD bonds	Issued via syndication
Fixed Rate (Mbonos)	MBONO Govt	Maturities: 1–30 years MXN bonds	Weekly auctions
Treasury Bills (Cetes)	MCET Govt	Zero Coupon Maturities: 1 week – 1 year	Weekly auctions
Inflation-linked (Udibonos)	MUDI Govt	Maturities: 1–30 years Reference index: MXUDI Index Most liquid: 5, 10, 20, 30 years	Weekly auctions
Derivatives	**BBG ticker**	**Description**	**Conventions & Settlements**
CDS	MEX CDS USD	Standard ISDA contract Coupon: quarterly	If triggered settled via auction
Interest rate swap	MPSW Curncy	Maturities: Up to 30 years Most liquid: 2, 5, 10 years	Fixed leg: 28 days Floating leg: 28 days, MXIBTIIE Index
Cross-currency swap (28d TIIE v. SOFR)	MPBSM Curncy	Maturities: Up to 30 years Most liquid: 5, 10 years	Local floating leg: 28 days, MXIBTIIE Index FX floating leg: 28 days, SOFRRATE Index
FX	**Traded Pair**	**Maturities**	
Spot	USD/MXN	n/a	
Forwards	USD/MXN	Up to 10 years; 1 year most liquid	
Options	USD/MXN	Up to 15 years	

Source: Bloomberg Finance L.P.

markets like Brazil, Poland, South Africa, Turkey, and Indonesia have similar instruments subject to local regulations and restrictions. Meanwhile, the available instruments in frontier markets are more limited and focused mainly on cash bonds, currencies, and simple derivatives (if any).

3.10 RISKS ASSOCIATED WITH SOVEREIGN DEBT DERIVATIVES

While sovereign debt derivatives offer valuable tools for hedging and strategy implementation, they introduce risks distinct from cash instruments. Managing these requires careful attention to counterparties, margining, and legal frameworks.

Counterparty Risk: All over-the-counter (OTC) derivatives, such as CDS and interest rate swaps, expose portfolios to the risk that the counterparty defaults on its obligations. This risk can be mitigated by trading through central counterparties (CCPs) or using collateral agreements. Even so, residual exposure remains. More so in volatile markets when there may be gaps before collateral is posted, leading to potential loss. Assessing counterparty credit quality, negotiating robust ISDA documentation, and maintaining diversified exposures are central to mitigating this risk.

Margin and Collateral Requirements: Futures, cleared CDS, and centrally cleared swaps require both initial and variation margin. Market volatility can trigger sudden margin calls, forcing managers to liquidate positions or raise cash at unfavorable times. Collateral requirements can differ by instrument—exchange-traded futures and options have standardized terms, while OTC trades may be subject to bilateral negotiation. Effective cash and collateral management is therefore essential when deploying derivatives.

Liquidity and Roll Risk: Derivatives also carry liquidity and roll risk. Even contracts with high average daily volume can experience sharp liquidity drops during market stress, widening bid-ask spreads and increasing execution costs. Futures contracts have roll dates where positions must be renewed, introducing roll yield considerations and cheapest-to-deliver (CTD) uncertainty. Similarly, single-name CDS and CDX indices roll periodically, which can cause pricing gaps between the old and new series, potentially creating basis shifts against other portfolio positions.

Basis Risk: Derivatives may not perfectly track the underlying cash instrument or index they are replicating. This *basis* can arise due to market technicals, liquidity, or settlement mechanics. For example, CDS spreads can diverge from cash bond spreads if there is a major buyer or seller of cash bonds. In interest rate derivatives, differences between swap rates and government yields can also create persistent basis exposure.

Legal and Regulatory Considerations: Derivative use is subject to complex legal documentation, such as ISDA master agreements, credit support annexes (CSAs), and jurisdiction-specific regulations. The enforceability of netting and collateral arrangements can vary by country, posing particular concerns in emerging markets where legal systems are less predictable. Regulatory regimes such as Dodd–Frank in the US and the European Market Infrastructure Regulation (EMIR) in Europe impose mandatory clearing for certain derivatives, trade reporting requirements, position limits, and restrictions on eligible counterparties. These rules can affect costs, execution venues, and permissible trading strategies, and they differ across jurisdictions, requiring careful compliance monitoring.

Leverage and Portfolio Impact: Finally, all derivatives introduce embedded leverage into a portfolio, amplifying both gains and losses relative to cash instruments. This leverage can be explicit, as with futures contracts where a small margin supports a large notional exposure, or implicit, as in options and swaptions, where delta exposure changes with market moves. These can lead to rapid changes in portfolio risk profiles, particularly if market conditions shift unexpectedly. Portfolio managers must ensure that leverage from derivatives remains consistent with mandate constraints and investor risk tolerance. Without disciplined position sizing and robust risk controls, leverage can exacerbate drawdowns during market stress. Stress testing and scenario analysis are therefore essential to understanding the full impact of derivative exposures, particularly during adverse market moves.

3.11 SUMMARY

This chapter surveyed financial derivatives linked to sovereign debt and their roles in portfolio management. It explained how single-name CDS transfers sovereign credit risk without owning the cash bond and how CDX indices provide diversified, tradable baskets for hedging or tactical exposure. It then reviewed interest rate derivatives, including interest rate swaps (to set duration and curve posture), futures on government bonds (for liquid, capital-efficient beta), options and swaptions (to express convexity and volatility views), and FRAs (to lock in short-rate expectations).

While financial derivatives have many practical portfolio uses, they come with their own set of risks that must be explicitly managed. These include counterparty and collateral/margin requirements, legal and documentation risk, roll and carry dynamics, and model/valuation risk for options. Mexico's bond and derivatives markets illustrate the range of sovereign debt instruments available for investors to use in their portfolios.

This concludes Part One on the investable universe. Part Two now turns to fundamental sovereign analysis and legal considerations for investors when lending to sovereigns.

NOTES

1. As of June 12, 2025, www.investing.com (accessed 29 July 2025).
2. A novation is a mechanism to transfer a CDS contract from one party to another, effectively exiting the original contract and replacing it with a new one involving the new party. Compressions are the reduction of redundant CDS contracts with the same reference entity to simplify positions and mitigate counterparty risk.
3. Other sovereign CDX indices are much less liquid and include the iTraxx SovX CEEMEA Index covering 26 countries in Central and Eastern Europe, the Middle East, and Africa; and the iTraxx SovX Asia Pacific Index, including 10 reference entities from the Asia and Oceania regions.
4. See IHS Markit, *CDS Indices Primer.*
5. See ISDA, *Credit Event Process* and Haworth, *Guide to Credit Events and Auctions* on the credit event process. The ISDA listed events are reduction in the rate of interest or amount of principal payable (which would include a "haircut"), deferral of payment of interest or principal (which would include an extension of maturity of an outstanding obligation), subordination of the obligation, and change in the currency of payment to a currency that is not legal tender in a G7 country or a AAA-rated OECD country.
6. See Markit, *Credit Event Auction Primer* for further details and examples of calculations at each stage.
7. See ISDA, *Greek Sovereign CDS Credit Event FAQs* and Jones, "$3bn Greek CDS Settlement."

8. In case of a restructuring credit event, the new version of the index starts trading from the day following the Event Determination Date. Restructuring credit events result in the impacted entity "spinning-out" of the index, resulting in the investor holding a position on the new index version and a single-name CDS contract on the restructured entity.
9. See J.P. Morgan, *EM Local Markets Guide* for an overview by country.

REFERENCES

Bank for International Settlements. *OTC Derivative Statistics*. 2023. https://stats.bis.org (accessed 29 July 2025).

Haworth, Helen. *A Guide to Credit Events and Auctions*. Credit Suisse Research and Analytics, 2011.

ISDA. *The Credit Event Process*. International Swaps and Derivatives Association, 2025. https://www.isda.org (accessed 29 July 2025).

ISDA. *Greek Sovereign CDS Credit Event FAQs*. International Swaps and Derivatives Association, 2012. https://www.isda.org (accessed 29 July 2025).

IHS Markit. *CDS Indices Primer*. 2021. https://www.ihsmarkit.com.

J.P. Morgan. *EM Local Markets Guide*. 13th ed. J.P. Morgan Emerging Markets Research, 2022.

Jones, Sam. "$3bn Greek CDS Settlement." *Financial News London*, March 28, 2012. https://www.fnlondon.com/articles/3bn-greek-cds-settlement-20120328 (accessed 29 July 2025).

Markit. *Credit Event Auctions Primer*. 2010. https://www.ice.com/publicdocs/Credit_Event_Auction_Primer.pdf (accessed 22 August 2025).

PART TWO

Credit and Contract Analysis

CHAPTER FOUR

Fundamental Sovereign Analysis

HAVING COVERED the tools for accessing sovereign exposure, we now explore how investors select countries and investment themes to invest in. This is where fundamental analysis comes in. It evaluates the macroeconomic drivers and credit quality of various sovereign issuers to identify the most compelling opportunities and to avoid those with deteriorating prospects or elevated default risks.

We begin Chapter 4 by outlining the various data sources and economic indicators available to portfolio managers for assessing sovereign credit and macroeconomic risks. Next, we summarize the analytical frameworks for fundamental analysis, including a range of tools and techniques that cover structural drivers, balance sheets, and macroeconomic factors. A selection of standard models used to enhance these analyses is reviewed together with applications to bond investment strategies.

Building on this analytical foundation, Chapter 5 delves into sovereign credit ratings and details the indicators analysts look at when evaluating a country. These credit ratings enable investors to categorize countries quickly and facilitate comparisons across countries and issuers from other asset classes. This is followed in Chapter 6 by a review of early warning indicators that help identify economies that may be vulnerable to different types of sovereign crisis, including currency, banking, and liquidity risks. We also discuss sovereign debt sustainability analysis and how to determine whether a country has high and unsustainable debt. This can be particularly relevant for investors to avoid sovereigns with high levels of default and restructuring risk.

For a clear understanding of how to apply these concepts, each section features examples from three sample countries: Country A, a developed economy; Country B, an emerging market; and Country C, a frontier market. Using these examples, the chapter examines various economic and credit developments and explains how they inform investment strategies.

4.1 DATA AND ITS LIMITATIONS

We start with a brief discussion of the data that underpins investors' views on a sovereign. Investors have access to a wealth of data and analysis, and they need to differentiate between useful information (which may affect the fundamental credit and market price) and *noise* (extraneous or irrelevant data that obscures underlying patterns or signals). Markets often react to the release of both types of information, which portfolio managers need to assess and act upon, sometimes within a very short timeframe. This section discusses the various data sources for key economic and credit variables used in sovereign analysis.

4.1.1 Sources and Analysis

Data sources used in sovereign analysis include raw data, third-party databases, analyst reports, government presentations, rating agency assessments, and reports from multilateral organizations.

Raw data on economic indicators—such as growth, inflation, unemployment, and fiscal indicators—are usually publicly available on government websites, such as the central bank and the Ministry of Finance. Key data releases, along with market expectations, are also available on Bloomberg and Reuters. They are often market-moving and watched closely by traders and portfolio managers.

A host of third-party paid databases amalgamate this raw data, facilitating cross-country and time series analysis. Cross-country historical databases are also provided by the United Nations, World Bank, regional development banks, the International Monetary Fund (IMF, "the Fund"), Eurostat (the statistical office of the European Union), the OECD, and investor organizations like the International Institute of Finance (IIF), among others. Table 4.1 summarizes key sovereign debt databases.

Sell-side analysts and private-sector consultants continually assess macroeconomic, policy, and political trends. They closely monitor data releases and policy changes, often accessing local information sources. These reports are frequently updated and focus on the near term. Additionally, the sell-side produces thematic research on market trends. Investors can utilize these assessments to enhance their own in-house credit and macroeconomic analysis.

For most countries, local data sources are essential for capturing details about what is happening on the ground. Data availability can vary significantly between countries and can be particularly limited in emerging and frontier markets. Accessing local information through consultants and sell-side analysts who have local networks is vital for investors to form informed opinions on developments. Often, the sell-side also organizes in-depth country visits for small groups of investors.

Government presentations and official reports are another source of information. These are often distributed during issuer roadshows where government officials meet with investors to discuss macroeconomic and policy updates to generate interest in an upcoming bond offering. These meetings provide investors with a prime opportunity to access new information on government policy objectives and understand current risks

TABLE 4.1 Select Sovereign Debt Databases

Name	Database	Description
Bank for International Settlements (BIS)	**Debt Securities Statistics**	Quarterly dataset covering borrowing in debt capital markets, including tradable debt instruments. It distinguishes between debt securities issued in international and domestic markets and reports the market value or nominal/face value of securities.
Bank of Canada and Bank of England	**Debt in Default Database**	Information on different types of sovereign government debt in default. Estimates of the stock of government debt includes bonds and other marketable securities, bank loans, and official financing from 1960 onwards.
European Central Bank (ECB)	**Debt Securities Issuance and Service by EU Governments**	Eurostat database on the growth, stock and issuance of debt securities issued by euro area governments, corporations and monetary financial institutions.
Institute of International Finance (IIF)	**Global Debt Monitor**	Quarterly dataset tracking debt by sector across developed and emerging markets. Variables include the currency breakdown of sectoral debt, bond and syndicated loan redemption profiles, and the foreign ownership structure of local currency government bonds. A related dataset, the IIF's Frontier Markets Debt Monitor is published bi-annually and focuses on frontier economies.
International Monetary Fund (IMF)	**Fiscal Monitor Statistics**	Data from the latest IMF Fiscal Monitor Report covering annual fiscal and debt numbers across advanced and emerging countries together with IMF forecasts.
International Monetary Fund (IMF)	**Historical Public Debt Database**	Annual database on government debt produced and maintained by the IMF Fiscal Department.
International Monetary Fund (IMF)	**Global Debt Database**	Dataset comprising the total gross debt of the (private and public) non-financial sector. Variables include the private debt of corporates and households, central government debt, and general government debt.
Organization for Economic Cooperation and Development (OECD)	**Government Borrowing Outlook**	Dataset including debt stock and projections for OECD member countries. It also includes sovereign debt issuance trends in emerging markets and developing economies.
World Bank	**International Debt Report & Database**	External debt statistics for low- and middle-income countries that report to the World Bank Debtor Reporting System (DRS). It includes external borrowing and sources of lending by type of borrower and creditor, debt service deferred by bilateral creditors, and projected monthly debt-service payments owed to all bilateral creditors.

Continued

TABLE 4.1 Continued

Name	Database	Description
World Bank	**Quarterly External Debt Statistics**	Quarterly cross-country external debt data and select foreign assets of developed, developing, and transition countries. A breakdown by instrument and measures of short-term debt not easily available from other sources are included.
World Bank	**Quarterly Public Sector Debt**	Quarterly cross-country data on the public sector debt of developed, developing, and transition countries.

Source: Adapted from Abbas, S.A. and Rogoff, K. (2022)/Oxford University Press.

and opportunities. Creditors can raise any concerns and suggest corrective actions they would like to see, as well as discuss topics such as climate policies or geopolitics. Other avenues for official communication from the government include press conferences following central bank monetary policy meetings and after the annual budget is published.

In-depth country assessments can be drawn from a variety of sources. Rating agencies produce *Rating Action Commentaries* that explain the rationale behind any rating action, as well as *Country Assessments* related to their credit ratings. The IMF publishes *Article IV* country reports for surveillance countries and *Staff Reviews* for countries with active IMF programs. These documents include macro assessments, debt and scenario analyses, a review of the economy's main risks and vulnerabilities, structural reforms, and policy recommendations. Multilateral and regional development banks have similar reports concentrating on medium- to long-term structural issues such as the energy sector and infrastructure needs.

4.1.2 Data Quality and Transparency

Data quality, transparency, and their limitations are particularly relevant for sovereign debt investors.[1] Governments have significant latitude over statistics and can shape data collection, methodologies, and information disclosure. Investors and sovereign analysts, therefore, have to be especially careful about the accurate measurement of variables like growth, inflation, fiscal, and debt numbers.

Argentina is a case in point. From 2007 to 2015, the government was embroiled in a high-profile controversy regarding the credibility of its inflation and GDP growth figures. Numbers reported by the national statistics agency, INDEC (Instituto Nacional de Estadística y Censos), were considered to be substantially different from other indicators. For instance, independent analysts estimated that actual inflation was 10–15 percentage points higher during some periods. This had real implications for investors as inflation and growth numbers were inputs into the payout calculations from Argentina's GDP warrants.

Another infamous case was that of Greece in 2009, when the incoming administration revealed chronic and systematic misreporting of fiscal data. They estimated that the previous data on government debt had been underreported by approximately $30 billion, or 11% of GDP! These revelations marked the beginning of the Greek and Eurozone Debt Crisis that followed.

Sell-side analysts and credit rating agencies play a crucial role as curators of country data, which is especially valuable in these situations. They strive to cross-check data series and highlight inconsistencies, follow up with government officials to address data voids and gaps in coverage, and examine the consistency of reports while considering local conventions alongside global databases (such as identifying differences in fiscal years in accounting).

Hidden public debt is a particular concern for sovereign debt investors. Mozambique's (2016) hidden debt scandal triggered an economic crisis and led to an eventual default on all external commercial debt. It originated from three separate loans totaling $2 billion made between 2013 and 2014, which were incurred by three state-owned enterprises and fully guaranteed by the government. Of these, only one loan of $850 million to Ematum for building a tuna fishing fleet was disclosed and included in the estimate of public debt. In contrast, the remaining two loans were not publicly disclosed or approved by the Mozambique parliament until they were revealed to IMF staff in 2016.[2]

Generally, information on multilateral debt and publicly issued government bonds (both external and local) is relatively widely available. In contrast, detailed data on bilateral country-to-country lending, private bond placements, commercial bank lending, and contingent liabilities tend to be sparse due to the lack of public disclosure requirements, with only the involved parties having access to the terms.

The significance of this is underscored by China's lending to developing countries, the full extent of which remains unreported even in national statistics. Additionally, there is suspicion that this debt may be collateralized and senior to bonded debt, potentially violating negative pledge provisions in bond contracts (see Chapter 7).

For countries adhering to the IMF's Data Standards Initiative, all public liabilities should be reported.[3] Yet even IMF reports, in the context of their country surveillance and program negotiations, periodically reveal cases of data misreporting, some of which are more egregious than others.

4.1.3 Sample Country Data

Country A

Advanced economies like Country A typically have high-quality, extensive, and reliable data from credible institutions. Time series information is readily available and usually accessible electronically, with minimal revisions. There tends to be extensive street coverage of most indicators with detailed reports, macro modeling, and attention to granular data sources and their nuances.

Taking inflation data as an example, high-frequency data releases are available and decomposed into various sub-categories reflecting headline, core, energy, housing, and consumer goods inflation trends. Several sources exist to corroborate trends, and there are various statistical aggregations.

Country B

Emerging economies like Country B typically have good data availability standardized to international best practices. There may be gaps and definitional changes in some years, and data may be subject to periodic revisions. Information is often available electronically and regularly updated. There is generally good coverage by street analysts, detailed reports, macro modeling, and information from local sources that enhance quantitative analysis.

Following on with the inflation example, data is usually available monthly and disaggregated into broad categories like headline, core, and energy inflation. The central bank may compute a number of measures of core inflation, including some statistical techniques to trim outliers. Additional sources for data verification may be available in larger emerging markets.

Country C

Frontier market economies like Country C often have moderate to poor data availability, frequently featuring significant gaps in coverage. Time series data may be unavailable and is usually provided with long delays. Coverage may be inconsistent and might not be directly comparable with international standards. Data accuracy may be affected by limited institutional capacity and political interference. Street coverage is often patchy, making local information and on-the-ground assessments highly relevant.

Inflation data focuses on headline inflation, and only in some cases, core inflation measures. There is unlikely to be a detailed statistical breakdown or disaggregated inflation data.

4.2 THE PILLARS OF SOVEREIGN ANALYSIS

Fundamental sovereign assessment requires a multi-dimensional approach supported by several interconnected analytical pillars. The objectives are to assess a country's capacity to meet debt commitments, identify key macroeconomic drivers, and evaluate overall risk vulnerability. Given the wide scope, the analysis integrates a range of quantitative and qualitative inputs and is as much an art as it is a science.

The foundation of sovereign analysis is understanding the economy's key structural features, which serve as the basis for the nation's wealth. This determines the amount of debt the country can borrow, its medium-term repayment capacity, and susceptibility to domestic and global shocks. These systemic features are slow to change in the short term, but over time can shift due to policy choices, external factors, or fundamental shifts.

The next building block is the sovereign's balance sheet, which provides a snapshot of the government's stock of assets and liabilities. Extending this analysis to each sector of the economy helps paint a picture of the country's indebtedness and reveals any currency, maturity, and sectoral mismatches. Additionally, debt service indicators provide further information on debt repayment risks for the sovereign and each sector.

Macroeconomic analysis builds on these two pillars. This examines the economic performance of key variables like growth, inflation, the fiscal balance, the current account, currency, and financial sector indicators. These help identify the structural and cyclical factors that impact a country's ability to generate income, revenues, foreign currency, and to repay debt.

Macroeconomic models inform sovereign analysis by focusing on specific variables and their interconnections. These include models that forecast growth, predict inflation and unemployment, forecast currency trends, frameworks for anticipating central bank policy rate shifts, and fiscal accounting tools. Credit analysts use these models to form initial country assessments and explore evolving economic dynamics.

Sovereign analysts also examine government policies, available policy options, and the political leanings of those in power. Such decisions not only shape economic outcomes but also often extend beyond what would purely benefit the economy or sovereign credit. This contrasts with corporate credit analysis, where the primary goal is profit maximization and optimizing shareholder value.

These elements—structural features, balance sheet analysis, macroeconomic and policy analysis—form the foundation of fundamental sovereign analysis. To this, qualitative factors like politics, geopolitics, and social dynamics are added to create a comprehensive picture of a sovereign's creditworthiness (see Figure 4.1).

When an investor or analyst assesses any sovereign, they begin with these foundational pillars and refine their views as new information becomes available.

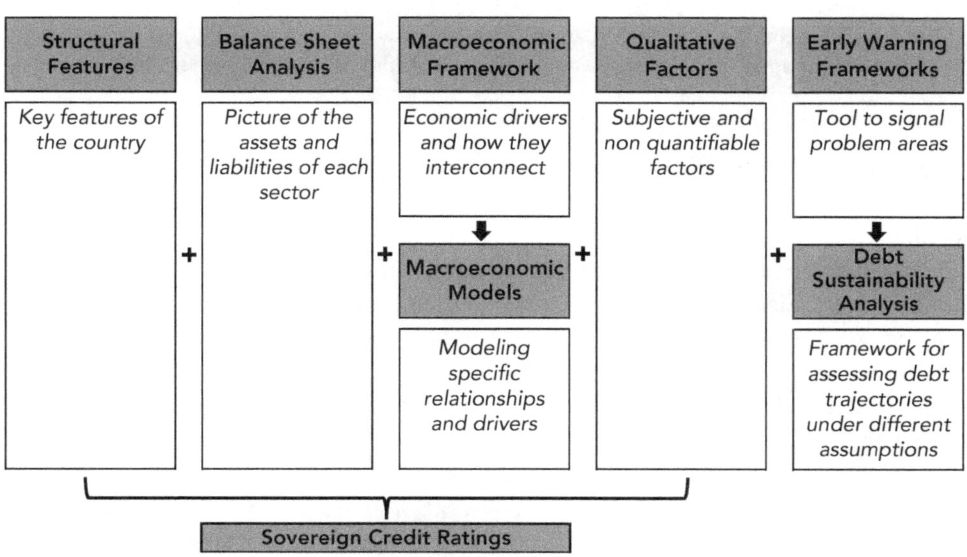

FIGURE 4.1 Analytical pillars of fundamental sovereign analysis.

Country A

In advanced economies like Country A, where credit risks are relatively low, the emphasis is on detailed economic trends and analyzing key economic relationships. This may include the stage of the business cycle, the Phillips Curve, or fiscal multipliers. Economists also look at how different sectors, such as the banking and financial sectors, are interconnected to assess the risk of asset bubbles or potential liabilities for the government.

Country B

For emerging economies like Country B, credit risk is higher, making balance sheet analysis crucial. This is combined with macroeconomic analysis, knowledge of government policies, and the impact of global shocks. Shifts in fiscal or exchange rate policies can have significant implications for the credit, macroeconomic variables, and debt ratios. Additionally, politics and institutional strength influence the overall assessment.

Country C

In frontier economies like Country C, balance sheet analysis takes center stage alongside government policy choices. This aids in determining whether the economy can repay its debt and whether it is pursuing responsible policies that will ensure this continues in the future. Qualitative factors such as political economy, geopolitics, institutional strength, and social dynamics are essential elements in determining sovereign creditworthiness.

Sovereign credit ratings are a tool used to combine the diverse indicators used in fundamental analysis into a single metric of credit risk. Chapter 5 examines ratings in further detail.

For all sovereigns, especially emerging markets and frontier economies, early warning frameworks are essential tools to avoid investing in countries at risk of crisis. These frameworks, discussed in Chapter 6, include indicators that have been empirically linked to various types of crises, helping to identify cases that require further analysis. This might involve a closer look at the source of the early warning, scenario testing, and risk assessments.

In-depth analysis of debt stock and debt sustainability can be used to supplement these frameworks. Debt sustainability analyses (DSAs) are highly adaptable and can be applied to assess different types of economies with varying financing structures. They're a crucial tool for evaluating default and credit risk in high-risk countries before making an investment. These are also covered in Chapter 6.

In the remainder of this chapter, we examine each of the foundational pillars in turn and explore them in greater depth.

4.3 STRUCTURAL FEATURES OF AN ECONOMY

Fundamental sovereign analysis begins with an overview of the key structural features of the economy. This encompasses the economic structure, global interconnections, financial market characteristics, demographics and social indicators, as well as natural resources and physical attributes. Qualitative indicators such as the governance and institutional framework, and politics and geopolitics are additional factors to consider. There may also be region-specific features to assess such as membership of a trade block or monetary union.

Table 4.2 illustrates select indicators for each pillar, which are applied to each of the sample countries below. Together, these provide context for the functioning of the macroeconomy and its sensitivities and vulnerabilities to shocks.

TABLE 4.2 Structural Indicators for an Economy

Pillar	Indicators
Economic Structure	Trend growth, GDP by sector and expenditure category, historical inflation rates, historical unemployment rates, share of public and private sector breakdown, state-owned enterprises and strategic sectors, commodity exposure and dependence.
Global Interlinkage	Trade openness, major trading partners, main exports and imports, terms of trade, membership of trade and economic blocs, exchange rate regime, exposure to commodities, sources and destination of capital flows.
Financial Architecture	Features of the banking and the non-banking-financial sector, size of pension and insurance fund sector, history of crisis, assets and liabilities.
Policy Framework and Institutions	Economic policymaking setup, CB independence, coordination between government ministries, inflation-targeting parameters, budget law parameters, approach to macroeconomic policymaking and government oversight.
Governance Indicators	Government effectiveness, voice and accountability, regulatory quality, political stability and absence of terror/violence, control of corruption, the rule of law.
Politics and Geopolitics	Political system, electoral framework, history of politics, geopolitical alliances and current memberships, strategic bilateral relationships, voting record on United Nations votes, history of sanctions.
Social Indicators and Demographics	Population breakdown, aging dynamics, composition of labor force by age and gender, skill and education breakdown of workforce, health and mortality indicators, inequality trends, history of civil rights, record on minority/gender/LGBTQIA+ rights.
Natural Endowments and Physical Features	Geography and landscape, natural assets, infrastructure availability and quality, susceptibility to environmental and weather-related risks, exposure to climate physical and transition risks.

Country A

Country A is a small, highly open economy with strong trade ties to the US and Europe. Services account for 80% of GDP focused on finance, professional services, and technology.

Trend growth is low at 1% alongside stable inflation at 2%. There is an independent central bank, government intervention in markets is minimal, and the exchange rate is floating. Fiscal accounts are transparent, and the budget is presented to parliament each year.

The financial sector is well-developed, featuring deep and liquid markets. Institutions are robust, characterized by high levels of accountability and transparency. The electorate is well-informed, and elections are conducted freely, fairly, and on time. Structural challenges include an aging population, growing income and regional inequality, and rising social tensions.

Country B

Country B is a large open emerging economy closely connected to the US, which accounts for 80% of exports. Services make up 60% of GDP, half of which is accounted for by automotive and electronics manufacturing.

Growth is moderate around 4% with structural challenges posed by low productivity and a large informal sector (about 50% of the workforce). Inflation is in the mid-single digits and is controlled by the central bank, which is often influenced by the government. The currency is floating, but the central bank intervenes when volatility is high or liquidity is low. Fiscal flexibility is limited, and the government has been running moderate to high fiscal deficits, often with undisclosed off–balance sheet transactions.

The financial markets are relatively well-developed for an emerging economy, characterized by a well-established cash and derivatives market. Institutional transparency is mixed, with the judiciary and public administration facing challenges from corruption and inefficiencies. Elections are timely and fair, although organized crime and gang violence are suspected of influencing outcomes in specific localities.

Country C

Country C is a frontier market economy heavily reliant on commodities, which make up around 80% of export revenues (mainly gold, oil, and cocoa). It has a large informal sector, employing around 80% of the workforce, and growth is volatile. The energy sector faces challenges, including frequent power outages, which also hurts industrial productivity.

Trend growth is high at 6–8% and inflation is in the low double-digits, with both indicators being relatively volatile. The exchange rate is pegged and managed by the government, which intervenes frequently. The government's fiscal capacity is limited, with low revenue mobilization (approximately 15% of GDP), which exacerbates debt vulnerabilities.

The financial system is underdeveloped, with limited banking penetration and shallow capital markets. The country's democracy is relatively stable, with peaceful elections, although election-related spending cycles dominate fiscal policy. The country struggles with high poverty rates, underdevelopment in rural areas, and a high susceptibility to climate shocks.

4.4 THE SOVEREIGN BALANCE SHEET

Understanding the government's balance sheet, including its assets, debt, and any contingent liabilities, offers insights into its associated financial risks and buffers. This sovereign balance sheet analysis can be expanded to other sectors of the economy, including the private financial and non-financial sectors, as well as the household sector.

The balance sheet approach for the country helps assess where leverage exists within the economy and where potential vulnerabilities may arise. Its usefulness was highlighted following the Asian Crisis of 1998, where solvency risks were initially posed by the non-financial corporate sector rather than the government or banking sectors. Assessing trends in the private sector, therefore, not only informs broad macroeconomic analysis but also helps determine the impact on the sovereign balance sheet through contingent liabilities and other left-tail risks.

Sovereign balance sheet analysis starts with examining recorded liquid assets. For most countries, this comprises foreign exchange international reserves, which are reported on a monthly or weekly basis. Other financial assets, such as sovereign wealth funds and national stabilization funds, are included if data is available; however, adjustments may be necessary for their liquidity.[4] Physical assets like land, buildings, infrastructure, and natural resources are typically excluded.

Next, we examine sovereign liabilities, which include government debt, known unfunded pension or social security obligations, intra-public sector arrears, and potential contingent liabilities. Data on government debt is published by the Ministry of Finance or the central bank, and can be compiled using country-specific and cross-country databases. Information on unfunded liabilities and arrears is more ad hoc and can be estimated through discussions with the Ministry of Finance, the IMF, and the World Bank country teams.[5]

Contingent liabilities refer to payment obligations or debts that may become the government's responsibility. Information on explicit government guarantees is often included in government debt figures. Implicit guarantees may arise from leverage in systemically important institutions, unforeseen spending related to natural or other disasters, government bailouts of unfunded pension and social security systems, banking sector bailouts, or state and local government debt. This information has to be pieced together by country analysts, with ranges estimated from scenario analysis outputs.

Balance sheet analysis can be similarly performed for each sector of the economy, including the bank and financial sectors, the non-financial corporate sector, and households. Data quality can vary widely across sectors and countries, and may be published with a lag for some variables. Supplementing the numerical analysis with in-country on-the-ground sources is therefore essential to get an accurate picture.

Information on the banking sector is generally detailed and collected by central banks and/or regulatory bodies in each country. Other sources are the IMF-World Bank Financial Sector Assessment Program (FSAP), which examines the risks in the financial

TABLE 4.3 A Sample Country Balance Sheet, $ Billions

	Country	
	Local Currency	Foreign Currency
Assets	455	475
Liabilities	315	505
Net	140	−30

	Central Government		Banking Sector	
	Local Currency	Foreign Currency	Local Currency	Foreign Currency
Assets	150	90	200	250
Liabilities	125	100	150	200
Net	25	−10	50	50

	Corporate Sector		Household Sector	
	Local Currency	Foreign Currency	Local Currency	Foreign Currency
Assets	80	125	25	10
Liabilities	30	200	10	5
Net	50	−75	15	5

sector of several countries, and the Bank for International Settlements (BIS), which provides data on financial sector soundness indicators and stress tests.

Information about the non-financial private sector varies by country. In some instances, data is available on the amount of leverage, currency exposure of debt, and rollover risks. The household sector typically has the least accessible information. The primary data sources are usually national expenditure surveys or credit data compiled by banks.

Table 4.3 illustrates a country's balance sheet and highlights potential areas of financial mismatches. These may include *currency mismatches*, such as when liabilities are denominated in foreign currencies while assets are predominantly in local currency; *maturity mismatches*, which occur when assets and liabilities have different terms, such as short-term versus medium or long-term; *sectoral mismatches* where assets belong to one sector of the economy and liabilities to another; and *solvency risks* when the value of assets falls below that of the liabilities on a sustained basis.

In Table 4.3, we see that the government's balance sheet is relatively healthy with a small net negative foreign currency position. While the banking sector has foreign currency leverage, it is matched by assets held abroad. There are substantial currency and rollover risks in the non-financial corporate sector, as they owe debt in mostly dollars and have assets in domestic currency. Meanwhile, the household sector has low leverage. The country is borrowing about $30 billion from overseas on a net basis, which indicates that currency risk may be a factor to monitor.

4.4.1 Sample Country Balance Sheet Analysis

Country A

Country A's balance sheet shows a complex yet stable macro-financial picture. As of 2024, gross government debt is around 100% of GDP, with financial assets, including foreign exchange reserves, around 30–35% of GDP. While the government primarily issues long-duration, local-currency-denominated debt, its rising debt stock and growing interest burden expose it to refinancing risk in a higher-interest-rate environment.

Banking sector total assets of over 450% of GDP indicate a large, international financial system. Cross-border exposures pose currency and maturity mismatch risks, but regulations and liquidity requirements help reduce systemic risks. The non-financial corporate sector holds debt around 75% of GDP, compared with 50% of assets, exposing it to rollover risks.

Household debt is about 85% of GDP, predominantly in fixed-rate mortgages, which limits near-term rollover risk; however, expiring fixed terms could expose borrowers to higher rates. Meanwhile, household financial assets exceed 200% of the country's GDP, providing strong buffers. Overall, the country exhibits a highly financialized economy, with elevated gross leverage across sectors underscoring the need for active risk monitoring.

Country B

Country B's balance sheet reflects a moderately leveraged economy with some exposure to external and market-based risks. As of 2024, general government gross debt was approximately 48% of GDP, supported by a conservative fiscal framework and modest primary deficits. Approximately 40% of government debt is denominated in dollars, posing moderate currency risks. Contingent liabilities stem from SOE debt (~10% of GDP) and compare with foreign currency reserves of 15% of GDP.

Banking sector assets are small by international standards at 55% of GDP, and largely funded in domestic currency, limiting systemic currency mismatch. Non-financial corporate debt is around 30–35% of GDP, with a significant share issued in foreign currency and in offshore markets. This exposes firms to currency mismatches and refinancing pressure when the currency weakens or global credit conditions tighten. Household debt remains low at approximately 16% of GDP, with limited exposure to variable-rate risk.

Country C

Country C's balance sheet is strained by high government debt, commodity dependence, and currency depreciation risks (50% in 2024). Public debt accounts for ~93% of GDP, with 50% denominated in foreign currency, which poses a high risk of default. Contingent liabilities include energy sector debts (~5% of GDP), compared with foreign exchange reserves of 4% of GDP.

The banking sector exhibits stress with non-performing loans (NPLs) at 21.8% and a large exposure to government debt. The corporate sector is moderately levered with debt of 10% of GDP and export revenues from gold, oil, and cocoa supporting debt service. Household leverage is low and poorly documented due to informality. The country's balance sheet warrants detailed debt sustainability analysis and monitoring of early warning indicators for default risk.

4.5 MACROECONOMIC ANALYSIS

We now turn to macroeconomic analysis for sovereigns and its application to investment strategies. Macroeconomics provides the context for understanding growth dynamics, interest rate movements, exchange rate fluctuations, fiscal dynamics, and changes in credit risk—all of which are key drivers of sovereign bond valuations and returns.

4.5.1 Economic Variables

The entire field of macroeconomics is dedicated to modeling economies, business cycles, and the interdependencies among macroeconomic variables. The main components of analysis focus on the interplay between several core pillars and forecasting their future trajectories: Economic activity encompasses growth, the output gap, and inflation. Fiscal policy concentrates on the budget balance, breakdown of government expenditure, taxation, and debt dynamics. Monetary policy highlights inflation targets, policy rates, and central bank mandates. The external position evaluates the current account, capital flows, exchange rate dynamics, and foreign currency reserves. Financial sector assessments consider the health of both the banking and non-banking financial sectors.

Understanding the empirical sensitivities of macroeconomic variables to domestic and global shocks enhances forecasting. For example, a drop in oil prices may affect commodity exporters very differently than commodity importers. A sharp depreciation in the exchange rate may have a larger impact on inflation for highly open economies compared to countries with a lower share of trade openness. Countries with a history of hyperinflation may have built-in rigidities in wage and price setting, which affect how food price shocks translate into future inflation, etc.

Sovereign analysts consequently select the relevant variables and models to focus on depending on the country and stage of the business cycle. In advanced economies like Country A, analysts may focus on business cycle indicators such as unemployment, growth, and consumer credit trends. In emerging market economies like Country B, the focus might be on inflation rates, the current account, and fiscal balance. Frontier markets like Country C may require attention to debt levels and foreign exchange reserves coverage.

In this way the focus of macroeconomic analysis is adapted to each country and economic context. Investors then utilize macroeconomic data releases and economic assessments to create a dynamic picture of the economy, continually updating their views on the sovereign macro and credit outlook.

PRO TIP: *Identify the main economic and financial variables to monitor for each country and set up alerts to monitor them.*

4.5.2 The IMF's Macroeconomic Framework

A useful reference is the IMF's macroeconomic framework, which captures linkages between various sectors of the economy in a way that is internally consistent.[6] The methodology employs a financial accounting approach that links economic identities of relationships between macro variables iteratively to ensure consistency across various sectors. In doing so, it facilitates the analysis of the current state of the economy, forecasts macroeconomic variables, and assesses the impact of government policies.

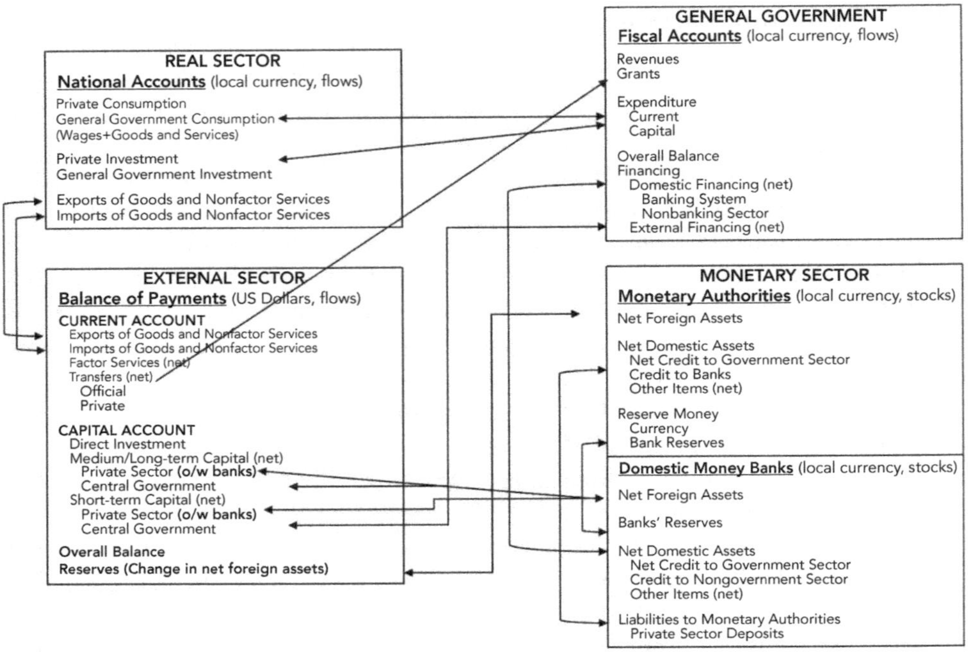

FIGURE 4.2 The IMF's macroeconomic framework. SOURCE: Gottschalk (2013)/International Monetary Fund (IMF).

Figure 4.2 provides an overview of the IMF's macroeconomic framework. Note that each component of the macroeconomic framework interacts with the others. These frameworks form the basis for IMF surveillance of member countries and for IMF financing programs. They are an integral part of the inputs for IMF policy advice and for sovereign debt restructurings. As such, they are especially important for bond investors to understand.

Studies suggest IMF growth and fiscal balance forecasts tend to be optimistic for IMF program countries. Investors have also questioned the real exchange rate forecasts used in restructuring cases. Critiques highlight that forecasting errors in the IMF's macroeconomic frameworks can be significant.[7] This may be due to drawbacks in the methodology, such as the assumption of exogeneity of variables in each identity, difficulties in predicting behavioral relationships between economic variables, or biases in IMF forecasts.

Considering this, IMF macro frameworks should be viewed as a preliminary guide to the economy rather than a precise tool for forecasting. They are valuable for cross-checking government economic forecasts, especially when they diverge from the assumptions used in the IMF tables. Rather than relying on them, investors should conduct their own macro assessments distinct from those of third parties. These should be enhanced with models for forecasting growth, inflation, credit growth, and the exchange rate, among others.

4.5.3 Sample Country Macroeconomic Analysis

Country A

Country A's economy is relatively resilient, with growth at 1.5%yoy annually after a sharp contraction during the COVID pandemic. Inflation is high at 3%yoy given energy price shocks, but is gradually decreasing following central bank policy rate hikes.

The government has tightened fiscal policy to −3% of GDP, from peaks of −12% of GDP during the pandemic. The balance of payments is fully funded, with a −4% of GDP current account covered by capital account inflows.

Macroeconomic analysis is focused on the drivers of inflation, the policy path of central bank rates, and currency dynamics.

Country B

Country B's economy is recovering from a period of high inflation alongside moderating growth. Growth rates are 4%yoy from an 8%yoy contraction during the pandemic. Inflation at 4.5%yoy is above the inflation target of 4%, despite steep central bank policy hikes.

Fiscal deficits are manageable at −2% of GDP, following previous highs of −4% of GDP during the election year. The current account is balanced, supported by manufacturing exports and remittances, and the capital account is stable.

Further analysis is focused on inflation dynamics, the trajectory of central bank rates, currency trends, and contingent liabilities from state-owned enterprises (SOEs).

Country C

Country C's growth is strong at 8%yoy following growth rates of only 0.5%yoy during the pandemic. Nonetheless, this growth remains dependent on commodities and is relatively volatile as a result. Inflation is elevated at 15%yoy, driven by currency depreciation and rising energy costs. Policy rate increases to 30% have helped, but have also led to fiscal financing pressures due to the increasing costs of short-term local currency debt.

Fiscal deficits are substantial at −10% of GDP, with the interest bill representing a large portion of expenditures. Consequently, public debt ratios are on an unsustainable path, exceeding 93% of GDP, a significant portion of which is denominated in foreign currency. Currency depreciation has triggered a drain on reserves, despite the current account deficit being moderate at −3% of GDP, and there is a real risk of capital controls.

Sovereign analysis is concentrated on fiscal financing needs, rollover risks, debt sustainability, and recovery rates in the event of a default.

4.6 USING MACROECONOMIC MODELING TO INFORM BOND INVESTMENT STRATEGIES

The diverse economies that make up the sovereign asset class mean there is no single macroeconomic model that applies to all countries in all situations. The sovereign debt investor must therefore use a variety of economic models, question existing behavioral relationships, and consistently be on the lookout for structural changes, especially in the aftermath of significant global or domestic shocks.

Together with macroeconomic analysis, macroeconomic models inform bond valuations and returns by linking economic conditions to changes in interest rates, yield curves, credit spreads, and currency movements. Let's review some common applications for investing in sovereign bonds. Part Three provides a more detailed discussion of these investment strategies for bond portfolios.

> ***PRO TIP:*** *Identify trade themes for each country and list any additional analysis required to action them.*

4.6.1 Interest Rate Strategies

The pillars of macroeconomic analysis for fixed-income investors are growth and inflation forecasts. These can be used to predict recessions, overheating, and changes in the central bank's policy rate. For instance, an economy growing above its potential may experience inflation rising above target rates. Conversely, an economy growing below potential may see declining inflation. A third scenario is where growth slows, but inflation increases, putting a stagflationary impulse on the economy. Economic models like the Phillips Curve, which links inflation to economic slack, may be used to forecast these relationships between growth and inflation.

Once a view on the macroeconomic path is formulated, the investor looks to predict the behavior of the central bank and interest rates. Policy forecasting models, such as the Taylor Rule or dynamic stochastic general equilibrium models, can forecast the trajectory of central bank policy rates. The anticipated path of policy rates can influence the path of market interest rates and the level and shape of the sovereign yield curve.

For instance, strong growth and rising inflation typically steepen the yield curve, increasing long-term yields. This is because the central bank is expected to raise policy rates in the future to bring inflation back toward the target. Conversely, fears of a recession can lead to a flattening or an inversion of the yield curve based on the expectation that the central bank will need to lower policy rates to support growth.

Portfolio managers compare macroeconomic forecasts and model results with market expectations and adjust their portfolios accordingly. If they expect interest rates to rise and the yield curve to steepen, they may reduce exposure to long-term interest-sensitive instruments. Conversely, they may increase exposure if they anticipate interest rates to fall and the yield curve to invert or flatten. The example of Brazil over 2021–2022 illustrates this in practice.

Example: Brazil 2021–2022

In 2021, Brazil's Consumer Price Index (CPI) inflation surged to over 10%yoy, driven by rising global commodity prices and a depreciating Brazilian real. The central bank operated under an inflation-targeting framework with a mandate to anchor inflation expectations around a 3% midpoint target. Even as inflation expectations rose, the central bank's policy rate remained at 4.25% in early 2021.

Economists and markets looked to forecast inflation and the forward policy path. Inflation forecasts were based on Phillips Curve models, macroeconometric models, and CPI index decomposition. The Phillips Curve suggested that inflation in 2021 should average about 7.5%yoy, significantly underestimating actual inflation, which was closer to 10%yoy. This underestimation was attributed to the effects of currency depreciation that were not accurately incorporated in the model.

Macroeconometric models, such as vector autoregression (VAR) models, forecast inflation based on growth, past inflation, the policy rate, and the currency. These predicted inflation rates to be around 9%yoy, closer to actual outcomes. Accounting models that decomposed CPI index components and forecasted each separately, and also estimated inflation to be elevated and below 10%yoy. Meanwhile, market-based indicators, such as breakeven inflation rates from inflation-linked instruments, similarly suggested high and sustained inflation.

The next step was to forecast the central bank's policy rate path. Modified Taylor Rule models incorporating the impact of currency pass-through pointed to a policy rate hike to 15%. The eventual outcome was interest rate increases from 4.25% in February 2021 to a 20-year high of 13.75% by August 2022. The central bank's hiking path was moderated in practice due to fiscal concerns. Even so, the central bank's statements were hawkish, emphasizing vigilance and the need to anchor expectations, indicating that policy rates would remain high for some time.

Investors traded these developments in a number of ways. Those that believed that the central bank would hike more than the markets anticipated decreased interest rate exposure in their portfolios by selling government bonds or paying interest rate swaps. Others who expected the central bank to stop short of market expectations due to fiscal concerns increased exposure by buying government bonds or receiving interest rate swaps.

4.6.2 Exchange Rate Strategies

Currency movements are another area of focus for investors. This is particularly important for sovereign debt investors, as currency fluctuations directly affect returns, debt sustainability, and the perceived creditworthiness of a country. Macroeconomic analysis of external accounts and various currency models can help predict exchange rate trends.

The balance of payments, the current account balance, and foreign exchange reserves of an economy can influence currency stability and foreign exchange rates. Countries with persistent and rising current account deficits may experience currency depreciations, while those with significant capital account inflows can witness currency appreciations.

Currency models are broadly categorized into fundamental, behavioral, and market-based approaches. Each model captures different currency drivers and forecasts movements over various time horizons.

Fundamental models include the Purchasing Power Parity (PPP) and Real Effective Exchange Rate (REER) approaches. They focus on the long-term economic drivers of currencies and identify exchange rate overvaluation and undervaluation by comparing spot rates to long-term benchmarks.

Behavioral Equilibrium Exchange Rate (BEER) models estimate the *equilibrium* exchange rate using econometric methods and compare it to current REER rates. They are commonly used by the IMF and central banks and serve as the foundation for valuation-based relative value FX trades.

Portfolio Balance Models forecast exchange rates based on the relative supply and demand for domestic and foreign assets. They emphasize capital account flows, such as foreign investor holdings of local debt and sovereign risk premia, in determining exchange rates.

Investors rely on signals from these models to determine whether a currency is overvalued or undervalued, and whether it is expected to move in one direction or the other. They may enhance their macroeconomic analysis with technical and flow-based insights into the currency markets. Portfolio managers can then use hedging instruments like FX swaps to mitigate currency risks in anticipation of potential currency depreciation or increase currency risk if they expect currency appreciation. The example of Turkey in 2018 outlines how the use of currency forecasts can help investors position themselves amid volatile markets.

Example: Turkey 2018

In mid-2018, the Turkish lira depreciated by more than 40% against the USD within a few short months. The depreciation occurred against a volatile economic backdrop driven by high inflation, unconventional monetary policy, and rising geopolitical risks.

Traditional currency models indicated that the lira had overshot fundamentals even after taking into account the weak macroeconomic indicators, worsening external balances, and decreasing foreign exchange reserves. In particular, the BEER and FEER model estimates suggested that the currency was approximately 20–25% undervalued.

Despite this, investors remained hesitant to invest in the lira as the central bank had adopted unorthodox monetary policies, refusing to raise interest rates because they believed it would exacerbate inflation rather than control it. Eventually, the central bank capitulated and hiked rates, raising the effective policy rate by over 1,100 basis points. Even so, heterodox policymaking persisted and inflation surged rapidly, resulting in further currency depreciations from 2020 to 2022.

Overtime foreign investors reduced exposure to Turkish assets shorting the lira and selling onshore holdings in Turkish government bonds. This illustrates that even when valuations are cheap for a given asset, the macroeconomic backdrop and policy stance are critical for investors to build positions in a given sovereign.

4.6.3 Credit Risk Strategies

Investors utilize macroeconomic metrics along with models of debt sustainability, early warning frameworks, and credit ratings to evaluate the credit risk linked to an issuer. This helps underpin credit risk strategies in sovereign bonds.

Macroeconomic indicators such as debt-to-GDP ratios, primary fiscal balance, and interest payments relative to revenues impact sovereign credit risk. Rapid increases in fiscal deficits and debt burdens elevate credit risk and may lead to widening credit spreads on government bonds. Conversely, improving budget balances and implementing credible government policies to reduce debt may lower credit risk and tighten credit spreads.

A high credit risk relative to market pricing may lead to the selling of bond exposures or hedging the credit risk using CDS. Conversely, a decline in credit risk and expectations of credit rating upgrades may encourage portfolio managers to add sovereign bonds and/or increase credit risk exposure through derivatives. The example of South Africa is a case in point where deteriorating fiscal metrics resulted in an eventual downgrade from investment grade to high yield.

Example: South Africa 2017–2020

South Africa faced significant fiscal challenges over 2017 to 2020. Economic growth was weak, public expenditures were rising, and fiscal deficits were projected to reach increasingly larger figures. At the same time, President Zuma was contending with political pressures related to state capture scandals.

Analysts forecasted the effects of deteriorating macroeconomic factors and the fiscal deficit on debt ratios, as well as the weaker institutional backdrop affecting the sovereign's creditworthiness. The budget deficit ultimately rose from approximately 3.9% of GDP in 2018 to 6.3% of GDP in 2019, while debt ratios increased from 50% of GDP in 2017 to 63% of GDP in 2020.

In November 2017, S&P downgraded South Africa's foreign currency rating from investment grade to high yield. This was eventually followed by the other credit rating agencies, Moody's and Fitch, in 2000. The downgrades led to wider credit spreads for the South Africa complex, with five-year CDS spreads increasing from 180 basis points in mid-2017 to around 400 basis points by mid-2020, reflecting the market's higher perception of credit risk. At the same time, the currency weakened by about 30%, while local yields increased by about 350 basis points.

Investors had positioned themselves for the deteriorating credit fundamentals by selling South Africa government holdings and by buying CDS, getting ahead of the wider credit spreads before the ratings downgrade from investment grade to high yield.

4.7 QUALITATIVE FACTORS

Sovereign analysis extends beyond quantitative metrics like growth, debt ratios, and fiscal deficits. Qualitative and subjective factors can also significantly influence a country's macro trajectory, government policies, and creditworthiness. Political stability, institutional quality, governance, geopolitical risks, social dynamics, and policy credibility are all qualitative variables that capture nuanced but potentially crucial risks.

Other qualitative drivers can be equally relevant. In particular, governance and corruption can have a direct impact on fiscal transparency, revenue collection, and investor confidence. This has played out in many countries, both developed and developing. The example of South Africa from 2017 to 2020, when President Zuma faced accusations of corruption and state capture, is just one such incident. Another relates to the loss of market confidence due to perceptions of unsustainable policy choices as discussed in the example of the UK below.

It's also crucial to factor in geopolitical considerations, including the risk of war and conflict, when analyzing sovereign risk. This is particularly important for investors buying sovereign debt in countries like Ukraine, which has been embroiled in a long-standing conflict with Russia, or issuers in the Middle East, given the region's complex geopolitics.

Example: UK 2016–2022

In the UK, the Brexit referendum in 2016 changed the economic and trading landscape the country had operated under for decades. A series of leadership crises ensued with five prime ministers over 7 years, the same number as over the previous 37 years.

The importance of policy credibility, even in developed markets, was highlighted with Liz Truss's election in 2022. Her mini-budget, which focused on unfunded tax cuts, triggered market panic, leading to a widening of five-year UK CDS spreads and a sharp spike in government bond yields. The swift policy reversal by the next PM, Rishi Sunak, restored stability.

While the long-term impact of Brexit is yet to be realized, higher trade costs and the relocation of financial services to Europe have already had a negative impact on the macroeconomy. Even so, this episode demonstrates how strong institutions in advanced countries can quickly readdress a temporary loss of market confidence. In contrast, emerging and frontier markets have much fewer degrees of freedom to recover from policy mistakes.

4.8 SCENARIO ANALYSIS

Scenario analysis and risk factor assessment help investors understand the vulnerabilities in the economy and their potential impacts. Some common scenarios to consider include elections, geopolitical events, and the impact of natural disasters. Macroeconomic shocks to currencies, growth, and fiscal accounts can also be useful in assessing their effect on the economy and its vulnerabilities.

Other scenarios to evaluate include assessment of financial and asset market bubbles in the equity markets, housing market, or specific sectors (like technology). Incorporating the impact of climate change can further illuminate transition and adaptation risks and the need for mitigation.

Investors should also consider the risk mitigants and backstops available to an economy. These include financial buffers in the form of savings and foreign currency reserves, low sensitivity to global shocks, policy space, and flexible policy frameworks that allow fluid responses to unforeseen developments and shocks.

Strategic bilateral and multilateral relationships are additional considerations. In normal times, they may drive foreign direct investment, while in times of stress, they may lead to direct financial support. The potential for IMF programs during sovereign crises should also be evaluated, as some countries have stronger relationships with the IFIs and are geopolitically more strategic. These countries are more likely to access funds with relatively greater ease and less conditionality than others.

Understanding the *known risks and mitigants*, along with the *known unknowns*, when approaching fundamental sovereign analysis helps prepare investments and portfolios for changes in economic conditions and potential macroeconomic shocks. Part Three delves deeper into how these investment decisions are shaped.

4.9 SOUTH AFRICA CASE STUDY

We now examine the case of South Africa and apply what we have learned about conducting fundamental analysis. For many emerging and frontier markets, a deep understanding of debt composition and debt service is necessary, as detailed below. Together, these enable analysts to understand the sovereign credit risk better.

South Africa is an upper-middle-income emerging market with a GDP of $400 billion, a per capita GDP of $6,253 (as of 2024), and a Ba2/BB-BB foreign currency sovereign credit rating. The Ministry of Finance (also known as the National Treasury) and the central bank's websites regularly provide government debt and macro statistics.[8]

The economy is diversified, featuring a mix of advanced financial services, a robust mining and natural resources sector, and a substantial informal economy. It has deep capital markets, strong legal institutions, and an inflation-targeting central bank (the SARB), operating under a credible monetary policy framework. The country is highly integrated into global trade and financial markets through its commodity exports and capital flows into the local currency bond market.

Despite these strengths, South Africa faces persistent structural challenges, including high unemployment, inequality, infrastructure deficits, and energy constraints. Its young demographics offer long-term potential, but governance issues and political uncertainty related to coalition dynamics and state-owned enterprise reform continue to weigh on investor confidence.

South Africa's GDP growth has averaged below 2% over the past decade, with recent gains hampered by electricity shortages, logistics bottlenecks, and subdued investment.

Inflation has moderated significantly, falling below 3% in mid-2025, allowing the South African Reserve Bank (SARB) to begin easing policy from its 7.5% peak. The rand is stable, supported by disinflation and improving external balances, though it remains sensitive to global risk sentiment. The current deficit is small at −0.6% of GDP in 2024, while FX reserves at $66 billion cover roughly 5.5 months of imports. Fiscal consolidation remains gradual, with the consolidated budget deficit projected at 4.6% of GDP in FY2024/25.

Turning to debt and leverage, the gross national government debt is high, at 78% of GDP, with 70% of GDP comprising domestic debt and 8% of GDP comprising foreign debt, based on the residency of holders (Table 4.4). A significant portion of government debt is marketable, accounting for approximately 69% of the country's GDP. Additionally, the government has provided financial guarantees amounting to 9% of GDP for public

TABLE 4.4 South Africa's Debt Statistics, Q1 2025

Government Debt	**Mn ZAR**	**% GDP**
Gross National Government Debt	5,693,471	78.2
Domestic Debt	5,091,703	70.0
Marketable	5,060,451	69.5
Government Bonds	4,510,965	62.0
Treasury Bills	549,486	7.5
Non-marketable	31,252	0.4
Foreign debt*	601,768	8.3
Marketable	450,791	6.2
Non-marketable	150,977	2.1
Other Debt	46	0.0
Financial Guarantees by the Government	678,995	9.3
External Debt	**Mn $**	**% GDP**
External** Debt	173,051	40.6
Foreign Currency Debt***	94,756	20.6
General Govt External** Debt	81,683	23.8
Central Govt	63,602	18.6
Public Corporations	17,571	5.0
Monetary Authorities	510	0.2
Nominal GDP mn ZAR	7,278,690	
Nominal GDP mn $	399,219	

Source: Haver Analytics, *Source*: South Africa National Treasury, South African Reserve Bank.
Notes: *Currency basis; **Residency basis; ***2024

corporations such as Eskom, the state-owned electricity utility. Long-term public debt sustainability hinges on raising potential growth and containing SOE-related liabilities, particularly from Eskom and Transnet.

The total external debt for the economy accounts for 41% of GDP, while the total foreign currency debt represents 21% of GDP. This indicates significant non-resident ownership of local currency debt. Total public sector external debt accounts for 24% of GDP, with the central government being the largest contributor. The difference between the foreign debt of the national government, at 8% of GDP, and the public external debt, at 19% of GDP, further highlights that nearly half of the substantial non-resident participation in the local currency debt is in central government securities.

The National Treasury also reports the ownership of domestic bond securities. Short-term debt (defined as less than three years) comprises 11% of the total stock, with most of it held by banks and private non-financial corporations, such as mutual funds. Long-term debt (defined as debt with a maturity of more than three years) accounts for the majority of domestic debt, with non-financial corporations owning approximately half of the total, and the remainder held by the Public Investment Corporation (which manages the South African Government Employees Pension Fund), banks, and other funds.

Data on holdings by fixed and floating-rate debt indicate that 73% of government bonds are fixed-rate, with the remainder being floating-rate debt. The ownership of each bond series is reported in greater detail, distinguishing holdings among the foreign sector, monetary institutions, insurers, pension funds, and other financial institutions. With this information, bondholders can evaluate which series exhibit a higher concentration of foreign holders, long-term buy-and-hold investors, and which may be more susceptible to withdrawals or rollover risks.

For sovereign investors, South Africa presents a profile of moderate credit risk with high liquidity, offering opportunities through selective positioning tied to fiscal discipline, SOE reform, and macro stabilization. Investors can gain exposure to South African sovereign assets through government external and local bonds and a range of derivative instruments, including 5-year CDS, IRS (up to 10 years), FRAs, and ZAR spot and forward contracts. The state-owned electricity corporation, Eskom, also issues external and local currency debt, some of which are guaranteed by the government.

The types of bonds issued by South Africa include:

- External USD bullet bond: SOAF 4 ¼ 05/15/35
- Local law ZAR bond: SAGB 8 ⅞ 02/28/35
- Local law ZAR inflation-linked bond: SACPI 3.45 12/07/33
- Local law ZAR Treasury bill: three-month T-bill
- Eskom USD bullet bond: Eskom 8.45 08/10/28
- Eskom ZAR bond: Eskom 8 ½ 04/25/42
- Eskom ZAR government guaranteed bonds: Bonds issued under the Domestic Multi-Term Note (DMTN) program

4.10 SUMMARY

This chapter reviewed the building blocks of fundamental analysis for sovereigns. It covered the structural elements to look for when assessing an economy, how to examine a country's balance sheet, and various aspects of macroeconomic modeling for an economy. The use of these models to inform bond investment strategies was also discussed, together with historical examples.

Importantly, fundamental analysis should be viewed as a video rather than a snapshot. Investors continually update their views on a country as new information and data are released. This forms the basis for their investment and credit perspectives, necessitating additional analysis if conditions change.

Building on this analysis and combining the various indicators, we have sovereign credit ratings. These ratings are used to quickly compare credit risk across countries and different asset classes. This is what we examine next.

NOTES

1. See Gonzalez-Garcia, *Improving Sovereign Financing Conditions*, on how data transparency can change borrowing costs.
2. See Mustapha and Olivares-Caminal, *Improving Transparency of Lending*, and IMF and World Bank, *G20 Note on Public Debt Recording*, for further details on Mozambique's "Tuna-bond" scandal.
3. The IMF's Data Standards Initiative encourages countries to publish economic data promptly and with prescribed requirements. There are three tiers: the Enhanced General Data Dissemination System (e-GDDS), the Special Data Dissemination System (SDDS), and the SDDS Plus. See the IMF's Dissemination Standards Bulletin Board (DSBB) at www.imf.org for further information.
4. Cross-country sources include the Global SWF Database and the Sovereign Wealth Fund Institute.
5. The IMF maintains the Public Sector Balance Sheet Database, which includes estimates of public sector assets and liabilities for a cross-section of countries. However, there is substantial heterogeneity in data quality and coverage.
6. See IMF Institute, *Financial Programming and Policy*, and Easterly, *An Identity Crisis?*
7. See IMF IEO, *IMF Forecasts*.
8. https://www.treasury.gov.za/ (accessed 29 July 2025) and https://www.resbank.co.za/en/home (accessed 29 July 2025).

REFERENCES

Abbas, Ali S., and Kenneth Rogoff. "A Guide to Sovereign Debt Data." Appendix in *Sovereign Debt: A Guide for Economists and Practitioners*, edited by S. Ali Abbas, Alex Pienkowski, and Kenneth Rogoff. Oxford: Oxford University Press, 2022.

Easterly, William. *An Identity Crises? Testing IMF Financial Programming*. Center for Global Development Working Paper No. 9, 2002.

Gonzalez-Garcia, J. Rodrigo. *Improving Sovereign Financing Conditions Through Data Transparency*. IMF Working Paper WP/22/230. Washington, DC: International Monetary Fund, 2022.

Gottschalk, Jan. *Macroeconomic Frameworks and Financial Programming*. Washington, DC: International Monetary Fund, 2013.

IMF Independent Evaluation Office (IEO). *IMF Forecasts: Process, Quality, and Country Perspectives*. Washington, DC: International Monetary Fund, 2014. https://ieo.imf.org/en/Evaluations (accessed 29 July 2025).

IMF Institute. *Financial Programming and Policy: The Case of Sri Lanka*. Washington, DC: International Monetary Fund, 1996. https://www.imf.org (accessed 29 July 2025).

International Monetary Fund and World Bank. *G20 Note: Improving Public Debt Recording, Monitoring, and Reporting Capacity in Low and Lower Middle-Income Countries: Proposed Reforms*. Washington, DC: IMF and World Bank, 2018. https://www.worldbank.org (accessed 29 July 2025).

Mustapha, Shakira, and Rodrigo Olivares-Caminal. *Improving Transparency of Lending to Sovereign Governments*. ODI Working Paper No. 583. London: Overseas Development Institute, 2020.

CHAPTER FIVE

Sovereign Credit Ratings

SOVEREIGN CREDIT RATINGS provide forward-looking assessments of a country's *ability and willingness* to fully and promptly meet its debt obligations.[1] A nation may have sufficient resources at a given time, yet be unwilling to make repayments due to the sacrifices involved. Conversely, a government might be firmly committed to repaying creditors but lack the financial capacity because of budgetary constraints. These ratings serve as a concise measure of a sovereign's creditworthiness and the risks investors face when lending to its central government.

Credit ratings allow investors to compare credit fundamentals across issuers and categorize sovereign bonds into various risk tiers. They can indicate improvements or declines in an issuer's credit quality and permit investors to transact and adjust positions before these changes are reflected in the market pricing. Additionally, client mandates use ratings to define the investible universe and describe what is permitted and what is excluded in terms of exposures.

In global financial markets, credit ratings serve various regulatory and operational roles. These include determining the risk weights of government bonds for Basel capital requirements, establishing collateral eligibility of government securities in central bank monetary operations, and assessing index eligibility of sovereigns.

Sovereign credit ratings are issued by rating agencies such as Moody's, Standard & Poor's, and Fitch. Investors can also create their own credit ratings to reflect their perspectives on sovereign fundamentals, the future trajectory of the macroeconomy, political and geopolitical implications, and other factors influencing creditworthiness.

This chapter examines sovereign credit ratings, including the ratings scale, methodologies, and differences between the three major agencies. It discusses the difference between domestic and foreign currency ratings, default ratings, and the integration of sustainability considerations in assessing creditworthiness. The chapter ends with a discussion of market-implied credit ratings and whether, and when, agencies have a market impact.

5.1 CREDIT RATING AGENCIES

The three leading global credit rating agencies (CRAs) are Moody's Investor Services (Moody's), Standard & Poor's (S&P), and Fitch Ratings (Fitch).[2] They categorize credit risk into ordinal letter grades that reflect a comparative assessment of the risk of default. Issuers rated AAA through BBB are the highest quality and are considered investment grade. Credits rated BB and below are classified as high yield, speculative, or non-investment grade. The third category, CCC or lower, describes sovereigns with a high likelihood of default or those currently in default (see Table 5.1).

TABLE 5.1 Rating Agencies Long-Term Issuer Foreign Currency Ratings

Category	Interpretation	Moody's	S&P	Fitch
Investment Grade	Highest Quality	Aaa	AAA	AAA
	High Quality	Aa1	AA+	AA+
		Aa2	AA	AA
		Aa3	AA−	AA−
	Strong payment capacity	A1	A+	A+
		A2	A	A
		A3	A−	A−
	Adequate payment capacity	Baa1	BBB+	BBB+
		Baa2	BBB	BBB
		Baa3	BBB−	BBB−
Speculative Grade	Likely to fulfill obligations, ongoing uncertainty	Ba1	BB+	BB+
		Ba2	BB	BB
		Ba3	BB−	BB−
	High risk obligations	B1	B+	B+
		B2	B	B
		B3	B−	B−
	Vulnerable to default	Caa1	CCC+	CCC+
		Caa2	CCC	CCC
		Caa3	CCC−	CCC−
Default	Near or in default	Ca	CC	CC
		C	C	C
		C	SD / D	RD
				D

Source: Adapted from Moody's (2023b), Standard and Poor's (2023a), Fitch Ratings (2023b).

Applying the ratings scale to the sample countries we discussed in Chapter 4, Country A's rating would likely range from AAA to A, Country B's from BBB to BB, and Country C's from B to CCC.

Ratings are generated for both issuers and instruments, across short-term and long-term maturities, in both foreign and local currency debt, and for bonds and loans. Long-term sovereign credit ratings align with the typical maturity of the sovereign's debt, which is 5–10 years. Short-term ratings pertain to credit assessments for the upcoming 12 months.

Rating outlooks complement letter ratings and reflect a six-month to two-year trend for the credit. A negative outlook indicates a potential downgrade, while a positive outlook indicates a potential upgrade. For event-driven rating changes, the CRAs issue credit or rating watches, which have a shorter time horizon for resolution (typically 90 days).[3] The letter rating, outlook, and credit watch are usually accompanied by in-depth credit reports that include the latest macroeconomic forecasts, policy implementation, and additional risk analysis.

Let's use Brazil's sovereign credit rating to illustrate the different ratings. As of May 2025, Brazil's foreign currency long-term rating was Ba1 with a Positive Outlook from Moody's, BB with a Stable Outlook from S&P, and BB with a Stable Outlook from Fitch. These ratings align with the country's respective local currency long-term rating. S&P and Fitch assess the foreign and domestic currency short-term rating as B.[4] Brazil's complete country report is available on each CRA's respective website for subscribers.

Credit ratings are periodically reviewed based on the CRA's internal schedule and country-specific dynamics. CRAs publish a calendar of rating reviews for the EU sovereigns (per regulations). Timelines for other regions can be estimated from the previous review and serve as a signal for potential rating changes and related market impacts.

PRO TIP: *Monitor the timing of CRA ratings actions and review positions and market pricing ahead of time.*

For investors, sovereign ratings from the CRAs have both advantages and disadvantages. Their benefits include independent ratings assessments conducted by specialists focused on specific countries and regions.[5] CRAs often have unique access to government officials and data that is not readily available to the market. Additionally, analyst ratings are typically reviewed by internal rating committees to ensure consistency and comparability across countries.

Limitations include infrequent rating reviews (typically one to two annually) that may not reflect rapidly changing credit conditions. Agency analysts might have differing views from those of investors on qualitative issues, such as a government's willingness to repay debt, the policy implementation of a new administration, or the risk of civilian unrest. CRAs might also apply different criteria for rating changes compared to investors, especially when issuers transition from investment grade to high yield (or vice versa).

5.2 A FRAMEWORK FOR MODELING SOVEREIGN CREDIT RATINGS

Many sovereign debt investors seek to create in-house credit ratings with enhancements tailored to their investment horizons and styles. These supplement CRA ratings and have the advantage of incorporating investor views and implementing new information quickly. The in-house approach also enables early forecasting of CRA ratings changes, which may impact market spreads and trading conditions.

Modeling sovereign credit risk involves evaluating a country's ability and willingness to fully and timely repay its commercial debt obligations. In its simplest form, quantitative indicators (as shown in Table 5.2) are combined to score each sovereign. These are overlaid with qualitative and subjective indicators to establish the sovereign's creditworthiness.

The main categories used in sovereign ratings include economic strength, fiscal performance, external vulnerability, monetary and financial sector strength, and institutional quality.[6] The most critical for credit worthiness include total government debt as a percent of GDP, total external debt as a percent of GDP, short-term debt as a percent of GDP, debt service as a percent of revenues, external debt service as a percent of exports, foreign exchange reserves in months of short-term debt and imports, the fiscal balance as a percent of GDP, and external financing needs as a percent of GDP.

Qualitative and subjective indicators can be equally important. They include evaluations of political and geopolitical risks, the likelihood of social unrest, and the sovereign's history of defaults and restructurings. Measures assessing credit risks related to climate change, biodiversity depletion, and natural disasters are also included where data is available.

There are several approaches to aggregating these indicators into sovereign credit ratings. A scorecard approach assigns values to each variable, normalizes the indicators, and aggregates them using a weighted formula. For instance, public debt ratios can be categorized on a scale of 1 to 10 depending on the range, or a Z-score can be calculated to reflect comparative rankings across countries. This can be done for all the variables under review. Each factor can then be weighted and aggregated. For example, a 30% weight can be assigned to economic strength, a 30% weight to fiscal strength, a 20% weight to external metrics, and a 20% weight to institutional quality. The cumulative score is then mapped to a rating category.

Another approach is to use regression-based models to predict ratings or default probabilities. These models estimate sovereign credit ratings or the probability of default based on various macroeconomic and credit indicators. These may include the fiscal balance, debt ratio, and FX reserves coverage of imports, to name a few. Ordered logistic models are typically used because of their simplicity and suitability for predicting ordinal rating categories.

Principal component analysis (PCA) can also be used to evaluate the main factors driving sovereign ratings and spread returns. The results are mapped to historical ratings to assign country-specific ratings and forecast future movements. Findings from the analysis can also be utilized to assign weights in scorecard frameworks.

TABLE 5.2 Select Variables Used by CRAs

Category	Moody's	Standard & Poor's	Fitch
Institutional / Political Factors	■ Institutional framework and effectiveness (rule of law, control of corruption, government effectiveness) ■ Policy credibility and effectiveness (inflation level and volatility) ■ Track record of default	■ The effectiveness, stability, and predictability of the sovereign's policymaking and political institutions ■ The transparency and accountability of institutions, data, and processes ■ Adjustment factor: The sovereign's debt payment culture; external security risks	■ Composite governance indicator from the World Bank Governance Indicators (rule of law, government effectiveness, control of corruption, voice and accountability, regulatory quality, political stability and absence of violence) ■ Years since default ■ GDP per capita ■ Share in world GDP
Economic Factors	■ Growth dynamics (GDP growth, growth volatility, competitiveness) ■ Scale of economy (nominal GDP) ■ National Income (GDP per capita) ■ Adjustment factors: Diversification, credit boom	■ Income levels (GDP per capita) ■ Growth prospects (trend, 3-year forecasts) ■ Economic diversity and volatility, exposure to natural disasters or other physical risks ■ Coverage and reliability of statistical information	■ Real GDP growth ■ Real GDP growth volatility ■ Consumer price inflation
Fiscal Factors	■ Debt burden (general government debt % GDP, general government debt % revenues) ■ Debt affordability (general government interest % revenue, general government interest % GDP) ■ Adjustment factors: Debt trend, general government foreign currency debt %, general government debt, other public sector debt % GDP, public sector financial assets or sovereign wealth funds % GDP	■ Fiscal flexibility (net government debt % GDP, fiscal balance % GDP, revenues % GDP) ■ Long-term fiscal trends and vulnerabilities (government assets % GDP, revenue base) ■ Debt structure and funding access (government debt burden, interest cost % revenues) ■ Contingent liabilities and likelihood they become government debt (from banking sector, non-bank financial sector, state-owned enterprises, public-private partnerships, etc.)	■ Debt burden (debt % GDP, debt % revenue) ■ Debt affordability (interest % revenue) ■ Adjustment factors: debt trend, composition of foreign currency debt, public sector debt and assets

Continued

TABLE 5.2 Continued

Category	Moody's	Standard & Poor's	Fitch
Monetary / Financial Factors	■ Included under institutional factors	■ Exchange rate regime and independence of and ability to coordinate monetary policy with fiscal and other economic policies ■ The credibility of monetary policy (inflation control etc.) ■ Depth and diversification of the domestic financial system and capital markets	■ Money supply ■ Banking sector soundness and supervision: Fitch Bank Systemic Risk and Macro Prudential Indicators
External / Vulnerability Factors / Susceptibility to event risk	■ Political risk (domestic and geopolitical political risk) ■ Government liquidity risk (fundamental metrics, market funding stress) ■ Banking sector risk (strength of banking system, size of banking system, funding vulnerabilities) ■ External vulnerability risk (current account balance+FDI as % GDP, external vulnerability indicator, net international investment position % GDP)	■ The status of a sovereign's currency in international transactions ■ External liquidity and ability to meet obligations to nonresidents ■ External position showing resident's assets and liabilities relative to the rest of the world ■ Balance of payments trends and terms of trade volatility	■ External balance sheet and debt ■ Reserve currency flexibility ■ Official international reserves ■ External debt service ■ Balance of payments: Commodity dependence Current account balance+net FDI

Source: Adapted from Moody's (2022), Standard and Poor's (2017), Fitch Ratings (2023a).

These approaches have the advantage of utilizing measurable variables within a predefined framework or model. This reduces subjective biases and facilitates cross-country comparisons across a large number of countries. However, limitations include the assumption of linear relationships, which may overlook more complex interactions. Aggregation bias from combining numerous variables may also be a factor. They also ignore qualitative rating drivers that can be especially important in determining sovereign creditworthiness.

Sovereign credit analysts can utilize in-house sovereign credit ratings to cross-check ratings from agencies. They can forecast future ratings movements based on the CRA models, flag improving and deteriorating credits, and highlight alpha opportunities in countries where the market has not yet reflected the anticipated changes. Credit analysts may also consider sovereign credit ratings as a ceiling for rating corporate and other exposures from the country. This is grounded in the idea that the government serves as the lender of last resort for issuers based in a country, owing to its taxation, money printing, and policymaking capabilities.[7]

The ease of using a single metric to signal credit risk must be balanced against the reality that sovereign credit assessments are complex, multi-dimensional, and dependent on country-specific contexts. Sovereign credit ratings, including those produced by the CRAs, are not merely a mechanical result of input variables, weights, and aggregation methodologies. This means that detailed macroeconomic and fundamental assessments must supplement credit ratings models to obtain a fuller picture of the credit quality of the underlying sovereign.

5.3 RATINGS METHODOLOGY OF THE MAJOR CRAs

Each CRA has a unique definition and methodology for sovereign credit ratings. Moody's emphasizes the expected loss given default, which depends on the probability of default and the expected recovery from the resolution of the default.[8] Standard & Poor's focuses on the likelihood of default without considering the magnitude of the loss. Fitch's ratings provide an ordinal ranking of credit quality and default vulnerability, and they are not linked to a specific statistical probability of default.

The methodologies for generating credit ratings overlap in the criteria and factors examined (see Table 5.2). The differences lie in the relative weights, emphasis on specific credit drivers, and rating definition. Additionally, there are various approaches for overriding quantitative data with qualitative information, different treatment of foreign and local currency ratings, government guarantees, and the integration of variables related to long-term sustainability.

For example, Moody's and S&P incorporate a broad set of structural factors, including the structure of the economy and competitiveness. S&P and Fitch seem to place relatively more emphasis on assessing the contingent liabilities of the government, particularly those arising from the banking sector. Meanwhile, Moody's framework categorizes susceptibility to event risk more explicitly.

Moody's sovereign ratings begin with a numerical scorecard based on four broad factors: economic strength, institutional and governance strength, fiscal strength, and susceptibility to event risk. Each factor is divided into sub-factors and aggregated sequentially to yield a scorecard value expressed as a range and translated into an alphanumeric score. The ratings committee then incorporates country-specific factors, any instrument-specific considerations, and adjusts for peer comparisons. The final credit rating is the result of a committee discussion and vote[9] (see Figure 5.1).

S&P employs a five-pillar framework that includes institutional, economic, external, fiscal, and monetary assessments (see Figure 5.2). Each pillar is evaluated on a six-point

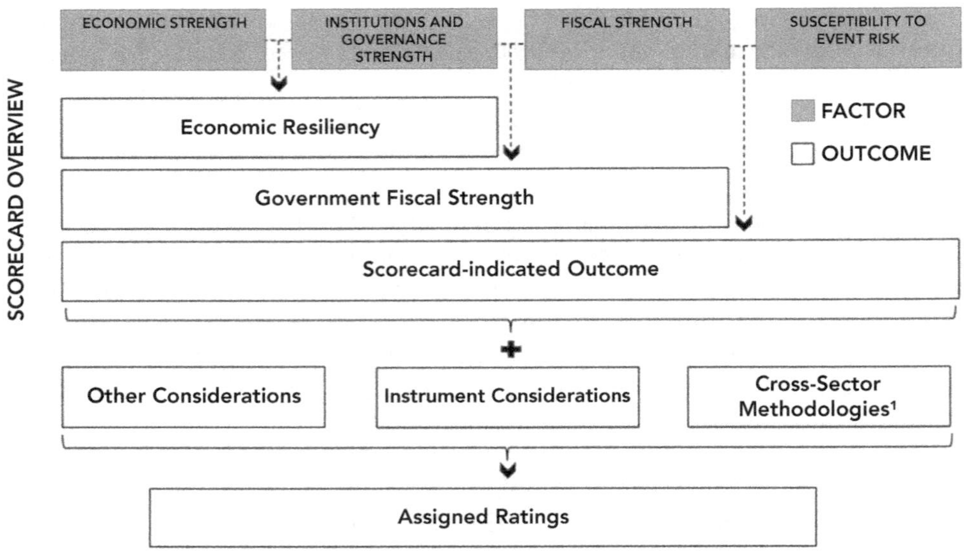

FIGURE 5.1 Moody's sovereign methodology framework. SOURCE: Moody's (2022)/Moody's.

1/*Note*: Some of the methodological considerations described in one or more cross-sector ratings methodologies may be relevant to ratings in this sector.

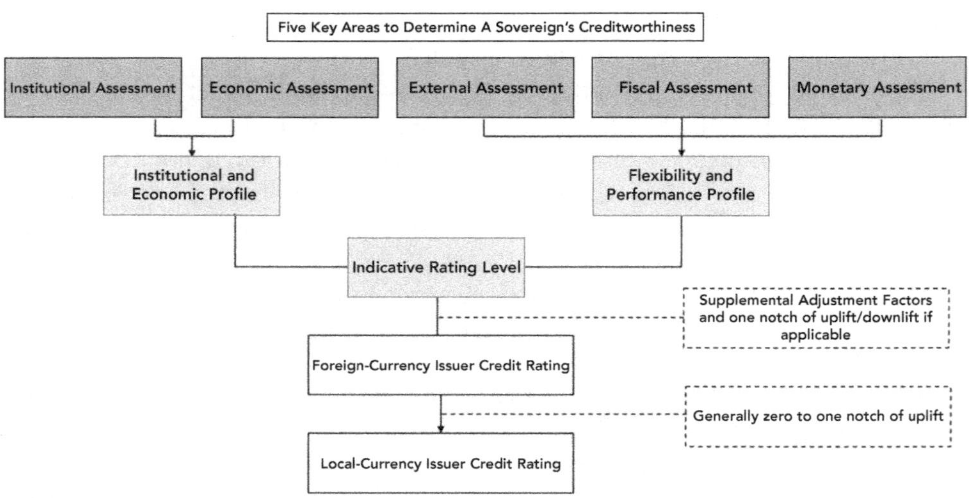

FIGURE 5.2 S&P's sovereign issuer credit rating framework. SOURCE: S&P Global Ratings (2017).

numerical scale from 1 (strongest) to 6 (weakest). The average of the institutional and economic assessments reflects S&P's views on the country's institutional and economic resiliency. The average of the external, fiscal, and monetary assessments is combined to form the country's flexibility and performance indicator. These two averages are integrated into a matrix to determine an indicative rating level. The final sovereign credit rating usually falls within one notch of the indicative rating level unless there are exceptional supplemental characteristics, such as a very high debt burden or a very high government liquid asset position.[10]

Fitch combines quantitative outputs from its Sovereign Rating Model (SRM) with qualitative overlays to determine its credit ratings (see Figure 5.3). The SRM is a multiple regression rating model that includes 18 key variables across four analytical pillars: structural features, macroeconomic performance and policy indicators, public finances, and external finances. Weights are determined by an OLS model, and the three-year average is used for most input variables. The result is a score calibrated to the long-term foreign currency rating scale from "AAA" to "CCC+," which forms the basis for the sovereign rating.[11]

Fitch then overlays these scores with qualitative adjustments that are not fully captured in the SRM. These adjustments have a potential notching range of +2/−2 for each of the analytical pillars mentioned above, with a maximum total rating adjustment of +3/−3 for each rating (except in exceptional circumstances). One benefit of Fitch's approach is that it distinguishes the quantitative factors in the model from the subjective judgments made by analysts, and it includes the rationale for any qualitative adjustments in its ratings report. An interactive version of the model is also available for subscribers.

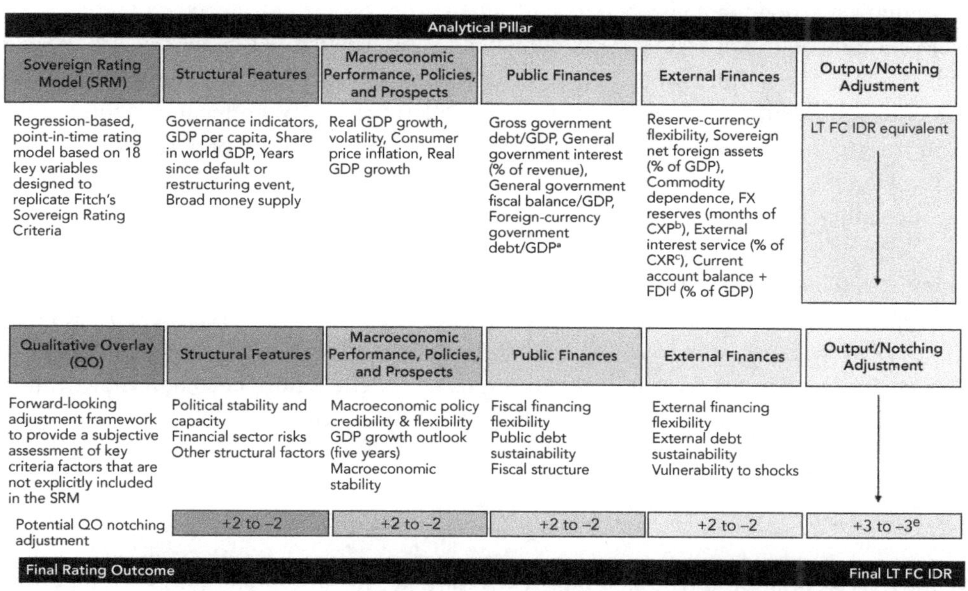

FIGURE 5.3 Fitch sovereign rating criteria. Source: Fitch Ratings (2023a)/Fitch Ratings.

Note: a: GGD = Gross Government Debt; b: CXP = Current External Payments; c: CXR = Current External Receipts; d: FDI = Foreign Direct Investment; e: Except in certain circumstances when, at the judgment of the committee, notching can be extended.

5.4 DOMESTIC VERSUS FOREIGN CURRENCY DEBT RATINGS

The industry convention refers to the *foreign currency long-term rating* as the sovereign credit rating; however, sovereign credit risk can differ based on the currency of the debt. Domestic currency debt might be easier to service due to the government's taxation and seniorage powers. The sovereign can also financially repress the domestic financial sector and control domestic policy frameworks that affect convertibility risk. This distinction may be especially important for countries with fixed or managed exchange rate regimes.

Moody's does not differentiate between local and foreign currency ratings except in rare instances. These instances include a persistence of limited capital mobility and external financing constraints, which create a distinction between the government's ability and willingness to repay creditors in local versus foreign currency. They note that "Any difference of more than two notches would be very rare."[12]

Standard & Poor's begins with the foreign currency rating and then applies an uplift for the local currency rating. In cases where the default risk is perceived to be lower in local currency debt, they may apply a one-notch upgrade, provided certain conditions are met. These conditions include independent monetary policy with a free or flexible exchange rate regime, deep local currency capital markets with capitalization typically above 20% of GDP and secondary market trading, as well as institutional and fiscal flexibility. There can be several notch differences between the foreign and local currency ratings, particularly if there is a high risk of default in the former but not in the latter.[13]

Fitch's methodology also begins with the assumption that the local currency rating will generally align with the foreign currency rating. While the two ratings are typically indistinguishable for investment-grade issuers, they may diverge more significantly in the categories of default or near-default ratings. Differences between local and foreign currency ratings may arise due to strong public finance fundamentals, preferential treatment of local currency debt, deep domestic capital markets, low and stable inflation, exchange rate flexibility, and relatively lower local currency debt burden.[14]

Taking S&P ratings as an example, as of June 2025, several countries have local currency sovereign credit ratings that exceed their corresponding foreign currency credit ratings. These include New Zealand (local rating at AAA versus foreign rating at AA+), Chile (local rating at A+ versus foreign rating at A), and Sri Lanka (local rating at CCC+ versus foreign rating at SD). In some situations where there have been domestic defaults, domestic currency ratings drop below foreign currency ratings.

5.5 DEFAULT RATINGS

When the risk of nonrepayment is high, CRAs downgrade sovereign ratings. Credit ratings below CCC indicate sovereigns that are in, or close to, default (see Table 5.1). These ratings are important for investors not only because they signal increased credit risk but also as portfolio guidelines often include minimum ratings criteria for issuers and securities.

An event of default (EoD) is viewed as a failure to pay interest or principal beyond the grace period or an exchange involving a deterioration of terms, such as a maturity extension, needed to avoid a traditional payment default.[15]

This definition is independent of whether creditors have pursued legal action, such as invoking EoD clauses, acceleration, or cross-default clauses. It emphasizes the coercive or involuntary aspect of investor participation in restructurings, rather than the net present value (NPV) of the offer. Even if there are sweeteners or NPV giveaways, creditor participation may depend on adverse terms associated with non-participation, making it voluntary only in name but not in reality. The issuer's motivation in preemptive debt exchanges is also taken into account when defining default, especially if it aims to avoid a payment default.

Each agency uses slightly different language for this general approach. Moody's EoD includes missed payments beyond the grace period, a distressed exchange of diminished value, or measures that enable the issuer to avoid default, as well as a forced change in the payment terms through currency re-denomination, indexation, or maturity extension.

Moody's clarifies that a tax on the coupon or principal of government debt instruments signifies a default, even if the action was not driven by an inability or unwillingness to pay. They also exclude missed payments due to technical or administrative reasons that are resolved within a short timeframe (one to two business days).

S&P assigns a selective default (SD) rating when there are missed payments on some, but not all, debt obligations. If no grace period is specified, they apply five business days for long-term obligations and zero business days for short-term obligations. A debt restructuring occurring a few quarters before maturity, where investors are asked to extend maturity with compensation through consent fees or higher coupons, is classified as proactive treasury management.

S&P's criteria for classifying distressed exchanges depend on the sovereign credit rating and whether the transaction is necessary to avoid default. Opportunistic exchanges are defined as transactions executed below par, where bonds trade at a discount, but the sovereign is likely to remain solvent even if the restructuring does not take place. For sovereigns rated BB− or higher, the debt restructuring would not be identified as distressed. For B+ or B-rated issuers, S&P would incorporate market prices or other indicators into their assessment, and for B− or lower rated issuers, the debt restructuring would be considered distressed.

Fitch's Restricted Default (RD) rating requires missed payments on public and unrated debt issued or guaranteed by the sovereign to private creditors. They define distressed exchanges as those offering diminished terms, a unilateral exchange or debt moratorium initiated by the sovereign, or an exchange necessary to avoid a traditional payment default. EoDs further include forced currency re-denomination unless creditors are given the option to be repaid in the original currency and on the original terms.

These categorizations of EoD mean that a missed payment (on principal or interest) that is cured before the grace period would not be classified as a default, while any delay beyond the grace period would be. For example, in 2022, Cameroon missed four external debt service payments to private creditors, which were subsequently cured within 18 days. Fitch did not classify these events as an EoD since the payments fell within the typical 30-day period.

A debt restructuring that triggers collective action clauses would be classified as involuntary, thus labeling it a coercive exchange and an EoD. The CRAs would also categorize a restructuring where the NPV of future debt streams is higher than the current market valuation but lower than the original par claim as a default.

In line with the criteria for a distressed exchange, an exchange characterized by high (or full) investor participation aimed at avoiding a sovereign default would be classified as an EoD. For instance, in 2022, Ukraine's bondholders agreed to postpone all coupon and principal payments on outstanding Eurobonds following the Russia–Ukraine war. Moody's labeled this as a distressed exchange because the payments were lower than the original commitments, and the transaction was intended to prevent the sovereign from ultimately defaulting on its payment obligations.

The assessment of debt-for-nature swaps is more nuanced. They can sometimes be classified as a distressed exchange. For example, Ecuador's 2023 debt-for-nature swap was classified by S&P and Fitch as an opportunistic restructuring and not a distressed exchange, as they expected the government to fulfill its financial commitments absent the transaction.[16] Meanwhile, Moody's categorized it as a distressed exchange because the securities were retired at a deep discount, even though participation by investors was voluntary.[17] On the other hand, Moody's did not classify Gabon's debt-for-nature swap as a distressed exchange (similar to the other agencies) since bonds were retired close to par and the buyback was not intended to avoid a default.[18]

Once a default occurs, none of the agencies explicitly covers the anticipated time in default, the mechanics of default resolution, or the range of expected recovery values. For this, investors must rely on their in-house analysis and research from the sell-side or third-party providers. We discuss these topics in Part Four.

CRAs come back into play once a restructuring has taken place. Specifically, exiting a credit default rating requires resolving a majority of creditor claims and occurs when the affected debt instruments have been modified, exchanged, or retired. Here, the CRAs make case-by-case judgments to determine whether a default has been cured. In general, the agencies tend to disregard residual amounts of unexchanged debt, especially if the defaulted instruments are retired or illiquid. However, unresolved debt becomes particularly relevant if there are litigious holdouts, as was the case for Argentina following its 2005 and 2010 debt exchanges.

A defaulted credit rating is usually upgraded one to two months after default resolution, typically once clarity is achieved regarding the participation rate and success of the exchange. For sovereign debt investors who see value in investing in securities emerging from default, the timing of ratings upgrades is crucial if portfolio guidelines restrict investment in defaulted securities. In these situations, proactively seeking client approval might enable them to purchase bonds before the upgrade occurs.

5.6 ENVIRONMENTAL, SOCIAL, AND GOVERNANCE (ESG) FACTORS

The integration of ESG variables in sovereign credit analysis is evolving, with CRAs increasingly emphasizing specific ESG drivers that have a significant impact on sovereign credit risk (see Table 5.3). As data availability improves and understanding of the impact of ESG variables on sovereign creditworthiness grows, these variables are expanding in scale and scope. Note that these differ from *ESG ratings or scores*, which assess sovereigns based on ESG outcomes and policies that extend beyond those pertinent to evaluating creditworthiness. We discuss the expanding ecosystem of ESG ratings and data providers in Chapter 19.

Some CRAs enhance their sovereign credit ratings with additional ESG-related assessments. Moody's provides two ESG scores for sovereigns. Issuer Profile Scores (IPS) gauge an issuer's exposure to ESG factors and serve as inputs to the scorecard/ratings process. Credit Profile Scores (CPS) measure the degree to which ESG factors impact an issuer's credit quality. For instance, environmental factors may influence the growth dynamics, debt burden, political risk, and external vulnerability of an issuer, with the magnitude reflected in the IPS and CPS.

TABLE 5.3 Select ESG Variables Used by CRAs

ESG Variable	Moody's	Standard & Poor's	Fitch
Environmental Risk	Carbon transition, physical climate, water management, waste and pollution, and natural capital	Climate transition risk, exposure to physical risk, policy frameworks for managing environment-related risks	Greenhouse gas (GHG) emissions and air quality, energy management, water resources & management, biodiversity & natural resources management, natural disasters & climate change
Social Risk	Demographics, labor and income, education, housing, health and safety, and access to basic services	Cohesiveness of civil society, inequality, health and safety outcomes	Human rights and political freedoms; human development, health and education; employment & income inequality; public safety and security; demographic trends
Governance Risk	Institutional structure, policy credibility and effectiveness, transparency and disclosure, and budget management	Transparency and reporting indicators, policy credibility and effectiveness	Political stability and rights; rule of law, institutional and regulatory quality, control of corruption; international relations and trade; creditor rights; data quality and transparency

Source: Moody's (2022), Standard & Poor's (2022), Fitch Ratings (2023a).

Fitch produces ESG Relevance Scores that flag the relevance and materiality of individually identified ESG issues for each credit rating. The scores range from 1 to 5 and do not make a value judgment on whether a sovereign is engaging in good or bad ESG practices. Additionally, Fitch notes that some inputs in its SRM model can be categorized as ESG variables, either directly or indirectly.[19]

S&P does not produce stand-alone ESG scores; instead, it considers the impact of ESG variables on the sovereign's ability to meet its financing commitments. Governance factors, in particular, have a close relationship with their institutional strength measure, while social indicators affect a country's resilience and economic strength. S&P highlights that the impact of ESG factors on creditworthiness can be uncertain and volatile, differing across regions, countries, and time horizons. They also emphasize that strong creditworthiness does not necessarily correlate with strong ESG credentials and vice versa.[20]

5.7 HOW GOOD ARE RATINGS AGENCIES AT PREDICTING SOVEREIGN CREDIT RISK?

In the aftermath of the 2008 Global Financial Crisis, the CRAs faced increased criticism for their excessively high ratings of US subprime mortgage-backed securities. A similar critique concerning sovereign ratings for the peripheral European nations arose following the European Debt Crisis.[21] This raises the question of how effective the CRAs are at predicting sovereign credit risk.

To answer this, we can examine the stability of sovereign ratings over time.[22] For example, is a AAA-rated sovereign still a AAA-rated sovereign in 3, 5, or 10 years? This is particularly important for portfolios with minimum credit rating requirements, such as investment grade or A-rated and above.

On average, 97% of AAA-rated sovereigns maintained their rating over a one-year horizon, but this figure declined to 85% over a five-year period. Relatedly, an AAA-rated sovereign has less than a 1% chance of being downgraded to BBB in five years, compared to an almost 20% chance for an A-rated sovereign. Meanwhile, the risk of losing investment grade from a rating of BBB− or lower is about 5% over a one-year horizon and increases to almost 15% over a five-year period.[23] So, rating stability is better for higher-rated sovereigns and deteriorates as the forecast horizon increases.

Another indicator of ratings performance is how well CRAs predict sovereign default risk. Sovereign foreign currency cumulative average default rates show that no sovereign rated AAA or AA has defaulted within the following 15 years. On average, about 4% of investment-grade rated sovereigns defaulted over the same period, compared to 31% of speculative-grade sovereigns. The predictive ability of CRA ratings is also evident in more granular sovereign ratings: the cumulative default probability increases from about 7% for A-rated sovereigns to 10% for BBB-rated sovereigns, 14% for BB-rated sovereigns, 42% for B-rated sovereigns, and 68% for CCC− (and below) rated sovereigns.[24] So, default prediction also changes by ratings category.

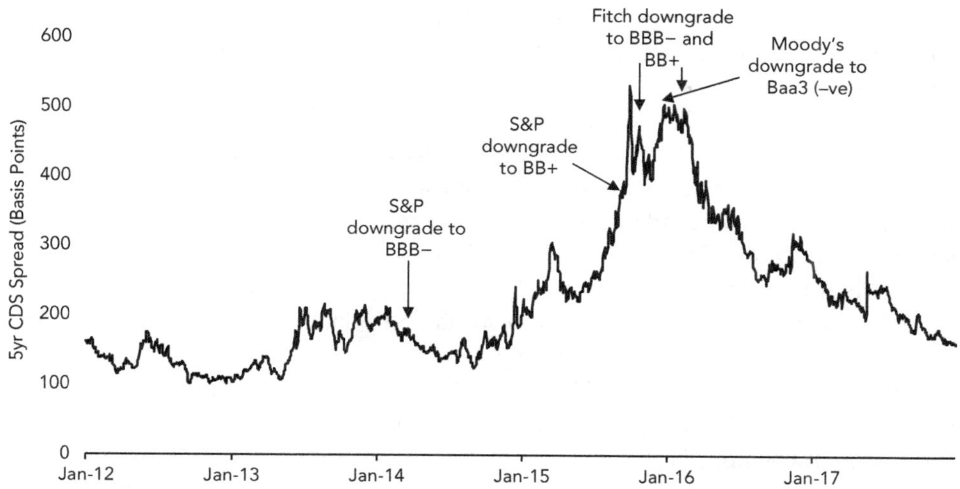

FIGURE 5.4 Brazil five-year CDS spreads and sovereign ratings downgrades. Source: Bloomberg Finance L.P.

The small sample size of sovereign defaults can skew probabilities in any given year and rating category. As a result, CRAs often report corporate transition and cumulative probabilities of default to inform trends for sovereign ratings. Corporate ratings have a larger sample size and closely align with sovereign ratings trends over long periods and across aggregated ratings categories. For example, the five-year cumulative probability of default for speculative-grade issuers between 1975 and 2022 is 13.8% for corporates and 13.3% for sovereigns.[25]

A third approach for assessing CRAs examines whether credit ratings correspond with the market pricing of credit risk. The general finding indicates that sovereign bond spreads and credit default swap prices often precede changes in CRA ratings. Markets typically anticipate downgrades by several months, and vice versa (see Figure 5.4).

The takeaway for portfolio managers is that sovereign ratings should be considered supplemental information rather than the sole predictors of credit risk. Tools to enhance the analysis of CRAs include in-house sovereign ratings models, early warning systems, debt sustainability analysis, and the use of market-implied credit ratings to evaluate what is already reflected in bond and CDS spreads.

5.8 MARKET-IMPLIED CREDIT RATINGS

Market-implied credit ratings (MICRs) estimate a sovereign's probability of default based on signals from bond prices and credit default swap spreads. They provide a high-frequency and real-time assessment of credit risk compared to sovereign credit ratings from CRAs.

MICRs are calculated by comparing an issuer's or security's trading price with that of other issuers within the same rating category. The average market-implied rating for an issuer is then contrasted with the long-term foreign currency rating of the senior unsecured bond. The *ratings gap* represents the discrepancy between the market-implied rating and the agency rating.

The instruments and tenors used in calculating MICRs depend on the rating category, liquidity, and availability of pricing matrices. For investment-grade sovereign issuers, five-year CDS spreads are used due to the standardization and liquidity of contracts. Benchmark cash bonds with 5- or 10-year maturities may be employed, although matching tenors and calculating on-the-run historical spreads can be more complex. For speculative-grade sovereign issuers, a combination of CDS (where they exist) and implied pricing from bond spreads is utilized. However, factors related to illiquidity and the lack of on-the-run instruments can pose challenges.

The ratings gap between MICRs and CRAs provides useful information as a starting point for identifying mispricing. Research from the corporate credit universe indicates that market-implied ratings can outperform rating agency ratings as predictors of default over shorter timeframes.[26] This is partly because market-based measures directly incorporate temporary shocks to credits, which CRAs tend to address using watches or outlooks rather than rating downgrades. Market-implied ratings also account for both cash-flow and discount-rate shocks to the credit, while CRAs primarily respond to cash-flow news.

The primary limitation of MICRs is that market spreads reflect other risks beyond credit risk. For instance, market technicals and liquidity can cause bond spreads to fluctuate. Moreover, financial market volatility can lead to excessive noise in MICRs and their implied ratings compared to CRAs. This is particularly true since CRA ratings are designed to be more stable throughout the business cycle rather than at a specific moment in time.

5.9 DO AGENCY RATINGS HAVE A MARKET IMPACT?

CRAs play a unique role in the investment ecosystem. Their certification services mean that, in many countries, their analyses feed directly into regulatory oversight functions, such as the calculation of Basel risk-based capital requirements. Their categorization of issuers into investment-grade and speculative-grade influences institutional demand for securities, index inclusion, and market liquidity. Client mandates often specify minimum rating requirements or investment-grade versus high-yield constraints. Moreover, CRAs' access to information provides valuable insights into data that are not publicly available.

The significance of this role underlies the nature and magnitude of the impact of CRAs on markets. The high correlation between CRA ratings and cross-country variations in spreads suggests that market participants and rating agencies have similar interpretations of the available data on sovereign credit risk. This is supported by academic empirical literature that finds CRA announcements generally impact sovereign bond spreads, CDS spreads, equity prices, and exchange rates.

Credit rating changes from a stable stance (as opposed to a negative or positive outlook/watch) have the greatest impact on market pricing. This may be due to the market already repricing risk when there is a change in the agency's outlook or watch, before the ratings change. Similarly, the surprise element is lower for changes from negative watch, perhaps because adverse news that triggers the negative watch is priced more quickly than is the case for positive ratings changes.[27]

Bond spreads are more sensitive to changes in CRA ratings when there is a risk of fallen angels (a decline in rating to high-yield) or the potential for rising stars (an upgrade to investment-grade). This is likely due to institutional mandates that limit the ability of asset managers to hold high-yield bonds within investment-grade mandates. It is no surprise, then, that empirical studies find the relationship between CRA ratings and spreads is stronger for speculative-grade bonds, which significantly respond to both upgrades and downgrades. Meanwhile, investment-grade bond spreads react more to ratings downgrades. Since the Great Financial Crisis of 2008, the empirical impact of agency rating announcements on spreads has decreased, although the relationship remains statistically significant.

PRO TIP: *Compare in-house and CRA ratings and monitor potential fallen angels (IG to HY) or rising stars (HY to IG) for portfolio positioning changes.*

Several real-world examples show how rating changes affect credit spreads, yields, and currencies. In 2015, Brazil struggled with a severe recession, high inflation, a worsening fiscal situation, and unstable politics. Deteriorating credit fundamentals ultimately led to CRAs downgrading the country from investment grade to high yield. Figure 5.4 shows how the ratings downgrade unfolded over several months, beginning with downgrades by S&P and eventually followed by Fitch and Moody's.

The downgrades significantly impacted market indicators, with Brazil's five-year CDS spread rising from around +200 basis points in mid-2015 to +400 basis points by early 2016, a roughly 60% increase. Losing investment-grade status resulted in capital outflows, which depreciated the currency by about 24% and raised yields on local bonds by about 400 basis points over the same time.

On the upgrade side, Greece regained its investment-grade status in October 2023 when S&P upgraded it from BB+ to BBB−. This improvement followed several years of fiscal consolidation, debt-to-GDP declining from 206% to 160%, and post-COVID recovery with GDP growth at ~5.7% in 2022. Greece's five-year CDS spread narrowed from ~100 bps to ~65 bps, a reduction of about ~35%, consistent with the spread reduction for investment-grade upgrades.

Chapter 14 takes a closer look at how changes in sovereign credit ratings affect markets. We explore how portfolio managers can evaluate the impact of forced sales triggered by rating changes. These forced sales result from institutional requirements for minimum ratings in sovereign bond portfolios and can significantly influence market repricing of sovereign risk.

5.10 SUMMARY

This chapter examined sovereign credit ratings and the methodologies used by the three main CRAs. It discussed ratings for domestic debt, defaults, and the integration of ESG factors in credit assessments. MICRs, the accuracy of CRAs, and whether CRA ratings have a market impact were also analyzed.

Despite questions about the timeliness of CRA ratings, the detailed analysis of credit risk data and the use of CRA ratings in institutional portfolio guidelines mean that CRAs play an important role in global financial markets. The takeaway for investors is that CRAs and their ratings, despite their shortcomings, cannot be ignored.

NOTES

1. Sovereign credit ratings are distinct from *country risk*, which covers the risks of investing in a country due to changes in the business environment, political backdrop, or policy framework.
2. Challenging the dominance of the Big Three CRAs are several country-specific and regional rating agencies. Examples include Dagong Global Credit Rating Agency (China), DBRS Morningstar, Scope Ratings (Europe), and the Japan Credit Rating Agency (JCR).
3. While negative and positive watches are less frequent than credit outlooks, they represent a stronger signal for markets as they are typically followed by a rating change within a couple of months (Binici, Hutchison, and Miao, *Are Credit Rating Agencies Discredited?*)
4. Ratings are as of May 27, 2025. Note that the short-term ratings do not strictly compare with the country's long-term ratings due to different scales.
5. As issuers solicit and pay for ratings, credit rating agencies are regulated to avoid conflicts of interest by the Securities and Exchange Commission (SEC) in the United States, the European Securities and Markets Authority (ESMA) in the European Union, and the International Organization of Securities Commissions (IOSCO) at the global level.
6. See Cantor and Packer, "Determinants and Impact of Sovereign Credit Ratings."
7. Exceptions may include large strategically important multinationals whose revenue base spans several countries and that have global political power.
8. Mathematically, expected loss = probability of default × (1 − recovery rate). For investment-grade and BB ratings, the recovery rate is assumed to be 100%. For single B issuers, it is 99%, and less than 35% for C-rated issuers. (See Moody's, *Rating Symbols and Definitions*.)
9. See Moody's, *Sovereign Rating Methodology* for further details.
10. See S&P, *Sovereign Rating Methodology* for further details.
11. See Fitch (2023a) for further details.
12. See Moody's, *Sovereign Rating Methodology*, p. 51.
13. See S&P, *Sovereign Rating Methodology*, p. 34.
14. See Fitch Ratings, *Sovereign Rating Criteria*, pp. 26–27.
15. See Moody's, *Rating Symbols and Definitions*; and *Sovereign Default and Recovery Rates*, S&P, *Global Ratings Definitions*, and Fitch Ratings, *Rating Recovery Path*.
16. See S&P, *Ecuador Research Update*.
17. See Moody's, *Ecuador Distressed Exchange Announcement*.
18. See Moody's, *Gabon Not Distressed Exchange Announcement*.
19. Fitch Ratings, *ESG and Sovereign Ratings*.
20. See S&P, *ESG Overview: Global Sovereigns*; and S&P, *ESG Principles in Credit Ratings*.
21. See IMF, *GFSR: Uses and Abuses of Sovereign Credit Ratings*.

22. Another measure is the average time in rating, such as Standard and Poor's Gini ratio (see S&P, *Global Ratings Definitions*, p. 12).
23. See S&P, *Annual Sovereign Default Study*. S&P's sovereign foreign-currency average transition rates are used here for reference, but Moody's and Fitch calculate similar matrices.
24. A lesser-used metric is the average default position (AP), which examines the extent to which defaulters are low-rated and non-defaulters are high-rated. Moody's finds that over 1983–2022, the typical sovereign defaulter was lower rated than 93% of all other sovereign ratings over a one-year horizon and 87% over a five-year horizon. Moody's, *Sovereign Default and Recovery Rates*.
25. See S&P, *Global Ratings Definitions;* and *Annual Sovereign Default Study*.
26. Hasan et al., "Market Implied Ratings," and Gredil, Kapadia, and Lee, "Information Content of Credit Ratings."
27. Binici, Hutchison, and Miao, *Are Credit Rating Agencies Discredited?*

REFERENCES

Bhatia, Ashok V. *Sovereign Credit Ratings Methodology: An Evaluation*. IMF Working Paper WP/02/170. Washington, DC: International Monetary Fund, 2002.

Binici, Mahir, Michael Hutchison, and Evan W. Miao. *Are Credit Rating Agencies Discredited? Measuring Market Price Effects from Agency Sovereign Debt Announcements*. BIS Working Paper No. 704. Basel: Bank for International Settlements, 2018.

Cantor, Richard, and Frank Packer. "Determinants and Impact of Sovereign Credit Ratings." *Federal Reserve Bank of New York Economic Policy Review* 2 (October 1996): 37–54.

Fitch Ratings. *Rating Recovery Path from Sovereign Defaults*. 2020. https://www.fitchratings.com (accessed 29 July 2025).

Fitch Ratings. *What Investors Want to Know: ESG and Sovereign Ratings*. 2022. https://www.fitchratings.com (accessed 29 July 2025).

Fitch Ratings. *Sovereign Rating Criteria*. 2023a. https://www.fitchratings.com (accessed 29 July 2025).

Fitch Ratings. *Rating Definitions*. 2023b. https://www.fitchratings.com (accessed 29 July 2025).

Gredil, Oleg R., Nishad Kapadia, and Jaehoon H. Lee. "On the Information Content of Credit Ratings and Market-Based Measures of Default Risk." *Journal of Financial Economics* 146, no. 1 (2022): 172–204.

Hasan, Iftekhar, Junbo Shen, Guoxiang Zhang, and Wai P. H. Poon. "Market Implied Ratings and Their Divergence from Credit Ratings." *The Journal of Financial Research* 46, no. 2 (2023): 251–289.

International Monetary Fund. "Chapter 3: The Uses and Abuses of Sovereign Credit Ratings." In *Global Financial Stability Report*, October 2010. https://www.imf.org (accessed 29 July 2025).

Moody's Investors Service. *Market Implied Ratings FAQ*. 2010. https://www.moodys.com (accessed 29 July 2025).

Moody's Investors Service. *Explanatory Comment: New Scores Depict Varied and Largely Credit-Negative Impact of ESG Factors*. 2021. https://www.moodys.com (accessed 29 July 2025).

Moody's Investors Service. *Rating Methodology: Sovereigns*. 2022. https://www.moodys.com (accessed 29 July 2025).

Moody's Investors Service. *Rating Symbols and Definitions*. 2023a. https://www.moodys.com (accessed 29 July 2025).

Moody's Investors Service. *Sovereign Default and Recovery Rates, 1983–2022*. 2023b. https://www.moodys.com (accessed 29 July 2025).

Moody's Investors Service. *Announcement: Moody's Considers Ecuador's Debt-for-Nature Swap Bond Buyback a Distressed Exchange.* May 2023. 2023c. https://www.moodys.com (accessed 29 July 2025).

Moody's Investors Service. *Announcement: Government of Gabon: Debt-for-Nature Swap Marginally Alleviates Refinancing Risk; Not Considered a Distressed Exchange.* August 2023. 2023d. https://www.moodys.com (accessed 29 July 2025).

Standard & Poor's. *Sovereign Rating Methodology*. February 23, 2022. https://www.spglobal.com/en (accessed 29 July 2025).

Standard & Poor's. *ESG Overview: Global Sovereigns*. 2021a. https://www.spglobal.com/en (accessed 29 July 2025).

Standard & Poor's. *Environmental, Social, and Governance Principles in Credit Ratings*. 2021b. https://www.spglobal.com/en (accessed 29 July 2025).

Standard & Poor's. *Annual Global Sovereign Default and Rating Transition Study*. 2022. https://www.spglobal.com/en (accessed 29 July 2025).

Standard & Poor's. *Global Ratings Definitions*. 2023a. https://www.spglobal.com/en (accessed 29 July 2025).

Standard & Poor's. *Research Update: Ecuador "B-" Ratings Affirmed on Debt-for-Nature Transaction; Outlook Remains Stable*. 2023b. https://www.spglobal.com/en (accessed 29 July 2025).

Standard & Poor's. *2022 Annual Global Sovereign Default and Rating Transition Study*. 2023c. https://www.spglobal.com/en (accessed 29 July 2025).

Standard & Poor's. 2022 *Annual U.S. Corporate Default and Rating Transition Study*. 2023d. https://www.spglobal.com/en (accessed 29 July 2025).

CHAPTER SIX

Risk Indicators and Debt Sustainability

CREDIT RATINGS are useful for integrating a wide range of macroeconomic indicators, but they represent only one tool among many. Investors can benefit from looking ahead to identify countries that may face challenges before these risks become fully reflected in macro projections, ratings, and market pricing. Early warning frameworks (EWFs) are beneficial in this regard by identifying shifts in sovereign credit variables that research has shown to be associated with sovereign crises, enabling timely monitoring and informed decision-making.

For countries with high credit risk and those close to or in default, investors can also gain insights from assessments of debt dynamics and repayment capacity. Sovereign debt sustainability analyses (DSAs) are forward-looking frameworks designed to evaluate a government's ability to meet its debt obligations without requiring external financial assistance or defaulting. For portfolio managers investing in sovereign bonds, DSAs are essential for assessing sovereign creditworthiness, pricing restructuring risk, and negotiating with a country's official and commercial creditors.

This chapter discusses risk indicators used in early warning frameworks and outlines the data and process involved in conducting a DSA. It reviews the frameworks of the International Monetary Fund (IMF) for market access countries (MACs) and low-income countries (LICs). The main factors in determining debt sustainability are described together with recent controversies where the IMF and bond investors have disagreed.

6.1 SOVEREIGN STRESS AND EARLY WARNING INDICATORS

Sovereign stress reflects the likelihood that a country faces payment or fiscal difficulties. It may signal a short-term liquidity or financing risk. It may also arise due to unsustainable or insolvent debt dynamics that could be mitigated if corrective policies are implemented in time. In extreme cases, it might indicate a potential default and a need for debt restructuring.

In practice, markets reprice sovereign debt instruments well before a liquidity crisis or default occurs. Therefore, accurately predicting sovereign stress episodes is crucial for the mark-to-market of debt portfolios. Here, the extensive literature on early warning frameworks proves helpful. This work examines historical sovereign, financial, and currency crises to derive signals for predicting future events.[1]

Stylized facts from the early warning literature show that banking and financial crises, exchange rate stress, global shocks, and periods of rapid debt accumulation often precede sovereign crises.[2] Crises are also linked to unsustainable macroeconomic policies, including monetary financing of fiscal deficits, extensive use of subsidies, poor debt management, and weak institutional and structural frameworks.

Table 6.1 presents several common indicators used in the literature.[3] Examining both levels and changes is illustrative to identify shifts in credit risk. For instance, the minimum level of foreign exchange reserves coverage is higher for countries with fixed exchange rates compared to those with a floating exchange rate regime; so, what matters is changes in the level of coverage rather than their absolute level. Two countries with the same total public debt ratio may display different vulnerabilities to crises if one has a significantly shorter debt maturity or a greater proportion of external indebtedness. Examining changes in the ratios can therefore flag if there are shifts in their credit risk profiles rather than looking at levels alone.

A scorecard approach can incorporate these, along with indicative thresholds, to signal different risks of sovereign stress. More extensive approaches use binomial logit/probit regression analysis to construct models that determine tipping points or stress. These methods tend to have higher predictive power than stand-alone variables. They can control for various fixed effects, including region, economic development, exchange rate regime, and commodity exposure, among others.[4]

Adopting a dynamic approach allows for the examination of interlinkages between variables and their systemic impact, and a better understanding of the risk of sovereign stress.[5] This can assist investors in minimizing both type I and type II errors—missed crises and false alarms—when making decisions regarding the scaling, size, and entry or exit of positions. When a country reaches "danger" thresholds, a closer look can be taken to determine whether there's a genuine risk.

PRO TIP: *Monitor risk indicators regularly, including changes in each variable. Supplement analysis with high-frequency data and news flow to identify sudden shifts.*

Investors should note that data availability in many countries, particularly in frontier markets, is often less frequent than in advanced and emerging markets. This limitation makes early risk assessments very challenging. In many cases, this results in considerable uncertainty in credit analysis, leading to wider variability in expected returns. This, in turn, prompts the market to demand structurally higher risk premiums.

TABLE 6.1 Select Early Warning Indicators

Sector	Indicator
Macro	Output Gap
	Real GDP Growth Variability
	Real GDP Growth vs. 5 year Average
	Inflation Rate
	Inflation Deviation from Target (or Average Historical Inflation)
	Standard Deviation of Inflation
	Domestic Savings % GDP
	Investment % GDP
Fiscal	Overall Balance % GDP
	Primary Balance
	Interest % GDP
	Revenue % GDP
	Interest % Revenues
	Expenditure % GDP
External sector	Current Account Balance % GDP
	FX Reserves in Months of Imports
	FX Reserves % Short-Term Debt (residual maturity)
	M2 % FX Reserves
	Gross External Financial Requirement % Reserves (or % GDP)
	Net FDI % GDP
	Portfolio Investment % GDP
	FDI Financing of the Current Account
	External Assets % GDP
Exchange Rate	Exchange Rate Volatility
	REER Over/Undervaluation
	PPP Over/Undervaluation
Public Debt	Total Public Debt % GDP
	Total Public Debt % Revenues
	Public External Debt % GDP
	Public Debt Service % Revenues
	Short-Term Public Debt % GDP
	Short-Term Public Debt % Total

Continued

TABLE 6.1 Continued

Sector	Indicator
External Debt	Total External Debt % GDP
	Total External Debt % Exports
	External Debt Service % Exports
	External Debt Service % FX Reserves
	Short-Term External Debt (Residual Maturity) % FX Reserves
	Short-Term External Debt % GDP
Private debt	Total Private Debt % GDP
	10 year Average Credit Gap: Current Debt – 10-year Average
	Domestic Credit % GDP
	Domestic Credit Growth %yoy
	External Private Debt % GDP
	NPLs %
	Loan to Deposit Ratio %
Debt dynamics	Real Interest Rate minus Growth
	1 year, 5 year, 10 year Domestic Bond Yields
	5 year, 10 year External Bond Spreads, Yields
Global	10 year Treasury Rate
	Oil Prices (level and % change) and Oil Price Sensitivity
	Commodity Prices (Metals, Wheat, etc.) and Sensitivity
	VIX Index

On the other end of the spectrum, EWFs may be too simplistic for advanced economies with complex economies and highly developed financial markets. For these countries, detailed analysis of financial sector risks (as covered by the IMF's Financial Sector Assessment Program [FSAP] and Bank for International Settlements [BIS] stress tests), analysis of potential asset market bubbles, and the assessment of global systemic shocks may be more relevant.

6.2 DEFINING DEBT SUSTAINABILITY

For investors in emerging and frontier sovereigns, thorough credit research and debt sustainability analysis are crucial to assess repayment and default risks.

A sovereign's debt is considered sustainable when it can meet its current and future debt obligations without restructuring, accumulating arrears, crowding out other essential fiscal expenditures, or implementing significant fiscal adjustments that undermine growth.[6] The concept encompasses both solvency and liquidity criteria and acknowledges that governments can influence debt sustainability through their policy actions.[7]

One approach defines sustainability as the condition in which the debt ratio remains unchanged. A stricter definition considers sustainability to occur when the ratio decreases below specified thresholds and over a defined timeframe.

Mathematically, the change in public debt is equal to:[8]

$$\begin{aligned} PDebt_t - PDebt_{t-1} &= \frac{1+r_t}{1+g_t} * PDebt_{t-1} + PB_t \\ &\approx (r_t - g_t) * PDebt_{t-1} + PB_t \end{aligned}$$

where:

$PDebt_t$ is the public-debt-to-GDP ratio in time t
PB_t is the primary fiscal deficit in percent of GDP in time t
r_t is the average long-term government bond yield in time t, and
g_t is the nominal GDP growth rate in time t

This states that debt is no longer growing when the difference between interest rates and growth $(r - g)$ is offset by adjustments in the primary balance (PB). Suppose the interest rates on government debt exceed GDP growth $(r - g) > 0$, public debt will increase as long as the primary balance does not counteract the impact of $(r - g)$. Conversely, if interest rates are lower than growth $(r - g) < 0$, public debt will decrease as long as the primary fiscal balance does not have a significant deficit.

In practice, determining when debt is sustainable also requires judgment. DSAs should therefore be closely linked to broader assessments of fiscal sustainability and macroeconomic scenario analysis.

Countries may face temporary shocks that impede their ability to meet payment obligations, even if their absolute levels of debt are low and manageable under normal circumstances. Governments can also alter policies to reduce debt ratios on a perilous trajectory. In some cases, debt ratios can remain high and serviceable for a long time even if they exceed thresholds usually associated with debt crises. The case of Japan is a case in point where high debt ratios have persisted for decades with little sign of sovereign debt sustainability issues or economic crises.

6.3 DEBT DATA

The starting point for any DSA is understanding the debt stack and debt servicing obligations of the sovereign entity. Debt statistics covering the amount, type of debt (fixed, floating, or inflation-linked), maturity, currency, governing law, and creditor characteristics are typically published by the Ministry of Finance or the central bank. Credit analysts should strive to obtain as much detail on these variables as possible, including by instrument if available.

The definition of what constitutes government debt is important. Most DSAs encompass the general government, which includes the central government, state and local governments, and essential government funds such as social security institutions. However, it is also vital to consider explicit guarantees (for state-owned enterprises, states, or municipalities), arrears, and contingent liabilities from the banking (or other) sectors.

Additionally, it is important to consider whether there is any collateralization of debt and if there are private loans or bonds that are not publicly listed. This information helps in understanding the seniority structure of the debt and which other creditors may play a role in any future debt restructurings.

The debt service schedule, which includes interest and amortization payments, provides insight into the immediate fiscal burden of debt. This can be further categorized by instrument, currency, holder (official versus commercial), and residency (onshore versus offshore). The magnitude and timing, especially if repayments are clustered, may provide insight into when stress events (like defaults or liquidity pressures) are likely to occur.

For sovereigns nearing default, debt service data can be utilized to ensure that payments are made and received promptly. The schedule can also be cross-referenced with CDS contract dates to identify potential trades in high-risk countries; for instance, increasing exposure via CDS when there is a window with no payments due.

6.4 IMF DEBT SUSTAINABILITY FRAMEWORKS

The IMF's Debt Sustainability Frameworks (DSFs) serve as a valuable starting point for analyzing a country's debt sustainability. The DSFs are deterministic templates that assess an economy's public and external debt trajectory based on a set of macroeconomic and policy assumptions. A baseline scenario undergoes a series of sensitivity (or stress) tests to provide a probabilistic upper limit for debt dynamics across various states of the world. Collectively, these elements form the foundation of the debt assessment.

IMF DSAs inform a borrowing country's ability to repay the Fund, and for countries facing debt distress, they outline the scope for debt restructuring and haircuts. These assessments are included in IMF Article IV Reports, Program Requests, or IMF Staff Reviews. For countries undergoing restructurings, DSAs may be updated and shared with creditors on a stand-alone basis before the country reports are published.

The IMF uses two distinct frameworks. The Sovereign Risk and Debt Sustainability Framework for Market Access Countries (SRDSF-MAC) is intended for lower-middle-income to high-income countries with market access.[9] The Debt Sustainability Framework for Low-Income Countries (LIC DSF) is designed for low-income countries accessing the IMF's low-cost financing from the Poverty Reduction and Growth Trust.[10]

These frameworks differ in methodology, country of coverage, and assessment of debt-carrying capacity. This arises as MACs rely on international capital markets for financing, and LICs depend on concessional finance.[11] The IMF is updating these frameworks, potentially consolidating them and incorporating new elements and parameters.

The Excel templates for both frameworks are available to the public on the IMF website (www.imf.org) and can be utilized by investors to conduct DSAs using their own assumptions. They can also be modified to include various scenarios based on investor perspectives, such as currency crises, banking crises, or the recognition of substantial contingent liabilities.

PRO TIP: *Use IMF DSAs as a starting point to assess debt sustainability, and carry out individual analysis for countries with a high risk of debt distress with your own assumptions and scenarios.*

6.4.1 Application to Market Access Countries (MAC-SRDSF)

The MAC-SRDSF assesses sovereign risk and debt sustainability over short-, medium-, and long-term horizons. It focuses on public and external government debt while incorporating country-specific factors such as investor composition and institutional quality. These inputs, along with probabilistic tools like debt fan charts, stress tests, and fiscal adjustment scenarios, are used to evaluate market refinancing risks and other vulnerabilities.

There are no fixed thresholds for determining debt sustainability. Instead, thresholds are probabilistic and specific to different time horizons. Indicative metrics include debt-to-GDP ratios exceeding 70%, gross financing needs greater than 15% of GDP, and interest-to-revenue ratios above 20%. These metrics are adjusted based on country-specific assessments of market access and currency stability.

Example: Argentina 2022

Argentina's 2022 DSA emphasizes the need for country-specific assessment and looking beyond the DSA numbers.[12] Following the 2020 restructuring, public debt was projected to gradually decline to around 64% of GDP by 2027, suggesting a moderate-to-high risk of sovereign stress.

Sovereign bond investors perceived the IMF baseline scenario as being too optimistic. They were additionally wary of Argentina's history of fiscal volatility and unstable relationship with the Fund. The market's assessment of a high risk of debt distress was quickly reflected in government bond valuations, which traded in the high 40s initially but dropped to the low 30s for several years following the restructuring.

Example: Egypt 2024

Egypt's 2024 IMF DSA highlights the importance of considering external support. In its 2024 Article IV and Extended Fund Facility program, the IMF projected that Egypt's government debt would stabilize around 65% of GDP by 2029, but that gross financing needs would remain high at 28% of GDP. The report highlighted risks associated with a significant dependence on external debt rollover and exchange rate pressures.[13]

Despite this, Egypt had strong multilateral support and concessional funding from bilaterals. As a result, the DSA concluded that debt was sustainable, although it carried high risks. The market's pricing of Egypt's USD-denominated bonds supported this assessment, with front-end bonds pulling to par while longer-maturity bonds remained well below.

6.4.2 Application to Low-Income Countries (LIC DSF)

The LIC DSF framework applies to low-income countries with a significant reliance on concessional financing. It classifies countries based on their debt-carrying capacity—strong, medium, or weak. It utilizes a composite indicator that includes real GDP growth, remittances, reserves, and the World Bank's Country Policy and Institutional Assessment (CPIA). The framework analyzes the present value of external and public debt over a 10-year horizon using a 5% discount rate. It assigns each country a risk rating ranging from low to moderate, high, or in debt distress.[14]

Debt sustainability thresholds are linked to the country's debt-carrying capacity (see Table 6.2). Stress tests conducted over a 10-year period determine the final risk rating and the amount of debt relief required.

Example: Zambia 2024

Zambia's 2024 LIC DSF assessment highlights one instance of significant investor disagreement with the IMF's assessment.[15] The LIC DSF numbers and threshold ratios did not indicate a high-risk rating, but nonetheless, the country requested significant debt relief.

In the debt restructuring negotiations, bondholders contended that the IMF's rating and conservative growth projections undervalued Zambia's copper export potential. The IMF's emphasis on shock absorption capacity contrasted with investors' expectations of quicker debt stabilization, leading to volatile bond pricing and delayed creditor agreement in the restructuring.

TABLE 6.2 IMF LIC DSF Thresholds

Debt-carrying Capacity	PV of PPG External Debt		PPG External Debt Service		PV of Total Public Debt
	% GDP	% Exports	% Exports	% Revenue	% GDP
Weak	30	140	10	14	35
Medium	40	180	15	18	55
Strong	55	240	21	23	70

Source: IMF (2018)/International Monetary Fund (IMF).
Note: PPG refers to public and publicly guaranteed debt.

6.5 GUIDELINES FOR INVESTORS

DSAs are only as reliable as their underlying assumptions and selected stress tests. Investors would therefore benefit from examining baseline assumptions for realism, comparing them to country-specific historical averages, and experiences from other countries. For instance, future primary balance adjustment targets can be compared to those achieved by other nations that have faced similar debt distress and fiscal consolidation plans.

The consistency of projections across macroeconomic variables should also be checked. For example, are real exchange rate assumptions aligned with inflation forecasts? Are fiscal revenue estimates consistent with fiscal multipliers? Are growth projections in line with fiscal consolidation targets? The basic drivers of debt dynamics should be examined, along with the extent to which macroeconomic variables like growth and inflation are projected to reduce debt ratios over time.

PRO TIP: *Pay attention to currency assumptions in DSAs, as well as macro-forecasts for fiscal adjustment, balance of payments flows and medium-term growth rates. Small changes in these parameters can have outsized effects on debt trajectories.*

When assessing an IMF program, understanding debt dynamics, including assumptions about rollover and refinancing, can help clarify aspects of the program. For example, is there an assumption of market access, and is a continuation of the IMF program likely? Relatedly, investors should evaluate whether any IMF program (if applicable) is likely to stay on track and if the conditionality is achievable and fully committed to by the government.

Ultimately, IMF DSAs inform IMF surveillance and program assessments. This may not always align with investor objectives, especially during a debt restructuring. Maintaining a critical perspective toward DSA final assessments ensures that investor viewpoints can be communicated to international financial institutions (IFIs) like the IMF and the government promptly. We discuss debt restructuring negotiations further in Part Four.

A more general point is that DSAs and the associated stress tests represent a partial equilibrium analysis that may result in an underestimation of left tail risks. Investors should conduct additional scenarios where applicable. These include assessing the risk of bank runs or unfunded contingent liabilities to enhance the analysis from DSAs. Such assessments can inform the evaluation of the risk of debt distress beyond the approach taken by the IMF frameworks.

Finally, investors may seek to expand beyond the traditional IMF DSA frameworks and include sustainability factors in DSAs. This is especially relevant for emerging and developing economies facing greater environmental risks. The incorporation of climate, nature-related, and social risks in sovereign DSA scenarios and stress tests is an emerging area of research.[16] Investors with sustainability and regulatory mandates to account for these risks would benefit from these frameworks. We discuss strategies for sustainable investing in sovereign debt portfolios in Chapter 19.

6.6 SUMMARY

Credit analysts must weigh the costs and benefits of focusing on high-frequency, widely available data, which allows for easier monitoring and cross-country comparison, versus a more comprehensive and in-depth country-specific approach, albeit with a lower cadence or longer time lag for updates. The use of EWFs coupled with DSAs for high-risk credits offers this balance for investment teams covering a large number of countries.

More broadly, macroeconomic and fundamental analysis, credit ratings, EWFs, and DSAs together help investors form a comprehensive view of the risks associated with investing in a given sovereign. These must be combined with the pricing and relative valuations of sovereign risk to develop an investment strategy for sovereign bond portfolios. This is what we turn to in the next chapter.

NOTES

1. See Berg, Borensztein, and Pattillo, "Assessing Early Warning Systems," and Chamon and Crowe, "Predictive Indicators of Crises."
2. See Koh et al., *Debt and Financial Crises.*
3. See Moreno Badia et al., "Debt Is Not Free," Appendix 4 for a detailed list of variables used in the literature.
4. Wijayanti and Rachmanira, "Early Warning System for Debt Crisis," find that for a sample of developing economies, the binomial logistic regression approach can predict 61.5% of the government debt crisis two years in advance.
5. For example, Manasse and Roubini, "Rules of Thumb for Sovereign Debt Crises," find that political instability and tight global financial conditions can aggravate domestic liquidity problems, increasing the probability of crises more than when looking at liquidity metrics alone.
6. This is distinct from debt solvency, which is a theoretical concept capturing when the net present value of the country's future stream of primary balances is in line with the net present value of all public debt obligations. Solvency doesn't factor in scenarios where solvent governments face repayment risks, and insolvent governments can survive through repressive policy measures before facing crises.
7. See Xavier et al., "Public Debt Sustainability" for an overview. IMF, *Review of the DSF for MACs* distinguishes between debt being unsustainable under *any* set of feasible policies (implying a debt restructuring is necessary), and one where the debt fails to stabilize under the *current* policy path (implying a macroeconomic or policy adjustment is needed).
8. This assumes seniorage, the income earned from issuing currency, is part of the primary balance. Seniorage may be a more relevant revenue source in developing economies, given relatively high inflation rates.
9. See IMF, *Review of the DSF for MACs.*
10. See IMF, *Guidance Note on the DSF for LICs*. The LIC analysis is carried out jointly with the World Bank.
11. See IMF, *Guidance Note on the DSF for LICs*, p. 8, for guidance on when to use the LIC-DSF versus the SRDSF-MAC.
12. See IMF, *Argentina: Second EFF Review.*
13. IMF, *Egypt: Third EFF Review.*
14. See IMF, *Guidance Note on the DSF for LICs*, p. 27, for further details.

15. World Bank Group, *Zambia DSA*.
16. See Kraemer and Volz, *Integrating Nature into DSAs*, and Maldonado and Gallagher, *Climate Change and IMF DSAs*.

REFERENCES

Berg, Andrew, Eduardo Borensztein, and Catherine Pattillo. "Assessing Early Warning Systems: How Have They Worked in Practice?" *IMF Staff Papers* 52, no. 3 (2005): 462–502.

Chamon, Marcos, and Christopher Crowe. "Predictive Indicators of Crises." In *Handbook in Financial Globalization: The Evidence and Impact of Financial Globalization*, edited by Gerard Caprio, 499–505. London: Elsevier, 2012.

International Monetary Fund. *Guidance Note on the Bank-Fund Debt Sustainability Framework for Low Income Countries*. IMF Policy Paper, 2018. https://www.imf.org (accessed 29 July 2025).

International Monetary Fund. *Review of the Debt Sustainability Framework for Market Access Countries*. IMF Policy Paper, 2021. https://www.imf.org (accessed 29 July 2025).

International Monetary Fund. *Argentina: Second Review Under the Extended Arrangement Under the Extended Fund Facility*. Country Report No. 22/322, 2022. https://www.imf.org (accessed 29 July 2025).

International Monetary Fund. *Egypt: Third Review Under the Extended Arrangement Under the Extended Fund Facility*. Country Report No. 24/274, 2024. https://www.imf.org (accessed 29 July 2025).

Koh, Chorching, Ayhan Kose, Peter Nagle, Franziska Ohnsorge, and Naotaka Sugawara. *Debt and Financial Crises*. World Bank Policy Research Working Paper 9116, 2020.

Kraemer, Moritz, and Ulrich Volz. *Integrating Nature into Debt Sustainability Analysis*. Centre for Sustainable Finance, SOAS University of London, 2022.

Maldonado, Franklin, and Kevin P. Gallagher. *Climate Change and IMF Debt Sustainability Analysis*. Boston University, 2022. https://www.bu.edu (accessed 29 July 2025).

Manasse, Paolo, and Nouriel Roubini. "Rules of Thumb for Sovereign Debt Crises." *Journal of International Economics* 78 (2009): 192–205.

Moreno Badia, Marialuz, Paulo Medas, Pranav Gupta, and Yi Xiang. "Debt Is Not Free." IMF Working Paper 20/1. Washington, DC: International Monetary Fund, 2020.

Wijayanti, Retno, and Sari Rachmanira. "Early Warning System for Government Debt Crisis in Developing Countries." *Journal of Central Banking Theory and Practice*, Special Issue from the 13th BMEB International Conference in Bali (2020): 103–124.

World Bank Group. *Zambia: Joint World Bank–IMF Debt Sustainability Analysis*. 2023. https://www.worldbank.org (accessed 29 July 2025).

Xavier, Debrun, Jonathan D. Ostry, Tim Willems, and Charles Wyplosz. "Public Debt Sustainability." In *Sovereign Debt: A Guide for Economists and Practitioners*, edited by S. Ali Abbas, Alex Pienkowski, and Kenneth Rogoff, Chapter 4. Oxford: Oxford University Press, 2019.

CHAPTER SEVEN

Bond Contracts and Legal Considerations

FINANCIAL TRAINING programs often miss a crucial element required to be a good investor: understanding bond contracts and their legal terms. The contractual terms embedded in bond documents inform investors of their rights and allow them to enforce their claims. These terms govern the legal jurisdiction for resolving disputes and outline the rules and procedures for amending the contract. In a default scenario, a contract's provisions can determine whether creditors recover 50 cents on the dollar or nothing at all. Collectively, the specifics of sovereign bond contracts influence bond prices, restructuring outcomes, and the risk of holdouts.

This chapter reviews the main features of foreign law government bond contracts and outlines considerations for bond investors. It examines several clauses essential for creditors to enforce their rights, including the choice between a trustee and a fiscal agent, collective action clauses, the pari passu clause, and negative pledges. The discussion also covers the legal framework for local law sovereign debt and considerations when investing in SOEs.

The chapter concludes with a discussion on the enforceability of sovereign debt contracts and the implications of sanctions on sovereign bonds. The term *"caveat emptor,"* or *"buyer beware,"* could not be more apt for investors purchasing sovereign debt. Sovereigns possess unique powers as debtors and are often subject to geopolitical policy changes. As such, even with their contractual rights outlined in bond documents, investors may find it hard to enforce them at all times.

7.1 THE SOVEREIGN BOND CONTRACT

We start with an overview of sovereign bond contracts, highlighting the key legal documents and stakeholders involved in the issuance and management of sovereign debt. The roles of bond indentures and prospectuses in defining the terms of the bond and the rights and obligations of issuers and investors are also reviewed.

7.1.1 Main Stakeholders

The main parties in a sovereign bond contract are the issuer (or borrower) at one end and the bondholders (or creditors) at the other. The issuer is a government entity, such as the Treasury, seeking to raise capital. It is responsible for making regular interest payments to bondholders and repaying the principal amount of the bond at maturity. Bondholders are the investors who purchase the bonds issued by the issuer. They receive regular interest payments from the issuer and the principal amount of the bond at maturity.

In between, several parties facilitate the transaction. A trustee is an independent third-party entity appointed to act on behalf of bondholders and protect their interests. A fiscal agent is an entity appointed to act on behalf of the issuer.

Other stakeholders include underwriters who assist the issuer in selling the bond to investors, the paying agent responsible for distributing coupon and principal payments to bondholders, and the registrar tasked with maintaining an up-to-date record of bond ownership.

Legal advisors ensure the bond is structured correctly and complies with all relevant laws and regulations. Credit rating agencies evaluate the issuer's creditworthiness and assign a credit rating to the bond issue. For sustainability-linked bonds, third-party certification organizations may also be involved.

7.1.2 The Bond Indenture and Other Documents

When a bond is offered for sale, there are several associated documents, including a bond prospectus, bond indenture, or offering circular.[1] The bond prospectus provides detailed information about the new instrument, including a description of the bond, the intended use of proceeds, the main risk factors, financial information about the issuer, any covenants, and relevant legal information. The aim is to equip potential investors with all the information they need to make an informed decision about whether to invest in the bond.

The bond indenture is a legal contract between the issuer and the bondholders that outlines the terms and conditions of the bond issue. It specifies details such as the principal amount, interest rate, maturity date, and payment terms. It lays out the governing law and any waivers, listing any covenants or contractual promises made by the issuer to the bondholders. The indenture also specifies events of default, remedies for bondholders, and the terms for modifying the contract. An offering circular is similar to a prospectus and is more commonly used in non-registered offerings in international markets.

Investors can access the prospectus in real time during the bond transaction by contacting the bank that underwrites the transaction. The bond indenture is issued after the sale is agreed and is available to investors through the trustee or the appropriate regulatory body. In practice, obtaining bond indentures can be challenging, especially for older bonds, those issued by irregular issuers, and those from frontier markets.

7.2 A CLOSER LOOK AT SOVEREIGN DEBT CLAUSES

Several debt clauses are particularly important for investors, which we examine more closely in this section. We start with a high-level categorization of reserve and non-reserve matters, as well as what constitutes an event of default. Next, we discuss clauses that allow bondholders to enforce their rights, including the governing law and jurisdiction, as well as whether there is a trust or fiscal agency agreement. We then examine terms that enforce bondholders and the payments owed to them, such as collective action clauses and the *pari passu* clause. We close with a discussion of legal terms that limit the action of sovereigns, such as negative pledges and waiver of sovereign immunity.

7.2.1 Reserve and Non-Reserve Matters

Provisions in a bond contract can be categorized into reserve, non-reserve, and trivial matters. Reserve matters are provisions that grant bondholders specific rights and protections in the event of default or restructuring. These include payment priority, Collective Action Clauses (CACs), negative pledges, cross-default clauses, and definitions of an event of default.

Non-reserve matters refer to provisions that ensure the bond contract is fair, transparent, and enforceable. These include the terms and conditions of the bond, the governing law of the bond contract, and the procedures for making payments on the bond. Non-reserve matters may also encompass events of default that do not relate to bondholder rights and protections, such as compliance with reporting requirements. Trivial matters are those that don't fall into either the reserve or non-reserve category.

Table 7.1 illustrates Mexico's 6.35% 2035 bond and outlines the main components of the indenture. It details the main provisions and their application in this specific case. While there are many similarities among sovereign bond contracts, the investor should be mindful that specifics matter. Even minor variations in provisions can significantly impact contract terms and enforceability in the event of default.

7.2.2 Events of Default

Sovereign bond contracts generally contain provisions detailing the circumstances that may lead to an event of default. The most common event of default is failure to make payments. This occurs when the issuer does not make interest or principal payments on the bond, following the designated grace period.

Events of default may include the breach of covenants requiring the issuer to meet specific financial or operational targets. Cross-defaults may be triggered if the issuer defaults on other debt obligations that contain cross-default clauses. Additional events of default may include the sovereign ceasing membership in the IMF, declaring a moratorium on its debts, or revoking necessary consents or laws for the performance or guarantee of the bonds.

TABLE 7.1 Summary of Mexico 6.35% 2035 Bond Indenture

Item	Details	Options	Mexico 6.35% 2035 Global Note
Issuer	Mexico government		The United Mexican States
Definitions	Defines the terms referred to in the document, for example what is meant by "external indebtedness"		
Governing Law	Determines the legal framework that will govern the interpretation and enforcement of the contract	NY, English or other	NY Law
Legal Jurisdiction	Specifies which courts will have jurisdiction over disputes arising from the contract	NY, English or other	Manhattan, New York City
Trust Indenture or Fiscal Agency Agreement		Trustee or Fiscal Agent	Trust indenture
Name of Trustee / Fiscal Agent			Deutsche Bank Trust Company Americas
Payment & Bond Terms	Specifies the amount, timing and frequency of interest that will be paid, the amount of principal that will be repaid at maturity, and other modalities of payment like the currency		Fixed coupon: 6.35% Coupon Freq: Semi-annual Maturity: 02/09/2035 Currency: USD Rank: Senior unsecured Amount Issued: $2.75bn Issue Price: $99.632
Events of Default	Specifies the circumstances under which the issuer will be considered to be in default on the bond contract. This can include failure to make interest or principal payments, breach of covenants, or other specified events		Failure to pay interest or principal after 30-day grace or Mexico declares a moratorium
Non-Reserved Matter Modifications	Rules and requirements for modifications of non-reserved matters		Single series: More than 50% of principal amount outstanding
Reserved Matter Modifications	Rules and requirements for modification of reserved matters		Single series: More than 75% of principal amount outstanding

TABLE 7.1 Continued

Item	Details	Options	Mexico 6.35% 2035 Global Note
			Cross series with single aggregated Voting: More than 75% of aggregate principal amount outstanding of all series affected with "uniformly applicable" treatment being met Cross series with two tier voting: More than 66⅔% of aggregate principal amount outstanding of all series affected, and more than 50% of aggregate principal amount outstanding of each series affected
Collective Action Clause	Specifies whether there are any CACs and which type	No CACs 1st Gen CACs 2nd Gen CACs 3rd Gen "enhanced" CACs	3rd Generation "enhanced" CACs (see voting thresholds under reserve matters)
Pari Passu Provision	Specifies details of the clause	Old vs. Enhanced	Enhanced pari passu
Terms of Other Bonds by the Issuer		Older CACs and thresholds, pari passu provisions	Prior to 2014
Covenants	Promises made by the issuer to the bondholders regarding the use of proceeds from the bond issuance and other aspects of the issuer's financial management	Restrictions on the issuer's ability to incur additional debt, limitations on the use of proceeds, and other provisions designed to protect the interests of bondholders	Negative pledge
Waiver of Sovereign Immunity		Yes No Selective	Yes

Source: Bloomberg Finance L.P.

Finally, sovereign bond contracts may contain force majeure clauses that permit the issuer to suspend payments in the event of a natural disaster, war, or other unforeseen circumstances. If the force majeure event persists for an extended duration, it may eventually trigger an event of default.

There may be gray areas in what constitutes a default, such as cases where the issuer makes the payment to the trustee or paying agent, but the bondholders do not receive it. This may be due to sanctions prohibiting receipt, as was the case for Russian payments in 2022 due to US sanctions. It may also be due to legal factors, as in the case of Argentina's 2014 default when New York Judge Griesa enjoined third parties from handling the payments.

Ultimately, whether an event of default has occurred depends on the terms listed in the bond contract. This forms the basis for enforcing creditors' rights in case of a default, including the right to accelerate repayment of the bond, demand immediate payment of all outstanding principal and interest, trigger cross-default clauses, or take legal action to recover their investment.

7.2.3 Governing Law and Jurisdiction

The governing law establishes which legal system and sets of rules apply to the bond contract. New York law and English law are two of the most common governing laws for sovereign bond contracts. While both laws share many similarities, there are some key differences summarized in Table 7.2. In general, New York law contracts tend to be more prescriptive and detailed in their approach to governing law. In contrast, English law contracts tend to be more flexible, allowing for greater consideration of the parties' intentions.

The legal jurisdiction determines which courts have the authority to hear disputes arising from the contract. This is crucial for enforcing judgments and seeking legal remedies in the event of a default. Exclusive jurisdiction designates a single court for the resolution of disputes, while non-exclusive jurisdiction permits creditors to pursue litigation

TABLE 7.2 Key Differences Between New York Law and English Law Bond Contracts

	NY Law	English Law
Governing Law	More prescriptive	Flexible and consideration of intention of parties
Jurisdiction	Laws of the State of NY, USA	Laws of England and Wales
Interpretation	More literal interpretation of contract terms	Emphasis on intent of parties and context
Enforcement and Centralization of Power	Both fiscal agents and trust structures although trust structures more common than in English law	Both fiscal agents and trust structures
Disclosure Requirements	Focused on legal and contractual features	More extensive disclosure requirements, especially financial reporting

in multiple jurisdictions. Additionally, there may be arbitration clauses that mandate the resolution of disputes through arbitration.

The governing law and jurisdiction are distinct. For instance, a bond issued under New York law must adhere to New York contract principles. If the bond designates English courts as the jurisdiction, disputes must be resolved there, even if governed by New York law. For investors, the selection of jurisdiction determines the procedural law that can make a lot of difference, particularly where there is ambiguity about whether some issues fall into the procedural or substantive law boxes. It also determines whether courts will enforce bondholder claims since bondholders may win legal cases but face challenges in enforcing rulings if the chosen court lacks leverage over sovereign assets.

In practice, issuers choose the governing law and jurisdiction, which limits recourse for investors in a specific bond sale. However, in some debt workouts, investors have managed to negotiate amendments to the jurisdiction and other legal terms to improve future enforceability.

7.2.4 Trust Versus Fiscal Agency Agreements (FAA)

Trustees and fiscal agents are key third parties involved in the issuance and management of sovereign bonds. A trustee is an independent entity appointed to act on behalf of the bondholders and protect their interests. Meanwhile, the issuer designates a fiscal agent to provide administrative and other services related to the bond issue. Both trustees and fiscal agents are appointed and compensated by the issuer at the time of issuance. Each has different roles and responsibilities, as reviewed in Table 7.3.

The trustee is responsible for ensuring that the issuer follows the terms of the bond indenture. This enhances transparency and information availability and offers investors an additional layer of protection. The trustee facilitates communication between the issuer and bondholders, provides a mechanism for dispute resolution, and helps avoid costly legal action. Meanwhile, a fiscal agent represents the sovereign issuer, handling tasks like making interest and principal payments, keeping track of bondholder records, and coordinating communications.

In the event of a default, the trustee has exclusive authority to enforce the bond contract. This requires a minimum percentage of bondholders to approve action and adequate indemnification. While the trustee is negotiating a restructuring agreement, individual bondholders are prohibited from pursuing any litigation. This reduces holdouts and safeguards the sovereign's assets during the negotiation.

The risk is that the trustee may abdicate their responsibilities or become hesitant to take action. The trustee may also demand excessive indemnities from bondholders before proceeding with legal action. In these cases, individual bondholders can only initiate legal proceedings after demonstrating that the trustee failed to meet their obligations despite the minimum quorum and reasonable indemnity being met.

This contrasts with a FAA, which usually doesn't have the power to enforce actions in the event of default. Instead, individual bondholders have the right to initiate legal proceedings against the debtor. In practice, exercising this right may be challenging for

TABLE 7.3 Main Differences between a Trustee and a Fiscal Agent

Role	Trustee Under Indenture	Fiscal Agent Under Fiscal Agency Agreement
Appointed by the issuer	✓	✓
Represent the noteholders in a fiduciary capacity	✓	×
Represent the issuer	×	✓
Note authentication	✓	✓
Secured offerings	✓	×
Monitor and ensure that all contractual obligations are carried out (secured and unsecured notes)	✓	×
Collection and payment of principal and interest to the noteholders	✓	✓
Issue stand-alone or program	✓	✓
Administer redemptions/maturities	✓	✓
Initiate appropriate actions if issuer does not meet obligations	✓	×
Arrange Noteholder meetings	✓	✓
Record keeping/tracking of notes proceeds	✓	✓
Collect and hold stipulated documentation	✓	×

Source: Adapted from Buchheit, L.C. (2018).

smaller investors given the cost and coordination needed. Bondholders, therefore, collectively benefit from the coordination and organizational services provided by the trustee structure.

Individual bondholders' rights to accelerate payment after a default are typically more limited under trust structures than under FAAs. Under a FAA, each bondholder can accelerate their own bond (but not the entire issue) without limitation. In comparison, trust structures limit the consequences of default to a single bond issue unless the quorum required for acceleration and cross-default of the entire issue is met, which is usually 25% of bondholders.

Trust structures ensure pro rata distribution among all bondholders of any amounts recovered through litigation, whether initiated by a single bondholder or a group. This sharing requirement discourages potential holdouts from pursuing litigation. In contrast, under a FAA that allows individual bondholders to litigate, the proceeds from litigation initiated by individual bondholders remain theirs alone.

A trust structure limits the risk of attachment on debt service payments. Payments received by a trustee are generally regarded as the property of bondholders as soon as they are received, and thus not subject to attachment by third-party creditors of the issuer. The risk of attachment concerning payments to fiscal agents is less clear. New York courts have at times classified the funds as property of the issuer (and thereby subject to attachment), and at other times as money held in trust for bondholders (and therefore not attachable).

FAAs are more prevalent in international sovereign debt transactions because they are slightly cheaper and simpler to implement than trust structures. Low-income countries, in particular, are sensitive to issuance costs and have utilized FAAs for sovereign debt issued under English law. Trust structures are more commonly used in sovereign debt instruments issued under New York law, as well as in more complex transactions.[2]

The use of FAAs and trust structures is not static, and sovereign issuers may switch modalities of issuance. Mexico (in 2014), Poland (in 2016), and Turkey (in 2018) have all switched from FAAs to trust structures. Meanwhile, the Philippines (2018) and Indonesia (2019) switched from trust structures to FAAs for their global bond issuances, respectively.

7.2.5 Collective Action Clauses

One of the most important legal provisions embedded in sovereign bond contracts are CACs. These provisions allow a qualified majority of bondholders to modify the terms of a bond without the consent of all bondholders.

CACs offer a mechanism for a coordinated approach to debt restructuring and help mitigate holdouts. This occurs when a minority of bondholders refuse to participate in a sovereign bond restructuring, hoping to extract better terms through litigation after other bondholders receive haircuts. Without CACs, issuers must individually negotiate with bondholders to modify the terms of a bond, which can be a time-consuming and costly process.[3]

CACs have evolved, motivated by the need for more efficient and orderly debt restructuring processes.[4] First-generation or series-by-series CACs enable a majority of bondholders within a single series to impose restructuring terms on non-consenting holdouts in that same series. Each bond series votes separately, with no cross-series aggregation. For reserved matters, the typical voting threshold is no less than 75% of the aggregate principal amount, while for non-reserved matters it is no less than 66⅔%. This means that holdout creditors must control a blocking stake of 25–34% in a single bond to prevent it from being restructured. First-generation CACs were first included in sovereign bonds issued by Mexico in 2003.

Second-generation or dual-limb CACs aggregate votes across different bond series. This enables bondholders of one or more bonds to compel bondholders in a different series into a restructuring if the voting thresholds are met in each series, provided that the same indenture governs all affected series. The usual threshold for consent on reserved matters of an individual series is 66⅔%, along with the additional requirement of agreement from a minimum number of holders across all series to be restructured (in aggregate). The aggregation constraint weakens holdout blocking strategies that require control of at least 15–25% of the *entire* issuance, rather than just a single bond series. Uruguay was the first country to issue Second-generation CACs, followed by Argentina.

Third-generation or single-limb aggregated CACs include additional tools to compel holdout bondholders into a restructuring. They permit a single aggregated vote across all affected bond series with the backing of typically 75% of holders. Consequently, the requirement for each series to approve the proposed amendment by a specified majority is removed. However, the mechanism does necessitate that the sovereign offers the same menu of considerations to all series impacted by the modification. This *uniformly applicable* feature is anticipated to protect intercreditor equity.

Third-generation CACs were introduced in 2014 and are now widely used by euro area and emerging market sovereigns. They have yet to be fully tested in courts, but investors have raised concerns about potential coercive tactics used by issuers, which we discuss in the next section.

Figure 7.1 summarizes voting for each generation of CAC with successively lower modification thresholds. Empirically, over 95% of the stock of international sovereign bonds includes some form of CACs, with only a small share (usually issued before 2003) lacking CACs. Of the outstanding stock of bonds, about 50% have Third-generation (aggregated, single-limb, or enhanced) CACs.[5] Nonetheless, bonds with series-by-series CACs continue to be highly relevant in distressed sovereign workouts.

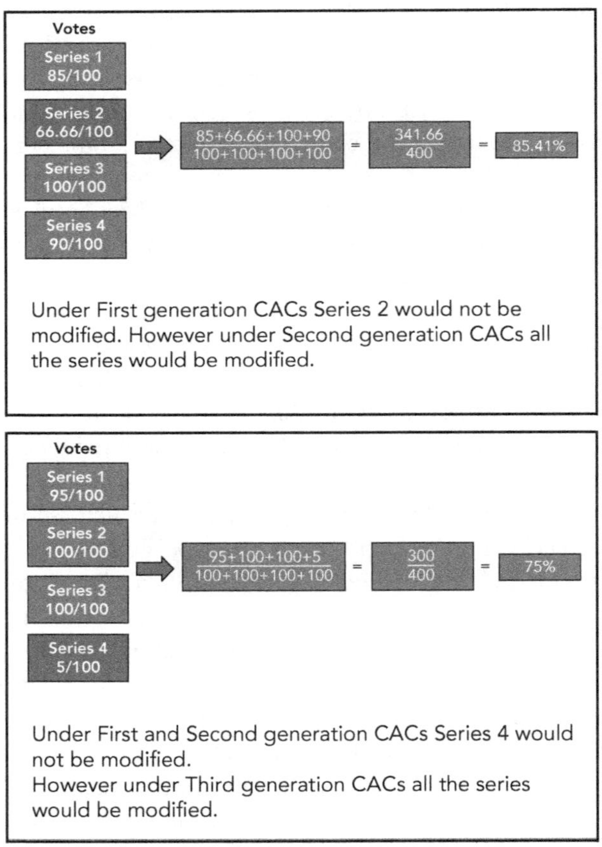

FIGURE 7.1 Example of amendments under different generations of CACs. Source: Cleary Gottlieb Steen & Hamilton LLP (2015)/Cleary Gottlieb.

For sovereign debt investors, understanding the nuances of CACs is not just about legal analysis—it is a fundamental factor in assessing default risk, bond pricing, and potential recovery values. Market pricing of bonds, liquidity, and creditor characteristics may vary based on CAC structure.[6]

Generally, newer single-limb aggregated CAC bonds trade at lower prices (wider spreads) than dual-limb CAC bonds because of the increased risk of restructuring. In contrast, First-generation or series-by-series CAC bonds trade at a premium due to a higher likelihood of successful holdout strategies. These differences become even more pronounced when sovereigns face high credit risk and are nearing default.

7.2.5.1 New Issues in the Use of CACs

There are several significant operational concerns regarding the use of the single-limb aggregated CACs. These involve the potential for issuers to employ the *Pacman strategy* and *redesignation*—both of which emerged during the 2020 restructurings in Argentina and Ecuador. Creditors contend that these strategies undermine the spirit of CACs and allow the issuer to manipulate restructuring terms unfairly.[7]

Under the Pacman approach, the sovereign uses multiple restructuring offers to obtain a super-majority of individual bond series sequentially, and then presents a slightly better deal through the aggregated super-majority process to restructure all bonds. This could allow for the restructuring of all bonds with significantly less than the super-majority support needed for aggregated voting, as every bondholder affected by the previous single series restructurings would vote to approve the aggregated proposal.

Redesignation enables the issuer to determine which series of bonds is included in the CAC vote, even after the exchange offer has closed. This could allow for the manipulation of the voting pool to ensure that the minimum voting thresholds are met for all individual series as well as in aggregate.

To address these concerns, both the Argentine and Ecuador restructurings adopted language in the new exchange bonds.[8] Even so, the limited adoption of this updated CAC language in new sovereign bond issuance means that these strategies could be used in future restructurings.

A separate issue is the *problem of ganging up.* In this scenario, holders of a particular series of bonds use their combined voting power in the aggregated pool to impose a disadvantageous deal on one or more other series. The potential for coercion arises because the uniformly applicable provision only requires a sovereign to offer the same consideration or menu of considerations. It does not imply that everyone would receive the same instruments, particularly those investors who voted against the proposal or exchange.

There are other open questions related to the use of CACs. One issue is whether bonds issued with aggregated CACs can be grouped with bonds featuring old CACs for voting purposes, which remains untested legally. Also related is the treatment of CACs if issuers that have issued under NY law switch to English (or other) law.[9] There is also the issue of whether a sovereign's local law bonds, if they have CACs inserted in them that are similar to the foreign law bonds, can vote in the aggregation.

Another question is whether CACs can be circumvented entirely by investors by pursuing and obtaining judgments before an issuer makes a restructuring offer to bondholders. This is particularly relevant in lengthy sovereign debt restructurings, where judgments against a defaulting sovereign could be obtained prior to the activation of CACs, allowing for separate negotiations on different terms than those offered to other bondholders. If feasible, this could seriously undermine the contractual framework intended to use CACs to limit holdouts.

A parallel issue relates to the comparability of treatment (CoT) between bondholders and those holding loans, as the latter typically lack embedded CACs and may be prone to holdouts. Also relevant is the CoT between bondholders and arbitration claims or the claims of tort victims for injuries the sovereign might have caused, for example, in a war.

These issues suggest that the details of CACs will remain a key aspect of restructuring negotiations for the foreseeable future.

PRO TIP: *Maintain a list of non-standard clauses (including CACs) in sovereign debt prospectuses and indentures as you come across them.*

7.2.6 The *Pari Passu* Clause

Another much discussed provision is the *pari passu* clause. The *pari passu* clause requires the issuer to treat all bondholders equally regarding payment priority in the event of a default or restructuring. The traditional *pari passu* clause gained prominence during the litigation against Argentina by holdout creditors represented by NML Capital Ltd. The holdout creditors argued that they were not being treated equally under the *pari passu* terms of the bond, as Argentina was paying bondholders who participated in the 2005 and 2010 restructurings but not the holdouts. The US courts sided with NML Capital and ruled that Argentina must pay holdouts ratably as it pays other bondholders.

The ruling raised questions about the meaning of the *pari passu* provision and whether the ranking interpretation or the payment interpretation was the correct interpretation of the provision.[10] The ranking interpretation asserts equal ranking (i.e., the relevant sovereign debt must not be subordinated to other debt); it does not assert equal payment. The payment interpretation stipulates that any payments made by the sovereign issuer on other relevant debt may only occur if ratable payments are also made on the sovereign debt in which the ranking provision is contained.

In 2014, ICMA modified the *pari passu* clause following the case. The change introduced an important *payment block* provision stating that creditors who did not participate in a restructuring would not be able to sue for equal treatment or claim priority over other creditors during the restructuring process. The modification also clarified that *equal treatment* does not mean identical treatment.

Together, these have provided greater flexibility for sovereign debt restructurings to proceed more smoothly without being held hostage by holdout creditors. Since 2017, the vast majority of sovereign issuances that have included single-limb aggregated CACs have also incorporated modified *pari passu* provisions.[11]

7.2.7 The Negative Pledge Clause

Next, we look at provisions that regulate the actions of sovereign issuers. A negative pledge clause safeguards bondholders by ensuring they're not structurally subordinated to other creditors. In simple terms, it prevents a sovereign borrower from using its assets as collateral for new debt without providing equal treatment to existing bondholders.

The strength and enforceability of negative pledges can vary. An *absolute prohibition* prevents the borrower from pledging assets or securing new debt under any circumstances. *Equal treatment, or pari passu collateralization*, means that existing bondholders must receive the same compensation or collateral granted to new lenders.

Another distinctive feature is whether the clause applies only to future borrowing or if it permits bondholders to seek compensation if an existing secured loan is found. This becomes relevant when a country fails to transparently disclose its borrowing activities, creating information asymmetries among creditors.

In sovereign bond contracts, the negative pledge provision applies to *relevant indebtedness*. This typically includes bonds, notes, debentures, loan stock, or other securities that can be listed or traded. The definition of relevant indebtedness may create gray areas. For instance, it is unclear whether it encompasses debt denominated in a foreign currency or debt sold in domestic markets.

Other areas for discussion include whether the indebtedness of central banks or state-owned enterprises (SOEs) falls within the scope of relevant debt. There is a related question of whether the assets of associated entities, such as SOEs, can be pledged even if there are no direct government exposures.

Understanding negative pledges is essential in an era where collateralized sovereign borrowing is prevalent. These include loans that are secured by central bank reserves,[12] commodity revenues,[13] or infrastructure assets. For sovereign bondholders, these arrangements create a risk of subordination, diminishing the pool of available assets in a debt restructuring.

Negative pledge clauses have not always been vigorously enforced, but there are some legal precedents. These include cases brought against the Republic of Congo concerning its oil-backed loans from China[14] and Mozambique regarding the implications of its gas-revenue-backed lending for its sovereign "tuna" bond issuance.[15]

7.2.8 Waiver of Sovereign Immunity

Another clause limiting the sovereign's power is the waiver of sovereign immunity. Sovereign immunity is a legal doctrine stating that a sovereign state cannot be sued without its consent. It is founded on the principle that a sovereign state should not be subject to the jurisdiction of another state's courts or tribunals.

A waiver of sovereign immunity signifies the sovereign issuer's agreement to relinquish its immunity from legal action in a foreign court or arbitration tribunal. This enables investors to sue the sovereign issuer in the event of a default or any breach of contract. The waiver may be limited in scope, may not apply to all types of legal actions or jurisdictions, and may include specific conditions or limitations to protect the sovereign's interests.[16]

Ultimately, the ability of bondholders to pursue legal action against sovereign debtors depends on the specifics of the governing law under which the instrument was issued. Under English law, a foreign entity is unlikely to have immunity from jurisdiction. Even so, English law bond contracts tend to include a waiver of sovereign immunity since it may be desirable to initiate legal proceedings in a country other than the United Kingdom.

Under New York law, sovereign immunity is closely linked to the Foreign Sovereign Immunities Act (FSIA). This US federal law, passed in 1976, governs the ability of foreign countries (and their instrumentalities) to be sued in US courts. It is important for investors as it lays out the framework for the general immunity of sovereign debtors from the jurisdiction of US courts, as well as the exceptions to those immunities.[17]

These jurisdiction-specific frameworks are particularly relevant for sovereign bond contracts where the sovereign issuer has not waived sovereign immunity. Examples include specific Venezuelan and Russian sovereign debt instruments issued under New York law, implying that the framework laid out under the FSIA would therefore apply.

7.2.9 Amending the Bond Indenture

The terms of a sovereign bond contract may be amended through negotiation and agreement between the sovereign issuer and the bondholders. The specific process varies based on the contract terms, the legal jurisdiction governing the bond, and the preferences of the involved parties.

Typically, it involves *notifying* stakeholders about the proposed changes; *consulting* with bondholders to discuss the changes and address any concerns or objections; *documenting agreements* with the amendments; obtaining *approval* through a vote or consent solicitation from the required percentage of bondholders, as detailed in the bond contract; and *implementing* and *incorporating* these changes into the bond contract.

In practice, making significant changes to the terms of a sovereign bond contract can be complex and time-consuming. Bondholders may have varying interests and priorities, which can make reaching a consensus on the proposed amendments challenging. In some instances, such as restructurings, the parties may need to engage in extensive negotiations and consultations to arrive at an agreement on the proposed changes.

Having addressed the main provisions in foreign law bond contracts, we now shift our focus to legal considerations in domestic sovereign debt.

7.3 THE LEGAL FRAMEWORK FOR DOMESTIC SOVEREIGN DEBT

The legal framework for domestic sovereign debt is complex. While external debt is typically issued under a sovereign debt contract governed by foreign law, domestic debt can be issued under various legal frameworks. These frameworks differ from country to country, as each state has its own legal and regulatory requirements governing debt issuance.[18]

In many countries, the constitution and domestic law establish the legal framework for sovereign debt. Public debt laws outline the procedures and requirements for borrowing money on behalf of the government, as well as the limits on the amount of debt that can be incurred. Statutes and regulations govern the issuance of bonds, the terms and types of bonds, and the procedures for resolving disputes between the government and bondholders.[19]

Before a public offering of domestic law bonds, the government may issue a prospectus or offering memorandum. This document outlines the terms and conditions of the bond, including maturity, coupon rate, and other key features, as well as the auction schedule and procedures (if applicable) and any pertinent legal provisions, such as the country's sovereign immunity or tax treatment of interest payments. If the debt offering is conducted through a syndicate of investment banks, there may be a formal indenture detailing the terms of the contract after issuance.

With domestic law, the terms of the bonds, the auction or syndication process, and the rights of bondholders are all subject to local legal frameworks. In the case of any disputes, the governing law for the bonds will usually be that of the issuing country. Disputes are resolved through the domestic judicial system, although some countries may include provisions for arbitration. International law may play a role if treaties and conventions exist that govern the treatment of foreign investors.

Domestic law issuance provides the sovereign with what is known as the *local law advantage*. This refers to the benefits a sovereign gains by having legal and regulatory jurisdiction over which it has significant control. A sovereign can influence bondholders' rights and remedies and alter the terms of its domestic law debt through legislation or executive actions without the consent of creditors.

Sovereigns have reprofiled domestic debt by extending maturity, reducing coupons or the face value, and modifying the currency and terms of payment. In some instances, currency controls have confined international investors' funds onshore, providing limited options for repatriation. Meanwhile, domestic investors, such as banks and pension funds, are captive to the government's terms.

Domestic law debt generally does not include CACs. There are select exceptions, notably euro area sovereign debt, which has included CACs in domestic law bonds since the Greek restructuring in 2012. Greece introduced dual-limb CACs through domestic legislation, enabling the government to cram down holdout creditors and move forward with the domestic debt restructuring. Legal challenges in domestic and international courts, as well as investment arbitration tribunals, were unsuccessful due to Greece's sovereign immunity, lack of legal jurisdiction, and the assertion that the restructuring was in Greece's public interest.[20]

All that said, there are some counterbalancing factors to the advantages of local law. Governments have an incentive to act fairly and transparently with investors to avoid a buyer's strike, particularly given the rising foreign participation in domestic markets. Domestic investors can be powerful within the country's political economy, and domestic law debt sometimes receives better treatment than debt issued in other jurisdictions. Furthermore, any changes to domestic legislation may be limited by the sovereign's constitution or its international obligations.

7.4 THE LEGAL FRAMEWORK FOR SOE DEBT

Sovereign debt portfolios often include exposures to SOE debt, whether guaranteed by the government or not. Foreign law debt issued by SOEs presents additional legal considerations compared to foreign law sovereign debt.

The legal framework of SOEs is corporate rather than sovereign, which impacts their legal status and restructuring framework. Unlike sovereign bonds, which are backed by a country's full faith and credit, SOE bonds are typically supported by the enterprise's cash flows and assets. Corporate insolvency law and bankruptcy proceedings apply in the case of a default, unlike sovereign debt, which requires a workout with creditors. See Table 7.4 for the main legal differences between sovereign and SOE debt.

The gray area arises when SOEs are strategically important, possess income streams that back government debt, or perform functions that can be perceived as government activities. In some instances, the underlying assets of SOEs (especially in the extractive sectors) belong to the sovereign rather than the operating entity. To complicate matters further, the sovereign often explicitly guarantees SOE debt. These debts frequently cross-default and are *pari passu* with international sovereign debt, blurring the line further.

Empirically, the legal treatment of SOE bonds in debt restructurings varies significantly across countries and situations. In some instances, SOE debt has been treated alongside the sovereign and restructured together—typically the case for SOEs that are strategic and of national significance. In other cases, SOE debt has been restructured separately, with

TABLE 7.4 Differences Between Government and SOE Bonds

Feature	Sovereign Bonds	SOE Bonds
Legal Issuer	Government (Treasury or Ministry of Finance)	State-owned corporate entity
Repayment Backing	Full faith and credit of the sovereign	Enterprise revenues and assets (unless explicitly guaranteed)
Legal Enforcement	No bankruptcy process, but lawsuits possible (e.g., Argentina case)	Can be restructured under corporate bankruptcy law
Governing Law	Usually English or New York law (for international bonds)	Local law or international law (depends on issuance)
Risk of Default	Sovereigns rarely default unless in severe crisis	SOEs can default more easily, especially if government withdraws support
Restructuring Framework	Handled through bondholder negotiations, CACs, and sovereign workouts	Can be handled via corporate restructuring, court proceedings, or sovereign intervention

bondholders navigating corporate-style restructurings instead of sovereign workouts. For bondholders, the key takeaway is to be ready to adopt a case-by-case approach and to critically assess the activities of the SOE and its relationship with the sovereign.

7.5 ENFORCING SOVEREIGN DEBT CONTRACTS

Sovereign debt restructurings are fundamentally different from corporate workouts. While corporate bonds are backed by tangible assets and a clearly defined legal framework for bankruptcy, sovereign bonds exist in a gray area of enforceability. Governments are immune from traditional bankruptcy proceedings, and enforcement mechanisms depend heavily on international legal structures, creditor coordination, and political will.

As a result, sovereign debt contracts are enforceable only to a certain extent. Creditors can obtain legal rulings, but practical enforcement through asset seizures and payment blockades is complex. It's also important to keep in mind that litigation can be profitable if there is a strong basis for legal action, but it requires a long-term commitment.[21]

For investors, the choice of governing law for bond issuance is significant. Foreign law bonds issued under English or New York law are more difficult for sovereigns to restructure unilaterally compared to local law debt. While CACs are reshaping enforcement risk and decreasing holdouts, many aspects of the single-limb aggregated CACs remain untested in courts. Lastly, geopolitics is increasingly a major factor in enforceability, with sanctions, the growth of Chinese strategic bilateral lending, and political rifts often overriding legal protections. These factors add to the complexity of investing in sovereign debt.

7.6 SANCTIONS ON SOVEREIGN DEBT

Aside from the contractual rights outlined in sovereign bond contracts, investors can encounter additional legal challenges. Sanctions on sovereign bonds constitute legal and regulatory restrictions that limit investors' ability to trade, hold, issue, or intermediate debt of targeted governments or entities. They have emerged as an essential tool of foreign policy, especially in the context of geopolitical conflicts, human rights violations, and illicit financial activities.

Sanctions take many forms. Blocking sanctions effectively prohibit all dealings related to sanctioned governments and their associated entities. Examples include US sanctions against Cuba, Iran, North Korea, and Syria. Restrictions on sovereign debt are another type of sanction, as seen in the case of US and EU sanctions against Russia and Belarus in 2022.

Sanctions may prohibit participation in new bond issues, while allowing secondary trading of existing debt. They may apply to various entities, including the sovereign, state-owned enterprises, corporations, and private individuals. Additionally, they may restrict access to international clearing systems (e.g., Euroclear, Clearstream). In some cases, the sanctioning government may issue general licenses to bondholders, authorizing for a limited time the ability of creditors to transact in the sanctioned entity's instruments.

For example, the 2022 US sanctions on Russia prevented third parties from processing Russian debt payments, even though the issuer had both the capacity and willingness to pay. During the CDS auction, special licenses allowed for the purchase and delivery of eligible Russian bonds.

In 2017, US sanctions on Venezuela prevented US bondholders from negotiating with the government to restructure defaulted debt. A clarification issued in 2018 allowed trading in PDVSA 2020 bonds due to the existence of US collateral in the form of CITGO shares.[22]

For sovereign bondholders, sanctions affect the liquidity, pricing, tradability, and potential index inclusion of the impacted bonds, and it is crucial to understand and comply with them to. We discuss the implications of sanctions for portfolios and guidelines for handling them in Chapter 14.

7.7 SAMPLE COUNTRY CONTRACTS

Bond contracts in our three sample countries will vary based on the type of debt that is issued.

Country A

Country A debt securities will largely be issued under domestic law and in domestic currency. As such the legal considerations for domestic law will apply. Aside from European sovereigns, most advanced economy domestic law debt does not have CACs. There may be a small amount of debt that is issued under foreign law, in which case the bond indentures will govern the legal framework.

Country B

Country B debt is generally a combination of domestic law and domestic currency issued debt, and foreign law and foreign currency issued debt. In some cases, there may be domestic law foreign currency issued liabilities. The respective legal frameworks for domestic and foreign law debt would apply for each category of debt. Foreign law debt will be issued under New York or English law with new issuances having Third-generation CACs and the modified pari passu clause. Domestic law debt is unlikely to have CACs.

Country C

Country C debt tends to be mainly foreign law debt owed to international investors or concessional debt owed to official creditors. There may be domestic law debt mainly held by domestic creditors. For these countries foreign law indentures and frameworks would be in play. Being an infrequent issuer, the country's older bonds may have older generation of CACs.

7.8 SUMMARY

This chapter covered the main stakeholders and provisions in foreign law sovereign bond contracts. It flagged new emerging issues that are yet to be resolved in the use of Third-generation CACs and several aspects investors should take note of in future restructurings. The discussion also reviewed issues in domestic debt and SOE bond contracts, which are becoming increasingly important as the frequency of domestic law default rises.

Investors should be cognizant of the legal specifics of the bond contract before building positions in a given issuer and bond issue. As the legal landscape evolves, it is helpful to keep abreast of developments through industry and trade organizations like the IIF, which can collectively represent investors' views to the relevant counterparts.

NOTES

1. An agency agreement may also accompany the bond issue. This is a contract between the issuer and one or more agents that outlines the roles and responsibilities involved in administering the bond after it is issued.
2. Approximately 36% of new international sovereign bond issuances since October 2014 use trust structures, and approximately 93% are issued under New York law (IMF, *Fourth Progress Report on CACs*).
3. Peru (1990s) and Argentina (2001–2016) highlight how prolonged and litigious sovereign debt restructurings can become in the absence of CACs. In both these cases, holdout creditors pursued aggressive legal action, complicating debt settlements. In contrast, countries with strong CACs—such as Ecuador (2020)—achieved quicker and more orderly restructurings with high creditor participation.
4. See ICMA, *Standard CACs (2014)*; *Standard CACs under English Law (2015)*; IMF, *Strengthening the Contractual Framework*; *Progress Report on Enhanced Provisions*; and *Fourth Progress Report on CACs*.
5. IMF, *Fourth Progress Report on CACs*.
6. See Chung and Papaioannou, *Do Enhanced CACs Affect Borrowing Costs?*
7. See De la Cruz and Lagos, "CACs at Work."
8. These provided that re-designation of voting pools will only be permitted if (i) bondholders are given five business days after the exchange offer closes to withdraw their votes or (ii) the offer was approved by holders of more than 66⅔% of the aggregate principal amount of the originally designated pool. Moreover, to limit the use of Pacman strategies, thresholds for the use of aggregated CACs were introduced.

9. CACs generally work across multiple series issued under the same indenture. As a result, sovereigns usually are reluctant to put together a completely new indenture under a different law that would limit the benefits of cross-series aggregation. To get around this, some sovereigns include language in their New York law indentures that the sovereign can issue English law bonds. This would suggest that in those cases, CACs will be interpreted pursuant to NY law, although this remains to be tested legally.
10. See FMLC, *Pari Passu Clauses*, Buchheit and Gulati, "Restructuring Sovereign Debt after NML," and Makoff and Kahn, *Sovereign Bond Contract Reform*.
11. The exceptions have been some issuers (for example, Russia) issuing under English law. This may reflect the view that English courts are unlikely to interpret the *pari passu* clause as requiring that the issuer make ratable payments to creditors. In addition, there is the view that the English Courts would approach the grant of remedies differently from the approach taken by the US Courts in the Argentina case.
12. During Zambia's debt restructuring (2020–2024), bondholders raised concerns about whether certain bilateral loans—particularly those from China—were secured against central bank reserves or government revenues. The lack of transparency surrounding these agreements created uncertainty in Zambia's debt restructuring negotiations, making it difficult for bondholders to assess their recovery prospects.
13. Ecuador's past loans from China illustrate how collateralized borrowing can impact bondholders. During periods of fiscal stress, Ecuador pledged future oil exports to secure Chinese financing. While these loans helped the country access funding, they also meant that when Ecuador restructured its international bonds in 2020, bondholders had little access to oil revenues that were already committed to repaying Chinese creditors.
14. Kensington International sued the Republic of Congo (Brazzaville, 2005–2007) in the UK, arguing that the country had violated its negative pledge clause by pledging oil revenues to secure new loans from Chinese and other bilateral creditors. The UK courts ruled in favor of Kensington, freezing certain oil shipments as part of an enforcement action. However, practical enforcement proved difficult because Congo's new creditors and trade partners worked to shield the country's oil exports from legal claims. The case underscored the challenges of enforcing negative pledge clauses when sovereign assets are pledged in non-transparent ways.
15. Mozambique secretly issued $2 billion in state-guaranteed loans in 2013–2014, later revealed to be linked to undisclosed borrowing secured against future state revenues from offshore gas projects. When the hidden debts came to light (in 2016), bondholders accused Mozambique of fraudulently circumventing its negative pledge clauses, as the government-backed loans were structured in a way that gave lenders preferential repayment rights over bondholders. The scandal led to a broader sovereign default.
16. For example, premises of diplomatic missions, their archives and documents, and military equipment may be inviolable and out of reach of attachment.
17. Under the FSIA, foreign states are generally immune from the jurisdiction of US courts, unless one of several exceptions applies. These exceptions include cases involving commercial activity, property taken in violation of international law, torts committed in the United States, and cases in which the foreign state has waived its immunity. The FSIA also provides for service of process on foreign states and their agencies and instrumentalities, and sets forth procedures for obtaining jurisdiction over them. The law also establishes procedures for the attachment and execution of property of foreign states in satisfaction of judgments.
18. See IMF, *Issues in Restructuring Domestic Sovereign Debt*.
19. In countries that follow a common law legal system, the principles of contract law and property law may also apply to sovereign debt. This may include the legal requirements for entering into a contract, the obligations of the parties involved, and the remedies available in the event of a breach of contract.

20. See Box 2, IMF, *Issues in Restructuring Domestic Sovereign Debt* for further details. A related debate (relevant for euro area post-2013 sovereign domestic law bonds) is whether this type of local law adjustment can still be invoked when the bonds already include CACs (see Weidemaier, *Restructuring Italian Debt*).
21. NML Capital v. Argentina and Crystallex v. Venezuela showed that persistence can pay off. However, successful litigation took years (sometimes decades) and significant legal costs.
22. Congressional Research Service, *Venezuela: Overview of U.S. Sanctions Policy*.

REFERENCES

Buchheit, Lee C. "Trustee Versus Fiscal Agents for Sovereign Bonds." *Capital Markets Law Journal* 13, no. 3 (2018): 410–414.

Buchheit, Lee C., and Mitu Gulati. "Restructuring Sovereign Debt after NML v. Argentina." *Capital Markets Law Journal* 12, no. 2 (2017): 224–238.

Chung, Kay, and Michael G. Papaioannou. *Do Enhanced Collective Action Clauses Affect Sovereign Borrowing Costs?* IMF Working Paper WP/20/162. Washington, DC: International Monetary Fund, 2020.

Cleary Gottlieb Steen & Hamilton LLP. *Latest Developments Regarding CACs and Pari Passu Clauses.* Slide Presentation, 2015.

Congressional Research Service. *Venezuela: Overview of U.S. Sanctions Policy*. Washington, DC: Congressional Research Service, 2024.

De la Cruz, Antonio, and Ignacio Lagos. "CACs at Work—What Next? Lessons from the Argentine and Ecuadorian 2020 Debt Restructurings." *Capital Markets Law Journal* 16, no. 2 (2021): 226–248.

Financial Markets Law Committee. *Pari Passu Clauses: Analysis of the Role, Use and Meaning of Pari Passu Clauses in Sovereign Debt Obligations as a Matter of English Law*. London: FMLC, 2015. https://www.fmlc.org (accessed 29 July 2025).

International Capital Markets Association. *Standard Aggregated Collective Action Clauses (CACs) for the Terms and Conditions of Sovereign Notes*. 2014. https://www.icmagroup.org (accessed 29 July 2025).

International Capital Markets Association. *Standard Aggregated Collective Action Clauses (CACs) for the Terms and Conditions of Sovereign Notes Governed by English Law*. 2015. https://www.icmagroup.org (accessed 29 July 2025).

International Monetary Fund. *Strengthening the Contractual Framework to Address Collective Action Problems in Sovereign Debt Restructuring*. IMF Staff Report, 2014. https://www.imf.org (accessed 29 July 2025).

International Monetary Fund. *Progress Report on Inclusion of Enhanced Contractual Provisions in International Sovereign Bond Contracts*. IMF Policy Paper, 2015. https://www.imf.org (accessed 29 July 2025).

International Monetary Fund. *Fourth Progress Report on Inclusion of Enhanced Contractual Provisions in International Sovereign Bond Contracts*. IMF Staff Report, 2019. https://www.imf.org (accessed 29 July 2025).

International Monetary Fund. *Issues in Restructuring of Domestic Sovereign Debt*. IMF Staff Report, 2021. https://www.imf.org (accessed 29 July 2025).

Makoff, Gregory, and Robert Kahn. *Sovereign Bond Contract Reform: Implementing the New ICMA Pari Passu and Collective Action Clauses*. CIGI Papers No. 56. Waterloo, ON: Centre for International Governance Innovation, 2015.

Weidemaier, Mitu. *Restructuring Italian (or Other Euro Area) Debt: Do Euro CACs Constrain or Expand the Options?* UNC Legal Studies Research Paper, 2019.

PART THREE

Generating Risk-Adjusted Returns

CHAPTER EIGHT

Sovereign Bond Math and Portfolio Metrics

PARTS ONE and Two examined the sovereign debt landscape, covering various government securities, macroeconomic and credit fundamentals, and the legal framework for sovereign bond contracts. Part Three shifts to the financial side, focusing on how to generate returns and manage risks. This includes understanding risk metrics, portfolio construction, and investment strategies. It also examines how to effectively trade government bonds and the tools needed for successful portfolio management.

This chapter introduces the core analytical framework for bond valuation and the portfolio metrics used by professional fixed-income investors.[1] It starts with a classification of the key risks in sovereign bonds, highlighting how they vary with the issuer's credit profile, among other factors. It then covers valuation fundamentals, including present value analysis, bond yields, and bond spread measures.

With the basic pricing tools established, the chapter moves on to portfolio risk, including duration, convexity, spread duration, carry and roll-down, and volatility. Performance metrics are covered next and comprise alpha, portfolio beta, tracking error, and risk-adjusted returns such as the Sharpe and information ratios.

Throughout, the application of these tools in real-world portfolio contexts is emphasized, featuring numerical examples. By the end of this chapter, readers will be equipped with the concepts for strategic and tactical decision-making in sovereign bond portfolio management.

8.1 TYPES OF RISKS IN SOVEREIGN BONDS

An investor purchases a sovereign debt instrument to receive both a return *of* their capital and a return *on* their capital. The *return of capital* refers to the repayment of the principal or the initial investment outlay. In contrast, the *return on capital* encompasses the income stream from the coupon as well as any gain or loss resulting from fluctuations in the bond's price.

For example, if an investor holds a 10-year US Treasury bond with a 5% coupon, the simple return would include the principal and 10 years of coupon payments. Investors can also generate returns by trading the bond in secondary markets—selling when bond prices exceed the initial investment and buying when prices are lower.

The risk of not receiving payment of the principal and coupon is referred to as *sovereign credit risk*. This is what sovereign credit ratings and debt sustainability analyses look to assess. Countries that are perceived to have a high risk of non-payment offer higher yields and payments to investors as compensation, while the reverse applies to countries with a lower perceived risk.

Investors also consider various risks that impact the secondary market price of a bond. *Interest rate risk*, arising from fluctuations in interest rates, affects bond prices such that prices decrease when interest rates rise (and vice versa). This is because a fixed coupon bond loses value if interest rates rise, as new bonds offer higher coupons to investors. Consequently, previously issued bonds with lower coupons need to decrease in price to entice buyers.

Exchange rate risk arises when fluctuations in currency values impact bond valuations by altering the nominal value of the income stream. The proceeds from a sovereign bond issued in local currency, such as the Mexican peso, will be worth less in US dollars if the peso depreciates over time. This affects the return for both US investors and Mexican domestic investors, as the opportunity cost of their investment is now lower. In extreme cases, exchange rate risk can result in *convertibility risk* due to capital controls that limit investors' ability to recover their investment.

Inflation risk is closely tied to interest rate and exchange rate risk. Higher-than-expected inflation reduces the real value of a fixed-income stream. Over time, inflation is associated with rising interest rates and higher risks of currency depreciation.

Market risks, including *liquidity* and *technical factors*, can also affect supply and demand. New issues, buybacks, or forced sales may influence market dynamics, introducing volatility and impacting the valuation of sovereign bonds.

Investors may also face *legal and regulatory challenges* when investing in certain sovereign entities. For example, local law bond investors might encounter changes in government legislation that alter the legal terms of their contracts. Regulatory changes regarding collateral eligibility or pension fund investment rules can also impact bond prices and returns.

Sanction risks may arise from geopolitics. US sanctions on Venezuelan debt instruments in 2017 impacted bond investors' capacity to receive principal and coupon payments from Venezuela and limited their ability to sell Venezuelan government bonds in the secondary market.

Each sovereign bond carries a combination of these risks (see Figure 8.1). Developed market bonds, such as US Treasuries or German Bunds, have high credit ratings and extremely low credit risk. For these issuers, interest risk and market risk are the primary

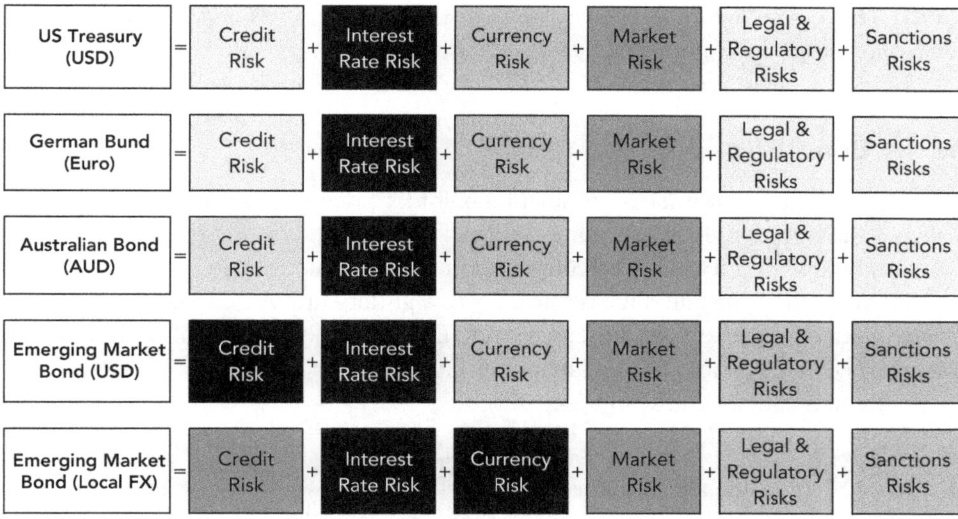

FIGURE 8.1 Risks in sovereign bonds. Note: Darker color denotes relatively more risk.

drivers of valuations. For international investors, these bond holdings also entail currency risk, as fluctuations in the dollar or euro impact returns in the home currency.

Emerging market sovereign bonds denominated in US dollars are primarily influenced by credit risk, US interest rates, and market risk. Meanwhile, for emerging market sovereign bonds issued in local currencies, the key factors include interest rates, currency dynamics, credit fundamentals, and market risks. Legal and regulatory risks may also be relevant.

By analyzing these different risks over various time horizons (short-, medium-, and long-term), investors can assess whether they are adequately compensated and determine whether to buy, sell, or hold their investments. To do this, investors start by calculating the bond's fair price, which we will focus on next.

8.2 BOND VALUATION METRICS

Understanding the value of a sovereign bond begins with mastering the foundational concepts of bond valuation. This section introduces the key metrics and mathematical tools used by portfolio managers to evaluate whether a bond is fairly priced, offering insight into its return potential and relative value. Topics include the time value of money and its application in calculating bond prices, the various definitions and uses of bond yields, the inverse relationship between bond prices and yields, and the importance of credit and market spreads in assessing sovereign credit risk. Together, these concepts form the analytical bedrock for pricing, comparing, and trading sovereign bonds across markets.

PRO TIP: *Calculate each of the metrics in this chapter for bonds in your portfolio and estimate the impact of price, yield, or spread changes.*

8.2.1 Bond Prices

A bond's *fair price* or *fair value* is the starting point for pricing a security. In its most basic form, it is the sum of the present value of all expected cash flows over the life of the bond.

For a bullet bond with a fixed coupon, principal paid at maturity, and no embedded options, calculating the fair value is relatively straightforward. All interest payments and the face value at maturity are added together to give the total cash flow of the instrument. This total is then discounted using an appropriate yield.

Mathematically, a bond's fair value is:

$$\textit{Bond Fair Value} = C\left[\frac{1-(1+y)^{-n}}{y}\right] + \frac{M}{(1+y)^n}$$

where:

C = semiannual contractual interest (in dollars)
y = semiannual yield
n = number of periods (number of years times 2)
M = par/face value in dollars

The appropriate yield is determined by examining the yields of comparable instruments, specifically those with similar maturity, ratings, and features.

The market convention is to quote bond prices as a percentage of their par or face value:

$$\textit{Quoted Price} = \frac{\textit{Dollar Price}}{\textit{Par Value} \times 100}$$

A bond trading at its par value is said to be trading at 100 or par (short for 100% of its par value). A bond trading below par is considered to be trading at a discount (less than 100% of its par value), while a bond trading above par is considered to be trading at a premium (greater than 100% of its par value).

Table 8.1 calculates the fair value of a 10-year bond with a par value of \$1,000 at maturity and a coupon rate of 8% at various yields. The bond's quoted price of 93.50 translates to \$930 for every \$1,000 of par value, while a price of 107.11 corresponds to \$1071.1 for every \$1,000 of par value.

If markets were completely efficient at all times, the market price of a bond would equal its fair price. In practice, the price of a bond can diverge from its fair value. Investors may disagree on the assumptions used for the fair value calculation, such as the discount factor. Other reasons include market technicals, liquidity conditions, new issuances, or

TABLE 8.1 Bond Valuation for a 10-Year Bond with 8% Coupon and Par Value of $1,000

Coupon Rate (%)	Maturity in Years	Par Value ($)	Yield (%)	Semiannual Coupon $ (C)	Semiannual Yield (y), %	Semiannual Maturity (n)	Present Value of Coupon Payments ($)	Present Value of Par Value at Maturity ($)	Fair Value / Price ($)	Price Quote
8	10	1,000	7.0	40	3.5	20	568.50	502.57	1,071.06	107.11
8	10	1,000	8.0	40	4.0	20	543.61	456.39	1,000.00	100.00
8	10	1,000	9.0	40	4.5	20	520.32	414.64	934.96	93.50
8	10	5,000	9.0	200	4.5	20	2,601.59	2,073.21	4,674.80	93.50

risk sentiment, among many others. Identifying when and why market prices deviate from fair value is the bread and butter of traders who buy, sell, and ultimately price sovereign bonds in the marketplace.

8.2.2 The Relationship Between Bond Prices and Yields

For plain vanilla bonds with no embedded options, the bond price decreases when interest rates rise and increases when interest rates fall.[2] Intuitively, when interest rates rise, new bonds provide a higher stream of payments compared to older bonds. Consequently, the prices of older bonds need to adjust for investors to continue holding them. The opposite occurs when interest rates fall.

Mathematically, we derive the same outcome from the formula for the present value of a bond's cash flow. When the required yield (or discount rate) increases, the fair value (or bond price) decreases, and when the yield decreases, the fair value increases.

In Table 8.1, when the required yield equals the bond's coupon rate, the calculated fair value equals the bond's par or face value at maturity. As yields increase, bond valuations fall below par, resulting in the bond trading at a discount. Conversely, as yields decrease, bond valuations rise above par, leading the bond to trade at a premium.

Another aspect of bond pricing is the concept of pull-to-par. This refers to the tendency of a bond's price to converge toward its par value as it approaches maturity, assuming there is no default or credit deterioration. This phenomenon occurs regardless of whether the bond was purchased at par value, a discount, or a premium and results from the inherent decline in time premium within the calculation of the bond's price.

8.2.3 Yield Measures

A bond's yield represents a measure of its return based on various assumptions regarding the holding period, cash flows, and reinvestment. Several measures of yield are used in analyzing sovereign bonds, including yield-to-maturity, yield-to-worst, current yield, and exit yield.

The *yield-to-maturity (YTM)* or *internal rate of return (IRR)* is the most common yield measure used in sovereign bond analysis. It serves as a standardized metric for comparing bonds with different maturities, coupons, or price levels. YTM is the yield that equates the price of the bond to the present value of the total cash flow from the investment:

$$YTM = r \text{ to solve } P = \sum_{n=1}^{N} \frac{C}{(1+r)^n} + \frac{M}{(1+r)^N}$$

where:

P = current bond price
C = semiannual coupon
M = face value
N = number of years

Calculating the YTM requires some iterations and trial and error. In Table 8.1, the YTM for the bond priced at 93.50 is 9%, as this is the yield where the present value of all cash flows from the bond is equal to the price. If instead the price were 107.11, the YTM would be 7%.

The *yield-to-worst* applies to bonds with embedded put or call options. It calculates the yield-to-maturity, the yield to each call date, and the yield to each put date, then takes the minimum of these yields. This measure is quite conservative and is particularly relevant for sovereign bonds with amortizing structures, which represent a tiny portion of outstanding sovereign bonds.

A simpler measure is the *current yield*, which divides the annual coupon interest by the bond price:

$$Current\ yield = \frac{Annual\ dollar\ interest}{Price}$$

The current yield for the 8% coupon bond with a par value of $1,000 selling for a dollar price of $934.96 is 8.6%. The current yield is a simple measure that doesn't take into account the bond's maturity or the principal payment. As such, its main use is as a quick screening tool.

The *exit yield* is another metric utilized by sovereign bond investors. It indicates the market-implied yield on newly restructured sovereign bonds and is derived from the market pricing of the new exchanged instruments. This metric signifies the expected returns post-default and plays a central role in default negotiations and in calculating the NPV haircuts that creditors are experiencing. We return to the exit yield in Chapters 17 and 18.

8.2.4 Spread Measures

The difference in yields between two metrics is the *yield spread,* or simply the *spread.* Spread measures enable fixed-income investors to evaluate sovereign bond yields in relation to benchmarks and risk-free options.

The *G-spread* is the difference between a bond's YTM and that of a comparable US Treasury bond. Sovereign bonds issued by countries outside the United States typically have higher yields than those of similar US Treasuries. This yield difference, or G-spread, serves as compensation to the bondholder for the extra risk associated with holding these bonds compared to Treasuries. Such risks may arise from differences in credit quality, liquidity, volatility, and the legal framework when investing in non-US Treasuries.

The *Z-spread* is another yield differential metric. Based on the term structure of interest rates, it represents the spread added to the zero-coupon US Treasury yield curve that equates a bond's cash flow to its market price. This metric is more precise than the G-spread, especially for bonds with irregular coupon and principal payments. It is primarily used for fair value analysis and peer comparisons.

For bonds with embedded options, investors use the *option-adjusted spread*, which adjusts the Z-spread for the options (call or put) in the bond structure.

8.3 ASSESSING A BOND'S RELATIVE VALUE

The price of a bond can change over time due to various factors. Changes in market interest rates can increase or decrease bond yields, which in turn affects their fair price. For instance, if US Treasury yields rise and US bond prices fall, foreign sovereign bond yields are also expected to increase, leading to a decrease in their prices.

Changes in the factors influencing the bond spread, such as credit risk, liquidity premia, or volatility, can also impact the price of a sovereign bond. If credit ratings decline in a particular country, investors will demand higher compensation for holding the sovereign debt, leading to an increase in the credit spread and consequently, sovereign bond yields.

Similarly, if there are regional risks and higher volatility, the spread differential for a sovereign compared to US Treasuries may increase, which could once again result in higher sovereign yields. Additionally, market technicals that affect liquidity and the supply and demand for a given country's bonds may also influence the yield differential, leading to changes in bond prices.

Portfolio managers and traders employ various techniques to evaluate changes in bond prices, yields, and spreads. In particular, to assess whether a bond is *undervalued* or *overvalued* in relation to its fundamentals and the market pricing of comparable sovereign risk. This evaluation of the *relative value* of a sovereign bond combines both art and science, incorporating market-based metrics and fundamental credit analysis.

Market-based metrics include *historical spread analysis, yield curve analysis*, and *peer-spread* comparisons. The average historical spread can be a straightforward indicator if credit fundamentals remain unchanged and there are valid reasons to expect mean reversion. Deviations from the average spread, such as ± 1 standard deviation from a rolling one-year spread, can indicate richness or cheapness. In practice, this simple measure is effective for short-term changes in bond spreads.

Intra-issuer yield curve analysis helps identify when specific bonds are trading rich or cheap compared to other instruments. These dislocations can occur due to liquidity, secondary market trades, tenders and buyback operations, or new issues. Traders can evaluate the value of any switches while taking market technicals and transaction costs into account.

Peer-spread comparisons can include other similarly rated sovereign issuers, countries with comparable characteristics, or those from the same region. For example, Nigerian bonds could be compared with Angolan bonds since both are commodity exporters with a similar single B rating and are located in Africa.

Peer-spread comparisons can also be made with quasi-sovereigns or corporate issuer spreads, which typically trade in line with those of sovereign issuers. This may include systemically important SOEs or similarly rated corporates. Note that peer-spread comparisons don't fully adjust for fundamentals and rely on mean reversion or historical market relationships to indicate mispricing.

Fundamental-based models of relative value utilize credit and macroeconomic variables to establish a fair value credit spread for a sovereign's bonds. A straightforward model may employ public debt ratios, fiscal balances, GDP growth, and FX reserves as independent variables to forecast fair value spreads using a cross-country panel of time series data.

For a given country's fundamentals, the model is used to estimate a fair spread. This fair spread is then compared with the market spread, and an assessment is made on rich/cheapness. For example, if the fair spread for Pakistan based on the model is +700 bps for a five-year USD bond, but the market is pricing it at +800 bps, the bond would be considered cheap compared with its fundamentals.

Another approach involves using the market-implied credit ratings discussed in Chapter 5. These market ratings can be compared with the credit ratings from the sovereign credit analysis, and a decision can be made about whether the market pricing is incorrect and likely to converge with that of the credit rating, or the other way around.

These approaches, along with perspectives on market risk sentiment and technical factors, help portfolio managers and traders evaluate bond market prices and identify potential opportunities to leverage for the portfolio.

8.4 PORTFOLIO RISK METRICS

At the portfolio level, sovereign bond investors must monitor a range of risk and performance metrics. These metrics enable investors to quantify and manage exposures to interest rates, credit risk, and broader market volatility. This section provides an overview of the key tools used to measure and evaluate risk in a sovereign bond portfolio.

Duration and modified duration capture interest rate sensitivity. Convexity measures second-order price sensitivity and becomes important during sharp yield movements. Spread duration provides exposure to credit spread movements, while carry and roll-down are key sources of income even in the absence of price changes. Volatility, calculated as the annualized standard deviation of returns, informs position sizing, stress testing, and overall risk budgeting. All these metrics are calculated at the bond level and aggregated to the portfolio level.

8.4.1 Duration and Dollar Duration

Duration is a fundamental concept in fixed-income analysis, measuring the sensitivity of bond prices to changes in interest rates. This metric helps portfolio managers estimate how a bond's value will change with movements in benchmark rates like US Treasuries.

Mathematically, duration is the weighted average of the present value of the cash flows from a debt instrument, with the weights representing the time period during which each cash flow is received. It can be approximated by the following formula:

$$Duration = \frac{P_L - P_H}{2\,(P_0)(\Delta y)}$$

where:

y = yield of bond
P_L = price of bond at slightly lower yield
P_H = price of bond at slightly higher yield
P_0 = initial price
Δy = change in yield

A duration of seven years means that a 100-basis point change in interest rates will change the bond price by 7%. Therefore, for a 7% coupon 10-year bond with a duration of 7 years, a 100-basis point increase in interest rates will reduce the bond price from 100 to 93, while a 100-basis point decrease in interest rates will raise the bond price to 107.

In practice, there are several measures of duration. *Macaulay duration* is the weighted average time to receive all the instrument's cash flows. *Modified duration* converts Macaulay duration into an estimate of the sensitivity of the bond's price to a 1% change in interest rates and is applicable to simple (or plain vanilla) bonds without options.

Effective duration computes duration for bonds with embedded options. *Key rate duration* evaluates the sensitivity of a portfolio or group of bonds to changes at a specific point on the yield curve. The portfolio manager selects the metric to consider based on the characteristics of the instrument or portfolio and the risks they aim to evaluate.

The coupon rate and the bond's face value affect duration. Bonds with low coupons have a longer duration compared to those with high coupons, while zero-coupon bonds have the highest duration, which equals the maturity of the instrument. Table 8.2

TABLE 8.2 Global Sovereign USD Bonds

Government	Bond	Coupon (%)	Yield (%)	Price	Duration (yrs)	Spread (bps)
United States	2/15/2035	4.625	4.5	101.1	7.9	–
Mexico	9/27/2034	6.750	6.2	104.1	6.9	171
Brazil	3/15/2035	6.625	6.7	99.3	7.3	226
Indonesia	10/12/2035	8.500	5.5	124.3	7.2	99
South Africa	11/19/2036	7.100	7.4	97.6	7.7	296
Egypt	9/30/2033	7.300	9.9	85.3	5.8	541
Nigeria	12/9/2034	10.375	9.6	104.9	6.0	514
Sri Lanka	5/15/2036	3.600	7.5	82.0	8.5	300

Source: Bloomberg Finance L.P.

indicates that a 4.625% coupon 2035 US Treasury bond has a duration of 7.9 years. In comparison, a 6.625% coupon 2035 Brazilian dollar bond has a duration of 7.3 years, and a 10.375% coupon 2034 Nigerian dollar bond has a duration of 6.0 years.

A bond's DV01 (or dollar value of a basis point) is a dollar measure of how much a bond's price changes for each 1 basis point change in interest rates. It is also referred to as the price value of a basis point or money duration. A higher DV01 indicates that the bond's price is more sensitive to interest rate changes, while a lower DV01 suggests the bond is less sensitive.

At the portfolio level, duration reflects how sensitive the portfolio's market value is to changes in interest rates. It is calculated as the market weighted average of the durations of its individual holdings instruments.[3] For example, the value of a $100 million portfolio with a duration of seven years will change by 7% if interest rates change by 100 basis points.

Translating this into a monetary value gives the *dollar duration*, which represents the change in the portfolio's value corresponding to a change in interest rates. In the previous example, the dollar duration is $7 million (7% × $100 million) for a 100 basis point change in interest rates. The relationship is assumed to be linear; therefore, if interest rates change by 50 basis points, the portfolio's value would adjust by 3.5% (7 years × [50/100 basis points]), equivalent to $3.5 million (3.5% × $100 million).

Dollar duration is a nominal measure of the interest rate sensitivity of a portfolio's value. Portfolio managers use it to assess the value at risk in the portfolio if interest rates change. It is also utilized to calculate the amount to trade when adjusting positions within a portfolio. This can involve meeting specific duration targets or maintaining a constant duration while changing the account's holdings.

Example: Changing the Duration of a Portfolio

A portfolio manager believes interest rates will rise more than what the market has priced in and wants to decrease a $100 million portfolio's duration from seven to six years. To achieve this, they would need to sell $1 million duration dollars [(7% – 6%) × $100 million] of the portfolio. The market value of any bond designated for sale would be equal to:

$$\textit{Amount to Sell} = \frac{\Delta \textit{Dollar Duration of Portfolio}}{\textit{Duration of the Bond Sold}/100}$$

If the portfolio manager chooses to sell a bond with a duration of seven years, they would sell:

$$\textit{Amount to Sell} = \frac{1\text{ million}}{7/100} = \$14.29\text{ million}$$

Example: Exchanging Bonds While Holding the Portfolio Duration Constant

For an issuer, Bond A is trading at a premium compared to Bond B while all other factors remain constant. To capitalize on the relative valuation change, the portfolio manager intends to sell Bond A and buy Bond B while maintaining the overall portfolio's duration constant.

Bond A has a price of 100 and a duration of 5, which means that a 100 basis point change in interest rates will adjust its price by $5 (5% × 100). Bond B has a price of 100 and a duration of 4, which means that a 100 basis point change in interest rates will adjust its price by $4 (4% × 100).

If the portfolio manager sells $10 million in market value of Bond A, the portfolio's dollar duration would decline by $500,000 (5% × $10 million). To maintain the same interest rate exposure in the portfolio, the manager would need to purchase $500,000 duration dollars of Bond B. This would require a market value of $12.5 million for Bond B ($500,000 / 4%).

Mathematically the amount to purchase would be:

$$\textit{Market Value of Bond B} = \frac{\textit{Dollar Duration of Bond A}}{\textit{Duration of Bond B}/100}$$

$$\textit{Par Value of Bond B} = \frac{\textit{Market Value of Bond B}}{\textit{Price of Bond B per } \$1 \textit{ of Par Value}}$$

Keep in mind that duration as a factor influencing bond prices becomes less significant for high-risk sovereign credits. For these issuers, bond prices are more affected by variables that drive credit risk and potential recovery.

8.4.2 Convexity

When large changes occur in interest rates, the relationship between interest rates and prices may not be linear, as duration measures assume. This relationship is better captured by *convexity*, which measures the curvature between prices and interest rates.

Mathematically, convexity refers to the second derivative of the impact of a change in interest rates on bond prices and indicates the rate at which duration changes as interest rates fluctuate. For managers of sovereign bond portfolios, convexity provides a more precise calculation of estimated price and value changes during periods of significant and volatile interest rate movements.

Positive convexity implies that the increase in price is greater than the decrease in price for significant changes in interest rates. Negative convexity means the decrease in price exceeds the increase. Most option-free bonds exhibit positive convexity. All else being equal, bonds with positive convexity provide greater upside during periods of falling interest rates and less downside during periods of rising rates, and vice versa.

8.4.3 Spread and Spread Duration

Spread duration measures how sensitive a bond's price is to a change in the credit spread. A spread duration of four years indicates that the bond's price adjusts by 4% when the credit spread changes by 100 basis points. A higher spread duration signifies greater sensitivity of the bond price to changes in the credit spread.

Example: Spread Duration Calculation

Bond A is priced at 100 with a spread duration of four years.

A 100 basis point increase in the credit spread reduces the price by \$4 (4% × 100), bringing it down to 96 (100 − 4).

Conversely, a 100 basis point decrease in the credit spread raises the bond's price to 104 (100 + 4).

Duration-times-spread (DTS) refers to the spread duration multiplied by the level of the credit spread. It accounts for the influence of spread levels on changes in credit spreads, providing a more precise insight into the spread sensitivity of an instrument. Similar to duration, spread duration can be aggregated and reported for the overall portfolio. This provides a measure of the portfolio's sensitivity to changes in the credit spread.

Example: Duration-Times-Spread

Bond A and Bond B both have a spread duration of 4, but Bond A has a spread of +50 bps while Bond B has a spread of +100 bps.

The use of spread duration would suggest that the price sensitivity to credit spread changes is the same for both bonds at 4%.

However, the DTS measure clarifies this to show a 2% change in price for Bond A for a 100 bps change in the credit spread, and a 4% change in price for Bond B for the same 100 bps change in the credit spread.

8.4.4 Carry and Roll-Down

Carry refers to the return generated from holding a bond over time compared to its financing cost. This return can be divided into income from coupon payments and gains or losses due to changes in the bond's price. Positive carry instruments are those where yields exceed the cost of financing, resulting in positive returns from holding the bond. Negative carry instruments are those where yields fall below the cost of financing, leading to losses over time.

Upward-sloping yield curves indicate that financing through short-term instruments occurs at lower yields compared to long-term instruments. This allows bonds to carry positively, with each maturity *rolling down* the yield curve. This roll-down results in price appreciation (lower yields = higher price) and positive returns. Yield curve stability is essential for investors to earn both carry and roll-down; therefore, interest rate changes and volatility pose significant risks to carry strategies.

8.4.5 Volatility

A common metric for measuring total risk in a portfolio is volatility. Mathematically, it represents the annualized standard deviation of a portfolio's returns over a specified period. Greater volatility indicates heightened uncertainty regarding return outcomes. In the case of sovereign bonds, volatility often arises from shifts in yields, spreads, currency fluctuations, or credit events.

Portfolio volatility can be historical (based on past returns) or implied (derived from market prices of options or credit default swaps). Importantly, it is used as an input to inform position sizing, stress testing, and overall risk budgeting. Investors monitor volatility at both the individual bond level and the portfolio level to ensure that risk remains within mandated constraints and is consistent with expected performance behavior.

> ***PRO TIP:*** *Calculate each of the portfolio level metrics in this chapter for your account and compare with the numbers produced by your firm's analytics to understand any differences.*

8.5 PORTFOLIO RISK AND PERFORMANCE METRICS

Risk and performance metrics are essential for evaluating sovereign bond portfolios. Alpha measures manager skill by capturing excess returns over a benchmark, while tracking error measures the deviation of a portfolio's returns in comparison to its benchmark. Meanwhile, risk-adjusted metrics like the Sharpe ratio and information ratio are particularly relevant for assessing active managers.

Portfolio managers are obsessed with these metrics. They examine them daily, often even before having their morning coffee, and continually consider the impact of market events, trades, and potential investments on their portfolio's performance.

8.5.1 Alpha

The simplest measure of performance is a portfolio's total return.[4] This is measured against the returns of a benchmark (if the portfolio has one) and referred to as the portfolio *alpha*. In the context of actively managed sovereign bond portfolios, alpha reflects the return from the portfolio manager's investment decisions such as country selection, curve positioning, or instrument choice.

Alpha is reported over a specified period (daily, weekly, monthly, quarterly, or annually) and is usually annualized and reported in percentage terms or basis points (bps). It can either include or exclude management fees, with *alpha excluding fees* and *alpha inclusive of fees* being common metrics.

8.5.2 Tracking Error

A portfolio's alpha does not account for the volatility of returns, which is an important element of performance. Tracking error (TE) measures the difference in risk between a portfolio's performance and its underlying benchmark. It indicates the deviation in positions taken by the portfolio manager compared to the index and serves as a gauge of how actively managed the portfolio is.

TE is calculated as the standard deviation of the portfolio's return relative to that of the index over a specified period (e.g., weekly, monthly, quarterly, and annually). *Ex post or historical TE* examines the past performance of a portfolio. Its primary use is to evaluate a manager's past performance. Consequently, it provides limited predictive information regarding the effect of current investment decisions on future portfolio performance.

Forward-looking TE utilizes factor models to decompose the drivers of portfolio returns alongside its risk factor positions. Also known as *ex ante TE* or *predicted TE*, the estimates can be produced for a range of risk factor positions and can help identify the impact of position changes on the TE of the portfolio. Forward TE metrics can also be estimated for specific macro and market scenarios, which helps to identify portfolio vulnerabilities. As such, they are an important risk management tool.

TE guidelines are determined by the asset owner and vary based on risk tolerance. A TE of zero represents a passive or benchmark strategy, involving relatively low risk compared to the benchmark. Larger TEs indicate more significant active management, higher risk tolerance, and alpha targets. TEs ranging from 75 to 200 bps are quite common for many actively managed government-benchmarked funds.

8.5.3 Risk-Adjusted Returns

For asset owners and portfolio managers, a primary objective is to generate a given level of alpha while minimizing its associated risks. The same alpha can be generated with different levels of risk as reflected by the volatility of returns and its concentration. For instance, portfolio managers can take a few big risks with high variation in their returns or many smaller risks with lower returns and lower variation. To take into account how alpha is generated, we look at risk-adjusted returns, which incorporates the volatility of returns into the performance calculation.

The *Sharpe ratio* is a measure of risk-adjusted returns for a portfolio over a specified time period. It adjusts the portfolio's returns using the risk-free rate (such as US Treasuries or other industry benchmarks) and divides this by the portfolio's return volatility:

$$Sharpe\,Ratio = \frac{R_p - R_f}{\sigma_p}$$

where:

R_p = portfolio return
R_f = risk-free rate
σ_p = standard deviation of portfolio return

The ratio can be calculated using backward- or forward-looking measures of returns. A higher Sharpe ratio is better, as it indicates higher excess returns, lower volatility of returns, or a combination of both. Sharpe ratios above 1 are considered to provide reasonable excess returns relative to volatility.

Another risk-adjusted return measure is the *information ratio*, which considers the portfolio's historical tracking error as follows:

$$Information\ Ratio = \frac{R_p - R_b}{TE} = \frac{Alpha}{TE}$$

where:

R_p = portfolio return
R_b = benchmark return
TE = historical backward looking tracking error
$Alpha$ = portfolio return − benchmark return

Intuitively, the information ratio indicates whether the portfolio manager is generating adequate excess returns for the risk taken. A higher information ratio is considered better, as it reflects consistent alpha generation and performance stability. Generally, an information ratio of 0.4–0.6 is regarded as good, 0.7 or higher as very good, and 1.0 or above as exceptional.

Both the Sharpe ratio and information ratios are useful metrics. Sharpe ratios may be more useful for asset allocation decisions compared to investing in risk-free instruments. Meanwhile, the information ratio may be more useful for evaluating active fund managers against their given benchmark.

8.6 OTHER PORTFOLIO METRICS

Several other portfolio metrics are useful to review. These include the portfolio beta, the contribution of a bond to portfolio metrics, and a portfolio's net asset value. We discuss each of these below.

8.6.1 Portfolio Beta

A portfolio's beta is an analytical metric that provides information about how risk behaves in the portfolio relative to the benchmark. A beta of 1.01 indicates that if the index value rises by 10%, the value of the portfolio holdings will, on average, increase by 10.1%.

Portfolio betas can be calculated for most risk factors, including the portfolio duration-beta and spread-beta, as follows:

$$Duration\ beta = \frac{Portfolio\ duration}{Index\ duration}$$

$$Spread\ beta = \frac{Portfolio\ spread}{Index\ spread}$$

A duration-beta of 1.05 indicates that if the duration of the index increases by 10%, the portfolio's duration will, on average, increase by 10.5%. A spread-beta of 1.07 indicates that if the index spread rises by 10%, the portfolio spread will increase by 10.7%.

8.6.2 Contribution of a Bond to Portfolio Metrics

Bond risk metrics can be measured as a function of their contribution to a portfolio's overall risk. This enables portfolio managers to appropriately scale portfolio positions while considering the impact on overall risk parameters due to the inclusion, exclusion, and weight of a particular bond.

A bond's *contribution to a portfolio's interest rate duration* is calculated by multiplying its market value weight by its duration. If the bond has a market value weight of 10% in the portfolio and a duration of 7 years, its contribution to the portfolio duration is 0.1×7, which equals 0.7 years.

The bond's *contribution to the portfolio's spread duration* is calculated similarly by multiplying its market value weight by its spread duration. If the bond has a market value weight of 10% in the portfolio and a spread duration of 6 years, the contribution to portfolio duration is 0.1×6, which equals 0.6 years.

The *contribution to alpha and tracking error* from an active position can also be calculated as shown in the example below.

Example: Contribution to Alpha and Tracking Error

Let's take a Colombia USD bond position in a $1 billion Emerging Markets sovereign bond portfolio. The anticipated overweight of Colombia is a 2% market value compared to the index, expected annual total returns for Colombia are 8% versus 6% for the index, and the return volatility for Colombia is 8% in contrast to 7% for the index.

The contribution to alpha from this position is calculated as follows:

Contribution to alpha = Colombia overweight × (Colombia sovereign total returns − Index returns)

Contribution to alpha = 2% × (8% − 6%) = 4 bps of alpha

The contribution to TE from this position is calculated as follows:

Contribution to TE = Colombia overweight × (Colombia return volatility − Index return volatility)

Contribution to TE = 2% × (8% − 7%)= 3 bps of TE

Together, these risk contribution metrics are used to place trade orders and evaluate whether the portfolio has sufficient or excessive risk from a given issuer or portfolio position.

8.6.3 A Portfolio Net Asset Value

A portfolio's net asset value (NAV) represents the value of the portfolio's holdings at a specific point in time. The market price for each instrument at the close of business is the standard metric used, with the NAV typically calculated daily. Mutual funds, closed-end funds, and exchange-traded funds (ETFs) must report NAVs daily, while separate accounts may report NAVs at specified intervals, such as weekly, monthly, or quarterly.

As inputs to a portfolio's NAV, bond valuations for portfolio holdings are continually reviewed and checked for outdated market quotes. This is particularly relevant for infrequently traded instruments where market quotes may not be regularly observed. In these cases, fair value estimates can be calculated using third-party or in-house pricing models.

8.7 SUMMARY

This chapter reviewed the main risks associated with sovereign instruments, the valuation of bonds, and the assessment of relative value. It covered fundamental portfolio risk metrics such as duration, convexity, and spread duration, as well as various methods for calculating portfolio performance.

The next topic we address is how to trade sovereign bonds in the primary and secondary markets, along with the guidelines investors should follow when developing trading strategies.

NOTES

1. For further information, see CFA Institute, *CFA Program Curriculum*; During, *Fixed Income Trading and Risk Management*; Fabozzi, *Fixed Income Analysis*; Fabozzi, *The Handbook of Fixed Income Securities*; Fabozzi, *Introduction to Fixed-Income Analysis*; Volpert, "Introduction to Bond Portfolio Management."
2. For bonds with embedded options, the relationship between prices and yields is more complex.
3. The duration of a group of bonds by sector, region, or rating can similarly be calculated by aggregating across instruments by group.
4. The Global Investment Performance Standards (GIPS) standardize how to calculate and present portfolio returns following the CFA Institute's industry-wide principles of reporting performance.

REFERENCES

CFA Institute. *CFA Program Curriculum Level I, II & III*. 2024. CFA Institute and Wiley.

During, Alex. *Fixed Income Trading and Risk Management: The Complete Guide*. Hoboken, NJ: Wiley, 2021.

Fabozzi, Frank J., ed. *Fixed Income Analysis*. 2nd ed. Hoboken, NJ: John Wiley & Sons, 2007.

Fabozzi, Frank J., ed. *The Handbook of Fixed Income Securities*. 9th ed. New York: McGraw-Hill, 2021.

Fabozzi, Frank J., ed. *Introduction to Fixed-Income Analysis and Portfolio Management*. Cambridge, MA: The MIT Press, 2024.

Volpert, Kenneth E. "Introduction to Bond Portfolio Management." In *Introduction to Fixed-Income Analysis and Portfolio Management*, edited by Frank J. Fabozzi, Chapter 43. Cambridge, MA: The MIT Press, 2024.

CHAPTER NINE

Trading Sovereign Bonds

PORTFOLIO MANAGERS get exposure to sovereign debt through various channels. The primary market is where governments raise funds directly from investors through new bond issuance. This process includes auctions, syndications, and private placements, with variations in issuance methods based on market development, debt management objectives, and the investor base. Primary issuance establishes the initial pricing and allocation of sovereign debt, offering investors opportunities to participate in scale and under preferential terms.

Once issued, sovereign bonds are traded in the secondary market. These serve as a vital platform for liquidity and price discovery. Investors who purchase bonds in the primary market sell them in the secondary market. More broadly, portfolio managers trade in secondary markets to adjust their portfolio positions, take profits, or minimize losses.

Secondary markets vary widely in size, volume, and efficiency across countries. They are shaped by the presence of market makers, settlement systems, investor composition, and legal and regulatory frameworks.

This chapter examines the mechanics of how investors gain access to sovereign debt instruments. It reviews the auction and new issue processes from the investor's perspective. It outlines the operation of secondary markets and discusses guidelines for trading and execution. It concludes with a discussion on liquidity and market technical factors.

9.1 PRIMARY MARKETS

Debt issuance in the primary market occurs through auctions, syndications, or private placements, where governments sell Treasury bills or bonds in exchange for funds.[1] We review each of these in turn.

9.1.1 The Auction and Syndication Process

Auctions are commonly used for issuing national currency securities due to their cost-effectiveness and transparency.[2] They can be Dutch style (single-price), where all winning bidders pay the lowest accepted bid price regardless of their original bid price, or multiple price (conventional), where each winning bidder purchases the security at their bidding price. Most auctions are conducted electronically and take place in four steps: announcement by the issuing entity, auction, bidding by investors, and issuance of securities.

Auctions can be combined with the syndication of benchmark bonds or tap sales. Syndication involves appointing a group of banks, known as bookrunners, to market and distribute a bond jointly. This is typically done to build outstanding volume and provide greater certainty of issuance quickly or to prevent collusion among bidding institutions.

The choice of instrument may determine whether issuance occurs through an auction or syndication. For example, Chile typically uses auctions for local currency issuance and syndication for hard currency issuance. It has also utilized syndication for domestic currency issuance of its social CLP-denominated bonds.

The syndication process typically includes the following steps:

- *Groundwork for a bond issue* includes obtaining the necessary authorizations from government departments or the national legislature.
- *Appointment of underwriters,* also referred to as "bookrunners." Underwriters are responsible for structuring the bond issue, establishing the terms, and ensuring regulatory compliance.
- *Credit rating*: Bonds receive ratings from credit rating agencies, offering investors an independent assessment of the issuer's creditworthiness and the bond's risk level.
- *Roadshow and marketing*: This involves presentations to institutional investors, asset managers, and retail investors to respond to questions and gauge interest in the deal.
- *Official announcement and price guidance*: The issuer announces the bond offering, which includes the total amount, maturity, coupon rate, and price guidance for each tenor.
- *Book building*: This is the process through which the underwriters receive feedback and indicative orders of interest from investors.
- *Deal launch and closing of books*: Official launch of the deal with final guidance on maturity, structure, coupon, and price. Investors confirm their final orders during the subscription period before the books close.
- *Allocation of orders*: The issuer and underwriters reach an agreement on the final allocation of bonds to investors. Based on demand, investors may receive all, some, or none of the bonds they subscribed to.
- *Issuance and settlement*: After the subscription process is finished, bonds are issued, investors are notified of their allocation, and their accounts are credited.
- *Management of the market after syndication*: Secondary market trading begins, and the bookrunners publish statistics on the deal's allocation, including regional distribution and types of investors (for example, institutional investors or *real money* versus hedge funds or *fast money*).

PRO TIP: *Plan ahead for auctions and new issues with a country-wide database of estimated issuance size and timing.*

9.1.2 The New Issue Process

The new issue process begins well before the official deal announcement. Sovereign analysts estimate the annual sovereign bond issuance for each country to gauge the expected supply coming to market. This information is compiled from budget deficit forecasts, historical issuance patterns, bonds maturing, and government announcements. The sell-side often publishes tables with this information.

Public information on upcoming issues and their potential size is available when issuers *file a shelf* registration statement. This regulatory provision allows issuers to register a new issue of securities with the relevant regulatory authority (such as the US Securities and Exchange Commission) without having to sell the entire issue at once. Seasonality in sovereign issuance means that the first and second quarters are the busiest, followed by the period between the end of summer and before Thanksgiving in the United States.

The roadshow presents an opportunity for investors to ask questions, learn about the credit and bond structure, and understand the use of proceeds from the issuance. Investors can express their preferences for tenor, currency, size of issuance, and potential structures. Credit analysts update their assessments immediately after the roadshow, as there is often a limited timeframe of a few days to a week before the deal launch.

At the price discovery and book building stage, investors assess the terms of the deal and evaluate whether it is attractive relative to its risk profile and similarly rated comparators. They discuss the deal with the bookrunners and share their views on size and pricing based on current market conditions and expected demand. This is an iterative process in which bookrunners gauge the market's overall interest and demand for specific tenors or price ranges. At this stage, it is unlikely that major features of the deal will change, such as the currency of issuance or the maturity bucket; instead, the focus is on the size and the price.

Once final price guidance is released, bond managers can confirm or adjust their orders. Large changes are not expected unless there is a significant change in the price guidance, issuance size, or market conditions. The issuer decides final allocations with the syndicate team, and depending on the demand (measured by the book-to-cover ratio), an investor may receive all or a portion of their order.

Bonds are typically issued with a concession to the existing curve and are expected to rally or increase in price after issuance. They are actively traded before, during, and after issuance, which is when secondary markets—a critical component of government bond markets—come into play. Following primary issuance, before bonds become *free to trade*, dealers quote *grays*, which indicate where they expect bonds to open in the secondary market once they become free to trade.

During the deal itself, existing bonds from the same issuer or those of peers may trade as portfolio managers create space for the new issue and raise cash or adjust risk positions.

After issuance, there may be buying from investors who are under-allocated to the deal or selling from investors looking to flip or profit from a price increase.

In rare instances, new deals may be pulled during or after the new deal process. This might occur due to unforeseen market conditions, new information about the issuer, or insufficient investor demand. Additionally, there may be situations where secondary market trading after issuance is poor due to aggressive final pricing or allocations in *weak hands*, accounts that look to flip the bonds immediately. This scenario does not bode well for future issuances and is something all parties involved in the transaction aim to avoid.

9.1.3 Private Placements

While most sovereign bonds are issued in public markets through auctions or syndicated offerings, some governments also raise funds through private placements. These are negotiated bond sales made directly to a small group of institutional investors and banks, typically without public disclosure or listing.

Frontier markets, low-income countries, and those in crisis may issue securities through private placements. The benefits include transaction speed, lower disclosure requirements, and confidentiality. For investors, private placements provide access to tailored sovereign risks, often with bespoke structuring, potentially higher yields, and enhanced covenants.

The issuance process resembles the new issue process, with the additional requirement of non-disclosure agreements and greater scope for interaction with the issuer. A private deal is generally viewed as a buy-to-hold investment, as once it is made, liquidity tends to be relatively low compared to publicly issued securities.

An example is Ghana's (2015) $1 billion Eurobond, which was issued via private placement with a $400 million World Bank guarantee. The deal was launched to reduce yields and foster investor confidence during a period of fiscal stress for the credit. The International Finance Corporation (IFC) and African Development Bank (AfDB) have also structured local currency private placements in Nigeria, Zambia, and Uganda to deepen domestic capital markets.

9.2 SECONDARY MARKETS

Secondary markets convert government securities issued in primary markets into tradable instruments, allowing them to be exchanged by buyers and sellers. They facilitate price discovery that reflects the balance of supply and demand, while also enhancing the liquidity and marketability of traded securities.

Primary and secondary markets are closely connected, with increased liquidity in secondary markets enhancing participation (and prices) in primary markets as securities become easier to trade. Meanwhile, transparent and consistent issuance in primary markets leads to better functioning of secondary markets through the establishment of a yield curve. This serves as a benchmark for new debt securities and anchors investors' and issuers' expectations.

Monitoring secondary markets is critical for successful transactions in primary markets, as new information is typically reflected in secondary market prices. For example, a large bond issuance might cause prices for the entire curve in the secondary market to fall, as the market requires a concession to absorb the additional supply. Suppose a bond is priced very cheaply (at a low price) in the primary market, and there is significant interest. In that case, it may rally in the secondary market, reflecting the actual demand for the instrument. Issuers, therefore, have a vested interest in how their bonds trade in the secondary market, given the symbiotic relationship between the primary and secondary markets.

9.3 TRADING SOVEREIGN BONDS

Efficient trade execution is a crucial aspect of managing fixed-income portfolios. Portfolio returns are calculated after trading costs, which can easily add up, and strategic trade execution can significantly reduce these costs.[3] Furthermore, portfolio managers can minimize transaction costs and obtain the best available price for a specific trade size, in contrast to the broader systemic risks that influence the portfolio returns.

Trading provides essential skills for understanding market dynamics, correctly pricing securities, and building networks within the industry. Many portfolio managers begin their careers as junior traders executing trades in the market, and then go on to manage their own accounts. A good starting point is to understand market regulations and trading platforms. Next is to review the life cycle of a trade, pricing conventions, liquidity, and market technicals, followed by a discussion of broad execution guidelines.

9.4 MARKET REGULATION

A solid starting point for a trader is understanding the rules of the game in the market where they are transacting. These include market regulations, trade requirements, and transaction protocols.

For example, in the United States, the Financial Industry Regulatory Authority (FINRA) establishes the mandatory reporting and compliance requirements for over-the-counter trades. Its Trade Reporting and Compliance Engine (TRACE) encompasses all transactions by member broker-dealers in TRACE-eligible securities. This information is summarized and disseminated at the end of each day, providing data on trade volumes and the most actively traded securities in each market segment. Similar regulatory requirements exist for all sovereign debt markets around the globe.

9.5 TRADING INFRASTRUCTURE

Bonds are traded over-the-counter, on electronic trading platforms, on exchanges, through auction systems, and directly party-to-party.[4]

9.5.1 Over-the-Counter Trading

Sovereign debt instruments have historically traded over-the-counter (OTC) between large broker-dealers acting on their clients' or their own behalf. The OTC market is decentralized with no physical location. Prices are undisclosed to the wider market beyond the two parties involved in the transaction, and there is no obligation to quote the same prices to all customers. Inter-firm relationships and counterparty risk are elements of trading in OTC contracts, with asset managers having a predefined list of cleared counterparties they can trade with.

A key reason why bonds trade OTC is the available customization. This allows for the diversity in the structure and characteristics of bonds, which may have different maturities, coupons, amortization profiles, currencies, and legal details. These factors, along with their less frequent issuance, make listing the current prices of fixed-income instruments much harder than for stocks.

Institutional investors sometimes negotiate transactions directly with one another without intermediaries. This approach may be used for in-kind transfers or the sale of substantial positions in portfolios. This mechanism may become more popular with advancements in DeFi platforms and technological infrastructure across financial institutions.

9.5.2 Electronic Trading

In recent years, electronic trading platforms have expanded as broker-dealer intermediation has declined and advances in computer technology have facilitated the growth of electronic market infrastructure.

Single-dealer platforms allow buy-side traders to transact with a specific dealer, effectively replacing a phone call with an electronic platform. Multiple-dealer platforms include Bloomberg's Electronic Trading (ET) platform, Tradeweb, and MarketAxess. These platforms connect buyers and sellers, display the best bids and offers across dealers, and provide various tools for trade execution and data analysis.

Electronic platforms provide a more structured and transparent environment compared to traditional OTC trading, thanks to real-time price quotes and trade information. They also improve liquidity by aggregating buyers and sellers across global markets. Operational errors, such as trading incorrect sizes or with unapproved brokers, are also minimized.

With the rise of electronic trading platforms, the distinction between OTC and exchange trading is becoming increasingly blurred. For instance, some electronic trading platforms enable dealers and certain non-dealers to execute trades directly through an electronic system, but only for authorized participants. Furthermore, the settlement of trades is left to the buying and selling parties. This contrasts with exchange trading, which is open to the public and where the exchange guarantees trade settlements.

9.5.3 Exchange Trading

Exchange trading (or all-to-all) platforms offer a centralized venue for bond trading, with standardized procedures and regulations. All market participants, including dealers, investors, and ETF traders, can transact with one another. Members can disclose their identity or choose to remain anonymous, which may provide advantages for some institutional investors.

Trading platforms can operate as request for quote (RFQ) or as order-driven models. An RFQ allows traders to receive price quotes and the associated volumes from multiple dealers, enabling them to accept or reject the trade offer. In an order-driven model, a trader submits an order subject to limits on price or spread, which is then matched to the quotes posted by counterparties. The trade is executed when both sides overlap.

There can be multiple counterparties, allowing large trade blocks to be broken up and cross-matching trades to execute automatically in real time. The increasing use of these platforms provides market participants with greater information on trade flow, with daily statistics available at the close of business. They also offer anonymity and help minimize trading costs.

The choice of trading platform and style ultimately depends on the specifics of the instrument, the size of the trade, market conditions, timing, and whether anonymity is preferred. Historically, relatively few sovereign bonds were traded on exchanges, exceptions being US Treasuries, which are listed on the New York Stock Exchange (NYSE) Bonds platform. However, this is changing with recent developments in electronic trading.

9.5.4 Auction Systems

Some countries utilize auction systems for the secondary trading of government bonds, especially for repurchase agreements (repos) and other short-term transactions. These systems allow participants to bid on bonds, often as part of liquidity management operations by central banks or other government entities. Although they are not a primary method for investor trading, auction systems contribute to the overall liquidity and pricing of government bonds in the secondary market.

9.6 LIFE CYCLE OF A TRADE

There are several stages involved in buying or selling an instrument, categorized into front office and back office procedures. The front office is responsible for market-facing activities and includes portfolio managers, traders, and strategists. The back office supports the trade life cycle after execution, handling settlement, recordkeeping, regulatory compliance, operational integrity, and reporting.

The front office initiates and executes the trade order. This order reflects the notional size, issuer, instrument, and targeted price range for the trade. The portfolio manager in charge provides the order, which may result from portfolio flows, rebalancing, or a change in strategy. Before the order is placed, it is checked for compliance with account guidelines and mandates.

Next is trade execution, which involves determining market liquidity for the trade size, assessing market technicals, price discovery, and agreeing on the sale with a counterparty.

The third stage is trade clearance, where the back office matches the agreed-upon details of the transaction, including the instrument, price, and size.

The fourth stage is settlement, during which the traded securities and funds are transferred between the seller and the buyer. The period between the trade execution date (T) and settlement is labeled as T + X, where X represents the number of business days between the trade date and settlement. For US Treasuries, the settlement is T + 1, while for other sovereign debt, it can be T + 2 or longer.

In some instances, trades may be executed correctly but fail to settle. This may be due to operational issues such as mismatched trade details (for example, the wrong ISIN, amount, or date) or delays in booking or transmitting settlement instruments; custody or account issues such as a lack of proper account setup with the central securities depository (CSD); insufficient securities or cash; and counterparty or legal issues such as settlement restrictions, missing documentation (especially in EM sovereigns), or trading sanctions. To stay abreast of these, traders should stay informed about issues related to trade clearance and settlement, particularly if there are repeated failed trades with the same broker or on the same security.

9.7 PRICING CONVENTIONS

Once a trader gets a trade order, they embark on a process of price discovery. This involves assessing market conditions, liquidity, and technicals to determine where the instruments should be trading.

Pricing conventions for government bonds vary based on the market, type of bond, and regional or national practices. Developed market government bonds tend to have more standardized pricing conventions due to the maturity and sophistication of the markets. Emerging markets exhibit greater variance: hard currency bonds generally follow the pricing conventions of the United States or Europe. In contrast, local currency bonds may adhere to different conventions based on local market prices.[5]

Typically, bonds are quoted either as a percentage of their par value, also known as face value, or in dollar terms. For instance, if a bond is quoted at 98, this means it is 98% of the bond's par value. Therefore, if the bond's par value is $1,000, the bond's price is $980. In some countries, bonds are quoted in yield terms (for example, the yield-to-maturity [YTM]—the internal rate of return if the bond is held to maturity, including all coupon payments and the redemption value).

The use of the *clean* versus *dirty* price varies by region and issuer. The clean price is the bond's price excluding any accrued interest, while the dirty price (or invoice price) includes accrued interest.[6] In the US, the pricing convention on Bloomberg and Reuters terminals is to quote the clean price, while in Europe, the convention is to quote the dirty price. When bonds are close to default (or have defaulted) and there is uncertainty regarding whether the next coupon payment will be made, bonds trade *flat*.

9.8 LIQUIDITY

Liquidity refers to the ease with which transactions can occur without causing a significant change in the price of a security. Government bonds are among the most liquid fixed-income securities in the financial market, with the US Treasury market regarded as the deepest sovereign bond market globally.

Common measures of liquidity include the *bid-ask spread*, which is the difference between the highest price a buyer is willing to pay and the lowest price a seller will accept (a narrower spread indicates higher liquidity). Also used is the *quoted size or clip*, which is the number of bonds dealers will buy or sell at the quoted bid-ask price (larger sizes imply higher liquidity). The traded volume is another metric, which is the total number of bonds transacted over a specific period (higher volumes signify greater liquidity).

Other metrics used include *market depth* (the size of orders at various price levels), *turnover ratio* (the total traded volume divided by the average market capitalization of bonds over a specified period), *price impact* (the way prices adjust in response to trades of a specific size), *time to execution* (the average duration for an order to be executed in the market), the *resiliency* (the speed at which prices return to their initial levels after a temporary shock), the *number of buyers and sellers*, and the *diversity* in characteristics and trading profiles of market participants.

In practice, liquidity is a dynamic variable that changes with market and issuer-specific conditions, as well as broader market technicals. Information on liquidity is regularly published by central banks, regulators, and exchanges. Some common indicators include the Barclays Liquidity Cost Score (LCS), Markit's Liquidity Score, and Intercontinental Exchange's Liquidity Indicators. Traders can monitor these liquidity metrics for specific bonds and issuers using dealer quotes that detail the bid-ask and size by bond on a daily and intraday basis.

In sovereign debt markets, if a bond is less liquid, traders are more likely to demand additional yield relative to what is justified by the country's macroeconomic fundamentals. A market or instrument is considered liquid if large-scale trading can occur without significantly impacting prices or volumes. Various factors can influence a bond's liquidity. These include the issuer's characteristics (frequent versus infrequent issuers, investment grade versus high yield credit) and the specific issue, such as notional size, outstanding float, whether it is a benchmarked bond (included in a bond index), and the time elapsed since issuance (with newer bonds generally having more liquidity).

The size and timing of the trade order can also impact liquidity, which tends to be lower for odd lots and trades conducted outside of market hours. More broadly, market liquidity often decreases ahead of holidays or month-end when dealers are looking to reduce risk, while trading around significant risk events can vary.

PRO TIP: *Monitor liquidity regularly including across asset classes as developments in one sector may quickly spill onto others.*

9.9 MARKET TECHNICALS

Bond markets can also be affected by *technicals*—factors influencing prices and traded volumes that are unrelated to the macroeconomic fundamentals of the issuer. Month-end technicals pertain to monthly index rebalancing and benchmark changes (inclusions and exclusions), which can drive prices higher or lower. ETF trade flows can amplify these effects, with prices rising for instruments on the buy list compared to those on the sell list.

Crowded positions and short squeezes characterized by large, similar-sided trades can drive prices and liquidity away from their fundamentals. Market dislocations can also occur when asset owners make significant portfolio shifts, such as transitioning from one asset class to another. Changes in ratings, especially movements between investment grade and high yield ratings, can result in substantial buying and selling demand. These changes may have broader spillover effects, impacting SOE and corporate issuers within the country or across similarly rated sovereigns.

Some market events act as natural liquidity providers. New sovereign issues and bond auctions enable investors to buy bonds at lower transaction costs compared to the secondary market. Often, these volumes are also larger. In addition, bond tenders allow investors to sell or reduce their exposure to specific instruments. Some issuers may also engage in direct buybacks in the secondary market, aiming to acquire blocks of specific instruments at the prevailing market price.

Government new issues, auctions, tenders, and buybacks also create their own technical factors in the market. New issues tend to reprice the entire issuer yield curve higher as the supply of new bonds lowers the prices of all bonds. Buybacks, where an issuer purchases large blocks of a specific instrument, can drive prices higher as they create an underlying bid below which bonds do not trade.

Tenders, in which an issuer makes an offer to all investors to reduce exposure to a specific instrument, may bolster bond prices by withdrawing supply from the market. If tenders occur alongside a swap and new issuance in a different area of the yield curve, the overall effect on the secondary market may be more calibrated.

These market technicals may provide traders with the opportunity to take the opposite side and benefit from price and volume dislocations. Note that in some cases, technicals may dominate fundamentals for extended periods, and even if contrary to fundamentals, they should be taken advantage of if suitable trades exist. Staying informed about market technicals more broadly, therefore, fosters a better understanding of market dynamics, improves trade execution, and may also present opportunities for profitable trades.

> ***PRO TIP:*** *Understand the core drivers of market technicals whether they are due to new supply, demand, ratings changes, or other factors.*

9.10 EXECUTION GUIDELINES

After the trader grasps the market conditions, liquidity, and technical details, they can start executing the trade. Next, we discuss broad guidelines for execution, including the relationship with the sell-side and best practices for transactions.

A sovereign bond trader operates within a financial ecosystem comprising brokers, dealers, sell-side traders, other buy-side traders, and electronic trading platforms. While some sovereign debt markets are liquid and highly transparent, others can be small, illiquid, and feature a limited number of players. These factors, along with the repetitive nature of market interactions, make it essential to understand the incentives, motivations, and risk positions of each player for effective trade execution.

Over time, building relationships with trading counterparties enhances trust, market insight, and information flow. Sell-side traders frequently post *trade axes* that indicate the securities they are motivated to buy or sell and in what sizes. *Trade runs* display the prices of lists of securities and recent trades, often accompanied by a narrative describing what is driving the market.

Pricing and volume information is also provided by electronic trading platforms either in real time or at the end of the day. A useful exercise for traders is to develop a system for understanding the data in axes, runs, and executed trades to form a mental picture of how the sell-side (or *the street*) is positioned, whether it is adding or reducing risk, and where.

At the outset, traders should understand the market conventions associated with the specific security they are trading. For instance, some sovereign bonds are traded based on yield, while others are based on price, and some markets quote levels as bid-offer, while others use offer-bid. Each sovereign local currency bond market has its own trading conventions, trading hours, and market holidays. These features of the sovereign bond market are regularly updated in annual reports like the J.P. Morgan Local Markets Handbook.

Assessing the market impact of a trade is sound practice. If a trade is substantial in size and/or highly illiquid, discussing the trading strategy with senior colleagues can be beneficial. For instance, when instruments are highly illiquid, the trader may seek to work with trusted counterparties, avoid platforms that publish details in real time, or opt for standard contracts rather than non-standard ones. If the trade size is large, the trader may break up the trade and execute it over time with a select group of counterparties.

The market convention is to quote bond prices based on a specific trading volume. For instance, 99.1–99.5 for 10 × 10 translates to a bid price of 99.1, which indicates the price at which the counterparty will buy the bond, and an ask price of 99.5, representing the price at which they will sell the bond, for a notional size of 10 million.

In contrast, a less liquid instrument may be quoted as 98–99 for 5 × 5 and may only have a few dealers willing to transact in the security. The variation in price and volume highlights that price discovery is a crucial aspect of trade execution, with best practices comparing at least three quotes before executing. For illiquid securities, traders should verify regulatory and internal compliance requirements regarding price discovery before execution.

Once the price and volume are agreed upon, the trade is executed according to the rules of the platform being used. The trader should ensure it is recorded immediately and correctly for the back office to process.

PRO TIP: *Review your firm's protocol for trade execution and the regulatory and compliance practices if trade errors occur.*

9.11 SETTLEMENT

The final stage of the trade is settlement. The settlement period for government bonds refers to the timeframe between the trade date (when the bond is bought or sold) and the settlement date (when the transaction is complete and payment is made). It is determined by market conventions and the operational capabilities of the financial market infrastructure in each country. It can vary by bond type, transaction (primary versus secondary), and clearance system.

There has been a trend toward shorter settlement periods to reduce counterparty risk and enhance efficiency, made possible by advancements in financial technology and the operational capabilities of market participants.

The standard settlement period for US Treasury securities is typically T + 1, which means the transaction is settled one business day after the trade date. In the European Union, the settlement period for euro-denominated government bonds varies, but T + 2 is common, indicating that the transaction is settled two business days after the trade date. The settlement period for Japanese Government Bonds (JGBs) is generally T + 2, while for UK gilts, it is typically T + 1. In emerging markets, the settlement period varies, with T + 2 and T + 3 being common. With technological advances, settlement periods are anticipated to decrease, enhancing market efficiency and lowering counterparty risks.

9.12 SUMMARY

This chapter reviewed primary issuance and the new issue process, as well as trading in secondary sovereign bond markets. It covered the main stages of a trade and provided guidelines on market pricing conventions, liquidity metrics, and market technicals. Broad execution guidelines were discussed, followed by an overview of settlement times.

With the basics of trading and how investors access sovereign debt securities under our belt, we move on to the investment goals and strategies that asset owners typically solve for when building their sovereign debt portfolios.

NOTES

1. Governments also issue non-marketable securities, such as savings bonds for households and other retail investors, and securities intended for government entities and pension funds. Kimmel, "Government Bond Markets."
2. Bremmer, Galai, and Sade, "Auctioning Sovereign Bonds."
3. These include broker commissions reflected in the bid-ask spread, custodial fees (charged by institutions that hold the securities in safekeeping), transfer fees (charged for moving the security between owners), and other hidden costs.
4. For further details, see Fabozzi, *Introduction to Fixed-Income Analysis*; Simko, *Strategic Fixed Income Investing*.

5. J.P. Morgan, *EM Local Markets Guide* is a valuable annual publication for the latest details by country.
6. For calculation methodology of accrued interest and day count conventions, see Chapter 4 in Fabozzi (2024).

REFERENCES

Bremmer, Michael, Dan Galai, and Orly Sade. "Auctioning Sovereign Bonds: A Global Cross-Section Investigation of the Price Mechanism." Manuscript, 2007. http://www.bauer.uh.edu (accessed 30 July 2025).

During, Alexander. *Fixed Income Trading and Risk Management: The Complete Guide*. Hoboken, NJ: Wiley, 2021.

Fabozzi, Frank J. *Introduction to Fixed-Income Analysis and Portfolio Management*. Cambridge, MA: The MIT Press, 2024.

J.P. Morgan. *EM Local Markets Guide*. 13th ed. Emerging Markets Research. New York: J.P. Morgan, 2022.

Kimmel, Christoph. "Government Bond Markets: Characteristics and Issues Related to Market Development." Draft paper, Deutsche Bundesbank, 2019.

Simko, Sean. *Strategic Fixed Income Investing: An Insider's Perspective on Bond Markets, Analysis, and Portfolio Management*. Wiley Finance Series. Hoboken, NJ: Wiley, 2012.

CHAPTER TEN

Investment Objectives, Strategy, and Vehicles

DESIGNING A SOVEREIGN bond portfolio starts with a clear understanding of the asset owner's investment objectives, investment strategy, and preferred investment vehicle. Every portfolio is grounded in understanding these elements, which, in turn, influence the portfolio construction process.

This chapter discusses each of these in turn. Investment objectives reflect client funding needs, stakeholder preferences, and regulatory requirements. They can range from absolute return maximization, beating a benchmark, and generating returns to match upcoming liabilities. Underlying these are the client's risk tolerance, portfolio constraints, and overall asset allocation.

Investment strategies translate investment objectives into practical frameworks for portfolio design and risk management. These include active management, passive investments, or liability-driven investing (LDI). Investment vehicles, such as mutual funds, ETFs, or separately managed accounts (SMAs), then determine how strategies are implemented, impacting cost, flexibility, transparency, and scalability.

Together, these decisions form the structural foundation upon which sovereign bond portfolios are constructed and managed.

10.1 INVESTMENT OBJECTIVES

Understanding a client's investment objectives is the first step in building a suitable investment portfolio.

Sovereign debt, with its long range of maturities and varied credit ratings, is well-suited to meet numerous client investment objectives and portfolio strategies. Some asset owners target risk-adjusted returns with performance targets and maximum loss criteria. Others concentrate on a specified return during each period to meet contractually specified liabilities. Clients may additionally have non-pecuniary objectives, such as promoting decarbonization or achieving specific sustainability targets.

The portfolio's mandate specifies the client's investment objectives, as well as the main performance criteria and targets the investment manager is expected to achieve. In addition to securing the funding for the mandate, understanding the details of the client's broader asset allocation is helpful for the portfolio manager. This information provides a holistic view of the client's investment needs and informs the portfolio manager about their risk tolerance. It also assists in anticipating any changes in asset allocation.

For example, suppose the sovereign debt portfolio represents a small portion of the client's overall assets that are invested in risky sectors. In that case, they may prefer a conservative approach in the sovereign mandate. If they are considering increasing risk in their asset allocation, they might want to consider investing in emerging market sovereigns in dollars or local currency.

Being aware of when a client divides their sovereign debt allocation among multiple managers also helps portfolio managers gain insight into their competitors. Monitoring how and where they are taking risks in their portfolios allows investors to evaluate their own performance during various market cycles and understand if they are fulfilling their clients' expectations or falling behind.

This information builds a holistic picture of the asset owner's requirements and enables the investment manager to better meet their clients' needs. This, in turn, shapes the portfolio's investment strategy, which we will address next.

> ***PRO TIP:*** *Understand the role of your portfolio in the client's overall asset allocation to assess the potential for additional flows and to avoid doubling down on risks taken elsewhere.*

10.2 INVESTMENT STRATEGIES

Asset owners employ various investment strategies based on their objectives and risk tolerance. The most common approaches in sovereign bond portfolios are absolute return, benchmark-based, and liability-driven strategies. Each approach involves trade-offs regarding the portfolio's flexibility, complexity, and level of risk.

10.2.1 Absolute Return Strategies

Absolute return strategies aim to generate positive returns regardless of market conditions or index performance. They involve the active management of portfolio holdings, often utilizing a broad investable universe and limited portfolio constraints. The strategy aims for positive total returns across market cycles by employing dynamic duration, long-short exposures, derivatives, and cross-asset positions. Risk is managed by drawdown limits or volatility targets rather than tracking error.

Depending on the mandate, the investable universe can be very broad, as in a *go-anywhere* mandate, or it can be tailored to meet specific criteria. Benchmarks, if used, are typically cash indices or money market instruments. Absolute return strategies offer flexibility and can provide diversification benefits. They also demand high levels of skill in macroeconomic analysis, trade structuring, and risk management.

In the sovereign debt space, absolute return mandates often focus on a specific region, country, or rating group. For example, an absolute return strategy focused on Brazil may allow investments in sovereign bonds denominated in dollars, local debt, the Brazilian currency, Brazilian quasi-sovereign debt, Brazilian corporate debt, and equity exposures.

10.2.2 Benchmark Strategies

Benchmark-oriented strategies are the prevailing investment model among global sovereign fixed-income investors. This approach aims to match or exceed the performance of a sovereign bond index.

A sovereign bond index is a statistical composite that reflects the performance of a global selection of government debt securities. As benchmarks for the sovereign debt market, they can vary by region, maturity, currency, bond features, and credit quality, among other factors.

Government bond indices range from short-term cash indices to those that include sovereign bonds of various maturities across many countries. Table 10.1 lists the most widely used sovereign bond benchmarks, including the Bloomberg Barclays Global Aggregate Bond Index, the FTSE World Government Bond Index, and the J.P. Morgan Emerging Market Bond Index Global series.

Specialist indices include those focused on inflation-protected securities and frontier market government bonds. A growing category focuses on sustainable debt instruments that aim to reflect sovereign issuers' sustainability practices.

The index returns in benchmarked strategies serve as a barometer for performance. It enables portfolio managers to track their investments relative to the market and allows asset owners to monitor the performance of their asset managers against a common standard.

Benchmarked portfolios can be passively or actively managed. Passive strategies include pure bond index matching, which aims to replicate the benchmark as closely as possible. Another passive approach is enhanced indexing that targets and matches the benchmark's primary risk factors. A third passive strategy is enhanced indexing that mirrors the benchmark's major and minor risk factors.

Actively managed portfolios aim to generate excess returns compared to the index by taking directional views on risk factors that diverge from the account's benchmark. These include strategies with significant risk-factor mismatches and those with full flexibility. With more proactive decision-making, active strategies tend to have higher fees than passively managed strategies.

TABLE 10.1 Government Bond Indices

Coverage	Index Name	Key Characteristics
Global Indices	Bloomberg Barclays Global Aggregate Bond Index	Includes investment-grade government, corporate, and securitized bonds from developed and emerging markets worldwide.
	FTSE World Government Bond Index (WGBI)	Measures the performance of fixed-rate, local currency government bonds from over 20 developed and emerging market countries.
	J.P. Morgan Global Government Bond Index (GGBI)	Tracks the performance of fixed-rate, local currency government bonds issued by investment-grade countries around the world.
US Indices	Bloomberg Barclays US Treasury Index	Focuses on US Treasury securities, which include various maturities.
	Bloomberg Barclays US Aggregate Bond Index	A broad-based benchmark that measures the investment-grade, fixed-rate, taxable bond market in the US, including government and corporate bonds.
	S&P US Treasury Bond Index	Measures the performance of US Treasury bonds across different maturities.
European Indices	Bloomberg Barclays Euro Aggregate Bond Index	Includes Euro-denominated government, corporate, and securitized bonds from the Eurozone countries.
	FTSE UK Gilts Index Series	Tracks the performance of British government bonds (Gilts).
	iBoxx € Sovereign Eurozone Index	Measures the performance of Euro-denominated sovereign bonds from Eurozone countries.
Asian Indices	Markitt iBoxx ABF Pan-Asia Index	Tracks the performance of local currency government bonds from eight Asian markets: China, Hong Kong, Indonesia, Korea, Malaysia, Philippines, Singapore, and Thailand.
	J.P. Morgan Asia Credit Index (JACI)	Includes sovereign, quasi-sovereign, and corporate bonds from Asia, but its broader than just government bonds.
Emerging Markets Indices	J.P. Morgan Emerging Markets Bond Index Global (EMBI Global)	Measures the performance of USD-denominated government bonds issued by emerging market countries.
	J.P. Morgan Government Bond Index-Emerging Markets (GBI-EM)	Tracks local currency bonds issued by emerging market governments.
	Bloomberg Barclays Emerging Markets Local Currency Government Bond Index	Focuses on local currency government bonds from emerging markets.

TABLE 10.1 Continued

Coverage	Index Name	Key Characteristics
Other Regional and Country Specific Indices	BMO Canadian Government Bond Index	Measures the performance of Canadian government bond market.
	S&P/ASX Australian Government Bond Index	Tracks the performance of the Australian government bond market.
	Nikkei Japanese Government Bond Index	Measures the performance of Japanese Government Bonds (JGBs).
Specialized Indices: Inflation-Linked	Bloomberg Barclays US Treasury Inflation-Protected Securities (TIPS) Index	Tracks inflation-protected US Treasury securities.
	Bloomberg Barclays Global Inflation-Linked Bond Index	A global index tracking the performance of inflation-linked government bonds from developed and emerging markets.

Source: Bloomberg, Global Aggregate Index Methodology; FTSE Russell, WGBI Series; J.P. Morgan, EMBI Family of Indices Methodology; J.P. Morgan, GBI Family of Indices Methodology; S&P Dow Jones Indices, S&P U.S. Treasury Bond Index; S&P Global, iBoxx EUR Benchmark Index Methodology; BMO Global Asset Management, ZGB ETF Overview; Citi, Citi Fixed Income Indices; HSBC, Frontier Markets Bond Index with Adpated from J.P. Morgan et al., S&P Global.

10.2.3 Liability-Driven Strategies

Liability-driven investment (LDI) strategies design portfolio assets and income streams to meet future liabilities. They are typical for institutional investors like defined benefit pension funds and life insurance companies, which have a series of obligations at specific times. The investment approach focuses on matching duration and managing interest rate risk, while also ensuring steady income streams over time.

LDI strategies may include benchmarks aimed at monitoring performance among managers or fulfilling asset allocation criteria. They may also permit some portion of the portfolio to be actively managed to reduce the risk of losses and ensure the ability to meet upcoming liabilities.

10.3 INVESTMENT VEHICLES

Once an investor selects a sovereign bond investment strategy—whether absolute return, benchmark-based, or liability-driven—the next critical decision is choosing the appropriate investment vehicle. The vehicle dictates how efficiently the strategy can be implemented, affecting cost, liquidity, transparency, and operational complexity.

Options include mutual funds, exchange-traded funds (ETFs), and separately managed accounts (SMAs). Each option offers distinct advantages: mutual funds provide active management and diversification, ETFs offer intraday liquidity and lower costs, while SMAs allow for customization aligned with institutional mandates.

The choice of vehicle shapes portfolio execution, risk control, and responsiveness to market opportunities or constraints. The final decision depends on the asset owner's objectives, risk tolerance, investment horizon, and liquidity needs.

10.3.1 Mutual Funds

Mutual funds are legal entities that pool money from numerous investors to purchase a diversified portfolio of bonds. They are managed by professional fund managers and regulated by the appropriate national financial authorities. For example, in the United States, traditional open-ended mutual funds are regulated by the Securities and Exchange Commission (SEC) under the Investment Company Act of 1940.

Investors buy and sell shares in the fund, whose value is determined by its net asset value (NAV). This is the total value of the fund's assets minus its liabilities, divided by the number of shares outstanding. The term *open-ended* indicates that the fund is open to new capital and generally doesn't have a limit on the assets under management (AUM). This contrasts with closed-end funds, which issue a fixed number of shares and raise capital through an initial public offering (IPO).

Mutual fund investment strategies can be active or passive. Active mutual funds are managed to outperform the benchmark, meaning they aim to achieve higher total returns than the benchmark by a specified alpha target. On the other hand, passive mutual funds seek to replicate a given benchmark, providing asset owners with exposure to the overall market risk of the sector. They tend to have lower fees than actively managed mutual funds but forgo the potential of generating excess returns versus the benchmark.

The primary advantages of mutual funds include professional management, diversification benefits, and ease of buying and selling (as compared with an SMA). However, these benefits must be weighed against management fees, volatility due to daily fluctuations in the funds' NAV, and the absence of a guaranteed return.

Mutual fund structures differ around the world, reflecting variations in regulatory environments, market practices, and investor preferences. These variations can affect the fund's legal structure, tax treatment, investment strategy, and protections for investors. Table 10.2 summarizes mutual fund structures in select developed markets.

10.3.2 Exchange-Traded Funds (ETFs)

Bond ETFs maintain a diversified portfolio of bonds but, like stocks, trade on exchanges and provide intraday liquidity. They blend the diversified investment strategy of mutual funds with the convenience of trading associated with stocks, giving investors a flexible and efficient way to invest in a broad range of assets.

Similar to mutual funds, ETFs provide investors with access to a broad segment of the market, region, or strategy through a single transaction. One of the advantages of ETFs is their tradability; they can be bought and sold throughout the trading day at market prices, just like stocks. This offers liquidity and flexibility that is generally unavailable with traditional mutual funds, which are traded only at the end of the trading day at their net asset value.

TABLE 10.2 Mutual Funds in Select Developed Markets

Country	Description
United States	Mutual Funds: The traditional open-ended mutual fund in the US can invest in a variety of assets, including stocks, bonds, and other securities.
Europe	SICAV (Société d'Investissement à Capital Variable): Popular in European countries, SICAVs are investment companies with variable capital. They are similar to mutual funds but structured as companies where investors are shareholders. UCITS (Undertakings for Collective Investment in Transferable Securities): A harmonized regulatory framework that allows funds to operate freely throughout the EU, provided they adhere to strict investment and reporting requirements. UCITS funds can be structured as SICAVs or other forms. Both Luxembourg and Ireland are popular domiciles for investment funds, especially UCITs, due to their favorable regulatory regimes and tax laws. Funds can be structured as SICAVs or other legal forms suitable for open-ended funds.
United Kingdom	OEICs (Open-Ended Investment Companies): Similar to SICAVs, OEICs are structured as companies. They combine features of both traditional mutual funds and investment trusts, operating under a single pricing structure. Unit Trusts: A traditional form of mutual fund in the UK, where the fund is structured as a trust rather than a company.
Canada	Mutual Funds: Canadian mutual funds operate similarly to those in the US, offering a range of investment options across various asset classes. They are regulated by provincial securities commissions.
Australia	Managed Investment Schemes (MIS): In Australia, open-ended funds are typically structured as managed investment schemes, where investors hold units in the trust rather than shares in a company.
Japan	Investment Trusts: In Japan open-ended mutual funds are commonly structured as investment trusts. These funds are regulated under the Financial Instruments and Exchange Act.

Most ETFs are designed to track an index and typically have lower fees compared to mutual funds because of their passive management structure. They regularly disclose their holdings and tend to be more tax-efficient than mutual funds due to their unique framework and how transactions are executed, which minimizes capital gains distributions.

ETFs offer many advantages, such as diversification, liquidity, and generally lower costs, but they also come with risks. They can be more volatile than open-ended mutual funds due to their intraday tradability, causing values to fluctuate based on the performance of the underlying assets.

In addition, while intraday liquidity can benefit investors, it may also lead to *higher* trading costs and wider bid-ask spreads. This is particularly true for ETFs that track niche markets with lower trading volumes, making it more challenging to buy or sell quickly at the indicated market prices.

Market technicals can lead to purchases at a premium or sales at a discount compared to a more actively managed portfolio. This, combined with the compounding of daily returns, can create significant tracking errors relative to the index. Over time, this may result in the ETF underperforming its benchmark index, as no countervailing measures are implemented, unlike in actively managed mutual funds.

The combination of low fees, diverse offerings, and liquidity has driven substantial growth in ETFs. The range of government bond ETFs has expanded to encompass various countries, maturities, benchmarks, and investor objectives, including ESG investing.

The initial passive management bias of ETFs has been enhanced with more actively managed strategies, increasing competition with mutual funds and separate accounts. As a result, fee pressures have emerged throughout the complex, leading to the conversion of many mutual funds into ETFs.

10.3.3 Separate Accounts

Separate accounts, or separately managed accounts (SMAs), are investment accounts where individual investors directly own the securities. This differs from mutual funds or exchange-traded funds (ETFs), in which investors own shares of a pooled investment. This direct ownership provides a greater level of customization and personalization to meet the investor's unique goals and requirements.

Separate accounts are managed by professional investment firms or asset managers, usually on behalf of institutional investors, endowments, or high-net-worth individuals. These accounts can be tailored to meet the investor's specific investment objectives, risk tolerance, tax considerations, and ethical or social preferences. Investors may choose customized benchmarks or request the exclusion of certain issuers or sectors according to their preferences.

Direct ownership of individual securities in the account, rather than owning shares in a pooled investment vehicle, allows for greater transparency and control over investments. Owners can adjust their investment strategies based on changing financial circumstances or goals and actively participate in divestment decisions related to sanctions or credit downgrades.

Owners can monitor the performance of portfolio managers at the trade level due to high transparency and visibility, rather than relying solely on performance indicators at the account level. Additional advantages include potential efficiencies in tax management. For example, tax-loss harvesting strategies aimed at reducing tax liabilities can be more easily applied at the separate account level.

Separate accounts may incur higher management fees and transaction costs compared to pooled investment vehicles, especially for accounts that require significant customization. They usually have a higher minimum investment requirement than mutual funds and ETFs, which can restrict accessibility for some investors. Furthermore, the level of customization and management needed can make separate accounts more complex for both the portfolio manager and the asset owner to manage and understand.

10.4 SUMMARY

This chapter discussed the key building blocks of sovereign bond portfolio design: investment objectives, investment strategies, and investment vehicles. Investment objectives capture client funding needs, performance targets, and risk tolerance, all of which shape portfolio constraints and the balance between risk and return.

Investment strategies—such as active management, passive investing, and liability-driven investing (LDI)—translate investment objectives into practical portfolio frameworks. The choice of investment vehicle, whether mutual funds, ETFs, or separately managed accounts, determines how these strategies are implemented and affects cost, flexibility, and transparency. Together, these elements form the structural foundation for constructing and managing investable sovereign bond portfolios, which is what we turn to next.

REFERENCES

Bloomberg. *Bloomberg Fixed Income Indices*. https://www.bloomberg.com/markets/rates-bonds/bloomberg-fixed-income-indices (accessed 14 May 2025).

Bloomberg. *Global Aggregate Index Methodology*. Bloomberg Index Services Ltd., 2024.

Bloomberg. *US Treasury Index Methodology*. Bloomberg Index Services Ltd., 2024.

Bloomberg. *US Aggregate Index Methodology*. Bloomberg Index Services Ltd., 2024.

Bloomberg. *Euro Aggregate Index Methodology*. Bloomberg Index Services Ltd., 2024.

Bloomberg. *Emerging Markets Local Currency Government Index Methodology*. Bloomberg Index Services Ltd., 2024.

Bloomberg. *US TIPS Index Methodology*. Bloomberg Index Services Ltd., 2024.

Bloomberg. *Global Inflation-Linked Index Methodology*. Bloomberg Index Services Ltd., 2024.

BMO Global Asset Management. *BMO Government Bond Index ETF (ZGB) Overview*. https://www.bmogam.com (accessed 14 May 2025).

BMO Global Asset Management. *Management Report for BMO Government Bond Index ETF (ZGB)*. 2024.

Citi. *Citi Fixed Income Indices*. https://www.yieldbook.com/m/home/index.shtml (accessed 29 July 2025).

FTSE Russell. *World Government Bond Index (WGBI) Series*. London Stock Exchange Group. https://www.lseg.com/en/ftse-russell (accessed 29 July 2025).

FTSE Russell. *FTSE WGBI Factsheet*. FTSE Russell Research Portal, 2024.

FTSE Russell. *FTSE UK Gilts Index Series*. London Stock Exchange Group, 2024.

FTSE Russell. *FTSE UK Gilts Index Series Ground Rules*. FTSE Russell Research Portal, 2024.

FTSE Russell. *FTSE Frontier Markets Government Bond Index Series*. London Stock Exchange Group.

HSBC. *HSBC Frontier Markets Bond Index*. https://www.hsbcnet.com (accessed 29 July 2025).

IHS Markit. *iBoxx ABF Pan-Asia Index Guide*. 2024.

J.P. Morgan. *GBI Family of Indices Methodology*. Emerging Markets Research, 2024.

J.P. Morgan. *Asia Credit Index (JACI) Methodology*. Emerging Markets Research, 2024.

J.P. Morgan. *EMBI Global Diversified Index Methodology*. Emerging Markets Research, 2024.

J.P. Morgan. *GBI-EM Global Diversified Factsheet*. Emerging Markets Research, 2024.

J.P. Morgan. *Index Research Factsheets*. https://www.jpmorgan.com/insights/global-research/index-research (accessed 29 July 2025).

Nikkei. *Nikkei Japanese Government Bond Index*. https://indexes.nikkei.co.jp (accessed 29 July 2025).

S&P Dow Jones Indices. *S&P U.S. Treasury Bond Index*. https://www.spglobal.com/spdji (accessed 29 July 2025).

S&P Dow Jones Indices. *S&P/ASX Australian Government Bond Index*. https://www.spglobal.com/spdji/en/ (accessed 29 July 2025).

S&P Global. *iBoxx EUR Benchmark Index Methodology*. 2024.

CHAPTER ELEVEN

Constructing a Sovereign Debt Portfolio

BUILDING A SOVEREIGN debt portfolio within the parameters set by a client's mandate requires a systematic approach. The process starts with the portfolio mandate and investment guidelines. These codify the client's goals, risk tolerance, regulatory constraints, and other structural considerations into actionable parameters.

The second stage involves applying various portfolio construction frameworks to build risk positions. These include the classic mean-variance optimization framework, the cell-based approach, and multifactor models. The latter can be used to capture systematic exposures such as interest rate risk, spread risk, and macroeconomic sensitivities.

The next stage focuses on factors specific to the portfolio's investment strategy. For portfolios managed against a benchmark, this means understanding index characteristics and the practical challenges of tracking and beating them. For liability-driven investment (LDI) portfolios, it involves selecting suitable cash matching and immunization approaches.

With the main parameters of the portfolio in place, the investor sets risk targets and takes an investment view. This involves setting risk budgets, scaling positions, and defining stop-loss limits to manage downside exposure. This chapter explores these different stages. It also discusses the behavioral biases that investors may exhibit, highlighting the necessity for a disciplined, rules-based investment process.

11.1 PORTFOLIO MANDATE AND GUIDELINES

Every portfolio has a specified mandate and guidelines set by the client that cover the investment strategy, objectives, targets, constraints, and risk parameters. These are outlined in the legal documentation for the account or fund and provide the guardrails for investing. Other goals may be communicated as client needs or market conditions evolve.

Portfolio targets encompass alpha expectations, tracking error ranges, and other risk-adjusted return objectives as reflected by the Sharpe ratio or information ratio. Minimum investment requirements and diversification parameters may also be included.

Portfolio constraints may include ranges on risk metrics such as duration, spread, and credit exposure. There may also be limits on the leverage ratio, minimum and maximum cash exposure, and minimum liquidity requirements. Permitted instruments may include derivatives, currency exposure, and types of security structures.

Constraints can also encompass minimum rating requirements, limits on issuer concentration, and the size of any off-benchmark exposures. There may be exclusions of certain countries or sectors, such as tobacco, gambling, or weapons exposures. Other sensitivities may include prohibiting defaulted securities, setting maximum losses on individual positions, and having preferences against holding issuers with headline risks.

In establishing these guidelines, the asset owner reflects their goals, objectives, and risk tolerance. This informs the portfolio manager about the level and type of risk position acceptable in the portfolio.

11.2 MODEL PORTFOLIOS

Every client pitch that ultimately leads to a funded portfolio includes a model portfolio. Model portfolios represent the risk positions and investments that a portfolio manager would make based on a set of portfolio objectives and constraints. They can be customized to meet a client's investment goals, comply with the portfolio's guidelines and restrictions, and enable performance backtesting. The model also serves as a template for the actual trades the portfolio manager would execute once the account is funded.

Model portfolios can be created in Bloomberg, allowing for daily monitoring and assessment of trades and portfolio strategies. They serve as valuable tools for junior traders and portfolio managers to learn how to structure portfolios, execute trades that reflect their investment views, and evaluate performance.

Portfolio managers utilize model portfolios together with several tools to construct portfolios. These tools include mean-variance analysis, a cell-based approach, and multifactor techniques. Each methodology can be applied, and portfolio positions can be optimized using the model before trades are executed and live positions are established.

Next, we turn to these frameworks and discuss their use in constructing sovereign bond portfolios.[1]

11.3 MEAN-VARIANCE FRAMEWORK

A standard approach to portfolio construction is the Markowitz mean-variance analysis framework. This mathematical framework is designed for creating a portfolio that maximizes expected returns for a given level of risk. It considers the expected value and variance of an asset's return, as well as the covariance or correlation of returns between pairs of assets within the portfolio. In doing so, it takes into account an asset's risk not only in isolation but also based on how it contributes to the portfolio's overall risk and return.

In sovereign debt portfolios, the mean-variance approach can allocate risk among regions, countries, and securities. It can also evaluate off-benchmark allocations, debt exposures in foreign versus local currency, sovereign versus quasi-sovereign debt, and exposures to non-sovereign assets such as high-yield corporates.

The framework includes both the issuer's direct contribution to the portfolio's returns and the contribution from correlations with other exposures. As such, it provides a comprehensive view of the security's impact on the portfolio.

Let's consider an example of a portfolio manager assessing how much to allocate to Colombia 2031 USD bonds within an actively managed emerging market hard currency sovereign debt portfolio. The portfolio's positions consist of bonds from Peru, South Africa, and Egypt, as shown in Table 11.1. The portfolio aims for a target return of 7%, with the objective of enhancing the Sharpe ratio by adding another issuer.

The mean-variance optimization model is:

$$Maximize = \frac{w^T R - R_f}{\sqrt{w^T \sum w}}$$

where:

w: vector of asset weights
R: expected returns vector
R_f: risk-free rate (e.g., 4.0%)
$\sum$: covariance matrix

This is applied to solve for the weight of the Colombia 2031 bond that maximizes the portfolio's Sharpe ratio, subject to the following constraints:

Portfolio duration: 7 ± 1 years
Maximum single issuer weight: 25%
Target volatility: ≤10%

TABLE 11.1 Example of Colombia 2031s

Sovereign Bond	Expected Return %	Volatility %	Correlation with Portfolio	Global Credit Beta	Latin America Beta	Oil Beta
Peru 2031	6.2	8.0	0.85	0.85	0.60	0.20
South Africa 2032	7.0	10.0	0.75	0.95	0.10	0.55
Egypt 2029	10.5	15.0	0.60	1.20	0.05	0.80
Colombia 2031 (candidate)	**7.5**	**9.5**	**0.40**	**0.75**	**0.70**	**0.40**

The results suggest scaling the Colombia 2031 position to 18% of the portfolio. While it has a yield similar to the South Africa position, its addition enhances the risk-adjusted return due to lower volatility. By factoring in the correlation of this position with the overall portfolio, the allocation can be adjusted to better optimize risk-adjusted returns than if it were based solely on bond returns.

11.4 CELL-BASED APPROACH

The cell-based approach divides the portfolio benchmark into cells representing various characteristics of the benchmark. These cells can include duration, convexity, maturity, coupon, ratings, region, sectors, and subsectors, currency, and instrument structure, among other categories.

Passive investors replicate the index by matching exposures across as many cells as efficiently as possible. For example, suppose 30% of the market value of the index is in investment-grade rated sovereigns in the European region. In that case, the passive strategy will aim to hold 30% of the portfolio in the same or similar names. If the duration of the index is seven years, the cell-based approach would replicate the duration exposure by region and issuer.

Active managers use the cell-based approach to express their views on each risk metric and in every cell. Positions may be *overweight*, *underweight*, or *flat* compared to the benchmark, depending on whether the manager chooses to be long, short, or maintain the same exposure as the benchmark across all cells.

For example, if the manager holds a negative view on duration because they believe interest rates will rise, they may opt to be underweight duration compared to the index. They may also have a negative stance on Mexico's sovereign credit and therefore choose to be underweight both duration and credit spread by decreasing their Mexico holdings relative to the index. In this manner, the investor can align each component with their investment perspectives.

Once an initial allocation is made across each cell, the manager can assess the portfolio's overall risk and adjust each exposure accordingly. For example, they can verify that they are meeting their duration and spread targets for the portfolio. Additionally, they can utilize performance evaluation metrics, such as tracking error, to guide this process. If the tracking error is too low, the manager may need to increase risk (and vice versa) compared to the benchmark to enhance their chances of achieving the alpha target.

11.5 MULTIFACTOR APPROACH

The cell-based approach overlooks the correlation between each cell and, therefore, may overestimate or underestimate the risk taken at the portfolio level. The multifactor approach addresses these concerns by modeling an asset's expected return based on its primary drivers or risk factors. These models can incorporate macroeconomic factors such as global growth, inflation, or commodity prices; issuer fundamentals like debt ratios, fiscal balance, or reserves; or statistical factors such as the historical performance of the asset class relative to others.

Multifactor models are statistical tools that can be used for portfolio construction. One approach identifies the main return drivers of an asset and is called the *expected-return forecasting factor model.* The return drivers are used to build a portfolio with expected returns that should outperform its benchmark.

Another method is the *risk forecasting factor model,* a widely used multifactor model. This model predicts key risk parameters, such as interest rate risk and credit risk, and then adjusts portfolio positions to meet the required risk target. For instance, forecasts of decreases in interest rates may point to long-duration risk positions and reductions in credit risk exposures.

The multifactor approach has the additional benefit that it equips portfolio managers with insights into where and what type of risk is present in the portfolio. By breaking down the portfolio's ex post tracking error into different factors, it aids in identifying the allocation of risk. For instance, it may reveal that the portfolio is heavily weighted toward interest rate risk in the 10-year sector, with most of the risk stemming from investment-grade sovereigns. It might also indicate that the portfolio has significant exposure to oil price risk, primarily from commodity-importing countries in Asia.

They also enable portfolio managers to scale positions intelligently, considering the risk drivers in the portfolio. Suppose the portfolio manager in the example above is deciding whether to increase the allocation to Colombia 2031s to 22% from 18%. This may be based on positive credit developments or if the bonds have cheapened relative to their peers.

The portfolio manager looks at the returns from the bond and its main risk drivers. This may include the global credit beta (the sensitivity to EM credit spreads proxied by EMBI index spreads, given Colombia's status as an EM economy), Latin America beta (the sensitivity to Latin American regional spreads, as Colombia is in Latin America), and oil beta (the sensitivity to oil prices, since Colombia is an oil producer).

Table 11.1 suggests that increasing Colombia 2031s weight in the portfolio would only marginally increase the portfolio's risk factors. The exposure to global credit would remain moderate, as Colombia's loading is below the portfolio average. Latin American exposure will increase, reducing regional diversification. Oil beta will be affected only moderately. The impact on tracking error can also be calculated. Together, these inputs are utilized by the portfolio manager in their decision of whether to increase allocations to Colombia.

11.6 PORTFOLIO OPTIMIZATION

Once a portfolio has been constructed, its holdings can be optimized using an optimizer. This tool employs mathematical models that consider expected returns, risk targets, covariances among securities, and portfolio constraints to derive optimal allocations across positions.

The optimizer's objectives can be alpha targets, tracking error ranges, or maximizing total returns. Risk targets may include duration, credit spread, volatility, and diversification metrics. Portfolio constraints can encompass limits on duration and credit spreads, sovereign credit ratings, cash and liquidity ratios, or issuer exposure.

The optimization process utilizes techniques, such as the mean-variance approach and quadratic programming, to establish the optimal asset allocation for a specific level of risk and vice versa. The result is a set of weights for each security in the portfolio, along with the expected risk-return profile of the portfolio.

This allows investors to evaluate whether the portfolio aligns with their risk tolerance and investment goals. The optimizer also facilitates sensitivity analysis, illustrating how the portfolio's performance varies when input assumptions change. Consequently, it can be a valuable resource in the portfolio manager's toolkit.

PRO TIP: *Regularly evaluate and optimize portfolio risk positions, particularly after large changes in prices or shifts in market sentiment.*

11.7 MANAGING AGAINST A BENCHMARK

Portfolio construction for both passive and active benchmarked strategies starts with an understanding of the portfolio's benchmark or index. This involves detailed knowledge of the index construction and its risk characteristics. Portfolio managers should also be aware of certain aspects of managing against a benchmark that may impact their performance and alpha. This is what we will discuss next.

11.7.1 Index Characteristics

The first step involves understanding how the index is constructed. This includes the criteria guiding index constituents, entry and exit, weights, and rebalancing methodology.

Government bond indices, like other benchmarks, have clearly defined rules. These include issuer characteristics, acceptable credit quality, issue size, and instrument liquidity and traceability. Bond attributes, such as maturity, structure, currency of denomination, and coupon type, are also considered. The selection criteria, in turn, determine which securities and issuers are included or excluded. Table 10.1 lists the most common sovereign bond indices.

Bonds in an index are typically weighted by their market value. This means that issuers with larger outstanding amounts carry a greater weight in the index, subject to a maximum weight cap to enhance diversification. A limited number of government bond indices utilize GDP-adjusted weights to minimize exposure of benchmarks to more leveraged issuers.

Indices are governed by a decision-making body or index committee that administers and oversees the calculation of index metrics. They publish regular reports addressing planned changes in index constituents, weights, and methodology. The index committee consults with the market ahead of major changes and gathers information when significant policy changes occur. Examples include the imposition of sanctions, issuer defaults, or exclusions from the index. These consultations give investors a forum to express their concerns and offer feedback.

Indices are periodically rebalanced to incorporate new bond issues, adjust for maturing bonds, and factor in changes in bond prices. Rebalancing modifies the weight and exposure of the components in line with the index's objectives and inclusion criteria. The index manager publishes the new index weights and constituents before the rebalance period (typically at month-end or quarter-end for most indices). They may stagger the timing of entry and exit if weights (or market exposures) are particularly large.

For instance, the introduction of Chinese debt instruments into global sovereign debt indices in 2019 marked a significant change. Equally important was the inclusion of Middle Eastern sovereigns in the J.P. Morgan Emerging Market Bond Indices during the same year. Both were communicated to the markets several quarters before implementation and were introduced gradually into the benchmark.

Once the portfolio manager has a solid understanding of the index methodology, they need to understand its risk characteristics. The range of metrics includes the benchmark's duration, spread, yield, volatility, credit rating, regional exposure, maturity, and country weights.

For example, the index may have a duration of seven years, a credit spread of +400 basis points over US Treasuries, and a yield of 7%. It may have an average credit rating of BBB with regional exposure in Latin America, Asia, and Europe.

The portfolio manager breaks down each risk metric into different buckets to assess the various sources of the risks. For developed market indices the focus is on duration, key-rate duration, and volatility metrics by country. Meanwhile, for emerging market indices, the focus also includes the contribution to the benchmark spread and benchmark carry by country.

The sensitivity or beta of the index to global factors and asset markets can be estimated to provide insight into how it may respond to various global and financial market conditions. For example, the equity market beta indicates how the index's performance correlates with equity market performance. The oil beta measures the sensitivity of its return to oil prices. This information aids in understanding the return drivers, volatility, and overall performance of the index.

Investors also look at indices as a valuable tool for assessing the flows into and out of the asset class. Even if an investor meets their performance targets compared to their benchmark, poor index returns relative to the rest of the market may still lead to outflows (or inflows) from the asset class as asset owners adjust their positions. Therefore, indices for sovereign debt markets should be regularly compared to other financial market benchmarks to evaluate the relative attractiveness of the asset class.

PRO TIP: *Know your benchmark in as much detail as possible and evaluate the best and worst performers regularly.*

11.7.2 Practical Aspects of Managing Benchmarked Portfolios

From the outset, a benchmarked portfolio starts with a *drag* or a disadvantage compared to the benchmark. This is because indices are challenging to replicate perfectly. Indices do not account for transaction costs incurred when entering and exiting a trade, which means that active portfolio investments are executed at different price points from the index. They also do not consider any taxes that investors are liable to pay.

Moreover, index constituents may include issuers and bond issues that are difficult to access. These consist of one-off issuers or less liquid and buy-to-hold securities. This is a pervasive feature of government bond indices, given that the assets under management (AUM) benchmarked against them are several times the AUM included in the benchmark. These factors make perfect index replication impossible, requiring the portfolio manager to bridge the gap using alternative strategies, such as corporate or derivative exposures.

Understanding index rebalancing changes and their impact on portfolio risk positions is necessary to prevent inadvertent *drift* or changes in the active positions. This requires awareness of the index rules and regular monitoring of constituents.

For example, some indices exclude bonds with less than one year to maturity; in this case, any residual exposures become off-index and illiquid. Suppose there is a new issue that will be included in the benchmark at month-end. In that case, portfolio managers may incorporate the estimated new weight when placing their order for allocations. Additionally, if issuers violate index inclusion rules, investors might seek to adjust exposures before index rules lead to forced sales.

From time to time, indices can amplify technical factors in the market. Examples include index exclusions or inclusions due to rating changes, which may lead to forced selling or purchasing. Orphan issuers or issues may arise if they do not fulfill index requirements, such as the required size for benchmark inclusion (which varies by index and over time) or meeting the issuer criteria. High-income countries like Korea are excluded from some emerging market indices for this reason.

Index decisions to revise market access assessments can also create self-fulfilling prophecies, either reducing or increasing demand for issuers or instruments. Understanding these feedback loops helps portfolio managers navigate the impact of these changes on their portfolios.

11.8 BUILDING BLOCKS OF AN LDI STRATEGY

The first order of business in constructing a liability-driven strategy is to identify the liability profile. This involves understanding the timing, size, and nature of the liabilities the portfolio needs to meet. These could be insurance claims, annuities, guaranteed investment contracts, pension payments, or other financial obligations.

Next, the cash flow requirements must be outlined, including the timing and amount of each liability. The portfolio manager then selects the investment strategy for designing the portfolio. These strategies include the cash matching approach, immunization techniques, and a combination approach.

The cash matching approach builds a portfolio comprising bonds with coupon and principal payments similar to those of the liabilities. Each liability is matched in turn with a bond that has a similar payment profile until all liabilities are satisfied.

For example, if a pension fund needs to pay out $100 million in 30 years, the portfolio could invest in 30-year sovereign bonds. The specific investment amount in the bond would be adjusted based on the principal and coupon stream compared to the liability. Sovereign bonds, with their long maturities, are well-suited for this type of investing and are generally low risk compared to other assets.

A second approach is the immunization strategy, which aims to hedge interest rate risk for each series of the portfolio's liabilities. This is typically achieved by matching the duration of the portfolio with that of the liabilities, ensuring both move in parallel. The portfolio must be constructed so that the present value of its cash flows equals the present value of future liabilities.

The risk in immunization strategies is imperfect ex post duration matching. One reason could be non-parallel and arbitrary shifts in the yield curve. The *immunization risk* metric quantifies this risk and is a third factor that the portfolios must target. As interest rates change, the portfolio must be rebalanced to align risk and liability duration metrics.

The third approach combines cash matching with the immunization strategy. It creates a portfolio that is duration-matched and cash-matched for the initial years. This method ensures that liquidity needs in the short term are addressed by the initial cash matching, thus minimizing the immunization risk tied to changes in the yield curve. The primary disadvantage of this combined approach is that the cost may be higher.

The approaches outlined provide the main building blocks for LDI portfolios. To this, the portfolio manager adds strategic and tactical positions in line with their risk views, which we turn to next.

11.9 TAKING ACTIVE POSITIONS

With the frameworks for constructing a portfolio established, we now turn our attention to setting risk targets in actively managed portfolios. The process begins with identifying several relevant investment themes that are expected to influence asset prices. The portfolio manager analyzes how these themes may impact various asset classes, sectors, issuers, and financial markets as a whole.

Next, risk targets are established for the portfolio's main return drivers, including duration, spread duration, curve, volatility, and portfolio beta. Trading strategies are formulated in alignment with risk targets. Each investment position is sized considering credit risk, valuation, and correlations with other portfolio exposures. Market liquidity, technical factors, and prices are evaluated, and specific securities are traded as the final expression of the strategy.

TABLE 11.2 Steps for Taking Active Positions

Step No.	Name	Inputs	Expression
1	Identify themes	Macroeconomic drivers, policy views, politics, global economic factors, commodity prices and global markets, geopolitics, structural factors	2–3 themes that are expected to influence asset prices
2	Assess market impact	Deep dive into drivers, market risk sentiment, investor positioning, and idiosyncratic factors	2–3 sectors and issuers to express the trade in where it is not already priced
3	Formulate trade strategy and risk targets	Performance of financial instruments, risk metrics, expected gains/losses, market consensus	Targets for main risk metrics including duration, spread duration, curve, volatility, and portfolio beta
4	Sizing portfolio position	Market valuations, cross correlations with other portfolio exposures, impact on TE and alpha, cost of exiting position	Size of position, price range for entry and exit, gain/loss analysis
5	Select and trade securities	Market pricing across cash and derivatives, relative valuations, positioning, liquidity	Trade specific instruments
6	Monitor position	Gain loss, alpha and TE contribution, market conditions and broker runs	Decision to hold, reduce, or add to the position

Over time, the performance of this active position is monitored. Each trade and investment position will have an indicative stop/loss that acts as a guide for reducing losses or taking profits. These are continually reviewed and managed alongside the broader risks and returns of the portfolio. Table 11.2 summarizes these steps, which we explore in more detail below.

11.9.1 Investment Themes

Taking active positions begins with identifying investment themes expected to influence asset prices and, in turn, portfolio returns. The investor considers a wide range of inputs, including a country's macroeconomic drivers, global economic trends, commodity prices, government policy, politics, and geopolitics, to name a few.

Macroeconomic themes encompass opinions on growth and inflation, unemployment and consumption trends, the trade balance, credit growth, and household consumption. Closely related are perspectives on government policies, central bank decisions regarding interest rates, the fiscal balance, the currency outlook, and other facets of public policy.

The investor's assessment of global economic performance and inter-country policy dynamics serves as additional inputs. Particular attention is given to systemically important economies such as the United States and China, as well as global central bank policy rates. The investor may also have perspectives on the commodity price outlook, international trade flows, and global capital market trends.

Geopolitics and shifts in relationships between major economies may also be relevant. Regional and sectoral dynamics, along with spillover effects—both internal and external—from developments abroad may also be covered. Structural factors, such as long-term trends in sustainable investing, demographics, and consumer behavior, are additional topics that may influence and shape a portfolio manager's fundamental investment views.

11.9.2 Market Assessment and Impact

Alongside identifying investment themes, the investor assesses market sentiment to determine whether the market is risk-on or risk-off. They examine co-movements between the equity and fixed-income markets, how investors are positioned, the flow of funds across asset classes, the amount of uninvested cash in portfolios, and whether investors hold long positions in particular regions or issuers.

This helps analyze how investment themes may impact markets and various asset classes, subsectors, and issuers. For example, if the investor expects a recession in the United States, they may expect interest rates to fall, leading to higher US Treasury bond prices. Market valuations may not reflect this recession risk if other investors expect growth to remain strong and inflation to be moderate. They may be overweight growth-sensitive sectors and sectors with high credit risk.

The investor would then develop a trading strategy that would benefit from slowing growth and lower rates. They may go overweight in US interest rate duration and reduce exposure to growth-sensitive or high-yield credits. The perspective on the timing of the recession would shape their expectations regarding the shape of the yield curve and when market pricing may shift.

They may adjust exposure to countries that rely heavily on US trade, which may see their growth slow down and their credit spreads widen. If there are currency exposures in the portfolio, the investor may short the US dollar based on expectations of currency depreciation due to slower growth and lower interest rates.

In this way, the investor builds on their initial investment theme and translates it into a trading strategy that can be implemented in their portfolio.

11.9.3 Formulating the Trade Strategy

Translating the investment theme and market assessment into a portfolio trade strategy involves selecting the asset class and security that provides the best expression and return potential from the trade. Central to this is identifying which assets will be most affected and understanding what the market has priced in.

Identifying where the investor's views diverge from those of the market and other investors is essential for successful investing. If the views align, then the theme should be fully reflected in asset prices, leaving no tradable strategy to provide any upside for the portfolio. However, suppose there is a significant divergence in views. In that case, there is a possibility that asset markets will reprice if the investor's perspective proves correct, thereby generating positive returns for the portfolio.

Continuing with the previous example, a US recession is likely to impact the US Treasury bond market significantly. By examining the bond curve and Treasury yields, the portfolio manager deduces that the market expects a 30% chance of a recession within the next 12 months. Meanwhile, the manager believes the probability of a US recession is 70% over the coming year. This suggests the potential for gains from a position in the US Treasury market, as bond prices should rise if the investor is correct.

In this scenario, a long position on US Treasury duration would be beneficial for portfolio returns. The practical application of this trading strategy would be to set a target (or range) for the portfolio's duration, specifically from US Treasuries. This could be further refined with targets for key-rate duration and curve positioning to align with the investors' views on the timing of the slowdown and Federal Reserve interest rate cuts.

The numerical value for the duration target or range would consider several factors. These include the benchmark duration, the potential gains and losses from the position, the extent to which the investment view differs from consensus, market liquidity, and trade costs. We examine some of these in more detail later in this chapter.

The portfolio manager would assess existing positions to determine how closely the proposed change is correlated with them and whether it offsets their risk. Additionally, the portfolio manager would evaluate the impact of the investment theme on the portfolio and set targets for other risk metrics, such as volatility, spread duration, and currency exposure.

11.9.4 Sizing and Scaling Trade Positions

Translating a trade idea into a portfolio investment involves determining the size of the position within the portfolio and identifying the specific security to trade. The portfolio manager estimates the expected gains from the position, the potential losses, and the meaningful trade size for the portfolio. They then adjust the position accordingly. The goal is to build the portfolio with sufficient diversification so that no single risk position is the main contributor to risk-adjusted returns, and concentration risk remains low. See Figure 11.1 for a sample trade order.

Sizing a position in a portfolio starts with the investment objective of the portfolio manager. For instance, to increase the duration beta of the portfolio, boost exposure to a specific country due to positive developments, or reduce credit risk in oil-sensitive names due to a projected decline in commodity prices. The investor's goals and their level of conviction will determine the risk factors they target and the size of the trade.

Another input is the correlation of the trade position with other portfolio risk targets to assess the overall impact on the account. Here, the multifactor portfolio approach helps identify any portfolio-level effects that may be overlooked when using a single factor or cell-based approach. For instance, an increase in exposure to Colombia may inadvertently

Trade Details	
Trade Type	Buy (long position)
Issuer	Arab Republic of Egypt
Bond	USD 9.875% February 2029 Eurobond
ISIN	XS1968719756
Trade Size	$5,000,000 face value
Price	82.00 (clean), accrued = 3.75 → Total price = 85.75
Settlement	T+2 via Euroclear
Execution Venue	RFQ via Bloomberg ALLQ
Counterparty	Approved dealer (e.g., JP Morgan)

Stop-Loss and Risk Management Indicators	
Stop-Loss Level	If bond price falls to **$77.00** (clean), initiate a reduction of 50%
Target Price	Monitor for exit near **$90.00**, representing ~120–130 bps spread compression
Max Loss Tolerance	−3.5% at position level (~$175,000 unrealized loss)
Risk Bucket	Classified under: High-Yield EM USD
Liquidity Constraint	Do not exceed 15% of average daily volume (e.g., $35 m traded daily)

Portfolio Risk Implications	
Portfolio Overweight in % MV	0.5%
Expected Contribution to Yield	Adds ~6 bps to portfolio-level YTM, assuming bond YTM of 12%
Expected Contribution to Alpha	~3–4 bps
Expected Contribution to TE	~5 bps
Sizing	Calibrated to contribute ~1.5% portfolio-level tracking error

Risk Factor Sensitivities	
Global credit beta	High (1.2)
Oil beta	Moderate (0.8)
Region-specific risk	High EMEA exposure

FIGURE 11.1 A sample trade order.

raise the portfolio's oil beta and risk related to Latin American regional dynamics, as we explored earlier in the chapter.

Backtesting the trade using historical data is a valuable exercise. Also beneficial is forecasting the trade's impact on the portfolio's tracking error, information ratio, Sharpe ratio, and portfolio alpha. If a position contributes excessively to any of these variables compared to other trades, its size should be reassessed. Conversely, if the contribution is minimal, often referred to as a *mosquito trade*, its size should be rescaled. Before execution, the trading and execution costs should be estimated to determine whether the trade remains worthwhile.

The level of conviction in the trade idea, along with the potential upside versus downside from the position, should be considered. Higher conviction trades may warrant larger positions, while greater downside risks may lead an investor to moderate their position even if conviction levels are high. In these cases, the portfolio manager will need to consider the characteristics of the issuer, including volatility of returns, credit rating, and fundamental dynamics. These factors, along with the tradable entry and exit prices and liquidity of the instrument, will help determine the overall size of the position.

> ***PRO TIP:*** *Backtest trades before implementation to ensure you are taking the risk you think you are.*

11.9.5 Security Selection

The portfolio manager, along with input from the trader, selects the instrument that offers the best expression of the investment theme and strategy.

Market valuations and whether the bond is rich or cheap compared to its intrinsic value are important considerations. The choice of security may be driven by relative price differences between peers and compared to other bonds on the yield curve. Instrument selection may take into account price differences between cash bonds and derivatives.

Certain tenors may express the theme more effectively than others. For instance, a trade leveraging changes in central bank policy might be better represented in the short end of the bond curve rather than the very long end. A credit-risk trade where the sovereign's debt service payments accelerate after seven years may be best illustrated in the short end of the curve, up to less than seven years.

The portfolio manager may want to trade specific features of the security, such as the coupon rate, guarantees, or call/put options. For example, suppose there are upcoming elections in a high-risk sovereign. In that case, the investor might prefer to be positioned in short-maturity instruments with high coupons that are delivered offshore, rather than in long-maturity cash bonds. Alternatively, if investing in a high-yield sovereign issuer, preference may be given to bonds guaranteed by the World Bank or to collateralized instruments.

Other factors to consider include liquidity and transaction costs, both when entering and exiting the trade. Here, the float and traded size of the securities are essential variables to look at. Additionally, investor positioning, crowded trades, and the concentration of holdings in specific securities should be taken into account.

Once securities are selected, the *scaling-in* strategy is determined. This frames whether the trader executes the position gradually at different price levels or trades the full position at once. Scaling into positions allows for better risk management and potentially better average pricing. It may include setting predetermined order sizes and prices to incrementally trade the position if the price moves in favor of the trade.

11.9.6 Stop-Loss and Position Monitoring

Predefining when the investor will close the trade (the stop/loss) and when they will take profits is good practice for disciplined investing. This is influenced by the investor's price expectations, the security's volatility, and the maximum loss or gain they are willing to accept for that portfolio position. In Figure 11.1 the sample trade order defines the stop/loss and the expected contribution to returns.

Behavioral research suggests that investors are often biased toward doubling down on poor trades because they are unwilling to accept losses. Additionally, there are several other biases that investors exhibit, which are discussed in the section below. Having broad parameters for the trade position offers some guardrails against these tendencies.

During the life of a trade, the portfolio manager monitors the position within the context of the portfolio's overall risk metrics. Particular attention is paid to whether the strategy is working as anticipated, and if so, why or why not. How the position behaves relative to others in the account and whether it is as expected is an additional consideration. All of this falls under the risk monitoring and continual assessment aspect of portfolio management, which is another integral part of investing.

11.10 BEHAVIORAL SCIENCE RESEARCH

Socrates reportedly said, "To know thyself is the beginning of wisdom." For investors, understanding their triggers and biases can provide valuable insights into how they make investment decisions, identify potential blind spots, and assess their comparative advantages in trading. In this section, we shift to behavioral science, which has identified several concepts that explain how bond traders often act.

Existing positions and returns may influence investment strategies. *Loss aversion* describes the observation that investors tend to be more sensitive to losses than to gains, resulting in risk-averse behavior. This can lead to more conservative strategies or the tendency to hold onto losing positions to avoid realizing the loss. Similarly, the *endowment effect* refers to the tendency of investors to overweight and overvalue existing trades compared to market opportunities, focusing on trading their portfolio rather than considering all options in the investable universe.

Market participants also influence investors. *Herd behavior* occurs when traders follow the actions of others instead of making independent decisions. This can result in momentum trades, asset bubbles, and an extended deviation of market prices from their fundamentals.

Anchoring happens when investors depend on outdated reference points to make their investment decisions, even when new information is available. These anchors can include the original purchase price or fundamental valuation, even if market conditions change and require an update.

How information is presented and framed can affect trading behavior. *The framing effect* occurs when traders are influenced by the way information is presented, creating a bias toward a specific outcome. *Recency bias* happens when recent information is prioritized over historical data or long-term trends. This can lead to an overreaction to short-term market changes.

The availability heuristic refers to investment decisions being influenced primarily by specific news flow, overshadowing other essential factors that may not be making headlines. *Confirmation bias* occurs when investors focus on information that corroborates their existing views and beliefs, reinforcing their choices while disregarding conflicting data until it is too late.

Overconfidence can lead to excessive risk-taking and larger positions than justified by fundamentals and market analysis. Additionally, there may be overtrading based on minor changes in data that confirm previous beliefs.

These behavioral biases can influence investors' actions and contribute to market inefficiencies. Understanding these biases can help avoid common pitfalls and enhance portfolio decision-making.

PRO TIP: *Understand your biases and put in place systems to compensate for them.*

11.11 SUMMARY

This chapter reviewed the main components of building a sovereign debt portfolio and the different approaches that are taken. It covered issues related to managing benchmarked portfolios and LDI strategies. The way active positions, which indicate where the investor deviates from the benchmark, are implemented in portfolios was addressed. It covered how portfolio managers develop investment strategies and considerations for sizing and scaling trade positions. We continue this topic in the next chapter, where we discuss various investment strategies used in sovereign bond portfolios.

NOTE

1. For further details see Fabozzi, *The Handbook of Fixed Income Securities*, and Fabozzi, *Introduction to Fixed-Income Analysis*.

REFERENCES

Fabozzi, Frank J., ed. *The Handbook of Fixed Income Securities*. 9th ed. New York: McGraw-Hill, 2021.

Fabozzi, Frank J., ed. *Introduction to Fixed-Income Analysis and Portfolio Management*. Cambridge, MA: The MIT Press, 2024.

CHAPTER TWELVE

Active Investment Strategies

PORTFOLIO MANAGEMENT is an iterative and ongoing process throughout the life of the portfolio. As market risk conditions change and portfolio managers' views evolve, various tools and strategies are used to alter portfolio positions. Portfolio management, from this perspective, is similar to Jenga,[1] where the goal is to start with a solid foundation and adjust positions safely, all while considering the many external risks and potential future actions by other players.

This chapter introduces the main investment strategies employed by active sovereign bond managers.[2] In contrast to passive approaches, active strategies necessitate continuous monitoring of the markets, adjustment of portfolio positions, thorough fundamental and technical analysis, and disciplined execution.

Key strategies include duration and yield curve positioning. These reflect views on interest rates and aim to exploit shifts in the shape of the yield curve. Credit spread strategies seek value in sovereign risk premia. Country selection reflects differentiated views on fiscal policy, debt sustainability, and political trajectories. Relative value trades take advantage of price differences between instrument pairs. Cash-CDS basis trades capitalize on disparities between bond and credit default swap markets.

Other essential approaches include sovereign backstop trades, which anticipate support from sovereign entities for quasi-sovereign or other organizations. New issue strategies capture pricing concessions in primary markets. Liquidity premium trades take advantage of differences in market depth or tradability between issuers or instruments. Managers may also include off-index exposures to improve diversification and alpha, while remaining mindful of scaling and mandate constraints.

These investment strategies enable skilled active managers to capitalize on the diverse opportunities that sovereign bond markets offer for generating excess returns while effectively managing portfolio risks.

12.1 DURATION STRATEGIES

The directional view on forward interest rates is crucial for generating returns for sovereign fixed-income portfolios. Simplistically, if interest rates are expected to fall relative to current pricing, then the portfolio should have a longer duration than the benchmark. Conversely, if interest rates are anticipated to rise relative to market pricing, the portfolio should have a shorter duration than the benchmark.

Let's consider an example of a $10 million sovereign bond portfolio with a portfolio and benchmark duration of seven years. Its holdings consist of Country A's Treasury bonds, which are standard coupon-bearing bonds. A duration of seven years indicates that the portfolio's value would change by approximately 7% or $700,000 (7% × $10 million) if interest rates were to change by 100 basis points.

Suppose the manager expects a decrease in interest rates by 100 basis points over the next month, which is not yet reflected in the market. In that case, they may extend the portfolio's duration to eight years, one year longer than the benchmark's. This implies that if rates fall by 100 basis points, the portfolio's value compared to the benchmark will increase by $100,000 ($800,000−$700,000), representing 1% of the portfolio's market value.

The extent to which the portfolio's duration target diverges from the benchmark depends on the manager's conviction, the tracking error budget, the portfolio guidelines, and the duration ranges set by the client. In the example above, adding one year of duration represents a significant change in risk position, considering the potential impact on alpha of approximately 100 basis points. In practice, portfolio managers may make smaller adjustments, such as modifying duration by 0.1 or 0.2 years compared to the benchmark.

A portfolio's duration can be adjusted by selling longer-duration bonds, swapping long-duration instruments for shorter-duration ones, or using interest rate derivatives (futures, forwards, and swaps) to reduce rate risk. When deciding the scaling of the position and the particular security to trade, the portfolio manager evaluates its contribution to the overall portfolio duration.

This contribution is determined by multiplying the issue's market value weight in the portfolio by the instrument's duration in years. It highlights which bonds or sectors are most sensitive to fluctuations in interest rates and compares their current positioning to that of the benchmark. The portfolio manager would also consider other aspects of the trade discussed in Chapter 11, including the contribution to alpha, tracking error, downside risks, liquidity, and exiting the position.

12.2 YIELD CURVE STRATEGIES

The portfolio duration metric assumes a parallel shift in the yield curve, implying that all maturities shift by the same amount for a given rate change. However, in practice, there can be non-parallel shifts in the yield curve. A flattening of the yield curve indicates that the spread between yields at the long and short ends of the curve has decreased. Conversely, a steepening of the yield curve signifies that the yield spread has increased.

Curve changes can be further classified. Bear flattening occurs when short-end yields rise, thereby compressing the yield spread, while bull flattening happens when long-end yields fall, which also compresses the yield spread. Bear steepening occurs when long-end yields rise, widening the yield spread, while bull steepening occurs when short-end yields fall, further widening the yield spread.

Other non-parallel shifts in the yield curve are referred to as *butterfly shifts*. A *positive butterfly* is when short-term and long-term yields are higher than intermediate maturity yields. A *negative butterfly* is the converse: when short-term and long-term yields are lower than intermediate maturity yields.

These non-parallel shifts in the yield curve indicate that the portfolio's duration positioning along the yield curve is as essential as the overall portfolio duration. *Yield curve duration* measures the portfolio's sensitivity to changes in the yield curve's slope. It evaluates the differences in yields at various points on the yield curve, typically focusing on the 2-, 10-, and 30-year points. The difference between the 10- and 2-year yields is known as the short-end spread, while the difference between the 30- and 10-year yields is referred to as the long-end spread.

Key rate duration measures a portfolio's sensitivity to changes in yield for a specific maturity, while holding all other yields constant. This can be calculated for each point on the yield curve, resulting in a range of durations for each maturity. For sovereign debt portfolios, key rate duration is typically assessed for the 3-month, 1-year, 2-year, 3-year, 5-year, 7-year, 10-year, 15-year, 20-year, 25-year, and 30-year rates. These measures can be adjusted based on the maturity and liquidity of the bond curve in any given country.

There are three common yield curve strategies to align investments with interest rate and yield curve views. *Bullet* strategies direct portfolio holdings to a specific point on the yield curve, such as the 30- or 10-year maturity points. The expectation is that this particular point on the yield curve will experience the greatest repricing, all else equal. *Barbell* strategies concentrate holdings in two extreme parts of the yield curve, like the 5- and 30-year points. *Ladder* strategies maintain equal exposure across all maturities along the yield curve. Managers' views on yield curve movements compared with the current market positioning are crucial determinants of which strategy they select to optimize portfolio returns.

12.3 CREDIT SPREAD STRATEGIES

The credit spread measures the additional risk an investor assumes when investing in a sovereign bond instead of US Treasuries or German Bunds. A wider credit spread indicates that investors perceive a higher risk of default and thus require higher yields as compensation. Conversely, a narrower credit spread suggests a lower risk of default, resulting in lower yields being required.

The credit spread is especially important for sovereign debt portfolios that benchmark to indices from a selection of countries. Each country presents different credit risks, and the portfolio manager must decide which countries will improve, deteriorate, or remain unchanged. The credit spread of the index is calculated as a weighted average of the credit spreads of the individual securities. Spreads for sub-groups classified by region, rating, maturity, or other criteria can be similarly determined.

Credit spread strategies involve assessing whether credit spreads for a country, region, or sub-group are likely to rise or fall compared to market pricing. Suppose an investor holds a negative outlook on a country's credit due to worsening fiscal and debt conditions. In that case, they may anticipate its credit spread widening, resulting in increased yields and lower prices on sovereign debt. To reflect this in their portfolio, they might reduce exposure to the country by selling bonds or buying CDS protection, which lowers the credit risk associated with that entity.

Now, suppose the portfolio manager believes that market risk sentiment is turning negative. In this situation, they may decide to reduce the overall credit spread exposure of the account relative to the benchmark to decrease risk. To align the portfolio with this perspective, they may decrease exposures for all issuers in the portfolio to be underweight compared to the index. A more efficient approach involving fewer trades would be to reduce specific holdings that may do poorly in this environment. For instance, high-yield issuers relative to investment-grade names. Alternatively, they may underweight the index's credit spread through the CDX Index (buying protection to mitigate risk) or by purchasing protection in single-name sovereign CDS.

The portfolio can also be adjusted to reflect broad thematic views on credit sectors. For example, suppose a rise in oil prices is expected. In that case, the portfolio can be positioned to go long on oil beta by overweighting issuers with a higher credit spread sensitivity to oil prices. Multifactor models can fine-tune this analysis by considering correlations with other positions to scale the position appropriately.

Similarly, if an investor anticipates a rise in regional credit spreads, perhaps due to a regional slowdown, they can adjust the portfolio to underweight issuers from that region. For instance, during the Eurozone sovereign debt crisis, some investors reduced their exposure to the high-debt economies in the periphery (Portugal, Italy, Greece, and Spain) while increasing their holdings in the core economies of Germany and France.

These building blocks for credit spread strategies can be fine-tuned with cell-based and multifactor portfolio construction tools to ensure the portfolio manager has the specific type and scale of credit risk they seek in the account.

PRO TIP: *Set up systems to monitor potential investment strategies (duration, yield curve, spread) in the portfolio and flag entry and exit points.*

12.4 COUNTRY SELECTION TRADES

One application of the credit spread strategy is country selection, effectively overweighting or underweighting sovereigns with improving or deteriorating metrics. Fundamental sovereign credit analysis helps identify countries where market credit spreads are misaligned with the fundamental drivers of credit and, in turn, with credit spreads.

For example, there may be differences between the in-house sovereign credit rating and those from credit rating agencies or the market-implied credit rating. This serves as the basis for adjusting the portfolio position against the benchmark. Investors consider these inputs, evaluate which risks are not priced into the markets, and determine whether to go long or short on the issuer.

An essential consideration in country selection is employing cell-based and multifactor approaches to monitor the impact of specific positions on overall portfolio risk metrics. This ensures that each exposure is not regarded in isolation but represents the best expression of both idiosyncratic, country-specific factors and the broader investment strategies of the portfolio as a whole.

For example, if an investor is optimistic about Mexico's credit trajectory. In that case, they should also be aware that adding Mexican exposures may increase the portfolio's overall interest duration since Mexican bonds generally have a higher duration than similarly rated bonds from lower-rated emerging markets. Additionally, this may heighten the portfolio's sensitivity to US growth since the Mexican economy relies heavily on US trade and tourism flows.

The scaling of the Mexican position and the security choice must incorporate these factors. Portfolio construction and risk management tools provide valuable inputs for this exercise, especially for assessing the position's impact on the portfolio's forecasted tracking error and alpha.

Another consideration when investing based on country drivers is determining which asset class best represents the investment theme and the risks the investor seeks to capture. Figure 8.1, which shows the risks in different sovereign bonds, is a helpful starting point. The best expression of the Mexico trade could be the Mexico USD sovereign bond market, the local sovereign bond market, the Mexican corporate bond market, the currency (i.e., the Mexican peso), or the local equity market.

Investors select the optimal exposure across these asset classes based on portfolio guidelines and by estimating the expected risk-adjusted return over a specified period for each sector. For instance, suppose a credit rating upgrade is anticipated. The investor may add hard currency exposure through USD sovereign bonds, as the spread impact will likely be most significant in that market. If similar credit rating upgrades are expected for SOEs and corporates, the investor may increase exposure to SOEs like Pemex instead of the sovereign.

However, if a structural decline in inflation is expected, followed by a structural decline in interest rates, the portfolio manager may consider going long on local sovereign bonds. Suppose a trade agreement between the US and Mexico is anticipated, and the Mexican peso has depreciated (or is fundamentally *cheap*) ahead of the negotiations. In that case, the best expression of the trade may be to go long on the currency.

By using this approach, portfolio managers can choose the investment strategy that maximizes risk-adjusted returns given their investment view.

12.5 RELATIVE VALUE STRATEGIES

Fixed-income markets are not always fully efficient. Prices can deviate from equilibrium levels for extended periods due to various factors. These include temporary influences like short-term supply and demand imbalances, liquidity drivers, and other market technicals. Announcements, rumors, and other news can also affect pricing and flow dynamics, creating opportunities for investors.

Relative value strategies exploit price inefficiencies between bonds from the same issuer or between issuers with similar characteristics. They emphasize the differences in spreads or *basis* between instruments instead of their fundamental valuation. The underlying assumption is that the market will eventually return to an expected *normal* spread basis. Due to this, relative value trades should have a timeline in mind for calibration. Investors should also be aware of any structural factors that may reset the historical relationships upon which the trade relies.

In *intra-market* trades, investors identify mispriced bonds from the same issuer relative to its yield curve. The corresponding investment position should benefit from an eventual movement toward the curve. For example, if there is a large seller of the seven-year Peru sovereign bond, it may trade with a wider spread compared to the remainder of the Peru sovereign curve. The driver of the spread differential is not fundamentally based but results from demand and supply imbalances. As the market absorbs the sales, the spread should eventually tighten to align more fairly with the curve.

In *inter-market* trades, investors compare bond spreads from similar issuers to identify deviations from historical trends. For example, they may trade country pairs with comparable credit ratings or spread drivers, such as investment-grade sovereigns like Chile and Peru, or Asian issuers like Indonesia and the Philippines, or frontier countries like Sri Lanka and Pakistan. These trades may exploit technical mispricing or anticipate fundamental changes in credit rates due to improving or deteriorating market dynamics.

Traders and brokers use several *rich/cheap* metrics to monitor relative value trades. These metrics utilize historical data to track deviations in spread, basis, and curve relationships to identify these trades. Figure 12.1 illustrates some standard relative value charts that are used in rich/cheap monitors.

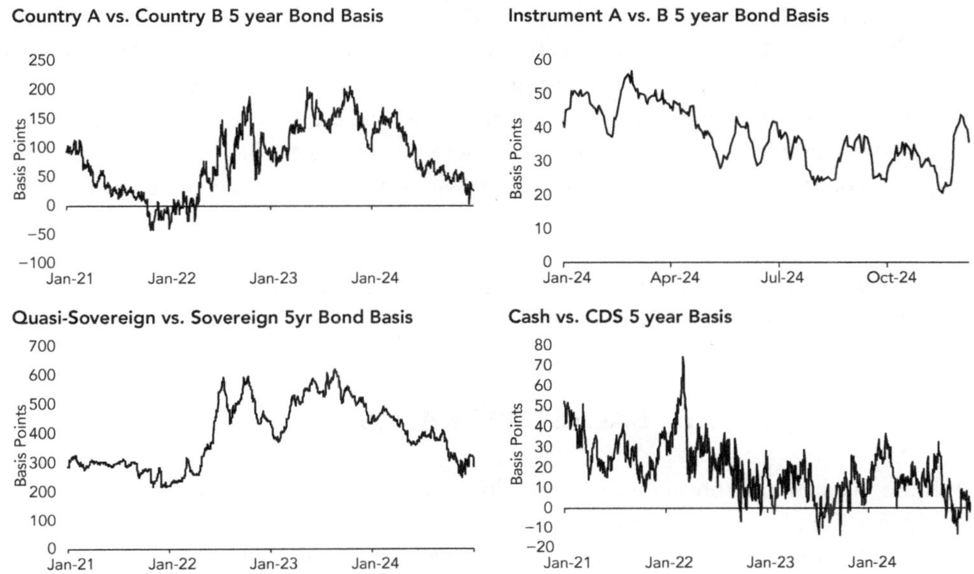

FIGURE 12.1 Relative value trades. Source: Bloomberg Finance L.P.

12.6 CASH-CDS BASIS TRADES

The cash-CDS basis refers to the difference in spread between a sovereign cash bond and the corresponding matched-maturity credit default swap (CDS). A positive cash-CDS basis indicates that the bond's spread is wider (price lower and yield higher) than the corresponding sovereign CDS. This suggests that the cash bond is *cheaper* than the CDS for acquiring the same credit risk exposure. Conversely, a negative cash-CDS basis means the bond's spread is tighter than the CDS, making obtaining the same credit exposure more expensive.

The cash-CDS basis can vary based on the dynamics of supply and demand, liquidity, market technicals, and investor perceptions of sovereign risk. In some instances, the basis may be a structural feature of the market, for example, when there are significant cash buyers of the issuer, such as sovereign wealth funds or retail investors. Additionally, the basis can fluctuate due to temporary factors such as new issues, tenders, or buybacks.

Sovereign debt investors can take advantage of dislocations in the cash-CDS basis by employing a cash-and-carry strategy, also called basis trading. In these strategies, if the basis is positive, the portfolio purchases the cash bond (long credit) and buys protection on CDS (short credit), assuming the spread will remain constant or narrow. If the basis is negative, the portfolio sells the cash bond (underweight credit) and sells protection on CDS (long credit) because the spread will likely widen.

Another use for the cash-CDS basis is in decisions on whether to increase exposures through cash or CDS. If the basis is positive, the portfolio manager might add cash bonds; if negative, they may add CDS and US Treasuries to replicate the cash bond risk exposures.

Key considerations in cash-CDS basis trades include the size, depth, and liquidity of the cash and derivatives markets, the potential for sharp price adjustments in both markets, and whether ad hoc factors such as new issues or tenders could quickly reprice the cash bond curve.

PRO TIP: *Set up systems to monitor relative value, cash-CDS, and quasi-sovereign basis trades that flag potential trade opportunities.*

12.7 SOVEREIGN BACKSTOP TRADES

Sovereign backstop or moral hazard trades look to take exposure in issues or issuers with the expectation of sovereign support. These positions typically benefit from an additional spread pick-up compared to investing in the sovereign bond, helping to offset liquidity (and potentially other risk) differences.

Sovereigns are often the lender of the last resort for issuers in their domain, effectively offering a backstop to those credits. The nature of the backstop and whether the sovereign guarantee is explicit or implicit is critical for assessing the additional risks associated with these backstop trade strategies.

Explicit guarantees are those encoded in bond contracts and recorded in government letters of guarantee, circulars, and legislation. As such, they can be legally enforceable in a court of law. They include sovereign guarantees for bonds of quasi-sovereigns, strategic corporates, and states and local governments. For example, the government of South Africa has explicitly guaranteed select bonds issued by its state-owned electricity supplier, Eskom.

Implicit guarantees include government financial support not explicitly listed in bond contracts or government documents. They may result from historic support from the sovereign or because the entity is systemically important, leading to expectations of a bailout if needed.

For instance, some investors believe that the government of Mexico implicitly guarantees bonds from its state-owned energy company, Petróleos Mexicanos (Pemex), given the government's historical support for the entity. As a result, Pemex cash bond spreads have historically traded close to the sovereign curve relative to its stand-alone credit rating.

Sovereign debt portfolios may take exposure to sovereign backstop trades as proxies for the sovereign. Even bonds with explicit sovereign guarantees, akin to sovereign credit risk exposure, trade with a basis to the sovereign curve. In other words, they trade at wider spreads to the underlying sovereign bond curve, leading to a pick-up in spread. This may be due to liquidity differences, the legal distinction between the issuer and the guarantor giving rise to potential delays in payment, or market technicals related to the issuer.

These securities, therefore, offer a vehicle to pick up spread for similar credit default risk in exchange for some of the other risks listed above.

Closely related are trades in issuers with implicit sovereign guarantees. It is essential to keep in mind that these do not have the same credit risk as the sovereign. Investors should make their own assessment of the extent of the sovereign backstop there is likely to be and scale exposures accordingly. As such, implicit guarantee trades are very case-specific, with room for differences in views between investors.

A common implicit guarantee trade is taking exposure to systemically important quasi-sovereigns (state-owned enterprises) instead of exposure to the sovereign. The investor goes long the quasi-sovereign security and underweight (or short) the sovereign exposure, effectively trading the quasi-sovereign basis. The view is either that the basis will remain constant and offer carry versus holding the sovereign position, and/or the basis will narrow, driving positive total returns for the portfolio.

Everything else being equal, a shift in the historical quasi-sovereign spread basis provides the opportunity for a relative value quasi-sovereign trade, as transitory changes should eventually correct. Other considerations include market liquidity, volatility, and credit quality differences between entities.

12.8 NEW ISSUES

When an issuer comes to the primary market to sell bonds, they typically price bonds slightly cheaper than the existing bond curve. This *new issue premium (NIP)* is paid to encourage investors to participate in the deal and ensure the issuer can raise the full amount they want to issue. The NIP also compensates existing holders for declines in the price of existing securities due to additional market supply.

NIPs for sovereign bonds can range from as little as +1 bps for the large developed markets to 50–100 bps for emerging and high-yield markets. They depend on market conditions and investor demand as measured by the bid-to-cover ratio.

Investors can harvest the NIP by adding exposure through new issues rather than purchasing bonds on the secondary market. Some investors trade the NIP by placing outsized orders for new issues and quickly flipping the purchase. Generally, flip trades are considered poor form, particularly in oversubscribed deals (i.e., where the bid-to-cover and demand are high), but they still occur.

It is essential to remember that not all new issues perform in the secondary markets post-deal. This may be due to the tight deal pricing, oversupply of bonds, a poorly managed deal, or if market conditions turn negative. The implication for portfolio managers is that harvesting the NIP is not a home run strategy for generating alpha. Instead, new issue orders should be placed considering credit fundamentals, portfolio objectives, and targets.

PRO TIP: *Maintain a database of new issues by issuer and track their pricing in secondary markets versus the issuance size, initial price offer, and bid-to-cover ratio. This provides useful information when the issuer comes to market next.*

12.9 HARVESTING LIQUIDITY PREMIUM

Some securities from the same issuer may trade at a lower price than their peers due to their lower liquidity. This illiquidity concession may hold even after adjusting for bond characteristics like coupon, maturity, and callability. It may be due to the security's structure, e.g., loans versus bonds, traceability (e.g., seasoned versus non-seasoned bonds), or the issuance market (private or publicly issued).

Investors may invest in these instruments to pick up additional spread while maintaining credit and other risk factors similar to those from more liquid exposures. In doing so, it is good practice to consider the share of illiquid exposures in the portfolio and view the investment as a buy-to-hold position. Thinking about the natural exit from the trade is also helpful in avoiding being trapped in unsaleable positions.

These considerations point to short-term exposures that naturally term out, instruments with put options, and adding exposures in securities from core benchmark constituents. The best practice is to ensure that total illiquid exposures are a small share of the overall exposure by the issuer and the portfolio.

On the other end of the spectrum, it also pays to be in liquid exposures when the opportunity presents itself. Bonds that are frequently repurchased or have a small tradeable float tend to have higher transaction costs and are harder to trade. When possible, tendering those bonds in exchange for more liquid on-the-run instruments or cash is often the best strategy for the portfolio. Similarly, rolling CDS and CDX positions into the on-the-run instrument is usually the best course of action from a tradability and transaction cost perspective.

12.10 ISSUES IN OTHER CURRENCIES

Sovereign debt is often issued in several currencies, including the US dollar, the euro, the pound sterling, and the Japanese yen. Investors can compare the currency-hedged yields for bonds from the same issuer and assess whether there is a pickup in spread for taking a position in a different currency. From time to time, this pickup remains even after considering differential liquidity, transaction costs, and market depth, which offers a scope for generating additional returns from the same sovereign issuer.

12.11 OFF-INDEX EXPOSURES

If their portfolio guidelines allow, investors may add exposure to securities not in their benchmark or asset class. These exposures may offer excess returns relative to the benchmark but have a higher tracking error. Moreover, any significant losses may be hard to explain to clients.

Off-benchmark exposures can be of different types. The first includes sovereign issuers that are in the investible universe but do not meet the benchmark criteria. These may not be included in the benchmark due to size, liquidity, or structure. Examples include explicitly guaranteed sovereign bonds or bonds issued with a smaller-than-benchmark size.

Countries may not meet the benchmark criteria for inclusion. For example, Singapore and South Korea are not part of most emerging market indices due to their high income levels but trade similarly to other emerging market instruments. Derivatives of benchmark entities are also off-benchmark exposures, as most indices include only cash exposures.

Another group of off-benchmark trades involves issuers from the same country, region, and jurisdiction but from a different part of the capital structure. Examples include state and provincial debt, select quasi-sovereign bonds, or corporate issuers domiciled in the same country. Sometimes, the sovereign may explicitly guarantee the bond issue or implicitly backstop the entity for strategic or systemic reasons. These bond issues may price off the sovereign curve and trade with a spread to the sovereign. The returns may also have a high correlation with that of the sovereign but may also be driven by other idiosyncratic factors.

A third category of off-benchmark investments is those in a different currency or legal denomination. Sovereign debt investors can add exposure through USD sovereign bonds, local currency sovereign bonds, or the local currency. Depending on the portfolio index, these exposures may be off-benchmark exposures. While they may correlate highly with the underlying benchmark, there will be a higher tracking error than taking positions in the benchmarked exposure.

Finally, investors may invest in trades in sectors other than the benchmark. The underlying principle is that these trades have positive expected absolute returns. Examples include exposures to high-yield corporate bonds, municipalities, or commodities.

Off-benchmark trades increase tracking error. Consequently, portfolio managers need high conviction and should scale positions appropriately to limit downside risks for the portfolio. They should also have a solid explanation of why the position is in the portfolio and why there are no other suitable benchmarked alternatives.

This is particularly important for trades in different asset classes from the investible universe of the portfolio. Failed trades and losses are especially difficult to explain if the manager has gone off-piste. On the flip side, gains may also be challenging to champion if the client has inadvertently duplicated the exposure through other parts of their asset allocation. For example, if a sovereign debt manager invests in US high-yield debt, when the client also has a separate mandate for US high-yield debt.

12.12 SUMMARY

This chapter explored the exciting world of taking active positions in sovereign debt portfolios. How portfolio managers implement their views and the various strategies they employ are essential for generating excess returns and effectively managing risk.

Active investment strategies rely on a solid portfolio foundation and careful, incremental changes as market conditions evolve. Practical strategies include duration and yield curve positioning, credit spread strategies, country selection, relative value trades, and cash-CDS basis trades. Additional methods include sovereign backstop trades, new issue strategies, liquidity premium trades, and selective off-index exposures. Together, these enable skilled managers to capture opportunities for excess returns while maintaining effective risk control.

Another important aspect of portfolio management involves a set of routine yet vital tasks needed to maintain portfolios. This is what we turn to next.

NOTES

1. Jenga is a game where players take turns removing wooden blocks from a tower and stacking them on top, trying to avoid making the tower fall. The game is named after the Swahili word "kujenga," meaning "to build."
2. See CFA Institute, *CFA Program Curriculum*.

REFERENCES

CFA Institute. *CFA Program Curriculum Level I, II & III*. 2024. CFA Institute and Wiley.

Fabozzi, Frank J., ed. *The Handbook of Fixed Income Securities*. 9th ed. New York: McGraw-Hill, 2021.

Fabozzi, Frank J., ed. *Introduction to Fixed-Income Analysis and Portfolio Management*. Cambridge, MA: The MIT Press, 2024.

CHAPTER THIRTEEN

Portfolio Maintenance, Risk Management, and Performance Attribution

PORTFOLIO MANAGEMENT encompasses more than taking risks and making investment decisions. It includes a series of daily maintenance tasks essential for the efficient and smooth operation of the account. Rebalancing ensures that there is no unintended drift in portfolio positions due to price movements or changes to the account's AUM. Monitoring cash levels and liquidity ensures that anticipated flows in and out of the account can be managed correctly. Rolling FX hedges, CDS, options, and derivative positions help maintain the targeted risk in the portfolio.

Risk management, monitoring investment positions, and adherence to compliance are other critical elements. At the portfolio level, this involves tracking risk metrics against portfolio guidelines and the portfolio manager's risk targets. There may also be risk targets set at the firm level that need to be followed. Scenario analysis helps forecast portfolio returns under various conditions and guides whether there is too much or too little risk, and where. At all times, the portfolio must follow compliance guidelines, and any issues that are close to being breached should be flagged.

This chapter reviews portfolio maintenance tasks and risk management tools used in sovereign debt portfolios. It also examines portfolio performance evaluation and attribution frameworks. These help assess whether the account is performing as expected and whether the assumed risk profile is appropriately reflected in performance outcomes. They also help monitor whether portfolio managers are meeting their alpha and tracking error objectives relative to the client's mandate and compared to their industry peers.

13.1 PORTFOLIO MAINTENANCE

Regular portfolio maintenance is essential for maintaining the integrity of the portfolio's strategic positioning. We begin by examining key portfolio maintenance practices, including rebalancing, which involves adjusting positions that may have unintentionally drifted from their targets due to price or index weight changes. Next, we discuss cash and liquidity management, which ensures the portfolio can meet redemptions, fund new investments, or navigate periods of market stress. The section concludes with a discussion of rolling FX hedges, CDS, and other derivative exposures that the portfolio may hold.

13.1.1 Rebalancing Positions

Portfolios should be monitored periodically and *rebalanced* to align with the investor's original targets. Positions may deviate from targets due to account inflows and outflows, changes in security prices, adjustments in index weights, or shifts in instrument liquidity.

Rebalancing can occur over any period, with month-end rebalancing of indices serving as a pivot point. Often, an investor may choose not to rebalance a position due to trade size or because they prefer to let the trade run longer. This decision should be made actively by the portfolio manager, as position drift over time can lead to significant changes in risk profiles and investment strategies.

13.1.2 Cash Management

Cash includes highly liquid assets with very short maturities of 90 days or less, such as money market instruments, bank deposits, and short-term government securities like Treasury bills. The Securities and Exchange Commission's (SEC) definition of cash is broader. *Cash and cash equivalents* are defined as securities that can be easily converted into known amounts of cash with minimal risk of a change in value.

Portfolio guidelines often specify minimum and maximum limits for cash and cash-like instruments that can be efficiently utilized for outflows or trades. Within these boundaries, the percentage of cash a portfolio manager targets depends on their risk appetite, investment time horizon, and the extent to which the portfolio is *fully funded* or invested. A high risk appetite may justify maintaining lower cash balances as the investor increases risk positions in the portfolio. Conversely, a pessimistic outlook on the markets or cash flows might require higher cash balances to mitigate risk and prepare the portfolio for outflows.

Managers may increase their holdings of cash and cash-like instruments in anticipation of client withdrawals. Such withdrawals are often communicated in advance if they are substantial or included in a mutual fund's daily flows if they are smaller. Portfolio managers may accumulate cash ahead of potential market uncertainty or to capitalize on possible price dislocations—referred to as having *dry powder* in the portfolio. Additionally, cash may be raised in preparation for new bond issues or private transactions.

Daily reports displaying estimated cash flows over the next 5, 7, and 10 business days help monitor cash positions across portfolios. This assists in planning how much cash needs to be raised, invested, or put to work in the portfolio.[1]

13.1.3 Liquidity Management

A portfolio's liquidity indicates how easily and cost-effectively positions can be sold. This is particularly important for mutual funds with liquidity rules that allow daily withdrawals.

The SEC classifies highly liquid assets as those that can be converted into cash in less than three business days. Moderately liquid assets can be converted into cash in three to seven calendar days. Less liquid assets can be sold within seven calendar days. Illiquid assets require more than seven calendar days to be sold.[2]

These classifications can be used to categorize a portfolio's holdings to assess the overall liquidity of the investments. The SEC limits illiquid holdings in a mutual fund to a cap of 15% of the net asset value, though investors may choose to remain well below this limit. Additionally, investors may opt to pursue barbell strategies with liquidity buckets—allocating a significant portion to the illiquid bucket to earn a high rate of return, balanced against a considerable allocation to the cash bucket for potential withdrawals.

Daily liquidity and cash monitoring reports calculate anticipated cash needs for portfolios on a rolling basis. Together, these enable managers to ensure that the portfolio's overall liquidity is sufficient and appropriate for any potential withdrawals. Expected cash flows should take into account the timing of daily trade settlements to facilitate an accurate estimate of future cash and liquidity needs.

13.1.4 Rolling FX and Derivative Positions

Sovereign bond portfolios often include FX and derivative exposures implemented via short-dated contracts. Maintaining and rolling these positions is a key aspect of portfolio management. This ensures that risk exposures remain aligned with the portfolio strategy and that derivative instruments function as intended.

Portfolios may have FX risk from strategic positions or by holding bonds denominated in currencies other than the investor's base currency. The portfolio manager may opt to maintain direct FX exposures or hedge them using forward contracts, currency swaps, and non-deliverable forwards (NDFs).

Rolling these FX exposures is crucial, particularly in portfolios that use short-dated instruments such as monthly or quarterly forwards. The roll entails closing expiring contracts and entering new ones with longer maturities. This process may result in roll costs or gains, depending on the forward curve and the spot-futures basis.

Similarly, other derivative exposures, such as CDS or CDX indices, require ongoing maintenance to ensure their effectiveness. CDS and CDX contracts, which typically have five-year tenors, are periodically rolled into new on-the-run contracts to maintain duration and basis alignment with the underlying bond exposure. Any shorter-dated CDS exposures, like three-month, six-month, or one-year exposures, should be regularly reviewed and rolled if they align with credit and risk views.

Successfully managing these exposures requires coordination among portfolio management, risk, and operations teams. Accurate measurement of exposures, effective counterparty management, and compliance with regulations and collateral rules are crucial.

Misalignment in hedge timing or sizing can introduce unintended risks, while missed rolls can leave the portfolio risk positions vulnerable. Effective hedge maintenance not only maintains intended risk exposures but also contributes to smoother performance. This reduces tracking error and enhances risk management—particularly in volatile or stressed market conditions.

PRO TIP: *Ensure you have daily reports for cash, liquidity, rebalancing, rolling derivatives and FX hedges, risk targets, and compliance management.*

13.2 ESSENTIALS IN THE PORTFOLIO TOOLKIT

Portfolio managers rely on a set of essential tools to fine-tune exposures, enhance returns, and manage risk more effectively. This section explores three core components of the sovereign bond investor's toolkit: managing cash positions, using leverage, and employing derivatives. Each of these tools serves a different purpose—whether improving portfolio efficiency, expressing tactical views, or optimizing capital usage—but all require careful governance, monitoring, and alignment with portfolio mandates.

13.2.1 Making the Most of Cash

Cash and liquidity management involves more than just meeting the portfolio's minimum cash and liquidity requirements. In sovereign debt portfolios, investors can structure short-term investments to yield additional returns above money market rates with low volatility while remaining invested in relatively liquid and safe instruments.

As a reminder, cash or cash-equivalent instruments are AAA-rated sovereign instruments with a maturity of 90 days or less. One way to enhance returns is to shift into similarly rated instruments with comparable maturities in foreign currencies. Therefore, if the portfolio is a US dollar–denominated fund, the investor may consider GBP-denominated or EUR-denominated AAA-rated money market instruments to capture excess returns if currency-hedged returns are higher.

The hedging mitigates currency risk and ensures that the currency exposure of portfolio returns remains in the home currency. For example, a Japanese one-month Treasury Bill hedged back into US dollars may offer an additional advantage compared to a one-month US Treasury Bill with relatively lower additional risk.[3] These opportunities evolve over time and in response to global market conditions. Therefore, monitoring hedged money market rates in AAA-rated sovereigns facilitates enhanced returns on cash invested in the funds' denominated currency.

Another way to enhance returns from cash is to invest in longer-maturity instruments. Extending maturity typically results in higher term premiums in upward-sloping yield curves. This additional yield is generally associated with similar credit risk for AAA-rated issuers and for short-term maturities.

This strategy allocates a portion of the portfolio to AAA sovereign assets with maturities greater than 90 days and less than 1 year. The exact maturity extension depends on the portfolio manager's risk appetite, investment strategy, and the relative liquidity of the instruments. Roll-down, carry, and the liquidity of various points on the yield curve can help the investor determine which maturities to focus on.

Diversifying into other AAA or high-quality instruments can further enhance returns while introducing some additional credit and liquidity risk. This may involve incorporating commercial paper or short-dated corporate paper from highly rated issuers. Assessing the liquidity of these instruments, along with conducting a credit analysis of the issuer, is typically part of this strategy.

Combining the strategies mentioned above can enhance returns from cash and cash equivalents while posing a limited increase in credit or liquidity risk. Therefore, these strategies serve as valuable tools for investors to supplement risk-adjusted returns.

13.2.2 Using Leverage

Leverage refers to using borrowed funds to invest in securities, leading to a higher market value than what can be achieved with cash alone. Essentially, the investor believes they can generate a higher return than the cost of borrowing the funds, thus enhancing the portfolio's excess returns. Leverage can be created through derivatives such as interest rate and credit swap agreements (see below), as well as collateralized arrangements like repurchase agreements.

A repo or repurchase agreement involves the sale of a bond with a commitment to buy it back at a specified date and price. In return, the seller receives collateral as security, typically in the form of high-quality, cash-like instruments, along with interest on the loan, determined by the repo rate. The collateral can be used to purchase additional securities, leverage the portfolio, and generate excess returns. Another advantage of repurchase agreements is that, with short-term repos, the portfolio can quickly access cash by buying the bond back from the borrower, facilitating better cash balance management.

Repos should be carefully structured to account for counterparty and credit risk. They should be executed with trusted counterparties, especially if the collateral is not delivered out. Collateral should be marked to market regularly, ensuring that price changes require posting additional funds. The seller may also aim to have a buffer against declines in the collateral's price by using a repo margin, which is the collateral's value minus the loan's value. This margin typically ranges from 1% to 3% but can be higher for riskier instruments.

Portfolio guidelines dictate the extent and conditions under which leverage is permitted in a given fund and are closely monitored due to the heightened risks involved. Specifically, leverage can amplify the sensitivity of the portfolio's returns to changes in duration and credit risk, among other effects. These are crucial for the portfolio manager to understand when using risk management and portfolio optimization tools. Consequently, the choice to use leverage in a portfolio relies on the investor's risk tolerance, their market perspective, and the comparative returns of a cash-only strategy versus one that employs varying levels of leverage.

13.2.3 The Use of Derivatives

Financial derivatives are invaluable tools for managing a range of risks in fixed-income portfolios. They allow portfolio managers to leverage a portfolio if desired, enabling them to make directional bets on the prices of the underlying securities.

The range of financial derivatives is diverse and includes instruments such as interest rate futures and swaps for managing duration, credit default swaps for managing credit risk, and FX derivatives for managing currency risk (see Chapter 3). As such, they can serve as a valuable tool for managing risk and creating leverage in sovereign debt portfolios, provided client guidelines allow their use.

The advantage of managing risk with derivatives compared to the underlying cash position arises from lower transaction costs in the derivatives market compared to the physical market. Cash bonds typically have larger bid-ask spreads and lower liquidity in the secondary markets than derivatives.

Derivatives enable investors who cannot obtain allocations from bond issuers in the primary market to replicate risk and achieve similar exposures in their portfolios. Since the AUM of benchmark holdings is lower than the AUM they are benchmarked against, derivatives play an integral role in managing risk in fixed-income portfolios. Furthermore, they can be customized to address the specific risks that investors wish to manage, such as reducing duration at the seven-year point on the curve or adjusting the key rate duration of a portfolio to align with their views on duration and convexity.

In some cases, selling the underlying cash position has tax implications that financial derivatives do not face, and it often disrupts other risk factors within the portfolio. For example, if a sovereign portfolio manager wanted to reduce South Africa's interest rate duration in a portfolio, selling a South African bond would impact both the duration and credit spread of the portfolio. This contrasts with using an interest rate swap to decrease duration while keeping the credit spread of the position and portfolio unchanged.

In sovereign debt portfolios, credit default swaps (CDS) can be utilized to manage credit risk in several ways. First, single-name CDS can be bought or sold to adjust credit exposure to a specific name. In the example above, if the portfolio manager wanted to keep the portfolio's duration constant but aimed to reduce the credit spread risk associated with South Africa, they could purchase CDS protection on South Africa without selling the underlying bond. They can then add US Treasury exposure to enhance the portfolio's duration.

Single-name CDS can also be structured so that contract terms and maturity align with the investor's credit views. For example, if there is an election in four years where credit risk may increase, the investor may seek to sell protection in standardized CDS contracts for up to four years or shorter. This is not always feasible with cash bonds, as the required maturities may not have been issued.

Relatedly, CDS contracts can also be customized for specific dates to mitigate the risks associated with credit events, such as elections or significant upcoming payments. These non-standard contracts are advantageous when an issuer may be approaching default or is encountering a significant policy shift that investors want to safeguard against.

Sovereign CDX indices can be a vehicle to short or go long the benchmark, representing either a structural or temporary position. For instance, the CDX EM series includes large, liquid emerging market sovereign issuers. The portfolio manager may use CDX to leverage or short the portfolio if they maintain a structurally positive or negative outlook on the EM asset class or credit risk more broadly. Other CDX indices, such as the CDX IG and CDX HY series, can be employed in a similar manner.

Derivatives can also quickly increase or decrease risk without the need for numerous trades and incurring high transaction costs. For instance, if there is a significant inflow, the portfolio manager can temporarily add risk exposures through derivatives while traders purchase cash exposures, which may take time to execute. Alternatively, if there is negative market news, derivatives can be employed to reduce risk while traders attempt to execute cash trades.

It should be noted that some sovereign debt portfolios, particularly those following a conservative investment strategy, may not allow leverage and derivatives, or may have specific rules and constraints on their use. Client guidelines and portfolio constraints should always be consulted before using these strategies.

13.3 RISK MANAGEMENT

Risk monitoring is an ongoing responsibility and a critical element of portfolio management. Its goals include mitigating portfolio losses while maximizing returns, identifying positions that are misaligned with portfolio constraints and investor-defined targets, and flagging outsized risks that may disproportionately impact returns.

Daily review of portfolio risk positions ensures trade orders are executed and accurately reflected in the portfolio. Monitoring alpha and tracking error enables investors to assess whether the portfolio's performance aligns with expectations based on risk strategies and market movements.

Examining daily performance enables investors to determine whether the risk *they perceive matche*s what is reflected in the portfolio. This alignment may differ if the correlation between assets changes or if there are shifts in the sensitivity of asset prices. The result may be a discrepancy between the ex ante risk and the realized or ex post risk in the portfolio. Monitoring risk positions, market movements, and the behavior of portfolio and benchmark returns helps to understand these changes and take corrective actions.

Risk reports include summary statistics to monitor the overall portfolio. Specific items include the percentage of cash, liquidity by bucket, issuer concentration limits, leverage ratios, exposure across ratings buckets, and the share of defaulted securities. The indicators can be tailored to client constraints, investor-selected parameters, and internal firm-wide limits. Together, they assist the portfolio manager in ensuring that their portfolio adheres to the required client guidelines and establishes guardrails for internal firm risk management.

Another component of risk assessment is scenario analysis, which examines how the portfolio behaves under various states of the world. Common scenarios include modeling the impact of large changes in interest rates, a sell-off or rally in the equity markets, significant swings in commodity prices, and major shifts in global growth. These scenarios help identify potential risk exposures that could be mitigated based on the likelihood of different states of the world. Portfolio managers can use this information to reduce those risk exposures or hedge the portfolio's returns in tail scenarios.

For sovereign debt portfolios, credit risk monitoring can be integrated with portfolio positions and risk reports. Issuer concentration limits can be established for high-risk credits or by rating categories. Credit analysis can notify portfolio and risk teams if they anticipate a downgrade to high-yield or an upgrade to investment grade. These adjustments can be proactively incorporated into risk targets, and positions can be modified, ideally before any changes in market pricing.

Macroeconomic forecasts can be integrated, and scenario analysis can be customized accordingly. For example, if economists expect a high likelihood of stagflation, the risk scenarios can be modified to assess how the portfolio would perform in that context. Alternately, if there is an expectation of a region-specific shock or macroeconomic development, they can also be examined in a separate scenario.

In these ways, risk management helps ensure portfolio performance is achieved in the safest way feasible while adhering to the client's mandate requirements.

13.4 ADHERENCE TO COMPLIANCE

A well-managed portfolio must ensure that it adheres to compliance rules and guidelines at all times. These include requirements detailed in the client's investment mandate as well as regulatory requirements related to the investment jurisdiction. The asset manager may also face additional requirements set by its internal risk team.

It's crucial to review the monitors that flag potential compliance breaches in portfolios daily. These include cash and liquidity monitors, as well as alerts for accounts nearing key risk metrics like duration, spread, currency, credit rating, or derivatives limits. Trade execution systems should have these constraints built in for each account to prevent accidental trade orders. Following these parameters is essential for fiduciary responsibility and keeping active portfolio decisions aligned with clients' long-term goals and operational constraints.

13.5 PORTFOLIO PERFORMANCE AND ATTRIBUTION

A client's objectives and investment goals serve as the foundation for evaluating portfolio performance. Whether the focus is on capital preservation, income generation, maximizing total returns, decarbonization, or achieving any other defined target, the portfolio's stated purpose is central to the assessment of its and the manager's performance.

Portfolio performance is also essential for understanding whether active investments are delivering value beyond passive exposure. Chapter 8 discussed alpha, tracking error, and risk-adjusted return measures like the Sharpe ratio and information ratio. These metrics inform us about the overall behavior of portfolio returns but do not indicate the drivers of performance.

For that, we turn to performance attribution, which breaks down portfolio returns into their component sources, including country selection, security choice, currency, and other risk factors. The results help understand where risk is being taken in the portfolio, which strategies are working and which are not, and where further attention is needed.

Specifically, attribution analysis can reveal which country allocations contributed to or detracted from performance, which key rate duration positions generated alpha, which instruments performed compared to the index, and which ratings buckets outperformed or underperformed the benchmark. Disaggregation by currency can illustrate how foreign currency exposures performed, while a breakdown by sector can indicate how corporate exposures compared with SOE and sovereign positions. Attribution can also flag exposures that have an outsized impact on performance, which can be used to resize positions and improve portfolio diversification.

There are multiple models for performance attribution analyses.[4] The Campisi performance attribution model can be used to break down returns from countries and regions, as well as risk factors such as duration and credit spread.[5] In this model, the residual, after considering country and risk factors, is attributed to security selection or other unquantified factors in the model.

Table 13.1 presents a sample performance attribution table. The portfolio's alpha for the period was 82 bps, which breaks down into 3 bps from income (coupon) payments, 18 bps from Treasury duration, 54 bps from credit spread exposures, and 7 bps from security selection, or the choice of bonds to invest in.

The total can also be broken down by country. A total of 250 bps of performance came from the country allocation to South Africa. Of this, 75 bps is due to income, 100 bps from the Treasury component, 100 bps from the spread component, and −25 bps from security selection. These metrics can be further disaggregated into maturity buckets for the Treasury and spread components and can extend to include other risk factors such as currencies, local rates, and off-benchmark exposures.

The investor can use this information to test priors as well as to alter portfolio positions. For instance, they may decide to reduce credit spread risk and scale down the South Africa position, as it has performed as expected and may not have much room left to generate returns. They may look into the negative contribution from security selection and

TABLE 13.1 Performance Attribution for a USD Sovereign Bond Portfolio

Country	Income (%)	Treasury (%)	Spread (%)	Security Selection (%)	Total (%)
Argentina	−0.50	−1.00	3.50	0.25	**2.25**
Brazil	0.50	1.00	2.00	0.25	**3.75**
Colombia	0.00	2.00	0.50	0.00	**2.50**
Dominican Republic	0.25	2.00	0.40	0.10	**2.75**
Ghana	0.10	0.50	−0.25	0.00	**0.35**
Indonesia	−0.25	−1.00	−0.35	0.15	**−1.45**
Mexico	−0.25	−1.00	−0.35	0.15	**−1.45**
South Africa	0.75	1.00	1.00	−0.25	**2.50**
Turkey	−0.50	−0.50	−1.00	0.10	**−1.90**
Zambia	−0.50	−1.00	1.25	0.00	**−0.25**
Total	**0.03**	**0.18**	**0.54**	**0.07**	**0.82**

TABLE 13.2 Factor-Based Performance Attribution

Risk Factor	Account	Benchmark	Portfolio Alpha
Yield Curve	100	50	50
Sovereign Credit Spread	100	25	75
Corporate Credit Spread	50	75	−25
Currency	25	0	25
Volatility	40	25	15
Total	**315**	**175**	**140**

how they could have improved. They may also realize that the contribution to overall alpha from this one position is too large and decide to rescale accordingly.

Factor-based performance attribution models break down returns into systemic risk factors. This may include changes in the level and shape of the yield curve, credit spreads by country or region, corporate or quasi spread risk, volatility, and exposures to derivatives (e.g., swaps or futures). Table 13.2 illustrates an example where the portfolio alpha of 140 bps is disaggregated into 50 bps from yield curve strategies, 75 bps from sovereign credit spread exposure, −25 bps from corporate exposures, 25 bps from off-benchmark currency exposures, and 15 bps from volatility risk.

Portfolio managers can utilize this information to fine-tune their risk positions, country allocations, and security selection. The attribution analysis can also indicate whether correlations among assets are functioning as the investor expected or has historically experienced. Performance attribution tables are a mainstay of most client reports on portfolio positions and performance, and are an essential part of the monitoring process of investment managers.

13.6 PEER ASSESSMENT AND MANAGER EVALUATION

Asset owners periodically evaluate their portfolio managers based on alpha, tracking error, and the Sharpe ratios of their portfolios. The most apples-to-apples comparison involves assessing the performance of managers with the same portfolio mandate. Large asset owners often employ this approach to diversify the risks associated with any particular investment manager. Additionally, it can serve as a basis for further allocations into the asset class.

Relative performance among managers can also be evaluated by examining public mutual fund data. Available on Bloomberg, this information is updated automatically as performance data is released. While each fund may have slightly different constraints and, in some cases, benchmarks, they should generally be comparable within a given asset class. For example, emerging market sovereign debt portfolios denominated in US dollars are usually benchmarked against the J.P. Morgan EMBI group of indices. They should be similar in their risk constraints and, as a result, performance criteria.

Table 13.3 illustrates an example of the available data in Bloomberg. This data allows for comparisons over long periods for portfolios with similar benchmarks and investment strategies. It also categorizes performance by quartile, enabling fund managers to monitor their performance rankings. This indicator is crucial for both asset owners and managers. Achieving a position in the 1st quartile for 1, 3, 5, and 10 years is a goal many strive for and a metric that many asset owners consider when selecting managers.

Table 13.3 shows that Fund 1 has consistently been a 1st quartile performer, while Fund 2 has been a 3rd quartile performer over the past five years. However, it has recently outperformed its peers and is now in the 1st quartile. Managers can use this information to delve deeper into the source of the outperformance.

PRO TIP: *Regularly analyze portfolio attribution and conduct peer performance and assessment of peer positions.*

Given the competition, it is beneficial for portfolio managers to monitor the performance of their peers. Beyond alpha, deeper insights can be gained by examining competitors' reported fund positions, which are available with a lag. Information on country

TABLE 13.3 Peer Relative Performance

Fund Name	Benchmark	AUM $bn	YTD	1 Year Alpha	1 Year Quartile	5 Year Alpha	5 Year Quartile
Fund 1	EMBIGD	$10,000	198	250	1st	200	1st
Fund 2	EMBIG	$2,000	175	225	1st	125	3rd
Fund 3	EMBIGD	$12,000	210	150	2nd	140	2nd
Fund 4	EMBIGD	$3,500	185	100	3rd	150	2nd
Fund 5	EMBIGD ex China	$5,000	90	75	4th	100	4th

exposure and security selection is available and helps to create a clearer picture of where an issuer's holdings and bonds sit across the market.

Econometric analysis can be conducted to disaggregate peers' returns into risk and country factors. This analysis can reveal whether competitors hold long or short durations, have a beta to oil greater than or less than 1, are overweight or underweight in a given country, maintain high allocations to cash, or are concentrated in a specific instrument. These insights provide understanding of the sources of their performance and how peers diverge from a given manager's own positions. They also assist in predicting future performance of competitors, assuming no changes in their reported positioning.

13.7 SUMMARY

In this chapter, we reviewed the essential tasks required for portfolio maintenance, including managing cash, liquidity, and derivatives exposures. It examined approaches to risk management and compliance adherence. The discussions also revisited portfolio performance metrics and analyzed strategies for portfolio attribution and peer assessments. These tools are critical for managing portfolios that are constantly evolving in response to shifting market conditions and changing risk perceptions.

Another key part of managing portfolios is navigating risk during volatile periods. To do this effectively, portfolio managers need specialized tools and techniques that take time to learn but are vital for guiding portfolios through varying market conditions. These will be reviewed in the next chapter.

NOTES

1. For case studies, see Vanguard, *A Framework for Considering Cash.*
2. US Securities and Exchange Commission.
3. There are other risks in this position, such as counterparty risk, which should be taken into consideration.
4. To see examples of how to calculate performance attribution, see Fabozzi, *Introduction to Fixed-Income Analysis.*
5. Campisi, "Primer on Fixed Income Performance Attribution."

REFERENCES

Campisi, Stephen. "Primer on Fixed Income Performance Attribution." *Journal of Performance Measurement* 4, no. 4 (2000): 14–25.

Fabozzi, Frank J., ed. *Introduction to Fixed-Income Analysis and Portfolio Management*. Cambridge, MA: The MIT Press, 2024.

U.S. Securities and Exchange Commission. https://www.sec.gov/ (accessed 14 May 2025).

Vanguard. *A Framework for Considering Cash in Your Portfolio*. April 16, 2024. https://corporate.vanguard.com/content/corporatesite/us/en/corp/articles/framework-for-considering-cash-in-portfolio.html (accessed 31 July 2025).

CHAPTER FOURTEEN

Trading a Portfolio Through Risk Events

PORTFOLIO MANAGERS often face sudden changes in market dynamics, resulting in increased volatility in asset prices and risk conditions. Events such as Federal Reserve interest rate cycles can have significant effects on financial markets and risk sentiment more broadly. Country-specific developments can have a powerful impact on sovereign bond prices and debt portfolios. Systemic events like the 2008 Global Financial Crisis and the 2020 COVID pandemic can cause widespread disruption and uncertainty across many sectors (see Figure 14.1).

As market conditions change, so too must portfolio risk positions. Managing a sovereign debt portfolio through crises and periods of volatility requires skill, hard work, guts, and resilience. Each situation is unique and may arise from systemic, country-specific, and thematic events. They can be prolonged or short-lived and have structural and temporal effects.

The diverse nature and changing aspects of these events require agility in portfolio management and a mix of investment strategies and approaches. We discuss these in detail in this chapter, covering available risk levers, hedging tools, and the guiding principles for navigating portfolios through volatility.

14.1 GUIDELINES AND PRINCIPLES

Crises and market volatility can represent significant risks as well as opportunities for investment portfolios. Portfolio managers and traders should develop the valuable skills of being nimble, maintaining a practical mindset, avoiding attachment to positions, and thinking analytically about the implications of unfolding events.

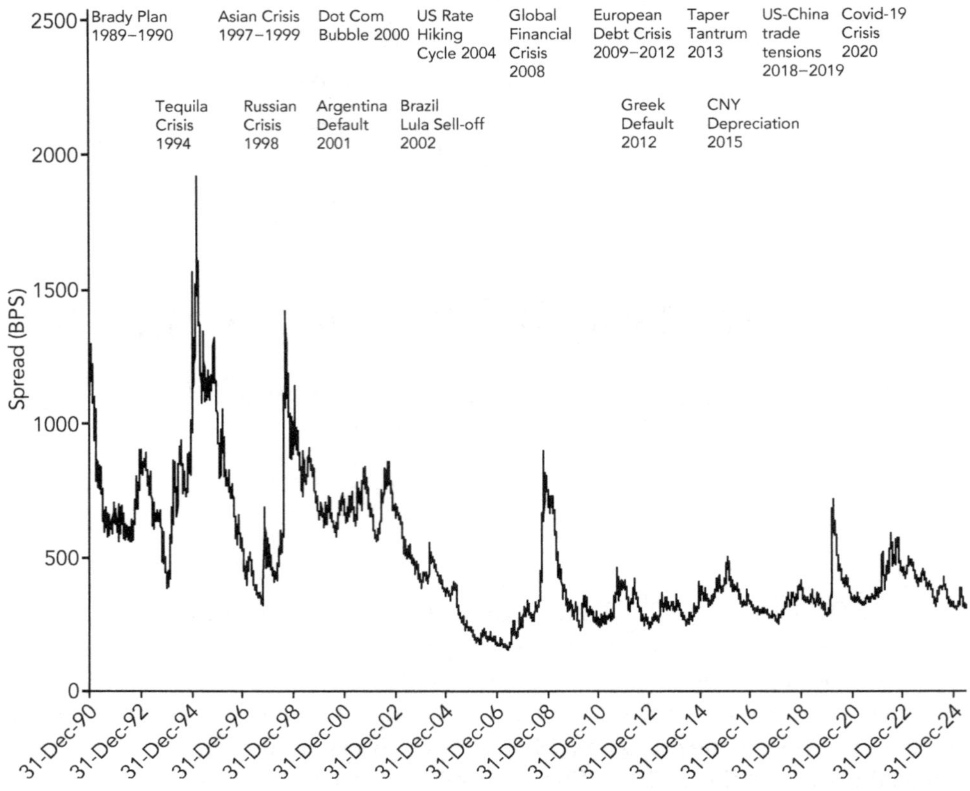

FIGURE 14.1 Sovereign crises through the years. Source: Adapted from J.P. Morgan, 2020.

During the initial stage of a crisis or volatility event, a baseline perspective on the implications of current events for risk factor positioning should be established. A common mistake is to accumulate information without processing it into an investment view. To avoid this, the investor must continually consider what the news flow means for the baseline investment view and the risk factor positions in the portfolio. This ongoing assessment, combined with market pricing and trading costs, will guide investors in making decisions about their portfolios.

When uncertainty is high, analyzing scenarios around the baseline helps clarify likely possibilities and evaluate alternative states of the world. This method is more effective than singular views and point forecasts, which can have a wide confidence interval and are subject to biases. The scenario approach also aids in identifying and considering potential tail scenarios.

Here, risk management reports and scenario models are valuable tools that provide essential insights into the portfolio's performance. These can be compared to ex ante views on performance and help reassess assumptions and adjust positions as needed.

Suppose there is a sharp sell-off in US Treasuries. In that case, the portfolio manager can assess whether the portfolio's performance corresponds to the performance based on ex ante scenario forecasts and their estimated priors. If not, they should investigate the causes of the mismatch. Were there elements of the actual scenario that the risk framework failed to model? Perhaps risk assets and correlations behaved differently than expected or did not follow their historical patterns. For example, the correlation between US Treasuries and US equities can be negative, flat, or positive depending on the nature of the shock and risk-off episode.

Another aspect to consider is whether the shock is transitory or structural. This helps determine whether prices should mean-revert or if they will find a new equilibrium. While this may be difficult to ascertain immediately, evaluating the pros and cons of all options enables a comprehensive analysis. If the shock is transitory, the best course of action may be to carry out tactical trades or to do nothing. If the shock appears permanent, further analysis may be required to understand the updated fundamentals and their implications for fundamental valuation.

For example, if bond market stress causes sovereign bond spreads to widen (and prices to drop), the investor would want to assess whether this indicates a high probability of payment default or whether other tactics are driving this price movement. The analysis would examine the cause of the stress, investigate the country's upcoming payments, and evaluate the available funding for debt payments. It may review what external assistance, like an IMF program, is available to help stabilize the government's finances. Together, this forms a picture of whether the drivers are fundamental or short-term, and, in turn, the implications for the risk of default.

There are some general pointers to consider when managing sovereign debt portfolios during periods of volatility and uncertainty. First, starting points matter. Depending on how the portfolio is positioned and the event's impact, it may need to reduce or increase exposure to one or more risk factors. Understanding where investments stand on this spectrum is beneficial. For instance, during episodes of market volatility, many managers may seek to add risk. However, suppose the portfolio is already long equity beta or credit risk. In that case, the decision must consider whether to increase risk further or if other positions should be sold alongside the purchases.

A second point is that doing nothing is still doing something. Some investors may feel safer not taking any action during periods of high uncertainty. This may be the right course of action, especially if lower liquidity and wide bid-ask spreads increase transaction costs and therefore the threshold for entering into trades. That said, doing nothing should be an active investment decision and not the result of paralysis. At a minimum, the investor should know what they would like to do if they could snap their fingers and understand why they can't or aren't taking action.

Third, scaling in and out of positions helps manage risks. Instead of going all in on a trade during periods of volatility, it is beneficial to scale into positions gradually. This approach means that if the market moves against you, the position at risk will be smaller than the targeted position. Additionally, it may help achieve a better average price for the position.

Fourth, stay aware of market technicals and what others might be doing. Gathering information from brokers, sell-side traders, other investors, and colleagues helps create an understanding of market dynamics and how asset prices could change. The ultimate goal is to anticipate shifts in pricing.

Fifth, it pays to be disciplined regarding stop losses and credit views. For various reasons, letting a position run longer than initially planned can be tempting. In a losing trade, the tendency may be to avoid realizing losses. In a winning trade, the inclination may be to keep the position open in hopes of further outperformance.

Discipline about stop losses and profit-taking is essential in normal market conditions, but it is critical during a crisis. Having a framework for valuations can safeguard against allowing biases to interfere with making the right decisions for the portfolio. If there is a compelling case for revising these limits, they should be incorporated into the framework to determine their implications for the investment decision.

A sixth guideline is to remember that managing portfolios through crises and periods of market volatility is a marathon, not a sprint. Keeping a level head, avoiding burnout, managing stress, and utilizing all available resources are integral to staying the course. Understanding one's investment style—whether one is risk-averse or risk-loving, how one handles losses, and when to enter positions during times of uncertainty—helps identify potential blind spots.

See Chapter 9 for a summary of common behavioral themes among investors and traders. This self-awareness can go a long way in managing portfolios effectively and efficiently during crisis episodes.

14.2 RISK LEVERS

In many instances, volatility episodes warrant a rapid adjustment of portfolio risk and positions. This may be to safeguard overall performance and take advantage of trading opportunities. Risk levers are instruments that enable the portfolio manager to do this quickly, at scale, and cost-effectively.

When choosing the appropriate lever, investors weigh the instrument's effectiveness to proxy for the risk they want to trade. If they're going to add interest rate risk, they may turn to interest rate swaps, or if they wish to add credit risk, they may turn to CDS indices. Investors are also mindful of whether historical correlations of the risk lever hold, or if there may be a structural break in the relationship.

Next, the executability of the trade is considered. If a market event occurs overnight after the market closes, the options for risk levers may be much more limited than during opening hours. The transaction costs of entering *and* exiting the trade are another factor. The best risk levers are low-cost, executable in large sizes, and found in liquid markets.

The hedge ratio, or the scaling of the risk lever to the risk metric, needs to be calculated and understood. This is informed by back tests of historical relationships and factor analysis to predict future movements. An additional input is the duration for which the risk lever will likely remain in the portfolio. Suppose the position is a bridge to the execution of other trades or is expected to be unwound when markets stabilize. In that case, the sizing and type of security will need to be adjusted as necessary. Together, these factors determine the instruments used and how much of the trade is executed for the portfolio.

Risk levers can be utilized in both risk-off and risk-on situations. In risk-off scenarios, investing in flight-to-safety instruments can be highly effective. For fixed-income portfolios, increasing duration via US Treasuries or German Bunds is a viable option. Even so, investors should bear in mind that historical correlations can often break down—particularly if the source of the risk-off is from developed country interest rate risk.

PRO TIP: *Correlations between hedges and underlying risks can change quickly and compared with historical relationships. Look forward rather than relying solely on past associations.*

Historically, gold has been viewed as a safe-haven asset, with prices rallying when global risks increase and vice versa. This role of gold has evolved, declining with the move away from the gold standard in the 1970s but resurfacing after the GFC due to rising government debt and inflation. With the increasing use of cryptocurrencies like Bitcoin, there is likely to be further evolution in what is considered a safe-haven asset in the global context.

Currencies often serve as effective risk levers due to the depth and low transaction costs of the forex markets. Depending on the macroeconomic context, the US dollar and euro are often used to adjust risk in a portfolio.

When crises are confined to particular countries, buying dollars while going short the local currency can be an effective hedge. However, if the shock is more global, the directionality of the currency hedge trade becomes situation-dependent. For example, suppose the shock arises from a recessionary trend in the US. In that case, adding US duration may be a more effective risk lever for the portfolio than adding US dollars, as the currency outlook could depend on global events occurring elsewhere.

Traditionally, the Japanese yen has served as a risk-off hedge during past crises. Japanese investors repatriate global investments during market volatility, driving movements in the currency. More recently, the correlation between the yen and other assets has become more context-specific as Japan's economic policies have evolved and retail asset allocation patterns have shifted.

Other macro strategies to hedge financial market risks include taking positions in VIX (the Volatility Index) options or ETFs that enable hedging against broader market volatility. These instruments increase in value as volatility rises, which can offset losses in portfolios with credit risk exposures during turbulent periods.

S&P futures serve as a powerful tool for adjusting portfolio risk based on expectations of equity market performance. By shorting S&P futures contracts, investors can counteract potential losses on their portfolio holdings. Conversely, going long on S&P futures can elevate risk in the portfolio and enhance returns if the market rallies. Because futures contracts provide significant notional exposure for a relatively small margin, investors can easily leverage the size of their portfolio.

Credit exposure can be quickly adjusted in sovereign debt portfolios by trading CDX indices. Adding CDX exposure increases the portfolio's credit risk across several issuers with a single trade, enabling the portfolio manager to boost the portfolio's beta rapidly. The same applies to reducing risk in the portfolio. Sovereign debt portfolios may also be able to buy and sell ETFs with underlying sovereign exposure to adjust credit risk exposure accordingly.

The range of macro hedges includes commodity futures in oil or gas that can help mitigate specific risks tied to fluctuations in commodity prices. For example, if a geopolitical shock impacts oil supply, going long on oil futures enables sovereign debt portfolios to increase their oil exposure and beta quickly. Similar options can be traded for various commodities, including energy, metals, mining, and soft commodities like wheat, soy, and rice.

Most risk levers are imperfect and will not fully hedge the portfolio in risk-off scenarios or replicate the underlying portfolio returns in a risk-on scenario. Therefore, any potential lever should be back-tested against the underlying risk metric to evaluate its effectiveness. This provides insight into hedge ratios (as noted previously) and the possible change in tracking error resulting from the trade.

During systemic crises, asset price correlations shift and may even break down, especially if price movements are significant or there are substantial policy changes. Consequently, hedge ratios and the co-movements between portfolio levers and the risk metrics they target should be reassessed to ensure risk levers perform as expected.

14.3 MANAGING IDIOSYNCRATIC SOVEREIGN RISKS

Crises are often linked to a specific country or issuer, prompting portfolio trades to mitigate or hedge against certain risks. Hedges for fixed-income portfolios can vary from simple instruments to intricate strategies. This section explores several techniques for managing sovereign debt portfolios subject to idiosyncratic or issuer-specific shocks. We address the management of sovereign debt portfolios during sovereign defaults in Part Four of this book.

Most sovereign crises don't occur overnight; they result from months of credit deterioration or the anticipation of a known event risk, such as an election. If the shock is permanent, portfolio targets must be reassessed with regard to the fundamental value of the instrument. If prices have already adjusted to reflect long-term fundamental valuations, the position can be monitored and adjusted over time.

Conversely, if prices have not fully adjusted, the exposure can be reduced. In fact, when there is a country-specific shock, the simplest hedge is often to sell the position. Avoiding over-layering the portfolio with a series of countervailing investments keeps portfolio construction clear, easy to interpret, and straightforward to monitor.

That said, very often a position cannot be sold due to illiquidity, high transaction costs, or regulations and sanctions. This is especially true for emerging and frontier market sovereigns, where markets are thin and spreads can widen rapidly, which can prohibit trading. In these situations, derivatives and reducing correlated country exposures can help manage overall risk in the portfolio.

Like broad portfolio risk levers, country-specific hedges should be continually reassessed as market conditions change. Often, idiosyncratic sovereign risks spill over and affect other countries and, in some cases, even the asset class itself. Contagion may happen due to fundamentals being impacted by the crisis or market technicals, such as raising cash or selling exposures from particular regions or issuers. Portfolio managers must remain aware of these risks at both the portfolio and asset class level and adjust their risk levers and hedges as necessary.

14.4 CREDIT RISK HEDGES

When adverse sovereign credit shocks occur, credit default swaps can be utilized to hedge against the credit risk while allowing the portfolio to maintain its position in the cash instrument. For example, if an investor wishes to hedge the credit risk associated with a five-year Indonesia USD bond, they can buy protection on the five-year Indonesia USD CDS. This strategy mitigates the credit risk from the bond exposure but leaves the interest rate risk from the cash bond exposure intact.

The portfolio manager may also reduce cash bond exposures from other countries with a similar risk profile. While imperfect, this approach can help manage overall risk exposure at the portfolio level, particularly if single-name CDS for the entity is unavailable. This type of cross-country asset sale often illustrates why a crisis in one country may spill over to others through financial markets, even when there are no direct fundamental linkages.

For example, during the Zambia sovereign debt crisis in 2020, frontier African sovereign credits were sold, leading to a drop in their bond prices as investors reduced credit risk across their accounts. These indiscriminate sales and their associated price overshoots represented buying opportunities for portfolios with the capacity to add African credit risk.

PRO TIP: *Sometimes the best hedge is to sell the position and bear the hit to the portfolio's profit and loss or PnL.*

14.5 DURATION HEDGES

If an investor wants to hedge duration risk from a particular security, they can use interest rate swaps, futures, and options as suitable risk levers. Interest rate swaps hedge the risk of rising interest rates by exchanging fixed payments on the bonds for floating payments (and vice versa). Futures contracts, such as US Treasury futures or Eurodollar futures, lock in the price for trading bonds in the future, protecting against adverse price movements. Options and other interest rate derivatives, like swaptions, provide the option to trade bonds at a specified price, thereby safeguarding against significant fluctuations in interest rates (see Chapter 3). For USD-denominated sovereign debt portfolios, these instruments can be employed to adjust duration for specific securities, issuers, and regions, as well as for the overall portfolio.

For sovereign debt portfolios denominated in local currencies, interest rate derivatives linked to the underlying sovereign can be utilized to hedge exposures. For instance, a Brazilian currency-based sovereign debt portfolio can mitigate Brazilian interest rate exposure by employing interest rate derivatives associated with Brazilian bonds as the underlying exposure.

For a portfolio of local currency sovereign bonds from around the world, country-specific derivatives can be utilized to hedge duration exposure. The specific instruments available depend on the development of the local currency market.

14.6 CAPITAL CONTROLS AND FX HEDGES

When a country faces a currency or debt crisis, there is a risk of capital controls being imposed or local law bond contracts being rewritten in the government's favor. This may result in funds being trapped onshore or local law bonds becoming worthless in terms of foreign currency. In these situations, derivatives can also help mitigate risks by replacing onshore exposures with offshore contracts that have the same underlying risk exposure.

For example, suppose an emerging market is expected to impose capital controls to prevent capital flight and currency depreciation. In that case, investors may look to convert local currency-denominated bonds into offshore interest rate swaps to receive payments offshore.

More broadly, the use of derivatives allows investors to separate the decision regarding local duration from that of currency risk. Investors may choose to hedge against currency exposure; that is, they might avoid exposure to the currency due to concerns about potential depreciation in the future and instead maintain only interest rate exposure. Alternatively, they may opt to assume both interest rate and currency exposure in derivative form. In this manner, derivatives facilitate more effective risk management of debt portfolios during both crisis and non-crisis periods.

Currencies can also be used to hedge other types of country-specific idiosyncratic risks. During risk-off periods, buying US dollars against the local currency can serve as an effective hedge, particularly if the currency has not moved in line with the local bond market. This situation can occur if the exchange rate is managed or if market contagion hasn't affected the currency market. The hedge can be executed through spot transactions as well as through foreign exchange derivatives like currency forwards, futures, options, and cross-currency swaps.

In general, currencies serve as better levers for sovereign debt portfolios with exposures in local currency debt compared to foreign-currency-denominated debt, as there can be high correlations between local yields and the currency. In countries with high levels of debt denominated in foreign currencies, there is often some correlation between currency movements and credit spreads. This arises as weaker currencies increase the debt burden of the economy, thereby raising the country's credit risk. The beta of credit spreads to currency movements can illustrate how closely the variables move together.

14.7 INFLATION HEDGES

In countries experiencing high inflation, investors may want to safeguard their portfolio's real value from erosion. For a given sovereign, inflation-linked bonds can protect against rising inflation. Derivatives such as inflation swaps, which exchange fixed payments for those linked to inflation, present another alternative. In many sovereign debt markets, inflation-linked securities are less liquid than their nominal counterparts, which must be considered when using them as a portfolio risk lever rather than as a dedicated allocation.

Inflation dynamics are country-specific, making it crucial to consider inflation drivers when selecting hedges. For example, if global oil price shocks drive inflation, US TIPS may provide broad protection. If inflation drivers are idiosyncratic, like a poor harvest, country-specific inflation-linked bonds or similar instruments might be more appropriate.

14.8 SOVEREIGN RATING DOWNGRADES

Sovereign credit rating downgrades impact bond prices, investor demand, and market sentiment. A decline in rating signals a deterioration in the issuer's credit quality and a higher risk of default. Investors, therefore, require higher yields as compensation. The overall effect on bond prices depends on whether the rating shifts from investment grade to high yield and the number of notches in the downgrade.

Ratings downgrades are typically not a surprise. They are communicated in advance through ratings watches or negative outlooks. Fallen angels—instances when ratings drop from investment grade to high yield—usually have the most significant impact on bond prices and market technicals. This occurs because issuers are removed from investment-grade bond indices, which leads to forced sales from benchmarked portfolios. Additionally, asset owners who are cautious about investing in high-risk issuers may instruct asset managers to divest due to concerns about further credit downgrades.

Investors can assess the extent of forced sales from fallen angels by examining the issuer's weight in each index. This can be compared with estimates of market positioning and the AUM relative to the index to provide a rough estimate of the outflows. Let's work through an example of the calculations involved.

Example: Forced Sales Calculations

A country has a 25 basis points (0.0025%) weight in an investment-grade sovereign index, which has $350 billion in assets benchmarked against it.

Positioning surveys suggest that the industry is between 10 basis points to flat compared to the index.

Upon a downgrade to high yield, forced sales may range from \$0.875 billion ($0.0025 \times \$350$) to \$1.225 billion ($0.0035 \times \$350$) to get to zero exposure.

In practice, actual forced sales may be smaller, as investors may not need to sell their positions immediately or at all. Conversely, forced sales could also be larger if the amounts benchmarked against the indices exceed estimates, due to separate accounts utilizing the benchmark, or because of direct sales from asset owners.

A valuable exercise for credit analysts is to monitor sovereign ratings and identify those at risk of upgrades and downgrades. They can evaluate the likelihood of rating changes based on their own fundamental analysis, compare these with market prices, and determine which issuers are mispriced.

Special attention can be given to fallen angels and the methodology each agency uses to determine downgrades to high yield. Replicating the agency methodology and monitoring the scores to see how close they are to making a rating change can help portfolio managers anticipate the actual agency downgrade.

The market typically begins repricing a fallen angel well before the actual downgrade by the rating agency. Additionally, rating agencies operate on different schedules for rating changes, leading to a staggered timeline for downgrades and exits from indices (which generally require ratings from two or more agencies). Consequently, markets do not fully reprice a fallen angel, resulting in a noticeable price impact when the downgrade ultimately occurs.

Moreover, prices typically overshoot relative to fundamental valuations. Investor positioning ahead of a potential fallen angel would benefit from being lighter on the way down, with the option to add risk (if needed) during the repricing. These effects are illustrated in Figure 5.4, which shows Brazil's 2015 downgrade from investment grade to high yield. The gradual widening of spreads ultimately peaked with the downgrade to high yield and eventually tightened over time.

14.9 SANCTIONS AND TRADE PROHIBITIONS

Sanctions and trade prohibitions represent a specific type of risk for portfolio managers to navigate. Portfolio managers and traders should gain a comprehensive legal understanding of the new rules and regulations before transacting in any securities or with issuers facing the prohibition. Sanctioned positions must be identified and coded within systems to ensure they are flagged automatically if any trade orders are mistakenly placed to trade them.

For benchmark investors, it is important to observe the actions of index providers and their treatment of sanctioned entities. Often, sanctioned or prohibited issuers become zombie positions in portfolios. Therefore, these exposures need to be hedged through the methods discussed earlier in this chapter. Additionally, there may be spillover effects on issuers closely associated with the sanctioned entity due to the risk of restrictions or market sales.

Comparing sanctioned exposures across competitors can provide insights for future risk-taking and performance. For example, portfolio managers with significant investments in sanctioned issuers often seek to offset performance losses through other positions. This may lead them to take on more risk in their remaining exposures by increasing positions or leveraging the portfolio.

Investors often lobby the government agency responsible for sanctions to lift them or provide exemptions for trading. Occasionally, these requests are granted, and if so, they are precise in their terms. These outline the instruments, dates, times, and counterparties permitted for the transactions. For example, the US sanctions on Russian debt following the Ukraine invasion in 2022 granted several exemptions for trading bonds and receiving interest payments for US-based investors.

14.10 SUMMARY

This chapter reviewed several tools and strategies for managing portfolios during volatile market conditions. It discussed broad guidelines and principles for portfolio managers when faced with challenging market situations. It covered various risk levers and hedges investors can use to mitigate risk in their portfolios. Specific events, including sovereign ratings downgrades and sanctions, were also addressed.

Navigating volatility and periods of heightened risk demands two core skills from portfolio managers: openness to new information and agility in portfolio management and investment decision-making. Next, we examine one of the most severe challenges they may face—sovereign positions turning distressed, culminating in default or debt restructuring.

REFERENCE

J.P. Morgan. *EM as an Asset Class in the Post-pandemic World*. Emerging Markets Research, 2020.

IV

PART FOUR

Managing Distressed Positions

CHAPTER FIFTEEN

An Introduction to Sovereign Defaults

THE TERMS *default* and *debt restructuring* can send a chill down the spine of any sovereign bond investor. This fear is not unfounded, especially considering that a historical method of debt restructuring was the harsh practice of bloodletting, the French monarchy's unfortunate habit of executing major domestic creditors. Nowadays, investors are more concerned about the deep red on their portfolio's profit and loss statements and the hit to their reputation as alpha generators.

In Part Four of this book, we turn to distress situations when the government seeks to amend its contractual obligations under bond contracts. We begin this chapter with a brief history of sovereign defaults and stylized facts observed around restructurings. Definitions of default are highlighted, including the differences between foreign and domestic law defaults. The related concept of sovereign debt crises is also addressed. This is followed by case studies of several notable sovereign defaults in recent history.

Chapter 16 goes on to describe the key players in sovereign debt restructurings and their motivations. It summarizes the various stages of the debt workout and what investors should watch for in each phase. Chapter 17 focuses on navigating sovereign bond portfolios in the event of sovereign distress episodes. It covers checklists for the investment team, portfolio hedges, index considerations, trading defaulted securities, and market technicals.

Chapter 18 goes on to examine exchange proposals and negotiations. It discusses the factors investors look at before accepting or rejecting an exchange offer. Negotiation tactics commonly used by the debtor and creditors in coming to an exchange agreement are outlined. The analysis also examines whether it pays to be a holdout. The chapter closes with a review of life after restructuring for the issuer, including market reentry and credit upgrades.

15.1 A BRIEF HISTORY OF SOVEREIGN DEFAULTS

Sovereigns have been defaulting since antiquity.[1] An early record of sovereign default occurred in 1294 when Edward I of England defaulted on war-related debts to Italian bankers.[2] In the centuries that followed, there have been several waves of sovereign defaults (see Figure 15.1).

In the 1820s, Latin American and European economies defaulted due to a combination of war, civil conflict, and financial crises. Another wave in the 1870s followed a decline in commodity prices and wars in Central and South America. The most significant wave occurred during the Great Depression of the 1930s, with defaults in both advanced and emerging economies.[3]

Since then, the Latin American debt crisis of the 1980s and the Asian financial crisis of the 1990s resulted in economic turmoil in many emerging market economies. The Russian default in 1998 and Argentina's default in 2001 were particularly notable due to their scale and the contagion effect on other economies.

Significant implications for sovereign debt markets and bond contracts followed. These included the growth of the securitized bond market and a greater focus on emerging market sovereign credit analysis. They also spurred the development of provisions in sovereign bond contracts to facilitate restructurings.

The post–World War II idea that sovereign credit risk was limited to emerging markets was challenged by the Eurozone sovereign debt crisis in 2009. During this episode, several European countries faced soaring borrowing costs, steep refinancing pressures, and rising debt levels. This threatened the stability of the euro, prompting EU-wide bailouts and austerity measures.

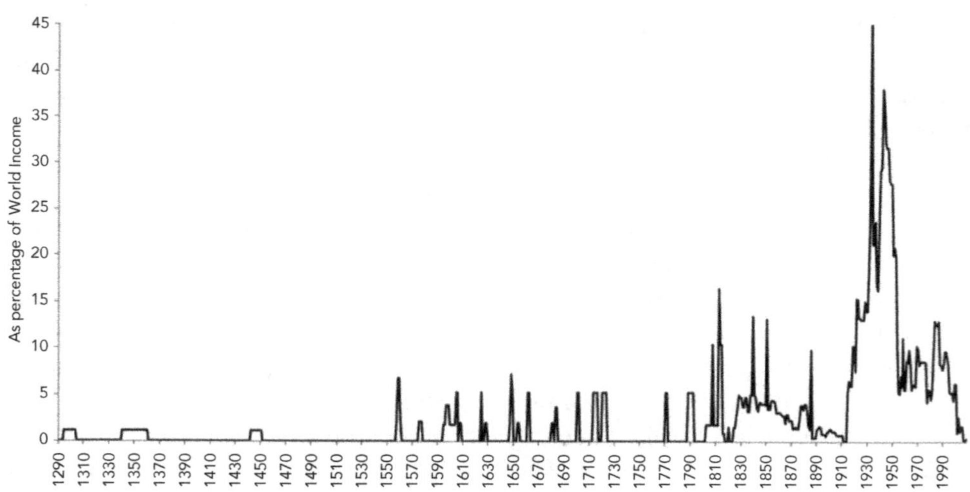

FIGURE 15.1 Sovereign defaults through history. SOURCE: Burdekin and Sweeney 2021/ EconStor.

Greece and Cyprus eventually restructured their debt, with Greece's 2012 default being the largest sovereign default in history. Extensive financial and economic support from the EU, ECB, and IMF was vital in preventing defaults in several systemically important European economies, including Italy, Spain, Portugal, and Ireland. The crisis exposed credit risks in advanced economies and the significant leverage of official lenders over sovereign governments during times of crisis.

In the post-COVID era, defaults in frontier emerging markets signal another potential wave of sovereign defaults. This time, the key questions revolve around how official lenders coordinate their response and the role of China in debt restructurings. At the same time, the substantial debt levels in advanced economies highlight the rising complexity of sovereign debt investing and the looming risk of future crises. Together, these are summoning bond vigilantes back to the market as enforcers of fiscal discipline.

15.2 WHY SOVEREIGNS DEFAULT

Sovereigns default for a number of reasons. A sovereign's ability to repay debt can be impacted by external factors such as wars, invasions, and military conflicts. The onerous reparations that followed Germany's defeat in World War I and the subsequent German sovereign default before World War II are one example. Natural disasters, trade shocks, and contagion from international financial crises[4] can also harm a country's ability to repay and service debt.

Poor macroeconomic management and weak public finances are also contributing factors.[5] The realization of contingent liabilities, particularly from the financial and banking sectors, can raise solvency concerns. Short-term liquidity risks stemming from rapid increases in interest rates or other unexpected events may also affect the sovereign's capacity to repay.

A sovereign's *willingness to repay* debt depends on the political economy its leaders face. Some governments hesitate to impose significant economic adjustments on their citizens to repay foreign or wealthy domestic creditors. Others are disproportionately willing to repay debt, even at a severe cost to the populace. This may be motivated by a desire to save face, minimize disruption to exports and trade flows, or because powerful groups hold a substantial share of government debt.

A case in point is Venezuela before the 2017 default. There, the government continued servicing external debt instead of using scarce dollars for essential imports, even though the economy faced severe shortages of medicines, food, and other necessities. The default was viewed as problematic for the oil-exporting economy due to the potential restrictions for the oil trade, and as the Venezuelan sovereign owned assets (like oil refineries) abroad. Moreover, the ruling military owned a large share of government bonds.

In some cases, sovereigns may default if debt is viewed as odious. In 2008, Ecuador's President Correa defaulted on two bonds, the 2012 and 2030s, arguing that they were illegitimate, although international third parties did not categorize them as such. The question of the legitimacy of the Iraqi debt incurred by Saddam Hussein also played a role in Iraq's debt restructuring negotiations in the 2000s, where recovery values for commercial creditors were in the single digits.[6]

Sovereigns may also default if there is a regime change or in the event of state succession. For defaults related to the breakup of sovereign entities, there is no unique and internationally agreed-upon mechanism to apportion debts. In the case of Yugoslavia's breakup in the 1990s, the IMF repartitioned debt based on the economic share of GDP. Even so, some debts were disputed, such as military-related loans, and the final settlement took nearly a decade to complete.

Sovereigns can involuntarily default due to sanctions, lawsuits, or legal constraints. International sanctions may limit a country's ability to repay debt or prevent bondholders from receiving payments. For instance, the 2022 US sanctions on Russia halted Russian debt payments from being processed, despite the issuer's capacity and willingness to pay, resulting in a payment default.

Legal rulings may also affect a sovereign's ability to service its foreign debt payments. During the litigation in NML Capital Ltd v. The Republic of Argentina, in June 2014, New York District Court Judge Griesa prohibited US financial intermediaries from assisting Argentina in paying existing bondholders unless Argentina also paid the holdouts. Argentina opted to default on the June 30 payment of the 2005 and 2010 exchange bonds rather than negotiate a settlement with the holdouts.

15.3 STYLIZED FACTS

Despite the long and well-telegraphed track record of sovereign default, actual defaults are relatively rare. The historical probability of default—or the odds of any given country defaulting in any given year—is low at around 2–4%.[7] This number has increased in recent decades and averages about 3% for defaults on sovereign external debt and 2% for defaults on domestic debt.

Sovereign defaults often arise in the context of sovereign debt crises. Empirically, about 20% of sovereign crises result in default.[8] Sovereign crises are extended periods of economic and financial stress, marked by substantial fluctuations in financial asset prices and heightened market volatility. Consequently, they can significantly impact portfolio performance, even in the absence of outright defaults and restructurings.

The duration of defaults, which refers to the time from when a sovereign defaults or announces a restructuring until the restructuring is settled, can vary from as little as a few months to over several decades. On average, external debt defaults take about 3.25 years to resolve, while domestic debt defaults average around 2.5 years.[9] Empirically, longstanding sovereign defaults, such as the repudiation of Tsarist Russia's debt following the Bolshevik Revolution in 1917, are rare and tend to be associated with regime changes.[10]

Selective defaults are the norm, with defaults on either domestic or external debt accounting for 70% of all defaults. Domestic defaults are characterized by financial instability and a high likelihood of banking crises. At the same time, external restructurings are associated with sudden stops in external financing, capital flight, and significant trade balance adjustments. Nevertheless, half of the countries that restructure domestic debt also restructure external debt, and one-third of countries that restructure external debt do so alongside a domestic debt restructuring.[11]

Creditor losses or haircuts in sovereign workouts average around 40% of face value. Domestic debt workouts are slightly more punitive, with net present value losses of 42%, compared to 37% for external debt restructurings. However, domestic defaults often involve smaller nominal debt values and typically take less time to resolve.[12]

Outright repudiation (100% haircut) is rare, with only 3% of defaults in the last 200 years since 1820 falling into this category.[13] Also rare are negative haircuts, where the NPV of debt is higher post-restructuring, as governments offer investors incentives to facilitate rolling debt or to avoid an outright payment default.

Between these extremes, there is significant variation in haircuts across countries, instruments, and over time. For instance, losses on sovereign defaults have ranged from as high as 82 cents on the dollar for the 1998 Russian default to as low as 5 cents on the dollar for the 2005 Dominican Republic default, where recovery was 95 cents on the dollar (see Table 15.1). Meanwhile, for the Ecuador 2020 restructuring, differences across instruments were close to 12 cents on the dollar.[14]

TABLE 15.1 Major Sovereign Defaults Since 1998

Country	Default Year	Total Defaulted Debt ($bn)	Foreign Currency (FC) or Local Currency (LC) Bonds	Recovery* (% of PAR)
Russia	1998	72.7	FC, LC	18
Argentina	2001	82.3	FC, LC	27
Dominican Republic	2005	1.6	FC	95
Ecuador	2008	3.2	FC	28
Greece	2012	264.2	FC, LC	24
Greece	2012	41.4	LC (euro)	37
Argentina	2014	29.4	FC	68
Ukraine	2015	13.3	FC	80
Venezuela	2017	36.7	FC	28
Argentina	2020	108.8	FC, LC	46
Lebanon	2020	31.3	FC, LC	17
Ecuador	2020	17.3	FC	27
Russia	2022	27.3	FC	28
Ukraine	2022	19.6	FC	22
Ghana	2022	13.7	FC, LC	41

Source: Adapted from Moody's (2023) Default Rates.

Notes: *Recovery is measured as the average trading price in % of the par value of the bonds at the time of the initial default event, 30-day post-default for missed payments, or around the close of an exchange for distressed debt exchanges.

Creditor losses result from a haircut on the principal or face value, a decrease in the coupon, and/or maturity extension. Aside from face value reductions, NPV losses can also be substantial due to coupon haircuts and maturity extensions. Empirically, NPV haircuts tend to be higher when debt stocks are elevated, in low-income countries, among first-time borrowers, and for sovereigns that have experienced geopolitical disasters such as wars, revolutions, or country break-ups. Large haircuts are also linked to prolonged sovereign debt crises and extended workouts.[15]

Preemptive restructurings that occur before a missed payment account for nearly 40% of debt restructurings. Historically, they are linked to significantly lower haircuts compared to post-default cases (18% versus 48%). Preemptive restructurings require a shorter duration for debt renegotiation (one year versus five years) and result in significantly lower output losses. Additionally, preemptive restructurings tend to enable quicker re-access to international debt capital markets.[16]

15.4 DEFINING DEFAULT

So far, we have been referring to sovereign defaults as if there is a unique definition of what constitutes a default. In practice, this is far from the case. Sovereign default events can be categorized by details in the bond contract, in terms of the NPV loss, by criteria used by rating agencies, or by those stipulated in CDS contracts. They can also be grouped into hard versus soft defaults, preemptive defaults, substantive defaults, selective or partial defaults, technical defaults, and involuntary defaults.[17]

What matters for investors is less the academic definition and more the events that may lead to portfolio losses or gains. These may arise from non-payment of coupons or principal, from securities being exchanged for those with lower value than their original claim, from rating agency decisions causing market pressure and forced sales, or from CDS contracts being triggered, which drives market repricing and an exchange of payments. Also important are the factors that breach bond contracts and are therefore enforceable in a court of law.

15.4.1 Events of Default in Foreign Law Sovereign Contracts

Foreign sovereign debt contracts clearly stipulate Events of Default (EoD). The most commonly understood is a *payment default*, which includes a missed interest or principal payment beyond the grace period.[18] Other contractual EoD include *debt repudiation*, where the sovereign rejects its obligation to pay; *debt moratoriums*, where the sovereign unilaterally halts payments; *covenant defaults*, such as violations of the *pari passu* or negative pledge clauses; *false representations*, including misreported data and lacking borrowing authority; and *cross-defaults*, which link two unrelated debt contracts so that a default under one constitutes a default under the other. Some sovereign contracts also define *policy-related events of default*, such as loss of IMF membership or breaches of debt ceilings.

Investors do not necessarily need to take action if there are contractual defaults and if inaction is the better option. In 2017, Venezuela missed payments on some bonds that contractually could have triggered an EoD for other bonds. Investors chose not to exercise their rights to accelerate or trigger cross-default clauses. Instead, they opted to receive payments on other bonds for as long as the sovereign could fulfill its payment obligations.

15.4.2 Preemptive and Substantive Defaults

The contractual EoD does not include situations where issuers impose losses on creditors within the existing contractual framework through collective action clauses. For instance, preemptive (pre-EoD) distressed debt exchanges can modify payment terms, resulting in less favorable conditions for the creditor within the existing bond contract. These can be just as significant for investors as contractual EoD.

Substantive defaults describe those where the haircut and losses imposed on creditors are significant. The severity is often measured in terms of the net present value of losses. Substantive defaults can occur both preemptively and following a payment default.

15.4.3 Rating Agency Criteria for Default

Rating agency definitions of default emphasize whether a restructuring leads to reduced financial obligations and whether such reductions are necessary for a sovereign to avoid payment default. They extend beyond the contractual definition of default and encompass events that may be contractually preemptive and legally consensual, including changes in domestic law that negatively affect payments. Examples include the use of collective action clauses, forced maturity extensions, currency redenomination, and indexation, among others. See the discussion on default ratings in Chapter 5.

A default rating by the agencies does not affect the contractual terms of the bond itself or the default criteria in Credit Default Swaps. However, ratings matter in that a downgrade to a default rating can trigger forced sales due to client mandate guidelines. This may influence the market pricing of bonds and lead to negative market technicals.

15.4.4 CDS Definitions of Default

Credit default swaps define *credit events* that trigger a payout from the seller of protection to the buyer of protection. These include failure to pay, obligation default, repudiation/moratorium, and restructuring, including through the use of collective action clauses. For standardized CDS contracts, the International Swaps and Derivatives Association Determinations Committees determine whether CDS has been triggered following a credit event.

Even if there is no contractual default and bondholders agree to an exchange, a country's CDS may still be triggered. A notable example is the 2012 Greek debt restructuring. ISDA ruled that the debt exchange constituted a credit event under CDS contracts, as the exchange led to a reduction in the principal amount of the original bonds, a delay in the payment of the original bonds, and the exchange was binding on all holders of the original bonds due to the use of retrofitted CACs. ISDA's determination was controversial because some market participants argued that the debt exchange did not constitute a default or a credit event under traditional definitions.

The triggering of CDS is significant for markets and investors. The outcome of ISDA's Determinations Committees can influence pricing for CDS and cash bonds and impact portfolio performance. In sovereign debt portfolios, CDS exposures are frequently maintained alongside cash bonds and can either offset or intensify losses from those positions.

15.4.5 Local Law Sovereign Defaults

Domestic or local law debt, like foreign law debt, is also vulnerable to default and restructuring.[19] That said, defining default in local law sovereign debt is not straightforward. Instead of a prospectus and debt indenture, the issuance of local law sovereign debt is governed by legislative statutes, guidelines, and administrative regulations, which are often undocumented and not easily accessible in a single, comprehensive resource (see Chapter 7).

Additionally, the sovereign has the authority to alter domestic law to modify debt contracts, overlook default, or impose restructuring terms on creditors with limited recourse. This may include mandatory reductions on principal and interest payments, as well as coercion through financial repression and capital controls. Sovereigns can reduce the real value of their obligations through inflation, currency conversion, or currency debasement. They may also employ tax policies, such as withholding taxes, to partially reclaim payments that would otherwise go to creditors.

Domestic law defaults are becoming increasingly frequent (see Figure 15.2).[20] In the 1980s, about 10% of default episodes involved domestic law debt, compared to around

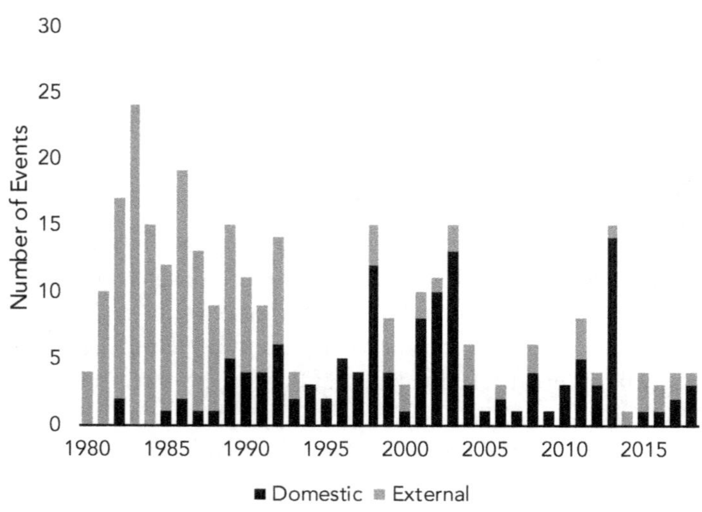

FIGURE 15.2 Frequency of domestic and external defaults. SOURCE: Adapted from Erce, Mallucci, and Picarelli, A Journey in the History of Sovereign Defaults.

70% in the 2000s.[21] Examples include Brazil in 1990, which experienced the largest recorded local currency default ($62 bn) due to the abrogation of inflation-linked indexes embedded in the original contracts, and Russia in 1998, when a $39 bn local currency default was accompanied by a selective default on foreign currency instruments. Defaults like Kuwait's in 1990–1991, which were on its entire stock of local currency debt while foreign currency liabilities were honored in full, are considered to be rare.

Domestic law defaults are complex and varied in their outcomes and resolution frameworks. Face value reductions are rare, with maturity extensions being the most common form of restructuring (in roughly 80% of the cases).[22] Despite this, the net present value losses for creditors can be significant.

In terms of timing, domestic debt restructurings take an average of 2.5 years to resolve. Even so, approximately 40% are resolved swiftly within six months.[23] Preemptive restructurings, where creditors were involved early, are gaining traction, as evidenced by Jamaica in 2013.

Sequencing tends to favor domestic restructurings before completing negotiations on external debt. For instance, Ghana (2023) carried out domestic debt restructuring before negotiating with external commercial creditors. This may be due to the ability of the sovereign to *financially repress* or cramdown domestic creditors, and as the vast majority of domestic law instruments do not have CACs.

15.4.6 Other Default Categorizations

There are several other default categorizations that bond investors may encounter.

Technical defaults encompass breaches of minor covenants, such as administrative errors, that do not lead to investor losses and are considered less significant by market participants. This category can also include situations where contractual defaults are rectified within a short timeframe. For instance if a payment delay occurs due to data or system errors, or if a non-payment is resolved quickly without an announcement of default.

Partial defaults occur when the creditor defaults on a portion of their debt, whether defined by currency, creditor, jurisdiction/law, or tenor. Examples include defaulting on external versus domestic debt, or on commercial loans rather than bonds.

This is distinct, although connected to *selective defaults,* where the issuer defaults on specific instruments or debtors even if they have the capacity to repay. Ecuador's 2008 default is considered a selective default as President Correa defaulted on the 2012 and 2030 bonds on the grounds that the debt was illegitimate. Meanwhile he remained current on the 2015 bond that had been issued under the previous Correa administration.

Ecuador's selective default is also regarded as a *voluntary* default because the country was considered capable of repayment. *Involuntary* defaults refer to situations where there is a willingness to repay but not the ability due to external factors beyond the issuer's control. For example, foreign sanctions or legal rulings can legally hinder sovereigns from servicing their external debt, as discussed previously.

Another term used is *soft versus hard* defaults. A soft default occurs when a country obtains permission from its bondholders to postpone payments through a consent solicitation and seeks to engage with creditors to negotiate debt restructuring in a constructive manner.[24] Examples of soft restructurings include Uruguay in 2003, where the sovereign engaged collaboratively with creditors, resulting in a high level of participation in the exchange (93%), even before the introduction of collective action clauses.[25]

In contrast, in a *hard default*, a country misses a payment without obtaining permission and may adopt an aggressive stance in dealing with its creditors. While this terminology does not have specific contractual implications or affect credit ratings or CDS contracts, it may be indicative of the timing, haircut, and outcome of any restructuring.

Argentina's 2001 default is often characterized as a hard default due to the combination of a payment default coupled with an aggressive restructuring posture. Recovery for the 2005 exchange was low at 27 cents on the dollar, and participation was low. It was eventually followed by 15 years of litigation by holdout creditors against Argentina. See the summary in Section 15.6.2.

15.5 SERIAL DEFAULTS AND RESTRUCTURINGS

Countries that have defaulted in the past are more likely to default again compared to non-defaulters with the same external debt-to-GDP ratio.[26] These serial defaulters are defined as countries that have experienced two or more default episodes since gaining independence. Factors specific to each country that contribute to serial defaults include vulnerability to natural disasters, weak institutions, political or geopolitical instability, and increased exposure to external financial shocks, among others.

Serial restructurings differ from serial defaults. They involve two or more restructurings during a specific default episode, defined as a period of at least 24 months without a default. Approximately one-third of sovereign defaults necessitate more than one restructuring, with an average of two restructurings needed to resolve a debt crisis.[27]

Serial restructurings highlight the repeated game aspect of sovereign debt negotiations. Restructurings that provide inadequate debt relief or insufficient corrective policies implemented by the government may trigger a series of interim restructurings, each causing smaller losses than the final resolution. Systematically higher yields following these restructurings may hinder the ability to roll upcoming debt payments, thus raising the likelihood of future restructurings.

A natural question for investors is whether it is worthwhile to lend to a previous defaulter. History suggests that, in some cases, compounding high interest rates and collateral can more than compensate creditors. Before the 1340 default, Edward III of England famously owed his Florentine bankers 10 times his annual fiscal revenues due to the aggressive conditions of the loans. However, by the time of default, his creditors had more than recouped the official outstanding debt of GBP150,000 and enjoyed two decades of high interest payments and profits from English wool duties.[28] Similarly, there is evidence of substantial (profitable) returns on short-term loans to King Philip II of Habsburg Spain, despite his notorious serial defaults.

Academic research finds that sovereign bonds of prior defaulters had significantly higher returns and greater volatility compared to benchmark UK and US government bonds, as well as compared to other countries that had never defaulted.[29] The findings suggest that investors are mainly compensated through higher coupons for the additional risk they take when holding bonds of volatile countries with poor credit histories.

PRO TIP: *Study previous sovereign defaults, crises, and restructurings as history often repeats itself.*

15.6 HISTORICAL SOVEREIGN DEFAULTS

We now turn to a series of historical sovereign default case studies—Greece, Argentina, and Ecuador—each chosen for the unique challenges they posed and the lessons they offer to sovereign investors. These cases highlight innovative legal risks, challenges from official creditors and government action, and the evolving role of collective action clauses. By examining how these crises unfolded and were resolved, portfolio managers can better understand the potential outcomes of restructurings and the strategies that can mitigate losses or capture value in distressed sovereign debt.

15.6.1 Greece 2012

The Greek sovereign default in 2012 marked a pivotal moment for sovereign debt investors.[30] As the largest sovereign restructuring in modern history (involving €206 billion of debt), it undermined the belief in the "no-default" status of advanced economies. It also exposed the risks associated with investing in sovereign entities without monetary sovereignty.

It redefined the role of official sector creditors in debt restructurings, with the *Troika*, consisting of the IMF, Eurogroup, and ECB, providing one of the largest bailout sovereign packages to date (an astonishing €280 billion). Even so, they faced increased criticism over the harsh conditions imposed on the Greek government, with then-Minister of Finance Yanis Varoufakis referring to the Troika's economic conditionality as "fiscal waterboarding."[31] The Troika, as official lenders, refused to take haircuts in the restructuring that followed, resulting in the burden of debt relief falling on private creditors, who experienced significant losses in net present value terms.

A unique feature of the Greek exchange was the introduction of collective action clauses (CACs) retroactively into Greek law bonds, setting a precedent that allowed legal frameworks to be altered post-issuance. With 85.5% of Greek debt holders participating in the exchange, the collective action clause was invoked, forcing the participation of holdout creditors (about €25 billion of the total bond stock of €177 billion). For investors, this episode underscored the importance of understanding bond documentation, the presence and type of CACs, and legal jurisdiction. It also highlighted the potential for coercive restructuring tactics and the willingness of sovereign nations to renege on their commitments when under distress.

The credit default swap (CDS) auction that followed also provided important lessons for investors. In the initial phase of restructuring, CDS was not triggered. However, following the retroactive insertion of CACs and the involuntary bail-in of bondholders, after considerable debate, ISDA ruled that a credit event had occurred. This process underscored the complexity of sovereign CDS contracts and the importance of clearly defined trigger events.

The origins of the default provided key lessons for policymakers and investors, namely to assess a country's fiscal numbers and debt dynamics critically. Greece's crisis began in October 2009 when the newly elected government disclosed that previously published government debt levels and budget deficits had been significantly underreported by as much as 11%.

The resulting loss of market confidence drove interest rates on Greek government debt higher, effectively shutting Greece out of the international capital markets. Successive rounds of fiscal austerity followed, leading to a prolonged economic slump, nationwide protests, and a debt-to-GDP ratio exceeding 160% by 2011.

The country eventually received large bailout loans from the *Troika* and initiated debt restructurings. Private bank debt was restructured in 2011 with a 50% haircut, amounting to €100 billion in debt relief. This was followed in February 2012 by a sovereign debt exchange proposal for Greek law government bonds, foreign law government bonds, and bonds issued by government-owned enterprises and guaranteed by the government.

With the majority of Greece's debt issued under local law, the restructuring occurred preemptively without a suspension of debt service payments. A total of €177 billion in local law bonds was tendered, along with €20 billion out of a total stock of €29 billion in foreign law sovereign debt and debt issued by state-owned entities. The haircuts were substantial, resulting in NPV losses of approximately 79% for local law bonds and 69% for foreign law bonds.[32]

15.6.2 Argentina (2001)

Argentina's 2001 default and subsequent restructuring is infamous for being one of the most contentious sovereign debt workouts in recent history.[33] Not only was the default significant in size—covering $82 billion of sovereign debt—the government's combative stance toward negotiations with bondholders diverged from the established convention in sovereign debt workouts.

The result was decades-long litigation with holdout creditors, including the landmark NML v. Argentina case.[34] The US court ruling in favor of the holdouts, which blocked Argentina from servicing restructured bonds until the holdouts were paid in full, highlighted the risks associated with *pari passu* clauses and the absence of an adequate mechanism to manage sovereign defaults in an orderly way.

Argentina's chaotic and lengthy restructuring saga has had enduring implications for sovereign debt markets. Argentina's sovereign bonds did not have CACs and so required unanimous consent for restructuring. The default paved the way for innovations in sovereign debt contracts, particularly the switch from unanimous consent to super-majority rule through CACs. Successive enhancements to CACs have been aimed at curbing holdout behavior, though recent changes are encountering resistance from creditors (see Chapter 7).

The lengthy and contentious litigation by holdouts, despite their victory, highlights the difficulty of enforcing sovereign debt contracts. The plaintiffs filed hundreds of suits, and many attempts were made to attach Argentina's assets in the U.S. courts, most of which failed. This reflected the high bar to collect assets from a foreign sovereign, given the U.S. Foreign Sovereign Immunities Act and similar laws enacted in other countries.

This raised the related question of whether it is beneficial to be a holdout creditor. In the case of NML v. Argentina, the size of the settlement resulted in a significant NPV payoff despite the length and cost of litigation. However, in other cases, like the Ecuador litigation following the 2008 default, it is less clear, as discussed in the next section. Even though courts eventually ruled in favor of the holdouts, the associated payout in Ecuador was much lower than expected.

Argentina's economic crisis of 2001–2002 set the stage for the default, which was accompanied by a sharp recession, a systemic banking crisis, the de-pegging of its currency, exchange rate devaluation, and political instability characterized by multiple leadership changes. Capital flight and excessively high interest rates on government debt increasingly hindered Argentina's ability to roll over its debt, leading to the announcement in November 2001 of its plan to restructure both local and foreign currency debt.

Initially, in December 2001, Argentina was able to restructure its US dollar and peso debt held by domestic investors into new government-backed loans. However, as the economic crisis escalated and all domestic contracts were eventually converted to pesos, Argentina was unable to complete the restructuring. It was not until 2005, four years later, that the government began the restructuring of its foreign debt.

In Argentina's 2005 exchange offer, the government adopted an aggressive stance, refusing to engage in good-faith negotiations with a committee of leading bondholders. The initial terms featured a 66% nominal haircut and the issuance of a GDP warrant, which implied an NPV haircut of 75% at market prices. Past due interest accrued since the 2001 default was only partially credited. There were no bona fide negotiations with creditors during the process, and the government's proposal lacked endorsement from the IMF, contrary to the usual practice in debt workouts. Additionally, there was a perception that the requested debt relief was not aligned with Argentina's capacity to repay and instead represented an opportunistic cramdown of bondholders.

The defaulted Argentine bonds did not have collective action clauses but instead required unanimous consent. This feature should have encouraged the country to seek debt relief that its bondholders would consider fair and reasonable. However, due to Argentina's approach, the participation rate in the exchange was low (76%) compared to levels achieved in other exchanges. Holdout creditors rejected the exchange, initiating a series of litigations against Argentina around the globe, most notably in New York. The outcome was years of legal battles, effectively closing Argentina off from accessing the international bond markets.

A reopening of its 2005 deal in 2010 brought the percentage of bonds under some form of repayment to 92%. Disputes with holdouts, most notably NML Capital, continued and became increasingly contentious and legally complex. In October 2010, NML filed its motion for the pari passu injunction mentioned above, eventually leading to Judge Griesa's extraordinary injunction blocking payments to all bondholders unless NML Capital and other plaintiffs were also paid. The result was a damaging default on all creditors in July 2014 when Argentina refused to pay the holdouts, and the court blocked its ability to pay the other bonds issued in the 2005 and 2010 exchange.

It wasn't until 2016 when the government of Mauricio Macri came into power that the case with holdouts was settled. NML received a settlement of $2.4 billion which was a 25% discount to the value of their legal claim, including past-due interest and post-judgement interest. As there is no public record of the price they paid for their claims, NML's profits cannot be reported. The settlement covered almost all of the 300 cases filed against Argentina in the U.S. courts and the total payment was in the area of $10 billion dollars.

Despite the infamy of this case, there are good reasons to view it as the exception rather than the rule for sovereign debt workouts. Argentina defaulted again in 2020, with very different outcomes. The subsequent debt exchange marked the first significant use of enhanced CACs to restructure a large, complex bond stock. The country swapped $65 billion in foreign law bonds with high creditor participation and minimal holdout risk. The potential for using Pacman strategies and redesignation of voting pools faced creditor resistance. It was subsequently followed by the adoption of new language in the exchange bonds to restrict their use in future restructurings.

15.6.3 Ecuador (2008)

In 2008, Ecuador's President Correa partially defaulted on two bonds, the 2012 and 2030s, for a total sum of $3.2 billion.[35] At the same time, he remained current on the 2015 bond, which was issued under his previous administration. The default was a surprise to the markets as the country's debt ratio was moderate at 27% of GDP, and it had the fiscal resources and foreign exchange reserves to continue servicing the debt. The President claimed the debt was illegitimate as past governments raised it, although international third parties did not categorize it as such.

Following the default announcement, bond prices plummeted, and the government repurchased almost 90% of the outstanding bonds at a deep discount. In doing so, Ecuador eliminated over $3 billion in external debt through this process, reducing its debt burden significantly at a price of less than $1 billion! The final recovery rate was estimated at 32–35%, making it one of the harshest haircuts for creditors in modern sovereign debt restructurings.

Eventually, Ecuador entered into a debt restructuring agreement with its remaining creditors, which involved exchanging existing bonds for new bonds with longer maturities and lower interest rates. While the majority of creditors agreed to the restructuring, a small group of holdout creditors refused to participate in the agreement and sued Ecuador in the US courts.

In 2012, a US court ruled in favor of the holdout creditors and ordered Ecuador to pay $1.4 billion in damages. Ecuador refused to pay the judgment, arguing that it was unfair and would have significant economic and social impacts on the country. The dispute between Ecuador and the holdout creditors continued for several years, with the two sides engaging in a legal battle in the US and international courts.

In 2016, Ecuador reached a settlement with the holdout creditors, agreeing to pay $112 million in damages in exchange for the dismissal of the lawsuit. The settlement was seen as a victory for Ecuador, as it was significantly less than the original judgment and allowed the country to avoid a potentially costly and protracted legal battle.

15.7 SUMMARY

This chapter laid the groundwork for managing distressed sovereign bonds in investment portfolios. After a brief historical overview of sovereign defaults, it outlined several stylized facts. These included the empirical probability of default, the average time for resolution, the average creditor loss or haircut, and empirical differences between domestic and external defaults.

Definitions of default were summarized, highlighting the differences between foreign and domestic law defaults. The chapter closed with a description of serial restructurings and defaults, and key takeaways for investors from notable sovereign defaults in Greece (2012), Argentina (2001), and Ecuador (2008).

For a sovereign facing a debt crisis or economic stress, there are several paths forward. In the vast majority of instances, governments look to work with creditors to restructure debt and come to a mutual agreement on the terms of the new debt contract. This is often a complex process involving many stakeholders and several stages, which we will discuss next.

NOTES

1. Eichengreen et al., "Public Debt Through the Ages."
2. Ash, "Great Defaults from History."
3. See Reinhart and Rogoff, *This Time Is Different*, for further details.
4. Reinhart, Reinhart, and Trebesch, "Global Cycles," find that the unconditional probability of sovereign default increases to 12% from an average of 2% if preceded by a sudden stop of capital flows.
5. See Martinez et al., *Sovereign Debt*, for a review of the literature.
6. Debt is defined as odious if it has been issued without the consent of the population, has brought no benefits to the population, and has been bought by investors knowing the funds would be misused (Kremer and Jayachandran, *Odious Debts*). Other candidates for odious debt include debts incurred under the regimes of Mobutu Sese Seko (Zaire, now Congo), Ferdinand Marcos (the Philippines), Anastasio Samoza (Nicaragua), and Franjo Tudjman (Croatia).
7. Tomz and Wright, "Empirical Research on Sovereign Debt," and Brauer, Martin, and Paja, *Emerging Market Sovereign Defaults Primer*. Note that there are two main approaches to calculating default rates. These are the average default probability for the face value of defaulted securities as a share of outstanding debt and the number of countries in default for a given universe. The aggregation methodology and whether the mean or median is reported can also affect the reported number.

8. Mitchener, Kris J., and Christoph Trebesch, "Sovereign Debt."
9. Erce, Mallucci, and Picarelli, *Sovereign Defaults at Home and Abroad.*
10. Other long defaults include Iraq (20 years) and Ivory Coast (12 years).
11. Erce, Mallucci, and Picarelli, *Sovereign Defaults at Home and Abroad.*
12. See Moody's, *Sovereign Default and Recovery Rates* for recent recovery rates by sovereign default episode. For reviews of the academic work on this topic, see Erce, Mallucci, and Picarelli, *Sovereign Defaults at Home and Abroad*; Graf von Luckner, Meyer, Reinhart, and Trebesch, *Sovereign Haircuts*; Tomz and Wright, "Empirical Research on Sovereign Debt"; Cruces and Trebesch, "Sovereign Defaults"; and Martinez et al., *Sovereign Debt.*
13. Graf von Luckner, Meyer, Reinhart, and Trebesch, *Sovereign Haircuts.* Debt repudiation occurred following the Cuban Revolution in 1959, China in 1949, Rhodesia in 1965, Zaire in 1979, Ghana in 1979 and 1982, and North Korea in 1976.
14. Waever, *Looking Back to Look Ahead.*
15. Graf von Luckner et al., *Sovereign Debt: 200 Years of Creditor Losses.*
16. Erce, Mallucci, and Picarelli, *Sovereign Defaults at Home and Abroad*, and Asonuma and Trebesch, "Sovereign Debt Restructurings."
17. See Ams et al., "Sovereign Default" for a review of the literature.
18. The exact grace period for a debt security will be specified in the contract. Coupon payments typically have grace periods ranging from 10 to 30 days, with short-dated instruments typically having no or much shorter grace periods (for example, 5 days). Grace periods for principal payments tend to be less common and shorter (typically, 5–10 days). Rating agencies also work with criteria for grace periods when they aren't stipulated explicitly in the debt contract.
19. IMF, *Issues in Restructuring of Sovereign Domestic Debt.*
20. See Erce, Mallucci, and Picarelli, *Sovereign Defaults on Domestic-Law Public Debt* and Moody's, *FAQ on Local Currency Sovereign Defaults* for a summary of the literature.
21. Erce, Mallucci, and Picarelli, *Sovereign Defaults on Domestic-Law Public Debt.*
22. Erce, Mallucci, and Picarelli, *Sovereign Defaults on Domestic-Law Public Debt.*
23. This is for defaults since 1980. See Erce, Mallucci, and Picarelli, *Sovereign Defaults on Domestic-Law Public Debt.* There are protracted cases, with almost one-third of domestic restructuring events lasting more than 3 years and 6% of them lasting more than 12 years.
24. The IMF's definition of constructive or *good faith* negotiations includes (i) engaging with the creditors at an early stage and throughout the restructuring proves, (ii) sharing relevant non-confidential information on a timely basis, (iii) providing creditors with the opportunity to give input on the design of the restructuring and individual instruments, and (iv) engaging with a timely formed and representative creditor committee (IMF, *Fund Policy on Sovereign Arrears*).
25. Moody's Investors Service. *Sovereign Default and Recovery Rates.*
26. See Asonuma, *Serial Sovereign Defaults* for a review.
27. Graf von Luckner, Meyer, Reinhart, and Trebesch, *Sovereign Haircuts.*
28. Ash, "Great Defaults from History."
29. Meyer, Reinhart, and Trebesch, "Sovereign Bonds since Waterloo."
30. For further details, see Papaconstantinou, *Game Over*; Varoufakis, *Adults in the Room*; Xafa, "Lessons from the 2012 Greek Debt Restructuring"; and Zettelmeyer, Trebesch, and Gulati, "Greek Debt Restructuring."
31. Smith, "Yanis Varoufakis."
32. In December 2012, the government bought back €31.9 bn of local law debt for €11.3 bn, implying a 63% loss as measured by trading prices. This was categorized by Moody's as a separate default under their classification criteria, although there was no missed payment. Of note, Greece continued to pay foreign law bonds that did not participate in the exchange. Moody's Investors Service. *Sovereign Default and Recovery Rates.*

33. See Moody's Investors Service. *Sovereign Default and Recovery Rates*; Makoff, *Default* and Porzecanski, "Why Was Argentina's 2001 Default So Contentious?"; and Silva, Campbell, and Ranieri, "Lessons from Argentina's Default" for further details.
34. For a summary of the Argentine litigation in the US, see Box 1 in IMF, *Strengthening the Contractual Framework.*
35. Moody's Investors Service. *Sovereign Default and Recovery Rates.*

REFERENCES

Ams, J., R. Baqir, Anna Gelpern, and Christoph Trebesch. "Sovereign Default." In *Sovereign Debt: A Guide for Economists and Practitioners*, edited by S. Ali Abbas, Alex Pienkowski, and Kenneth Rogoff, Chapter 7. Oxford: Oxford University Press, 2022.

Ash, Adrian. "Great Defaults from History, Part 372: The English Experience c.1300." *BullionVault*, July 22, 2011. https://www.bullionvault.com/gold-news/default_072220116 (accessed 31 July 2025).

Asonuma, Tamon. *Serial Sovereign Defaults and Debt Restructurings.* IMF Working Paper No. 16/65. Washington, DC: International Monetary Fund, 2016.

Asonuma, Tamon, and Christoph Trebesch, "Sovereign Debt Restructurings: Preemptive or Post-Default." *Journal of the European Economic Association*, 14, no. 1 (2016): 175–214.

Brauer, Jane, Lucas Martin, and Merveille Paja. *Emerging Market Sovereign Defaults Primer – A Survival Guide.* GEMs FI Strategy Viewpoint. Bank of America Global Research, 2022.

Burdekin, Richard C. K., and Richard J. Sweeney. "The Evolution of Sovereign Debt Default: From the Thirteenth Century to the Modern Era." *Journal of European Economic History*, 50, no. 2 (2021): 9–56. Claremont McKenna College Robert Day School of Economics and Finance Research Paper No. 3885237; Georgetown McDonough School of Business Research Paper No. 3885237.

Cruces, Juan J., and Christoph Trebesch. "Sovereign Defaults: The Price of Haircuts." *American Economic Journal: Macroeconomics* 5, no. 3 (2013): 85–117.

Eichengreen, Barry, Asmaa El-Ganainy, Rui Pedro Esteves, and Kris James Mitchener. "Public Debt Through the Ages." In *Sovereign Debt: A Guide for Economists and Practitioners*, edited by S. A. Abbas, A. Pienkowski, and K. Rogoff. Oxford: Oxford University Press, 2022.

Erce, Aitor, Enrico Mallucci, and Mattia Picarelli. *Sovereign Defaults at Home and Abroad.* European Stability Mechanism Working Paper Series, 60, 2024.

Erce, Aitor, Enrico Mallucci, and Mattia Picarelli. *A Journey in the History of Sovereign Defaults on Domestic-Law Public Debt.* International Finance Discussion Papers 1338. Washington: Board of Governors of the Federal Reserve System, 2022.

Gilman, Martin. *No Precedent, No Plan: Inside Russia's 1998 Default.* Cambridge, MA: MIT Press, 2010.

Graf von Luckner, Clemens, Carmen M. Reinhart, Josefin Meyer, and Christoph Trebesch. *Sovereign Debt: 200 Years of Creditor Losses.* 24th Jacques Polak Annual Research Conference, International Monetary Fund, 2023.

International Monetary Fund. *Fund Policy on Sovereign Arrears to Private Creditors.* Washington, DC: International Monetary Fund, 2002.

International Monetary Fund. *Strengthening the Contractual Framework to Address Collective Action Problems in Sovereign Debt Restructuring.* IMF Staff Report. Washington, DC: International Monetary Fund, 2014.

International Monetary Fund. *Issues in Restructuring of Sovereign Domestic Debt.* IMF Staff Report. Washington, DC: International Monetary Fund, 2021.

James, Harold. *The IMF and the European Debt Crisis.* Washington, DC: International Monetary Fund, 2024.

Kremer, Michael, and Seema Jayachandran. *Odious Debts*. NBER Working Paper No. 8953. Cambridge, MA: National Bureau of Economic Research, 2002.

Makoff, Gregory. *Default: The Landmark Court Battle over Argentina's $100 Billion Debt Restructuring*. Washington, DC: Georgetown University Press, 2024.

Makoff, Gregory, and Mark C. Weidemaier. Mass Sovereign Debt Litigation: A Computer-Assisted Analysis of the Argentina Bond Litigation in the U.S. Federal Courts 2002–2016, U.C. Davis L. Rev. Vol. 56 at 1233.

Malik, Hassan. *Bankers and Bolsheviks: International Finance and the Russian Revolution*. Princeton, NJ: Princeton University Press, 2018.

Martinez, Leonardo, Francisco Roch, Francisco Roldán, and Jeromin Zettelmeyer. *Sovereign Debt*. IMF Working Paper No. 22/122. Washington, DC: International Monetary Fund, 2022.

Meyer, Josefin, Carmen M. Reinhart, and Christoph Trebesch. "Sovereign Bonds Since Waterloo." *Quarterly Journal of Economics* 137, no. 3 (2022): 1615–1680.

Mitchener, Kris J., and Christoph Trebesch, "Sovereign Debt in the Twenty-First Century." *Journal of Economic Literature* 61, no. 2 (2023): 565–623.

Moody's Investors Service. *Sovereign Defaults Series: FAQ: The Increasing Incidence of Local Currency Sovereign Defaults*. 2019. https://www.moodys.com.

Moody's Investors Service. *Sovereign Default and Recovery Rates, 1983–2022*. 2023. https://www.moodys.com.

Papaconstantinou, Giorgos. *Game Over: The Inside Story of the Greek Crisis*. Scotts Valley, CA: CreateSpace Independent Publishing Platform, 2016.

Porzecanski, Arturo C. "Why Was Argentina's 2001 Default So Contentious?" *Americas Quarterly*, April 2024.

Reinhart, Carmen M., and Kenneth Rogoff. *This Time Is Different: Eight Centuries of Financial Folly*. Princeton, NJ: Princeton University Press, 2009.

Reinhart, Carmen M., Vincent Reinhart, and Christoph Trebesch. "Global Cycles: Capital Flows, Commodities, and Sovereign Defaults, 1815–2015." *American Economic Review* 106, no. 5 (2016): 574–580.

Silva, Ricardo E., Matthew Campbell, and Ana M. Ranieri. "Lessons from Argentina's Default on Its International Sovereign Debt." In *The Guide to Restructuring*, 3rd ed., edited by James K. Gallup and Mary L. Fitzgerald. Latin Lawyer, 2023. https://latinlawyer.com/guide/the-guide-restructuring/third-edition (accessed 31 July 2025).

Smith, Helena. "Yanis Varoufakis: Greece's New Finance Minister Takes on the Austerity Establishment." *The Guardian*, January 27, 2015. https://www.theguardian.com/world/2015/jan/27/yanis-varoufakis-greek-finance-minister-syriza-anti-austerity.

Tomz, Michael, and Mark, L. J. Wright. "Empirical Research on Sovereign Debt and Default." *Annual Review of Economics* 5 (2013): 247–272.

Varoufakis, Yanis. *Adults in the Room: My Battle with the European and American Deep Establishment*. New York: Farrar, Straus and Giroux, 2017.

Xafa, Miranda. "Lessons from the 2012 Greek Debt Restructuring." *VoxEU*, June 25, 2014. https://cepr.org/voxeu/columns/lessons-2012-greek-debt-restructuring (accessed 31 July 2025).

Zettelmeyer, Jeromin, Christoph Trebesch, and Mitu Gulati. "The Greek Debt Restructuring: An Autopsy." *Economic Policy* 75 (2013): 513–563. https://doi.org/10.1111/1468-0327.12014.

CHAPTER SIXTEEN

The Debt Restructuring Process

SOVEREIGN DEBT restructurings are complex, multi-stakeholder negotiations that determine how much investors recover when a government defaults. Unlike corporate restructurings, which are governed by bankruptcy laws and regulations, sovereign debt restructurings do not have a formal legal framework. Solutions must be negotiated between the sovereign and its creditors, often alongside economic crises, political pressure, and market turbulence.

This chapter explores the distinct aspects of sovereign restructurings. It examines the key players and their objectives in the restructuring process. An overview of the main phases in sovereign debt restructurings and key considerations for investors at each stage follows this. These include the prospects and nature of IMF involvement, creditor organization and information collection, release of the official macroeconomic framework, and official debt sustainability analysis. The restructuring envelope, the restructuring proposal, negotiation, and official offer and exchange are also reviewed.

16.1 DISTINCT ASPECTS OF SOVEREIGN RESTRUCTURINGS

Sovereigns are unique debtors with a wide range of powers that can influence the timing and outcomes of debt restructurings. They can affect the legal, fiscal, and financial landscape in which creditors operate. They can change domestic legislation, levy taxes, implement capital controls and price restrictions, and adjust the regulation and supervision of the financial sector.

Sovereigns can protect their assets from attachment and leverage geopolitical, official, and bilateral networks that private creditors cannot access. They also possess an informational advantage regarding their ability to repay and willingness to comply with required policy adjustments after restructuring.

At the same time, sovereign issuers face unique vulnerabilities. No bankruptcy code allows a sovereign to restructure its debts under a court's supervision and protection. This means obtaining debt relief is not unilateral and requires creditors' consent. Countries unable to reach a negotiated settlement may be shut out of the financial markets indefinitely. Holdout action may prolong debt restructurings and lead to costly litigation.

Sovereign debt restructurings are not merely transactions between the creditor and the government. They typically involve third parties, such as the IMF and bilateral creditors, who wield significant influence over outcomes, often more than private creditors. The seniority of multilateral funding means investors' claims are subordinated to IMF repayments. Additionally, IMF bailout programs determine the scale and terms of the debt relief requested by the government.

Moreover, sovereign restructurings frequently happen during economic and political crises. As a result, governments must often manage complex macroeconomic policy challenges, domestic political considerations, and geopolitical issues simultaneously while negotiating debt restructuring. This combination of factors further complicates debt negotiations.

These unique aspects make sovereign debt restructurings much more complex than corporate workouts, for both the debtor and private creditors.

16.2 KEY PLAYERS AND THEIR OBJECTIVES

Sovereign debt restructurings involve a range of stakeholders, each with its own interests and objectives. The ability of these stakeholders to collaborate and reach a mutually acceptable agreement is often a critical factor in a successful debt workout. The main players include the sovereign issuer, multilateral organizations, bilateral creditors, private sector creditors, and legal and advisory consultants.[1]

For the sovereign debt investor, a strong dose of skepticism is essential to evaluate the objectives of each player. What agents claim their motivations are may differ significantly from what their incentives entail and what their actions ultimately reveal.

For instance, governments frequently claim that they do not intend to default, only to reverse course and default within a short period. Similarly, so-called *investor-friendly* governments have often imposed severe restructuring terms on private creditors. These actions serve as a reminder that the stakes are high and nothing is off the table.

16.2.1 The Sovereign

The government entity responsible for restructuring and negotiating with creditors plays a crucial role in a sovereign debt workout. In most sovereign restructurings, the debtor is the central government, represented by the Ministry of Finance's Debt Office, which leads and coordinates the negotiation. The Central Bank, state-owned enterprises, and sub-sovereign entities may also be involved, working alongside the central government's restructuring program.

In the initial phase of a sovereign crisis, the government's primary objective is to stabilize the economy and negotiate external assistance from lenders such as the International Monetary Fund (IMF) (if available). After the acute phase of the crisis has passed, restructuring debt and restoring debt ratios to sustainable levels may occur.

The government's historical record of defaults and interactions with investors can indicate how it will approach the restructuring. If it has generally negotiated in good faith, this may continue. Investors may be approached and treated fairly if market access after restructuring is financially relevant for the country. The level of hardship faced by the population and the causes of the default may also be determining factors.

The political economy of crises and the context of default can influence the restructuring process. For instance, it may determine what type of debt is included in the scope of the restructuring and what is excluded. Geopolitics and contagion risk can affect whether external support from the IMF and bilateral creditors is available and its extent, as well as whether the program's conditionality will be strict or manageable.

16.2.2 The IMF, World Bank, and Third Parties

The IMF plays a central role in sovereign restructurings. As a lender of last resort, the IMF can provide governments with emergency financing and has been involved in the majority (77%) of sovereign restructurings since the 2000s.[2]

Specifically, the IMF's analysis of debt sustainability and macroeconomic policy serves as the foundation for determining whether a debt restructuring is necessary and, if so, its parameters. This analysis, together with the program's financing envelope, is utilized to identify the resources available for debt service and the medium-term macroeconomic trajectory of the economy. The IMF also collaborates with official sector actors and assesses whether any agreements with private and bilateral creditors meet the debt relief requirements of the program.[3]

Other multilateral creditors that may be involved include the World Bank and regional development banks. National and international organizations may also monitor, finance, and support the restructuring process. For example, during the Eurozone Crisis, the *Troika* of the European Central Bank, the European Commission, and the IMF worked together. They provided new financing programs for the crisis-hit peripheral countries and were instrumental in defining the terms of the Greece 2012 restructuring.

16.2.3 Bilateral Official Creditors

Countries often lend to each other in the form of bilateral loans.[4] These may serve geopolitical or strategic purposes, finance infrastructure projects, support exports from the creditor country, or provide development assistance.

Historically, these loans (when distressed) were restructured through the Paris Club, an informal group of 22 member countries formed to coordinate sovereign debt restructurings. With the rise of non–Paris Club lenders like China and India, these negotiations with developing economies are increasingly conducted under the G20 Common Framework. This is a debt restructuring mechanism launched in 2020 for official bilateral creditors to negotiate with low-income debtor countries to address unsustainable debt burdens.[5]

China is by far the largest bilateral creditor to developing countries, lending an estimated $1.3 trillion to 135 countries across Asia, Africa, and Latin America.[6] China's lending is distinct from that of other official creditors because it occurs through its state-owned banks and involves both public and private sector borrowers within the debtor country. This blurs the distinction of whether the creditor is public or private and whether the liabilities represent sovereign or private debt. Historically, China and its entities have negotiated as a bloc with the debtor country across all sectors, but this is changing with the G20 Common Framework.

With China's involvement, the rules governing debt restructurings are being challenged. While key principles of the Paris Club, such as comparability of treatment (CoT) and information sharing, remain intact, new questions are emerging. These encompass the seniority of multilateral lenders, the management of domestic debt, and the enforcement of CoT clauses. Additionally, the approach to debt relief appears to be shifting toward maturity extension rather than principal haircuts.

The IMF and official bilateral creditors are usually in the driving seat of debt restructurings, particularly if their exposure is significant. They collaborate closely during a sovereign debt restructuring and share information as bilateral creditors sit on the IMF Executive Board. An IMF program requires *financing assurances* from key official bilateral creditors before any IMF disbursements occur. These commitments ensure that the official bilateral creditors will provide debt relief and/or financing, allowing the country to repay the IMF and pursue a sustainable debt path. Any complication in this process may delay the IMF program and the debt restructuring.

16.2.4 Commercial Creditors

Commercial creditors consist of bondholders, banks, trade finance providers, and suppliers that finance the government.

Bondholders can be categorized into resident and non-resident holders, those holding foreign law versus local law debt, and by the currency of issuance. Additional categories include types of instruments, such as front-end bonds versus long-end bonds or those with specific types of CACs. These distinctions become relevant when there are trade-offs in the debt restructuring process, where different categories of instruments may be treated differently.

To better understand market technicals and holdout behavior, bondholders can also be classified by investment strategy. This can be disaggregated into institutional investors, distressed funds, hedge funds, and retail investors. Grouping by active versus passive or ETF mandates can also be helpful to understand trade flows and holding patterns.

Commercial creditors, particularly banks (both international and domestic), are often pivotal in debt restructurings, as their solvency can be threatened if their holdings are restructured. Identifying which parts of the debt stack will be restructured is essential, as this determines the need for bank support and potential domestic debt bail-ins.

Together, these help in assessing the macroeconomic impact of default and the scale of the required adjustment.

Commercial debt may also be owed to suppliers and providers of trade credit secured by exports or other assets. This debt may be senior to bonds, affecting the ability of bondholders to enforce claims. Useful sources for the size and details of these claims include IMF program documents and debt sustainability analysis reports.

16.2.5 Creditor Committees

Commercial creditors organize themselves into creditor committees at some point in the debt restructuring process. These committees play a crucial role by coordinating a common position among their members and negotiating with the government. The committee agrees on the amount of debt relief, the timing and structure of debt repayments, and any other conditions related to the debt restructuring. They also communicate with other stakeholders, such as official creditors, different commercial creditors, advisors, and rating agencies, to advance the debt agreement.[7]

Creditor committees comprise investors who share similar incentives, hold instruments with comparable characteristics (such as maturity or collateral), and/or have common institutional objectives and constraints. The committee chair is typically the investor with the largest position in the relevant bond series or the chair from the previous debt restructuring (if one has occurred). Once appointed, a chair invites other creditors with similar objectives to join the committee.

Often, more than one creditor committee exists, in which case an overarching committee coordinates decisions on behalf of all members. For example, in Ecuador's 2020 debt restructuring, there were three creditor committees: the "Ad Hoc Group," comprising major institutional holders of Ecuador's external sovereign debt; a "Steering Committee" (the "Minority Committee"); and an ad hoc group of holders of the 2024 bond.

16.2.6 Other Parties

Financial advisors provide sovereign issuers with advice and guidance on the restructuring process. They can develop the government's debt restructuring plan and run debt sustainability models. They often liaise with the IMF on behalf of the government and interact with creditors to assess what terms would be acceptable to them in exchange for a restructuring package.

Legal advisors include the government's team, creditor committee representatives, and independent firms that provide legal assessments and guidance on the restructuring process. Other third parties include index providers and credit rating agencies, who aren't directly involved in negotiations but may impact markets through their index and ratings actions.

PRO TIP: *Build contacts with the main players in the debt restructuring to gain insights on their motivations and to stay abreast of developments as negotiations progress.*

16.3 STAGES IN SOVEREIGN DEBT RESTRUCTURINGS

Sovereign debt restructurings have distinct stages. The first phase is the pricing of sovereign credit risk, particularly default risk, into markets. This often occurs well before an actual default or restructuring event and marks the beginning of the process for sovereign bond investors. As market valuations adapt to the new developments, investors update their portfolio strategies and views on the credit and adjust risk positions.

Meanwhile, for the sovereign debtor, the process begins with a recognition that a restructuring is necessary. Depending on the political economy the government faces, this may occur preemptively or after a payment default. There may also be a broader backdrop of a macroeconomic crisis that the government is looking to contain through an IMF program or support from bilateral creditors.

If there is an IMF program, the government negotiates loan terms and policies aimed at stabilizing the macroeconomy and debt dynamics with IMF representatives. Concurrently, official creditors organize and engage in multilateral and bilateral discussions regarding debt treatment. Private creditors also organize and conduct independent credit analysis, due diligence, and form creditor committees.

The next phase occurs over several rounds. Bilateral creditors may announce their views and provide the IMF with financing reassurances ahead of any program. If an IMF program is agreed, details are made public, and the first tranche of financing is disbursed to the country.

At some point, the restructuring envelope will be announced, along with the publication of the IMF's DSA and information on the government's macroeconomic plan. These topics are discussed with creditors through structured forums like the Global Sovereign Debt Roundtable (GSDR),[8] and investor calls involving the government, the IMF, and their advisors.

The sovereign and its advisors will also determine how to manage SOE, state, and local government debt. In most instances, they will establish parallel restructuring tracks, each with its distinct parameters and terms.

Following this extensive groundwork, the restructuring moves into the negotiation phase. This begins with a preliminary offer from the government that serves as the basis for discussions with each creditor committee. This part of the process may be quick or prolonged, depending on the specifics of the case. Once an agreement is reached, the government makes an official offer and initiates an exchange. After the exchange, the government evaluates the results and determines its strategy for addressing any holdouts.

The entire process can take anywhere from a few months to several years, and in some cases, decades, to complete. The average duration of sovereign debt restructurings is between 2.5 and 3.25 years, indicating that even in the best scenarios, an extended period of time is involved.

16.4 IMF INVOLVEMENT

A key question for investors is whether there will be external bilateral support or an IMF program.[9] These may stem the crisis altogether, reduce its scope, and impact the debt relief required from private creditors. The likelihood of bilateral support and an IMF program, its form (funded or unfunded), the size of any financing, and the timing are important factors that investors look to forecast.

IMF financing comes with strings or *conditionality*. This may include policy measures such as fiscal consolidation and subsidy reform, or structural reforms like the privatization of state assets and addressing corruption. These measures tend to be politically unpopular, challenging to implement, and often unappealing for governments to endorse.

Many governments kick the can down the road and resist IMF programs during the early stages of the crisis. As a result, conflicting news often arises about whether there will even be a request for an IMF program. Once the decision to engage with the IMF is made, the government and the IMF Mission Team go through a negotiation process. This forms the basis for determining the loan amount and the conditions for disbursements.

The country's relationship with the IMF, its record on conditionality in previous programs, and ownership of the policy adjustment plan serve as strong indicators of a successful IMF program. Important bilateral benefactors, such as the US, Europe, or China, along with contagion and geopolitical considerations, also play a role in influencing the scale, timing, and conditionality of any IMF program.

Investors learn about an IMF agreement through press releases and conference calls involving both the government and the IMF. They might be asked for feedback during the initial discussion phase but are not formally part of the negotiations. The specific terms of any agreed program are ultimately made public several months later, once the IMF board has approved the program.

IMF programs are not a panacea for sovereign debt crises, and even with the best intentions, they can fail. The program size may be small compared to the financing needed (or the financing gap) and the market's expectations. The diagnoses of the problem may be incorrect, and corrective policies may not be appropriately calibrated. There may be unintended or unforeseen changes that could impact the macroeconomic forecasts. The government's credibility and commitment to adhering to the program conditionality may be questionable. This means that private creditors need to assess the terms and details of any IMF program critically.

For investors, an IMF program can also be a double-edged sword. Multilateral claims are super senior to any other category of debt, and this subordination can be significant. This was demonstrated in the 2010 Greek restructuring, where the official sector refused to take haircuts, leaving the burden of debt relief to fall mainly on private creditors.

16.5 INVESTOR VIEWS AND CREDITOR ORGANIZATION

Investors may be approached to share their views with the government and engage with the IMF. This could happen in small groups or through structured formats like the Global Sovereign Debt Roundtable. The government's advisors might also contact investors to provide information about their holdings, expectations regarding recovery, and perspectives on the instruments offered in the exchange. Industry bodies such as the IIF can unify investor perspectives and communicate them cohesively.

Bilateral and other official creditors may also express their views on the debt restructuring. In some cases, they might provide the country in crisis with supplemental credit lines and funds separate from IMF financing.

Eventually, creditors begin to organize themselves and decide whether to join a creditor committee.[10] Several creditor committees may be formed based on the type of investor, their holdings, and objectives. These commercial creditor committees may seek to engage with bondholder committees to share information and strategies.

Investors should take into account several factors before joining a creditor committee. The first is to weigh up the power of collective bargaining compared to taking individual action. If the creditor committee holds a majority of assets, it might be able to negotiate more effectively with the debtor than the bondholder acting alone. Alignment with committee members' incentives is also relevant. In particular, whether the interests, expertise, and preferred outcomes of the committee match those of the investors.

Individual investors need to consider both their influence within the committee and the rules that guide its decisions. These rules outline how the committee will operate, including voting mechanisms and procedures for reaching consensus. Since decisions are usually made by majority rule (one vote per institution), the power of larger stakeholders is constrained. This makes alignment of investor incentives particularly important.

Creditor committees often hold an informational edge versus going it alone since debtors share information with members under a confidentiality agreement. Additionally, committee members may exchange their macro and DSA analyses with each other to reach a consensus on their strategy. This may help investors better evaluate any exchange deal and structure their post-exchange positions more effectively.

Even with these advantages, there are drawbacks. The cost of confidentiality agreements and the limited ability to trade positions during the restructuring may deter investors from joining. Investors may encounter additional participation costs, such as administrative fees and the time spent in committee meetings. Potential reputational risks may also arise if the restructuring is stalled or unsuccessful.

16.6 OFFICIAL MACROECONOMIC FRAMEWORK

The country's revised macroeconomic forecasts, debt statistics, and government measures to achieve debt sustainability are eventually made public. Typically, these appear in government presentations and IMF program documents. Investors need to understand the official numbers and compare them with their own independent credit analysis.

The government's macroeconomic projections and assumptions are a good starting point. Growth predictions should be evaluated in relation to the country's historical performance and the performance of other economies in times of crisis. The fiscal effort assumptions should be reviewed and compared with successful budgetary consolidations in the past or other countries. The currency assumptions, especially the real effective exchange rate trajectory, need to be reviewed for consistency with the dynamics observed in other crises. Assessing whether the economy has passed through the acute phase of the crisis or whether there is potential for further adverse shocks is also crucial to ascertain.

Ensuring the internal consistency of forecasts is essential. The projections should be assessed to see if they effectively consider feedback loops and spillover effects on other macroeconomic variables. For example, if a decrease in economic activity is predicted, are lower fiscal revenues expected in line with the fiscal multipliers seen in past slowdowns? Is the influence of currency fluctuations accurately factored into the estimation of inflation trends? If there are losses in the banking sector and an increase in non-performing loans, are these accurately represented in future credit trends?

The government's adjustment program needs critical evaluation regarding political feasibility and its estimated impact. For instance, does the country's political economy suggest that the adjustment policies will be implemented? If taxes are to be raised, will there be significant pushback from the population? Will trade unions and other pressure groups resist wage bill or public sector employment cuts? How will the opposition take advantage of the crisis? Might there be a shift in government or key officials, like the Minister of Finance or the Central Bank Governor?

The size, conditionality, and success of the IMF program (if one is negotiated), should be similarly assessed. Key parameters to examine include the macroeconomic adjustment strategy and its alignment with past adjustments by the country and other IMF programs. How stringent are the program's conditions, and is their implementation politically viable? Are there any elements that might pose challenges? Is the government dedicated to the full program, or is it merely pursuing a short-term solution to the crisis? These considerations could influence whether the program faces challenges in subsequent reviews and goes *off track*, or fails to fulfill its commitments.

The size of the IMF program and its ability to fill the country's financing gaps are critical factors that can either stem the crisis or exacerbate it. Historically, smaller programs than the market expected have faced challenges.

The likelihood of a follow-on IMF program after the initial program is also relevant. IMF programs aim to restore sustainability within three to four years, often relying on optimistic assumptions. However, there is a precedent for an extended IMF presence through serial programs. Understanding this helps investors gauge the country's medium-term credit prospects.

16.7 THE OFFICIAL DEBT SUSTAINABILITY ANALYSIS

The government, along with its advisors and the IMF, carries out a debt sustainability analysis (DSA). This document outlines details of the sovereign's indebtedness, its debt service schedule, and its various creditors. The analysis projects debt stock and required financing ratios for the baseline scenario using updated macroeconomic assumptions. Alternative scenarios to the baseline are estimated based on different assumptions and economic shock scenarios.

The DSA is often shared with investors ahead of the release of the full IMF program document. It is usually accompanied by conference calls for investors to ask questions, clarify the official assumptions, provide comments, and convey their opinions.

Several key factors must be considered in the DSA. The first is the choice of the DSA framework, as the IMF applies either the Low-Income Country Debt Sustainability Framework (LIC DSF) or the Market Access Country Debt Sustainability Framework (MAC DSF). The chosen framework influences the methodology for assessing debt sustainability and macroeconomic assumptions.[11]

The IMF determines the framework to use based on the World Bank country classifications, including its International Development Association (IDA) status and dependence on concessional financing. Nevertheless, there is room for judgment, especially for "blend" countries that have access to both concessional finance and market-based borrowing.

For Ghana's 2022–2023 DSA, the IMF used the LIC DSF due to IDA eligibility and the history of concessional borrowing. This was even though Ghana had significant market access and issued several Eurobonds before its debt crisis. Meanwhile, the IMF used the MAC DSA for Pakistan in 2025, showing how even countries with concessional loans can be classified as market-access countries when market risks are material.

The DSA's macro assumptions and variable forecasts should be critically evaluated for consistency and feasibility. The potential biases in IMF projections emphasize the necessity for investors to compare these figures with those from their own independent analysis. The stress tests and alternative scenarios should also be scrutinized for realism to ensure there is no unintended bias regarding downside risks. See Chapter 6 for a detailed discussion of DSAs.

The DSA can be used to calculate the amount of debt relief the government may be requesting and the breakdown between debt stock and flow relief. Although these details are not explicitly stated, they can be inferred from the numbers. For example, if the baseline debt ratios are 100% of GDP and the IMF's DSF guidance indicates sustainable debt ratios of 40–50% of GDP, then simplistically, the debt stock would need to be reduced by about 50–60%. This can be combined with other parameters included in the IMF program, such as the economy's gross financing needs, to estimate the liquidity relief required each year.

The DSA scenarios provide further insights into the debt stock and liquidity relief ranges. By evaluating the potential downside risks associated with the debt restructuring, the additional debt relief that may be necessary in an adverse scenario can be calculated. The distribution of this debt relief burden among various types of debt and debt holders is part of the restructuring envelope, which we discuss next.

16.8 THE RESTRUCTURING ENVELOPE

The primary purpose of the DSA is to determine the amount of debt relief required. Along with the IMF's macroeconomic stabilization plan, it establishes the *restructuring envelope*, which outlines the overall financial terms for the debt restructuring. This includes the size of haircuts, maturity extensions, interest rate adjustments, and other necessary modifications to align the country's debt burden with its ability to repay.

The restructuring envelope plays a crucial role in identifying which creditors will be bailed-in to provide debt relief and which types of debt will be restructured. For instance, it will clarify whether external and local debt will be included, and whether all maturities and instruments will be covered. It will determine if SOE and state debt will fall within scope and specify whether official creditors will be senior or bailed-in to the restructuring.

Typically, the restructuring envelope leaves out certain types of debt. It treats IMF and World Bank claims as super senior and excludes them. Senior debt, such as repo loans, and collateralized debt are also excluded and are often repaid before defaulting on bondholders.[12] Also excluded are trade credits, given the importance of trade finance for the economy, and treasury bills, given the need for short-term financing for the functioning of the government.

That being said, excluded claims are evaluated on a case-by-case basis, and there are several notable exceptions. A key example is the 1998 Russia default, when GKOs—zero-coupon ruble-denominated treasury bills—were restructured.

The factors driving the debt crisis and the structure of the debt stack will influence which type of debt is included in the restructuring plan. Key aspects include differences in legal jurisdiction (whether local or foreign law applies), currency (whether liabilities are in foreign or domestic currencies), residency (whether the debtor is a non-resident or resident), and the potential for negative feedback loops (such as the impact on the banking sector or access to markets).

Historically, domestic debt has been included on a case-by-case basis due to the political and economic impacts of restructurings on the banking and domestic financial sector.[13] Instead, financial repression, coercion, and legislative changes were often used to deflate local law and local currency claims in ways foreign law instruments cannot. These options were more limited if domestic debt was in foreign currency or had a higher share of non-residents.

More recently, domestic debt restructurings are increasingly unavoidable, raising the question of whether external debt should also be bailed-in. In these situations, governments must weigh the economic and political implications of including foreigners in the restructuring envelope against the risk of foreign holdouts and being locked out of international capital markets.

The historical precedent is mixed and underscores the case-by-case approach. Russia's 1998 default excluded foreign law bonds issued by the Russian Federation but restructured domestic law, as well as foreign currency and ruble-denominated instruments issued by the government. External creditors were also excluded in Jamaica (2010, 2013) because many global bonds lacked collective action clauses (CACs) and constituted only 30% of the outstanding debt stock.

Barbados (2018) is a notable counterexample. Although its external debt constituted only 20% of the total debt, the debt stock itself was high, amounting to 175% of GDP. As a result, external creditors also need to be bailed in to bring debt ratios down toward more sustainable levels. The government also pushed to distribute debt relief fairly among all creditors.

More recent examples have also been mixed. Domestic debt was included in the restructuring envelope in the Sri Lanka 2023 and Ghana 2023 debt restructurings but was excluded from the Zambia 2024 restructuring.

The restructuring envelope evolves alongside the negotiations. It may be modified if economic conditions change significantly and if powerful creditors advocate for the bail-in of other categories of debt. The latter has been the general direction of travel with China's involvement in the debt restructuring process.

16.9 THE INITIAL RESTRUCTURING PROPOSAL

Once the restructuring envelope is defined, the government releases an official restructuring proposal. This outlines the amount, method, and modality of debt relief being sought from creditors.[14] The release of the initial restructuring proposal marks the start of the formal negotiation process with creditors.

At this point, investors can assess the exact terms of the debt relief effort they are being asked for and may push back. They evaluate the DSA and IMF program and communicate any disagreements regarding the economic assumptions, macroeconomic framework, policy prescription, and debt sustainability methodology.

They may give alternative views on the restructuring envelope and the required investor effort reflected in NPV estimates. They may also provide comments on the new instruments and offer counter-proposals. Investor feedback is coordinated through the respective creditor committees and communicated to the government when negotiations begin.

16.10 NEGOTIATIONS

Restructuring negotiations can be straightforward if the debt treatment is simple and all creditors share the same interests. However, they can become extremely complex and challenging if there is a complicated debt stack with various creditors pursuing different goals. Typically, debt restructuring takes around two to three years, but the timeline can vary significantly. In reality, this phase can last anywhere from a few weeks to several months, or even years. This is also the stage where debt restructurings most often encounter roadblocks.

Governments negotiate with their official sector creditors and private creditors separately, holding distinct discussions within each group. Official sector negotiations are usually conducted within the Paris Club and G20 frameworks, with bilateral talks taking place in parallel. Private creditor negotiations occur through the respective creditor committees, as well as via one-on-one discussions with large holders.

Official creditors possess unique advantages over bondholders due to their role as IMF board members. They can influence IMF programs and debt relief recommendations before commercial creditors receive this information. This comes with the responsibility of providing *financing assurances* for fund disbursements and adhering to the IMF's DSA and debt relief requirements.

Official lenders pursue geopolitical objectives, extending negotiations beyond debt relief metrics. An official creditor might agree to debt relief similar to that of commercial creditors while negotiating access to critical infrastructure, ports, and commodities. This can complicate debt restructurings, particularly with strategic competition between official creditors. For instance, during the 2023 Sri Lanka debt restructuring, both India and China sought to maintain their geopolitical influence and access to strategic areas in the country. This added another layer of complexity to what was already a complex restructuring.

Commercial creditor committees negotiate for groups of creditors, conveying their questions, concerns, and suggestions while engaging in a dialogue with the government and its advisors. The recognition of the creditor committee is based on the principle that the sovereign will not make a formal offer to all creditors without the prior approval of the committee. Consequently, any disagreement on the DSA, initial restructuring proposal, or exchange offer must be resolved to avoid prolonged or blocked debt restructuring.

Given the need for IMF lending assurances, discussions with the official sector usually take place before negotiations with commercial creditors are finalized. Typically, the private sector follows the official sector, as investors have much less leverage to push for equal treatment once debt relief is granted. One notable exception is Suriname's 2023 restructuring, where bondholders proceeded with the complete restructuring of the two outstanding bonds. Meanwhile, the official sector provided flow relief during the IMF program, leaving the decision on principal relief to be made after the completion of the IMF program.

16.11 OFFER AND EXCHANGE

Once an *agreement in principle* is reached, the sovereign issues an official offer of exchange to creditors. This may involve exchanging old instruments for new bonds, where the former are retired or made less appealing. Alternatively, they may adjust the terms of existing bonds with minor modifications, which can include pausing coupon payments, a short maturity extension, or a slight reduction in the coupon rate.

A third approach combines upfront cash, new bonds for old ones, and issuing new instruments with state-contingent features. In Chapter 18, we cover the different types of exchange offers, negotiation tactics, and what investors look for when assessing different packages. We also discuss outcomes for investors who reject the exchange offer and hold out instead.

Once investors have made their choice and the exchange is settled, the agreement is finalized, and the official debt restructuring process is complete. Alongside these developments, markets reprice to reflect views on the restructuring and portfolio managers reassess their risk positions and issuer scaling.

16.12 SUMMARY

This chapter highlighted the unique aspects of sovereign debt restructurings and how they differ from typical corporate workouts. It explained the main players in sovereign debt restructurings and their motivations, including the government, the IMF, the official bilateral sector, commercial creditors, and other third parties.

The various stages in sovereign debt restructurings were assessed starting from the initial phase of the crisis, IMF involvement, creditor organization, the release of the official macroeconomic and restructuring assumptions, and the initial restructuring proposal. The discussion then covered the negotiations and the offer and exchange.

With a good understanding of the process and players, we now turn to how to manage bond portfolios during sovereign defaults and restructurings.

NOTES

1. Buchheit et al., "The Restructuring Process."
2. Waever, *Looking Back to Look Ahead.* Where the IMF is involved, the program is nearly always agreed upon before the debt restructuring is finalized. Usually, commercial debt restructuring is completed ahead of the first or second IMF review.
3. The IMF may also provide technical assistance, for instance, on reforming tax policy or financial sector stress tests, interact with regulators, and work with specialists on designing structural policies.
4. Bilateral lending can also be restructured, such as the $3 billion Eurobond issued by Ukraine in 2013 and purchased entirely by Russia.
5. The framework was initially established during the COVID pandemic for eligible countries to voluntarily request debt relief from official and bilateral creditors, under the purview of a funded IMF program. It is now used as a coordination mechanism for official and bilateral creditors on sovereign debt restructurings.
6. Reuters, "China Lent $1.34 Trln."
7. DeSieno, "Creditor Committees in Sovereign Debt Restructurings."
8. The GSDR brings together debtor countries and creditors. The objective is to build common understanding among key stakeholders on debt sustainability and debt restructuring challenges, and ways to address them. It discusses broad issues as well as aspects of specific restructurings to highlight implications for debt restructuring frameworks and approaches.
9. External support can take a variety of forms. For example, in 2014, Saudi Arabia, the UAE, and Kuwait pledged $23 billion in aid to Egypt following the ousting of President Mohamed Morsi. It included central bank deposits, energy subsidies, grants, and concessional loans.
10. For best practices for their formation and operation, see Institute of International Finance, *The Principles for Stable Capital Flows.*
11. See IMF, *Guidance Note on the DSF for LICs;* and *Staff Guidance Note for MAC DSA.*
12. In the 2020 restructurings of Argentina and Ecuador, repo loans were repaid in full with scarce foreign exchange reserves before the countries defaulted.
13. See IMF, *Issues in Restructuring of Sovereign Domestic Debt* for a discussion of the issues.
14. A sovereign can release the indicative restructuring proposals to a restricted group of creditors and creditor committees, or publish them on a public website. The former requires nondisclosure/stop-trade agreements from the institutions receiving material nonpublic information. The latter avoids the need for nondisclosure agreements but opens the government to criticism if the final terms are a lot worse than initially planned.

REFERENCES

Buchheit, Lee, Guillaume Chabert, Chanda DeLong, and Jeromin Zettelmeyer. "The Restructuring Process." In *Sovereign Debt: A Guide for Economists and Practitioners*, edited by S. Ali Abbas, Alex Pienkowski, and Kenneth Rogoff, Chapter 8. Oxford: Oxford University Press, 2019.

DeSieno, Timothy B. "Creditor Committees in Sovereign Debt Restructurings: Understanding the Benefits and Addressing Concerns." In *Too Little, Too Late: The Quest to Resolve Sovereign Debt Crises*, edited by Martin Guzman, José Antonio Ocampo, and Joseph E. Stiglitz, Chapter 9. New York: Columbia University Press, 2016.

International Monetary Fund. *Guidance Note on the Bank-Fund Debt Sustainability Framework for Low Income Countries*. 2018. https://www.imf.org (accessed 31 July 2025).

International Monetary Fund. *Issues in Restructuring of Sovereign Domestic Debt*. 2021. https://www.imf.org (accessed 31 July 2025).

International Monetary Fund. *Staff Guidance Note on the Sovereign Risk and Debt Sustainability Framework for Market Access Countries*. 2022. https://www.imf.org (accessed 31 July 2025).

Institute of International Finance. *The Principles for Stable Capital Flows and Fair Debt Restructuring: Report on Implementation by the Principles Consultative Group*. April 2022 Update. Washington, DC: IIF, 2022. https://www.iif.com (accessed 31 July 2025).

Reuters. "China Lent $1.34 Trln in 2000–2021, Focus Shifts from Belt and Road to Rescue Finance: Report." *Reuters*, November 6, 2023. https://www.reuters.com/world/china/china-lent-134-trln-2000-2021-focus-shifts-belt-road-rescue-finance-report-2023-11-06/ (accessed 31 July 2025).

Waever, Simon. *Looking Back to Look Ahead: Distressed EM Sovereign Credit Strategy*. Morgan Stanley, 2022.

CHAPTER SEVENTEEN

Navigating Portfolios Through Distress

FOR THE SOVEREIGN bond investor purchasing bonds at or close to par, sovereign debt restructurings are best avoided. Sovereign risk is rapidly repriced during distress episodes, and elevated market volatility complicates matters further. Fluctuations in bond valuations, even if temporary, can result in substantial losses or gains for sovereign debt portfolios. They also necessitate heightened attention to detail in trading. This makes the restructuring journey a rollercoaster ride with periods of significant uncertainty.

This chapter reviews the primary considerations for investors navigating portfolios through periods of sovereign debt distress and restructuring. The simultaneous and time-sensitive nature of the required tasks places substantial demands on investment teams. Given the extended duration typical of such processes, debt restructurings should be approached with a methodical framework and a long-term perspective. In short, they should be viewed as a marathon rather than a sprint.

17.1 PRICE DISCOVERY AND MARKET ADJUSTMENT

With the initial news of the crisis, the market enters a price discovery phase and reevaluates country risk. While there are no hard and fast rules governing how price dynamics evolve, studies on bond price dynamics in past debt crises provide valuable insights.

In most cases, bond prices drop sharply about two years before an actual payment default or restructuring (see Figure 17.1). They tend to overshoot eventual recovery, with prices at the time of default or restructuring being, on average, 26% lower. Prices usually hit rock bottom between the official announcement and the actual restructuring, typically about 32% lower than they were at the time of the announcement or default.[1]

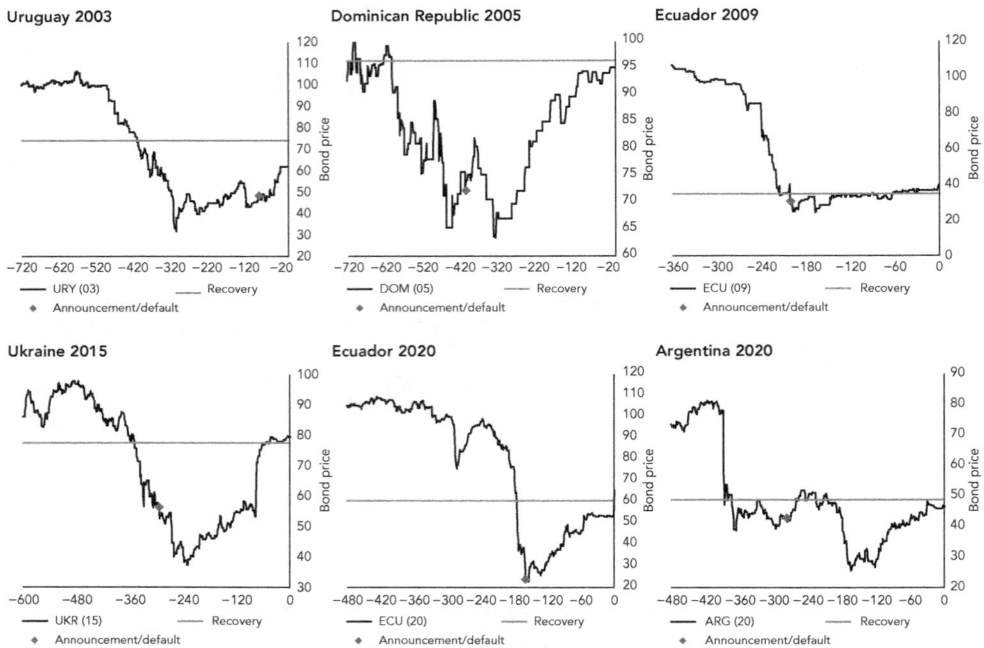

FIGURE 17.1 Average bond prices going into select sovereign restructurings. Source: Waever, Simon (2022), Bloomberg Finance L.P.

For investors, it is helpful to maintain close contact with leading market makers, brokers, and sources of local news. This allows access to daily runs, news updates, and trade axes (i.e., specific interests a trader has in buying or selling a security). In some instances, there may be only a few dealers trading the bonds, or market-making may shift to another jurisdiction. For example, following US sanctions on Venezuela in 2017, trading moved to Europe and the Middle East, where there were no restrictions.

When bonds are in default, trading moves to flat pricing, without additional payment of accrued and unpaid interest. EMTA announces the new pricing convention after consulting with broker-dealers and market representatives. Bid-ask spreads can be wide, with volatility high due to the increase in uncertainty that is typically associated with defaults. This can lead to stale price marks in portfolios and indices that need to be regularly reviewed by traders to ensure accuracy.

Adjustment in portfolio positions often leads to price differentiation across bonds along the sovereign curve. This differentiation may be based on contract terms, collateral, holdings by investor type, or cheapest-to-deliver characteristics. Relative price differences between the issuer and its regional or rating peers may emerge. Additionally, there may be changes in the pricing relationships between the issuer's sovereign bonds and those of SOEs, corporates, and CDS instruments.

Understanding the drivers of these changes and having a view on whether they are temporary or fundamentally driven will enable investors to take advantage of market opportunities and to avoid costly mistakes.

At the same time, new instruments may start trading and others may become more active, providing new ways to take (or reduce) risk. These include short-dated CDS contracts (such as one- and three-month CDS products) to capture periods when there are no coupon payments due, or CDX contracts that exclude the defaulted entity. Markets in recovery swaps, which enable investors to trade their views on recovery pricing, may also emerge. These serve as an additional tool for hedging portfolio exposures that can't be easily traded.

New market technicals may emerge, influencing pricing and trade dynamics. Forced divestments and selling pressure can result from client directives, rating downgrades, or index exclusions. Exposures may transfer from institutional holders to hedge funds or distressed creditors. Traders may capitalize on price fluctuations to shift exposures from one issuer and instrument to those with more favorable valuations or improved legal protections. Contagion and spillover to other issuers and assets may further intensify these dynamics.

Following the initial price discovery phase and shake-out of risk exposures, the market eventually adjusts and settles down. Even so, defaulted securities tend to be volatile and particularly sensitive to headline risk.

PRO TIP: *Debt restructurings are marathons not sprints. Set up internal systems to keep abreast of the various aspects (legal, compliance, risk, trading, analysis, client facing) and ensure information is shared, discussed, and debated.*

17.2 PORTFOLIO REVIEW AND RISK ASSESSMENT

Alongside price discovery and market adjustment, portfolio managers reassess their risk positions and investment strategies.

This starts with a review of issuer positions, sizing of exposures, overall portfolio risk metrics, and the performance impact from the event. Next, risk metrics should be recalibrated as significant price changes can affect the measurement of portfolio risk parameters. For example, the effective duration of defaulted bonds often drops to nearly zero, which has implications for portfolio duration, spread duration, and the portfolio beta to the benchmark. Measuring risk correctly from the affected instruments, therefore, allows for proper risk assessment and tracking at the portfolio level.

Depending on the portfolio's starting risk position and current market prices, the investment team may choose to reduce, maintain, or increase exposure to the impacted credit. Initially, the portfolio manager may focus on tactical trades and risk hedges as they recalibrate their fundamental views on the credit and gather more information on how the restructuring may evolve. However, if the restructuring and associated price changes significantly affect performance, especially in comparison to competitors, portfolio managers may need to reassess their risk positions and investment strategies entirely.

Market liquidity and transaction costs will determine the menu of executable trades. Generally, outright cash sales of the defaulted entity may be difficult or only possible at prohibitive costs. Instead, investors may consider prospective hedges such as buying CDS protection, using interest rate derivatives, and selling the currency against the dollar or euro (see Chapters 3 and 14).

Portfolio risks can also be adjusted by realigning other high-risk exposures in the account. This includes trading issuers at risk of fundamental or technical contagion, along with different names in similar rating buckets. Broader risk hedges such as US Treasuries, global interest rate derivatives, and G-7 currencies can also be used.

It is essential to reassess the scaling of affected bonds throughout the restructuring process, as market conditions and information availability shift. Here, a scenario-based approach is preferred over a point estimate approach, with probabilities for each scenario being adjusted as new information becomes available.

For example, the portfolio manager may brainstorm several outcomes along with their view on the price of bonds under each. They may apply probabilities to each scenario and calculate the probability-weighted average price based on their assumptions. Comparing this with current pricing tells them whether they are more or less optimistic than the market. As events unfold, these probabilities may be adjusted or additional scenarios added to the range of outcomes.

For investors with limited exposure to the distressed sovereign, there may be buying opportunities. These include affected credits and issuers that have been mispriced due to technical contagion. It may also include the defaulted cash bonds if prices seem to have overshot below the investor's expectations of eventual recovery. Exposure may also be increased through instruments directly linked to the affected issuer, such as CDS and recovery swaps.

Once portfolio managers have adjusted their initial positions, they continually review and recalibrate them. This is particularly essential during sovereign debt crises and related restructurings due to the frequent changes in market pricing, uncertainty, and news flow as negotiations proceed.

17.3 INFORMATION PHASE

Sovereign debt crises can range from a clear payment default to preemptive restructuring or a reassessment of prices in anticipation of a potential risk event. Collecting as much information as possible and confirming its nature is an essential initial step. If a trigger event (such as non-payment) has not taken place, the investment team should monitor payment obligations to ensure their timely receipt. Once a trigger event has occurred, an official announcement indicating that the government is working on a restructuring plan typically follows.

At the same time, the investment team should assemble a core group to oversee the restructuring and compile a checklist of tasks (see Table 17.1). This should include legal counsel, risk management, compliance, and client-facing professionals. The firm's internal stakeholders and portfolio managers with exposures in the affected issuer should be notified and regularly updated.

TABLE 17.1 Investor Checklist

1. Initial Phase
Account Holdings and Account Guidelines
Account Risk Diagnostics and Client Calls
2. Information Phase
Review Bond Universe and Indentures
Review CDS and CDX Contracts and Footprint
Review Market and Competitor Positioning
Index Guidelines and Scenarios
3. Trading and Price Discovery
Review Trading Protocol of Distressed/Defaulted Securities
Assess Market Technicals and Positioning
Monitor Portfolio Positioning and Risks
4. Assessment Phase
Communicate with Government, IMF, and Advisors
Assess IMF Reaction Function
Independent Credit Analysis and DSA
5. Organization
Decide Whether to Join a Creditor Committee
Consult with Legal Team if Holding Out
6. Assess DSA and IMF Program
Assess the Debt Restructuring Package
Assess the IMF Program and the Government's Adjustment Policies
7. Assess the Initial Exchange Offer
Negotiate Terms
Decide Whether to Accept the Proposal or Reject/Holdout
8. Reassess Portfolio Risk
Assess Market Technicals Following End of Restructuring (if Agreement)
Reassess Portfolio Risk and Country Exposure
If Holding Out, Continue Negotiations or Initiate Legal Proceedings

During the information gathering phase, the key tasks involve collecting account and client information, creating a list of the bond universe and indenture details, identifying all firmwide CDS and CDX exposures, reviewing CDS/CDX auction details, and evaluating index decisions and their impact on market technicals. Let's look at each of these tasks in turn.

17.3.1 Account Holdings and Constraints

A comprehensive list of all portfolio positions related to the issuer should be compiled. This includes all direct exposures, such as foreign and domestic bonds, derivatives, local currency exposures, private bonds, and loans; holdings of issuers domiciled in the country, including SOEs, state and local governments, corporates, and all government-guaranteed debt; as well as issuers domiciled abroad but that have significant operations or revenues from the country.

It is important to flag indirect or look-through exposures via CDX indices or other composites, and holdings that may be susceptible to contagion effects. These include issuers with close trade or financial ties, countries within the same region or ratings group, and portfolio substitutes with similar yields and risk profiles.

The exposures should be categorized by account type, detailing each client's mandate requirements and associated account rules. The investment team should identify accounts with low risk tolerance, those that cannot hold defaulted securities, or have a minimum ratings criterion. Clients with sensitivities to large valuation changes due to gain/loss restrictions and other accounting considerations should also be flagged.

Portfolio managers should also take note of accounts with higher risk tolerance, like distressed credit and hedge fund strategies. These portfolios may view the default and repricing of debt as a buying opportunity. These types of accounts more broadly drive the transfer of defaulted risk instruments from institutional mandates to hedge fund and high-yield strategies.

Account managers should share their understanding and assessment of the latest developments with all clients and pass along any client feedback to the investment team.

17.3.2 Bond Universe and Indentures

In addition to the account review, the trading team should compile a list of all outstanding sovereign bonds by instrument and issuer. For each instrument, include the financial structure (bullet, call features), maturity, currency of denomination, outstanding notional amount, and float. Amortization and coupon payment dates should be listed and used to create a debt payment schedule for monitoring missed payments.

Holding information should encompass the amounts held by domestic intra-government agencies (e.g., central bank, pension funds, social security funds), onshore entities (e.g., domestic banks), and offshore entities (foreign buyers). The foreign holding data can be disaggregated by fund type, such as institutional, retail, benchmarked, passive, distressed, or hedge funds. Additionally, publicly available mutual fund holdings can also be utilized to compile data on holdings of competitors and other investment managers.

Bond indentures should be examined to determine whether the legal documentation is favorable for a particular instrument or series. Key parameters include the governing law, the features of the trustee or fiscal agency agreement, the presence of collective action clauses (CACs) and their thresholds, any special clauses, acceleration and aggregation parameters, and cross-default and *pari passu* provisions. Traders can assess whether these differences are reflected in the market price and execute any favorable trades.

Bonds of related entities such as SOEs, corporations, state, and local governments should be included in this review. In particular, bonds with explicit guarantees should be flagged, along with details of their *pari passu* treatment with sovereign debt, and how the guarantees can be triggered and enforced. A list of any implicit guarantees is also helpful for identifying potential moral hazard trades. The latter arises since sovereigns often bail out systemically important entities or national champions like airlines.

17.3.3 CDS and CDX Exposures

Many sovereign portfolios replicate bond exposures through CDS or CDX. These exposures are directly affected by sovereign defaults, as missed payments trigger events in the underlying contracts. In the lead-up to a default, CDS pricing reflects the increasing risks of non-payment. CDS contracts may also influence bond pricing, as the cheapest-to-deliver instrument may be bid up when default becomes imminent.

The DTCC website provides a list of the market's CDS and CDX holdings. The triggers for the standard contracts should be recorded, particularly whether they include bonds *and* loans or only bonds. Specific cases or events, such as debt repudiation and involuntary restructurings through the use of CACs, may also trigger CDS even if no payment is missed.

CDS maturity dates in standard contracts can be matched against bond coupon and amortization payment dates. This determines which CDS maturities lack payment triggers, i.e., mature before any scheduled payments, versus those that do not and therefore carry greater payment risks. For instance, if there are no payments due in the next six months, followed by a large debt payment, six-month (and shorter) CDS contracts may present a better investment opportunity than longer-dated CDS contracts.

Reviewing the CDS auction process and auction date timing is also helpful. The ISDA voting committee's exposure to bonds and CDS can offer insights into the range of potential outcomes. Market pricing will highlight the *cheapest-to-deliver* bonds, and the holdings record may indicate who owns them, such as the type of holder or their region.

See Chapter 3 for more information on CDS and CDX exposures.

17.3.4 Industry-Wide Exposure

Restructurings of sovereign debt can significantly affect portfolios, depending on their price impact and scale. Knowing the industry's exposure to the credit and the affected instruments can offer valuable insights. Survey data compiled by J.P. Morgan on overall scaling suggest how portfolios are positioned relative to benchmarks, which can indicate the impact on managers' and mutual funds' performance. If the impact is substantial, it may lead to changes in their other asset holdings.

Information on holdings by instrument can indicate any potential impact on market technicals and the liquidity of specific bonds. It may also identify instances where investors have built up a substantial stake, allowing them to hold out and negotiate more favorable terms. This insight can inform the choice of the creditor committee and which investors to band together with at the negotiation table.

Understanding the characteristics and risk profile of holders offers further insights. Forced sales may be higher if holdings are primarily in benchmarked accounts, as they might not want to hold defaulted securities. If holders are mostly passive accounts, index decisions will have a bigger impact on market technicals. If distressed funds start buying bonds, valuations may signal cheapness and that prices have overshot expected recovery rates.

17.4 INDEX RE-EVALUATION

Index providers often exclude issuers due to defaults, liquidity issues, or pricing problems tied to sovereign crises. Decisions about index inclusion can trigger forced sales or buys, cause portfolios to be over- or under-weighted, and ultimately affect the performance of portfolios and investment managers.

To get a handle on index decisions, review the rules of major sovereign bond indices that include the issuer in question. Understand the conditions, criteria, and key indicators that index providers look at. In particular, focus on the criteria for inclusion/exclusion, the liquidity and trading volumes required, and how indices will mark prices if liquidity starts to decline.

Index teams usually reach out to market participants before making major decisions. These conversations help gauge the expected timing of any changes and whether they'll be rolled out gradually. It's also helpful to know under what conditions index providers would allow index inclusion in the future. Additionally, it's crucial to understand if there will be a sunset clause to exclude issuers if a default goes unresolved for an extended period.

17.4.1 Distressed Sovereigns in J.P. Morgan's EMBI Global Bond Index[2]

Every index has its own rules and guidelines for handling defaulted and restructured debt. This section looks at how J.P. Morgan's EMBI Global Bond Index treats distressed sovereign bonds, given that its universe of emerging countries has several historical defaults that can be learned from.

Defaulted bonds stay in the EMBI indices as long as there's secondary market trading, liquidity, price discovery (with two-way pricing), and investors can replicate the benchmark. If any of these conditions aren't met, the index team may consider excluding and phasing out the bonds.

This index eligibility is in contrast to high-yield and EM corporate credit indices, which typically exclude defaulted issuers. One fallout of keeping defaulted securities in is index distortion. This arises as defaulted and distressed securities disproportionately drive the index spread and volatility. It also means that institutional sovereign debt managers must cover defaulted sovereign credits, unlike in other asset classes, where defaulted securities are often outsourced and managed by distressed credit specialists.

When debt is restructured, old index bonds exit at the last traded price. Newly exchanged bonds enter the index at the same market value as the exiting old bonds, with no changes to accruals or notional amounts, and are treated like other new issues.

The index team determines the timing of inclusion based on the impact on the index and performance. For example, Ukraine's 2024 restructured bonds were added to the EMBI indices in a special rebalance mid-month due to their size and impact on the benchmark. In contrast, Zambia's 2024 restructuring was incorporated into the regular monthly rebalance schedule because it had a smaller face value.

There might be unusual circumstances that affect index decisions. Sanctions can lead to market disruptions, reducing liquidity and making it harder for investors to replicate the index. Additionally, there may be situations where investors risk serious damage to their reputation from being exposed to a particular issuer or country. Since these events are highly specific, index treatment often depends on the context.

After global sanctions hit Russia in 2022, major bond indices like J.P. Morgan's excluded Russia due to the significant market disruption of Russian securities, with the sanctions eventually triggering default. In contrast, US sanctions on Venezuelan debt in 2019 led to a more gradual withdrawal, with the default already having occurred and reflected in trading. This involved a two-month initial index watch, followed by a five-month phase-out of Venezuelan and PDVSA bonds from the EMBIG indices.[3]

17.5 INDEPENDENT CREDIT ASSESSMENT

Investors must independently assess the sovereign credit and the unfolding debt crisis to evaluate debt sustainability and calculate necessary debt forgiveness. This, in turn, enables estimating a range of potential recovery values and calibrating bond valuations to market pricing.

Credit analysts should begin with a thorough breakdown of the debt stack by holder, instrument, tenor, currency, and seniority. This serves as the foundation for identifying where the source of the debt issue resides and which elements are likely to be included in the restructuring envelope.

It also plays a role in understanding who the primary participants in the negotiations will be. For example, whether a bilateral lender like China will call the shots, or if a large institutional investor holds the bulk of the marketable debt.

If domestic debt makes up a large share, it will likely be part of the restructuring plan. If official sector debt is significant, private creditors may be bailed-in to give more debt forgiveness. If debt ratios are moderate but repayments are clustered, the country may require grace periods for coupon payments and maturity extensions, rather than a principal haircut in order to even out debt service payments over time.

The macroeconomic analysis, forecasts, and scenarios should be updated. This may feature a baseline reflecting outcomes based on current policies. Alternative scenarios can be developed from this baseline, like the economic path under corrective policies or an IMF adjustment program. Downside scenarios might address impacts from a currency or banking sector crisis, or worse-than-expected growth. Upside scenarios could evaluate support from bilateral or multilateral lenders.

It's essential to conduct an independent debt sustainability analysis (DSA) using these macroeconomic inputs. This will help pinpoint the scope of the debt issue, its origin (debt stock or debt service), and its main drivers (weak growth, currency depreciation, interest rates, or fiscal adjustment). Adding scenario analysis to the baseline debt trajectories can help gauge how severe the problem might become in the worst-case scenario compared to the best-case. See Chapter 6 on guidelines on how to carry out DSAs.

Using these guidelines, investors can estimate the debt forgiveness a country needs based on the IMF's published standards. The goal is to forecast the IMF's recommendation on the amount, timing, and type of debt relief required. By analyzing the principal and coupon haircut ranges, along with the maturity extension needed to meet IMF requirements, investors can get a sense of what debt relief might look like.

For example, for low-income countries, comparing debt stock and financing ratios from the DSA with IMF LIC DSF thresholds (see Table 6.2) can help estimate the NPV haircut that the IMF team may recommend. Recovery and NPV losses can then be calculated based on various assumptions for the face value haircut, maturity extension, new coupon stream, and grace period. These can be probability-weighted for different restructuring and macroeconomic scenarios and used as anchors to guide market price evaluations and inform investment decisions.

As the restructuring process unfolds, the credit evaluation, DSA, and recovery estimates should be updated regularly. This independent credit analysis and DSA can then be used to cross-check the official macroeconomic assumptions and forecasts, and (if needed) to challenge the official DSA calculations and results. See Chapter 16 for what investors should look for in IMF DSAs.

17.6 PORTFOLIO POSITIONING AND REASSESSMENT

Portfolio managers continually assess their risk and country positions, particularly during high-volatility events like sovereign debt restructurings. Once the market works through the initial price discovery, information, and credit assessment phase, portfolio managers can take a more triangulated view of the portfolio's country exposure and risk.

They can develop an investment strategy based on their expectations of recovery, the exchange offer, and how bonds will perform after the exchange. We discuss the factors investors consider when evaluating an offer in Chapter 18. Key components include the value of the offer, the fairness of the expected haircut, and whether bondholders are treated similarly to other creditors. They also evaluate government policy adjustments and whether these will lead to a long-term solution to the debt problem. These factors are often reflected in bond prices after the restructuring, which we will discuss next.

17.7 BOND MARKETS POST-RESTRUCTURING

The moment of restructuring, when the old debt is exchanged for new instruments, marks a critical inflection point for sovereign bonds. The newly exchanged bonds with updated terms undergo market calibration of their value and the sovereign's creditworthiness.

Portfolio managers reassess risk and portfolio strategies while deciding on new targets for the issuer and its instruments. Depending on initial holdings, benchmark weights, and the terms of the restructuring, a large number of bonds can trade and change hands as risk positions are adjusted.

While recovery values at the time of exchange are often used to benchmark a debt deal, the subsequent 12 months following a restructuring are equally crucial for portfolio returns. Empirically, post-restructuring bond prices tend to trade well below par (often 40–70 cents on the dollar) and exhibit considerable volatility linked to trading and macroeconomic risks.[4]

As the sovereign emerges from the crisis and investor confidence returns, prices appreciate and spreads tighten. This was the case in Greece (2012), where bonds traded in the 20–30 cent range immediately after restructuring. Over the next 12 months, they rebounded to 40–50 cents given ECB support, EU guarantees, and the anchor of the IMF program. Greece eventually returned to the primary markets in April 2014. The takeaway for investors is that if policy anchors are credible, bond prices may recover, even with deep investor hesitation haircuts.

That said, it is common for bond prices to underperform following an exchange. This may occur if there is no IMF involvement or there is a significant risk of the IMF program going off track. Bonds may also fail to rally if debt issues persist and there is a risk of serial restructuring.

Argentina's 2020 restructuring serves as a case in point where, following the exchange, prices were between 55 and 60 cents on the dollar, with average exit yields of 10.5%. Asset managers were already overweight the benchmark prior to the default and remained overexposed after the restructuring. This, combined with IMF friction, low reserves, and a lack of policy commitment to reforms, drove prices to the 30s by 2021, where they traded for the next few years.

Post-restructuring bond markets are, therefore, a by-product of numerous factors. While they are an important input into credit decisions, investors also examine fundamental valuations to reinforce their investment view. The government's new policies and commitment to any IMF policy programs are key inputs that help determine whether bond prices appreciate, depreciate, or remain stagnant over the long term.

Looking at the bigger picture, defaults usually hurt bond prices, but high coupons can lead to substantial returns over time. In reality, the total return on government bonds typically falls by around 15% following default events, but the long-term returns can still be positive (see Figure 17.2).

Typically, it takes around four years from the default for the cumulative total return to become positive. Furthermore, about 25% of defaults don't show a significant drop in total returns, and some investors see their capital grow by 50% within five years of the default. However, for the bottom 25% of defaults, there's still no recovery even after six years following the default.[5]

Identifying and maneuvering these differences is the task of sovereign credit analysis and navigating portfolios through the debt restructuring.

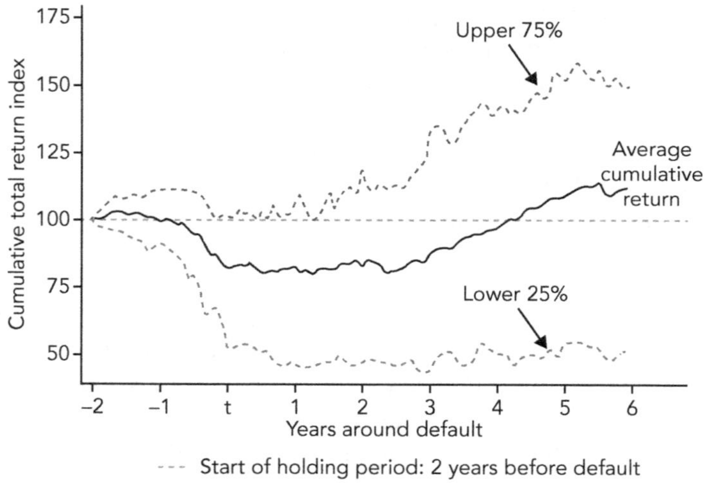

FIGURE 17.2 Bond returns around sovereign defaults. SOURCE: Meyer, J. et al. (2019)/World Bank Group.

17.8 SUMMARY

This chapter discussed how portfolio managers navigate portfolios through sovereign distress and restructurings. It described the initial phase of the crisis and how markets update prices and credit views. It covered trading protocols for defaulted securities and market technicals that may emerge due to bonds and securities changing hands in the aftermath of a sovereign crisis. The discussion also covered factors portfolio managers take into account when assessing their risk positions and investment strategies.

The analysis also reviewed the information that should be collected on account holdings, the bond universe, CDS auction protocols, and how index providers treat defaulted securities. The need for independent credit assessment was highlighted, and the potential areas where investors may be able to push back on official DSA and restructuring envelop assumptions.

The chapter concluded with an examination of investment strategies and bond market dynamics following a restructuring, along with an analysis of the total returns of restructured securities. These considerations form the basis for understanding how investors decide whether to accept an exchange offer—a topic we explore in greater detail in the next chapter.

NOTES

1. Waever, *Looking Back to Look Ahead*.
2. See J.P. Morgan, *EMBI Global Diversified Index Methodology* and J.P. Morgan, *Index Research Factsheets*.

3. One difference of note was that Venezuela's weight in the index was reduced to 0, driving the zeroing of the market valuation. Meanwhile, Russia was excluded entirely from the index, with its bonds priced at zero. This difference matters as the entity is still in the index, so investors may not have to be forced to sell the position depending on their account guidelines. Secondly, if sanctions are lifted, the index weight can be increased very quickly as opposed to the usually longer phase-in time when entities are excluded. This can have important implications for account performance if investors are void or if they had a stale "overweight" position.
4. Waever, *Looking Back to Look Ahead.*
5. Meyer, Reinhart, and Trebesch, *Sovereign Bonds since Waterloo.* Argentina (2001) and Ecuador (2008) are two recent cases of long-lasting creditor losses, where in Argentina it took investors until 2016 to breakeven, and in Ecuador about five years.

REFERENCES

Brauer, Jane, Lucas Martin, and Merveille Paja. *Emerging Market Sovereign Defaults Primer – A Survival Guide.* GEMs FI Strategy Viewpoint. Bank of America Global Research, 2022.

J.P. Morgan. *EMBI Global Diversified Index Methodology.* Emerging Markets Research, 2024.

J.P. Morgan. *Index Research Factsheets.* https://www.jpmorgan.com/insights/global-research/index-research (accessed 31 July 2025).

Meyer, Josefin, Carmen M. Reinhart, and Christoph Trebesch. *Sovereign Bonds Since Waterloo.* World Bank Policy Research Working Paper No. 9906, 2022.

Waever, Simon. *Looking Back to Look Ahead: Distressed EM Sovereign Credit Strategy.* Morgan Stanley, 2022.

CHAPTER EIGHTEEN

Outcomes of Sovereign Debt Restructurings

SOVEREIGN DEBT restructurings are high-stakes negotiations between governments and creditors, shaped by financial, legal, and geopolitical considerations. Private creditors face unique challenges in this process, including limited access to information and few avenues for enforcing claims.

This chapter reviews exchange offers and historical outcomes of sovereign restructurings. It outlines the strategies employed by both sovereigns and investors to strengthen their positions and explores whether it pays to be a holdout. The chapter concludes with a look at post-restructuring dynamics, including bond pricing following exchanges, issuers' exits from default ratings, and re-entry into capital markets.

18.1 OUTCOMES OF SOVEREIGN DEBT RESTRUCTURINGS

The range of outcomes from a sovereign debt restructuring depends on the severity of the debt crisis, creditor cooperation, multilateral support, and the government's macroeconomic adjustment policies. Contrary to popular belief, the interests of investors, the sovereign debtor, and the official sector are often aligned in that a rapid resolution is generally beneficial for all involved.

A successful restructuring with market re-entry is the goal of most sovereign debtors. Uruguay's (2003) debt exchange is considered the prototype. The government, facing a liquidity crisis, implemented a voluntary, investor-friendly debt exchange that quickly restored market confidence, allowing Uruguay to re-access markets soon after.[1]

Restructurings become more involved when there are large and unsustainable debt stocks. Soft restructurings may leave a lingering debt problem, leading to serial restructurings down the road. An overly harsh exchange offer may be seen as an opportunistic cramdown by the government, resulting in litigation with holdout creditors. Argentina's serial restructurings and the contentious court case brought by NML serve as a primary example. The fallout was a costly and prolonged legal battle that culminated in an eventual payout to the holdouts under a new government.

Complexity in debt restructuring outcomes increases as multiple creditors become involved. The presence of significant official bilateral lenders like China is altering the preexisting rules of the game, which the IMF and the Paris Club of creditors once dominated. The rising frequency of domestic debt restructurings, along with the lack of standardization in their treatment, adds further complications.

In certain instances, the government may not start a formal restructuring process but instead carry out informal debt buybacks at distressed prices in the secondary market. This approach is not a viable solution for resolving sovereign defaults, as there are usually not enough funds to repurchase the entire stock of tradable debt.

Finally, in a small number of cases, defaults remain unresolved when no restructuring takes place, leaving creditors to write off the debt indefinitely. For example, Cuba's indebtedness before the 1959 revolution was repudiated by Fidel Castro's government on the grounds that the debt was odious, and to this date has not been resolved.

18.2 TYPES OF OFFERS

An exchange offer typically provides bondholders with a menu of options to swap their existing debt for new instruments featuring revised terms. These options may include adjustments to maturity, coupon rates, principal claims, or the addition of extra payouts as incentives.

Par-for-par exchanges change the maturity date for new bonds with the same nominal principal. The maturity extension prevents nominal losses for investors and can help ease the government's short-term liquidity needs but may not provide sufficient debt stock relief.

A *discounted exchange* reduces the principal of the face value through a *haircut*. This can provide significant debt stock relief and enhance debt sustainability, but it may result in substantial losses for creditors. An excessively high haircut might lead to a rejection of the offer and holdouts.

A *coupon adjustment* lowers the interest rate on the instrument and may include grace periods for repayment. It decreases near-term liquidity needs for the government without a principal reduction but may not offer sufficient debt relief if debt stocks are high.

Value recovery instruments (VRIs) link bond payments with growth, tax revenues, commodity receipts, or other macroeconomic indicators.[2] They are often used when significant principal haircuts are on the table, when there are disagreements regarding macroeconomic assumptions, or when there is uncertainty about economic or political outcomes. They can be complex to value and not straightforward to monitor, as governments have an informational advantage concerning whether targets have been met.

In practice, exchange offers are tailored to fit the debt relief needs of the borrower and the preferences of the creditor. A standard approach is a package of bullet bonds with fixed coupons, where maturities are extended, principal claims face a haircut, and the coupon rate is adjusted. Sweeteners may include consent fees, VRIs, and the capitalization of past due interest.

For example, Ukraine's 2015 restructuring offered bondholders a package of nine bullet bonds with fixed coupons (7.75% compared to the 7.2% average on the old bonds), a four-year maturity extension, and a 20% reduction in principal. Investors received a GDP warrant, and past due interest was capitalized with a higher face value for the strip of bonds.

Another version includes amortizing bonds with step-up coupons. These bonds reduce rollover risks for the issuer and are often paired with coupon grace periods to provide liquidity relief. In Argentina's 2020 restructuring, principal haircuts were minimal, with the first principal amortization beginning in five years. Each bond had a distinct coupon step-up schedule, staggering repayments, and bondholders were offered amortizing bonds with a 1% fixed coupon in lieu of accrued or past due interest.

Some exchange packages cater to different risk preferences of investors. In Argentina's 2005 restructuring, bondholders were offered a choice between a low-coupon Par bond (exchangeable for 100% of the value of the investor's claim) and a high-coupon Discount bond (exchangeable for 33.7% of the value of the investor's claim, i.e., a 66.3% haircut). Both bonds were sinkers, featuring step-up coupons. In addition, GDP warrants were included as value recovery instruments.

There may be selective treatment of investors based on legal claims, holdings, and original maturity. For instance, instruments with higher thresholds for collective action clauses may be treated more favorably. Holders of already restructured debt may receive better terms, or those with short- versus long-maturity securities may be offered slightly different packages to encourage participation. Examples have been observed in the Argentina (2020), Ukraine (2015), and Ecuador (2020) restructurings.

18.3 EVALUATING THE EXCHANGE OFFER

Investors consider several criteria as they evaluate an exchange offer. These include the financial aspects of the deal, such as net present value (NPV) loss, the treatment of past due interest (PDI), and the value of post-restructured sovereign bonds. The legal structure and terms of the proposed instruments, and whether they are being treated on par with other creditors, are taken into account. The final assessment is then based on whether the debt relief offered is appropriate—neither excessive nor insufficient—and if the sovereign will be able to meet the obligations of the new bonds.

Evaluating whether an exchange offer provides value involves more than just math. The credibility of the government's post-deal economic strategy and the future trajectory of sovereign credit also play a crucial role. Additionally, the near-term market pricing of risk, the pricing of alternative investments available in the market, and the overall financial risk environment are significant factors. Collectively, these elements determine whether sovereign credit will continue to be a strategic fit for the portfolio or will need to be traded once the exchange is finalized.

> ***PRO TIP:*** *Focus on the role of the restructured debt in your portfolio, its expected performance, and how it measures up to alternatives with similar risk-return profiles.*

18.3.1 Creditor Losses: Haircuts and Recovery

Assessing any exchange offer begins with calculating the creditor losses implied by the package. This is determined using the NPV of the cash flows from each instrument (including past due interest, PDI), discounted at an appropriate interest rate.

One measure of loss is the *haircut*, which measures the extent of loss from the original claim. The market haircut (MH) compares the NPV of new debt with the *face or nominal value* of the old debt:

$$\textit{Market Haircut (MH)} = 1 - \frac{\textit{Present value of new debt}}{\textit{Face value of old debt}}$$

The NPV of new debt is discounted at the *exit yield*, which is the secondary trading yield immediately following the restructuring. For example, if the new bonds trade at 40 cents on the dollar and the face value of the old bonds was 100 cents on the dollar, the market haircut is 60% = (1 − 40/100) × 100.

An alternative measure is the NPV loss,[3] which compares the NPV of the new and old debt, both evaluated at the exit yield:

$$\textit{NPV Loss} = 1 - \frac{\textit{Present value of new debt}}{\textit{Present value of old debt}}$$

Using the previous example, if the pre-restructured bonds traded at 50 cents on the dollar, the NPV loss would be 20% = (1 − 40/50) × 100.

The NPV loss measure results in a lower estimate of losses than the market haircut methodology because it is discounted using the typically high exit yield. It is considered a better measure of the permanent loss incurred by creditors when evaluating an exchange offer. This is especially true for successive restructurings, where the market haircut approach can exaggerate losses.

The *recovery rate* is (1 − market haircut) and represents an estimate of the post-restructuring value of each instrument. This metric is easily observable and should reflect where the old bonds trade just prior to the exchange (once all details are known). In the example above, the recovery rate is 40% or (1 − market haircut).

Table 18.1 illustrates how the recovery and NPV of a bond can vary based on the principal haircut, maturity extension, coupon rate, and discount factor used. Generally, a larger face value haircut leads to a greater NPV loss. Still, even without face value

TABLE 18.1 NPV Calculations

	Original Bond	New Bond 1	New Bond 2	New Bond 3
Principal	100	100	70	100
Coupon (%)	10	5	5	5
Nominal value	200	200	140	225
NPV original interest rate	100	57	40	55
NPV new interest rate	139	100	70	62
NPV loss (%)		72	51	45
Market haircut (%)		50	65	69
Year 1	10	5	4	5
Year 2	10	5	4	5
Year 3	10	5	4	5
Year 4	10	5	4	5
Year 5	10	5	4	5
Year 6	10	5	4	5
Year 7	10	5	4	5
Year 8	10	5	4	5
Year 9	10	5	4	5
Year 10	110	5	4	5
Year 11		5	4	5
Year 12		5	4	5
Year 13		5	4	5
Year 14		5	4	5
Year 15		5	4	5
Year 16		5	4	5
Year 17		5	4	5
Year 18		5	4	5
Year 19		5	4	5
Year 20		105	74	5
Year 21				5
Year 22				5
Year 23				5
Year 24				5
Year 25				105

haircuts, NPV losses can be significant due to longer maturities and lower coupons on the newly restructured debt.

Even so, there is a tendency for investors to resist principal haircuts. This may stem from the visual impact of marking down losses and accounting requirements for maximum loss per period. Retaining the original principal value along with longer-maturity bonds provides investors with greater upside potential if the restructuring succeeds and exit yields decline. Additionally, if there is a risk of future restructuring, maintaining a par claim might also be advantageous.

Note that recovery and haircuts can vary by instrument, so for any given debt restructuring, a single ratio is calculated using the market capitalization-weighted average across all bonds restructured.[4]

18.3.2 Treatment of Past Due Interest

PDI is the interest that has accrued on a debt but has not been paid by the debtor. If a debt restructuring is preemptive, then this accrued interest (generally based on the coupon rate) will be small. However, after a prolonged default, PDI can be substantial, particularly when coupon rates are high. Venezuela, which defaulted in 2017, accrued PDI at a rate of $5 billion per year on $57 billion of bonds, reaching $35 billion by 2024! Consequently, the treatment of PDI can be a significant part of the compensation investors receive.

The calculation of PDI depends on the legal jurisdiction and whether bondholders have a judgment. Under New York law, pre-judgment PDI accrues at the coupon rate plus a pre-statutory rate of 9% on missed payments (interest on interest) based on the original face value of the debt. If debt holders receive a judgment, in federal court, PDI accrues at the then-prevailing weekly average one-year constant maturity (nominal) Treasury yield.[5] In English law, judges have discretion, but usually, the pre-judgment interest is a base rate plus 1%, and the post-judgment rate is 8%.

The treatment of PDI varies across restructurings. One common approach is to align its treatment with the restructuring terms of the overall debt. Another approach is to handle PDI separately, making it payable as a lump sum or as bonds with different terms and maturities from the rest of the exchange. Creditors can agree to forgive a portion of the PDI owed, accept cash or bonds, and agree to different terms than those applicable to the rest of the debt stack.

Empirically, there has been mixed treatment of PDI. Accrued interest received relatively favorable treatment in the Argentina 2020 and Ukraine 2015 restructurings but unfavorable treatment in Ecuador 2020 and Argentina 2005 restructurings.[6] In recent cases, there has been a shift toward paying PDI in bonds rather than cash, with examples of new bonds featuring shorter maturities and an increase in the total size of new bonds issued as part of the restructuring.

18.3.3 Exit Yields and Eventual Recovery

For portfolio managers, the value of the post-restructured sovereign bonds is a crucial factor in evaluating the exchange offer. This involves assessing both the near-term market valuation of the exchanged bonds and the intrinsic or fundamental value of the sovereign credit.

In the lead-up to an exchange settlement, as information about the offer terms becomes available, bond prices reflect the market's valuation of the deal. The exit yield, or secondary market yield, is used as an input to calculate the NPV haircut and estimate recovery. Higher exit yields indicate larger haircuts and lower recoveries are needed, or the belief that the sovereign credit will remain a going concern for some time.

Exit yields can also remain high for an extended period due to technical selling pressures, liquidity discounts, and market volatility. To look through these factors and get a handle on where the sovereign's yields should eventually settle, it helps to cross-check NPV calculations using alternative discount factors. These consist of yields on comparable distressed sovereigns, CDS-implied rates, or yields based on the country's fundamental credit rating post-restructuring.

Incorporating these factors into the assessment of the exchange offer allows investors to anchor value beyond short-term market dynamics. Views on the medium-term credit depend on whether the government's adjustment policies are likely to improve the sovereign's credit trajectory. This, in turn, hinges on whether the debt issue has been resolved or pushed down the road. Investor confidence in the fundamental credit would be reflected in lower exit yields and higher recovery values.[7]

Bondholders also consider market dynamics when assessing exchange bonds. Traders examine whether the offer has been priced in and identify mispriced instruments that present trading opportunities post-deal. They evaluate potential sales or buys as portfolio managers rebalance their positions. They also consider whether investors will view the restructuring as successful and want to hold the bonds or shift their positions.

Determining whether the newly exchanged bonds will be included in any sovereign index is a valuable consideration for this assessment. Index inclusion creates a natural demand for instruments, which in turn supports prices. Equally important is whether other issuers in the market provide better relative value and have better risk profiles. Together, this information assists portfolio managers in evaluating the value of the offer, formulating their trading strategy after settlement, and determining the eventual size of the position in the portfolio.

18.3.4 Inter-Creditor Equity and Comparability of Treatment

Before accepting an offer, creditors check to ensure that the offer is comparable to those extended to others. This principle of inter-creditor equity, or *comparability of treatment* (CoT), states that all creditors with the same seniority and legal claim should share the costs of debt relief equally, and no creditor should receive more favorable treatment than another.

When an exchange offer and counteroffer are made, the government, along with its advisors and the IMF, determines whether the necessary debt relief and CoT are met. If CoT is not met, the exchange offer will likely need modification until it is satisfied.

Measuring CoT is not straightforward, and there is no universally accepted calculation methodology. The lack of consensus among creditors—especially between official and private creditors—stems from differences in time horizons, lending objectives, interest rates, risk appetite, and leverage in the negotiation process. This leads to disagreements on the discount rate, exit yield, and whether to use the net present value or nominal value of the claim.[8]

Historically, CoT has been based on three criteria. The *change in net present value (NPV)* captures the time value of debt service payments before and after the restructuring.[9] The second criterion examines the *change in duration* before and after the treatment, where duration is measured as the weighted average time for all cash flows to be received. The third criterion evaluates the *change in nominal debt service* before and after the treatment, where the change is measured over the IMF program period associated with the restructuring.

The choice of discount rate affects the NPV and duration calculations. For low-income countries (LICs), the IMF uses a 5% discount rate that reflects the concessionality of official loans. For market-access countries (MACs), the IMF employs a sensitivity analysis based on various discount rates applied to both official bilateral and private creditors.

Instead of creating a one-to-one equivalence of treatment, the CoT assessment utilizes these criteria and considers creditors' preferences.[10] For instance, private creditors might prefer earlier repayments and, in exchange, may be open to accepting a higher NPV debt reduction through longer-duration instruments. Official creditors could be willing to significantly reduce the debt service during the IMF program period but may be reluctant to accept a nominal loss.

CoT is key to mitigating moral hazard. Theoretically, it diminishes the incentive for creditors to wait for others to restructure debt and/or disproportionately claim debt service payments made by the sovereign after a restructuring. In this way, CoT importantly enables official creditors to proceed with debt relief and offer financing assurances to the IMF for a program to commence before the details of the overall restructuring are known.

If private creditors move first, CoT enables them to seek debt treatment on at least as favorable terms as those given to others, or it may render their agreement ineffective. To implement this, exchange instruments can include enforcement and claw-back clauses. See the discussion below of Argentina's RUFO (Rights Upon Future Offer) clause. That said, once a restructuring is complete, it is rare for creditors to reopen discussions, even if holdouts or other creditors end up with slightly better terms.

Note that CoT focuses on the financial aspects of the restructuring and does not include any non-financial elements of lending. The latter can be a key objective for official creditors due to geopolitical alliances, access to strategic infrastructure like ports, and acquisition of key commodities such as oil or rare earth minerals. These factors may influence the parameters and timing of debt negotiations within the official sector and between bilateral creditors.

18.3.5 Other Considerations

Creditors also examine the legal structure of the new debt instruments and may negotiate provisions that give them flexibility in the event of future restructurings. Loss reinstatement clauses allow restructured creditors to present their original claims without impairment if there is a second round of restructuring of the same debt. Additionally, changes in the legal jurisdiction of the new bonds may facilitate future litigation in more favorable foreign courts.

Exit consents may also be used, allowing participating creditors to vote to amend non-financial terms of the old bonds, reducing their attractiveness to potential holdouts.

The tradability of both old and new instruments is also a factor. Exchanges may limit the transactability of old debt, making it prohibitive to hold, and may also increase the liquidity of new exchanged debt by registering them on exchanges and converting private debt into publicly marketable instruments.

18.4 SOVEREIGN STRATEGIES IN DEBT RESTRUCTURING NEGOTIATIONS

Governments employ various cooperative and coercive strategies to influence investor expectations and maximize participation in a sovereign debt restructuring.[11]

By managing information and controlling the narrative, they can shape investor sentiment and informally gauge their reaction function. Governments often present the restructuring as inevitable, emphasizing the potential downside risks if it does not proceed in a timely manner. Official projections used in the IMF DSAs may be conservative, justifying the need for additional debt relief. There may be potential leaks of restructuring terms or trial balloons to assess market reaction before a formal offer is made.

Negotiation tactics can include incentives as well as deterrents to encourage investor participation. Early consent may be rewarded with higher recoveries through payment of a consent fee, improved treatment of PDI, and preferential allocation in the exchange. This can be substantive as seen in Ecuador's (2020) restructuring where consenters earned a premium of about $12.[12]

The exchange offer can also be enhanced with upfront cash or credit guarantees from third parties. The Brady Plan of the 1990s is the poster child where defaulted sovereign loans were restructured into Brady Bonds guaranteed by US Treasuries.[13] VRIs and state-contingent instruments may be included to give participants upside if the economic outcomes exceed those predicted in the baseline.

There may be contractual improvements on the table such as a change in legal jurisdiction or altering the tradability of the security, for example, converting from a syndicated loan to publicly traded bonds. The restructuring may include loss reinstatement features that allow creditors' original claims to remain unimpaired if there is a second round of restructuring of the same debt.

Other clauses include commitments to equal treatment or provisions that grant participants the advantage of any better offer that may arise in the future. Examples include the comparable treatment clause in Paris Club Agreements and the RUFO clause utilized in Argentina's 2005 restructuring.

Sovereign debtors also have a number of sticks to encourage bondholder participation. The implementation of collective action clauses (CACs) enables a majority of bondholders to bind all investors to the terms of a restructuring. Retroactive legislation can incorporate CACs into local law debt and impose restructuring terms on dissenting creditors. Furthermore, successive generations of CACs have shifted power away from bondholders toward the debtor by reducing the thresholds necessary for modifications.

As noted in Chapter 7, there remains the potential for sovereign debtors to use redesignation strategies to change the voting pool after votes have been cast and Pacman strategies to sweep up non-consenting holders. While these methods have faced pushback from bondholders during Argentina and Ecuador's (2020) restructurings, they remain to be tested in courts.

Governments may also use exit consents to deter holdouts by worsening the non-financial terms of the old agreements bonds.[14] These may be used alongside preferential terms for early participants or those who consented in the vote.

In a nuclear option, the sovereign can threaten to walk away from the restructuring and not pay investors indefinitely. This can be a credible threat if the government in power is willing to be in a state of economic autarky or if its reliance on international capital markets is low and can be substituted with official sector or bilateral funding.

18.5 INVESTOR STRATEGIES IN DEBT RESTRUCTURING NEGOTIATIONS

Bondholders similarly have several strategic, legal, and financial tools in their arsenal to negotiate better debt restructuring terms and maximize recovery.

Bondholders can strengthen their bargaining position by presenting a unified front through creditor committees. These committees facilitate coordination and information sharing among investors. Collective bargaining provides individual investors with more clout than acting independently and may lower the risk of holdouts. Strength in numbers also means that if terms are unfavorable, there can be sufficient pushback to block the triggering of CACs (if applicable). This is supported by the unspoken contract that the government will not make an official exchange offer to all bondholders without the implicit consent of the creditor committee.

Whether working within a creditor committee or not, investors can challenge the DSA and the estimates of the debt relief required. They can dispute any unrealistic macro assumptions or debt sustainability thresholds employed. They can expose hidden assets or instances of financial mismanagement to contest claims that the country cannot provide better repayment terms.[15]

In some cases (Ecuador 2020), creditors have demanded an independent review of the DSA, arguing that conservative assumptions led to deeper haircuts than necessary. In other instances (Ukraine 2022), investors lobbied to include both upside and downside scenarios in the IMF DSA.

Creditors can propose innovative market-based solutions to enhance recovery while providing debt relief and assisting the sovereign in regaining market access. In Ukraine (2022), bondholders agreed to pause debt service in the immediate aftermath of the Russian invasion. When outcomes are particularly uncertain, they may suggest staggered restructuring phases that offer short-term debt relief or maturity extensions instead of permanent haircuts. This allows for the potential of higher future payments if economic conditions improve.

Bondholders can structure and propose VRIs. These instruments can bridge the gap between the government's ask, differences in assumptions, and the debt relief needed. They provide both sides flexibility if outcomes are better or worse than expected, offer bondholders potential gains in more favorable scenarios, and give additional debt relief if adverse outcomes are realized. In other cases, new instruments can be collateralized, or there may be debt-for-equity arrangements where shares in SOEs or infrastructure projects are exchanged for debt. All viable options should be explored and presented for consideration.

Bondholders can also utilize lobbying, the media, and political influence to shift public opinion and pressure sovereigns to enter negotiations and provide fair terms. Investors may engage with the domestic opposition in the debtor country to emphasize an alternative approach and/or negotiate a settlement once they assume power, as occurred in Argentina with the appointment of President Macri in 2015.

International investors can also work with their government representatives in the US Congress or the EU to oppose bailouts through the IMF if private creditors are not treated fairly. While it is crucial to utilize all available tools to reflect bondholder preferences, this has produced mixed results. Governments balance various objectives when interacting with their sovereign counterparts, and addressing the concerns of their domestic financial players is just one aspect.

There are instances where the sovereign debtor conducts informal debt buybacks instead of a formal exchange. These provide bondholders with an opportunity to exit their position with a partial (market-based) recovery. That said, the recovery (even if market-based) may be lower than from a negotiated settlement. Moreover, for most sovereign defaults, this is not a viable solution, as the government typically does not have the funds to execute this for the entire stock of tradable debt.

18.6 HOLDING OUT

Holding out during a sovereign debt restructuring—refusing to accept a proposed exchange offer to secure better terms—is a controversial, high-risk/high-reward strategy. For portfolio managers, the decision to hold out must consider legal leverage, litigation costs, creditor coordination, market conditions, and the sovereign's willingness and ability to pay.

The general rule of thumb is that a debt restructuring accepted by 90% or more of creditors should proceed. If the remaining bondholders are not bailed in via CACs, they may become holdouts who seek better payment terms. There is a difference between bondholders and creditor committees negotiating with the government and resisting any given offer, and holdout creditors. The latter benefits if debt relief is granted by other creditors, allowing the holdout to achieve a much higher recovery than what is offered to the broader market.

The holdout strategy requires legal leverage and the ability and willingness to litigate. A prerequisite is favorable bond documentation that has no CACs or includes those requiring small blocking positions, ensuring the bondholder is not automatically bailed in. This has become increasingly challenging with new-generation CACs requiring much larger exposures to block restructurings that are binding on all.[16]

Equally important is the governing law, such as New York or English law. Moreover, bond indentures issued under international law (as opposed to domestic law) may have a better scope for investors to obtain a judgment and enforce repayment. Whether the instrument is issued under a trust structure or a fiscal agency agreement also determines the ability and avenues for bondholders to pursue legal recourse.

If a sovereign faces pressure to resolve the default and regain market access, holdouts may find themselves in a stronger position to negotiate a settlement. NML Associates v. the Republic of Argentina is one of the most notable and publicized holdout cases in sovereign debt defaults. The government ultimately paid the holdouts after more than 14 years in default but only once a new administration took power in 2016. The new government sought to move past the extended litigation in New York courts and reestablish access to international capital markets.

That said, being a holdout carries certain risks. Litigation can be lengthy and extremely costly. Even if investors manage to secure judgments, they can be challenging to enforce. A country's international assets, such as embassies, consulates, and central bank reserves held at the Bank for International Settlements, are typically protected from attachment by national and international law. Furthermore, various practical techniques and tools, like redirecting payment flows or altering ownership structures, can be employed by sovereigns to evade the attachment of exports such as oil or other commodities.

This protection from attachment does not extend to property held for commercial purposes or owned by state-owned enterprises. In a landmark case for creditors, Crystallex (a Canadian mining company) argued and won a case against the Venezuelan sovereign. They contended that PDVSA's (Venezuela's state oil company) US subsidiary CITGO was an alter ego of the sovereign, and therefore, CITGO shares could be attached.[17] This is referred to as piercing the corporate veil and is incredibly difficult to do in practice.[18]

In extreme cases, sovereign assets can be protected by international law via special amendments. During Iraq's 2005 restructuring, the UN Security Council passed a resolution to immunize cash proceeds from Iraqi oil sales from attachment in all UN member states. The eventual recovery for commercial creditors was in the single digits, one of the lowest in recent sovereign debt restructurings.

There are additional practical challenges for portfolio managers when pursuing a holdout strategy. Mandate restrictions may prevent litigation or the holding of distressed assets. Bonds involved in legal proceedings face illiquidity and trading restrictions that need to be managed within the overall portfolio's risk. They also incur opportunity costs concerning portfolio returns, particularly in cases of uncertain and prolonged litigation.

Asset managers and owners may prefer to avoid reputational risks associated with holdout strategies. This is especially true if public opinion is against the holdouts, if the default correlates with economic hardship for the population, or if it was due to factors beyond the country's control, such as natural disasters or invasions.

18.7 LIFE AFTER RESTRUCTURING

After completing a debt restructuring, a sovereign focuses on restoring creditworthiness, regaining investor confidence, and reestablishing market access. The following section examines patterns in credit rating upgrades, changes in funding conditions, and the typical timelines for returning to international capital markets. For portfolio managers, understanding the post-restructuring recovery process is essential for identifying early opportunities in rehabilitated sovereign credits.

18.7.1 Credit Rating Upgrades

After a sovereign debt restructuring is completed, rating agencies judge whether the default has been resolved. Within one to two months, they reassess the sovereign credit rating, taking into account the terms of the restructuring. In some instances, if the debt relief is insufficient or the adjustment program is unrealistic, they may refrain from changing the rating, keeping it in the default category.

For investors, rating exits from default are consequential, as credit upgrades can drive position adds for rating-sensitive mandates. Active managers can estimate whether there will be a credit rating upgrade from default and seek prior permission from clients to add exposures ahead of the event and potential market repricing. See also the discussion in Chapter 5.

18.7.2 Regaining Market Access

Following a default, countries are often locked out from accessing debt capital markets.[19] When they can once again issue bonds in the primary bond markets and refinance maturing debt at reasonable yields, the sovereign is said to regain market access.

Access to domestic markets is typically regained sooner than access to external markets. This may be because well-functioning domestic capital markets are vital to recovering from crises. Government policies, such as financial repression and capital controls, can also shape the availability of domestic funding and demand for local debt.

For external markets, gaining market access takes longer. The typical time it takes is around four to five years, but there is significant variability. Some countries regain market access relatively quickly; for instance, Greece (2012) and Ukraine (2015) regained market access within two years of restructuring. Meanwhile, others remain locked out indefinitely.

There appears to be a correlation between the time it takes to recover market access and the severity of the haircut or loss experienced by bondholders. This is particularly true following haircuts greater than 50%. This may stem from a combination of reputational damage or the fact that larger losses signal deeper debt sustainability issues that take longer to resolve. Countries where default is perceived as beyond the government's control, such as in the case of natural disasters, tend to regain market access sooner, in about three years.

Market access often comes at the price of higher borrowing costs. On average, defaulters pay 3–4% more to borrow than non-defaulters, with spreads exceeding 5% for sovereigns that imposed large haircuts.[20] The higher coupons and more favorable contract terms suggest it may benefit investors to lend to serial defaulters despite the higher credit risk (see Chapter 15).

18.8 SUMMARY

This chapter focused on the outcomes of restructurings. It described the different types of offers debtors make and which are preferred by different categories of creditors. The discussion focused on how investors evaluate exchange offers, including the calculation of creditor losses and the treatment of past due interest. The relationship between exit yields and recovery, and how inter-creditor equity is assessed, was also described.

Negotiation strategies used by the sovereign and investors were reviewed. Carrots and sticks were described, together with the tools bondholders may utilize to engineer better outcomes for their clients. The risks and benefits of holding out were discussed together with some recent examples. The final section of the chapter covered life after restructuring, including the timing of credit rating upgrades and market re-access.

With this, we round up Part Four and now turn to Part Five, which discusses innovations and future trends in sovereign debt investing.

NOTES

1. Buchheit and Pam, "Uruguay's Innovations."
2. VRIs can be linked to commodities like the oil warrants issued by Venezuela in 1990, a basket of exports like Uruguay in 1991, future GDP as in Argentina (2005, 2010), and Ukraine (2015). The experience of creditors with VRIs has been mixed. See Lalo, *Important Innovations in Sovereign Finance* for an overview.
3. Also called the Sturzenegger and Zettelmeyer haircut (HSZ), this metric is used in much of the empirical academic literature. See Sturzenegger and Zettelmeyer, "Haircuts," and Martinez et al., *Sovereign Debt*.
4. Empirically, the average difference between the maximum and minimum haircuts across bonds is about 17% points, but it has been as high as 56%. Waever, *Looking Back to Look Ahead*.
5. This accrual applies even after the original maturity date of the bond. Post-judgement in NY (state) courts, it accrues at the statutory 9% rate, but as countries have the right to move suits to federal court, this rate has not been relevant historically.
6. In the Argentina (2020) and Ukraine (2015) restructurings, accrued interest was not subject to a haircut even as principal claims were. In Ecuador (2020), accrued interest was subject to a larger haircut than principal claims (14% versus 9%). In Argentina's (2005)

restructuring, any PDI accrued from December 31, 2001, onward was not recognized as a claim. Interest for the new exchange bonds accrued at the new, much lower, coupon rate from December 31, 2003, prior to the settlement of the exchange bonds. See Brauer, Martin, and Paja, *Emerging Market Sovereign Defaults Primer*, for examples of good, bad, and ugly treatment of PDI.

7. There is limited evidence that larger NPV losses bring the exit yield down. This goes against the idea that the bigger losses are inflicted on creditors, the lower the exit yield is due to fewer repayments.
8. See Lazard, *How to Make Sovereign Debt Restructurings More Effective*, for an overview of the calculation methodologies and the challenges of each approach. Buchheit and Gulati, "Enforcing Comparable Treatment," discuss enforcement in sovereign debt workouts.
9. The Paris Club compares the NPV of restructured claims with the NPV of existing old claims. An alternative methodology is to compare the NPV of restructured claims against the face value of the original outstanding claims. This would favor official creditors with low-interest concessional loans.
10. The Paris Club website calculates CoT across different restructuring packages, taking into account creditor preferences. See https://clubdeparis.org/en (accessed 31 July 2025).
11. Buchheit, "The Legal Context," and Buchheit et al., *How to Restructure Sovereign Debt*.
12. Brauer, Martin, and Paja, *Emerging Market Sovereign Defaults Primer.*
13. Other examples include insurance wraps for interest and/or principal payments by third parties such as the US International Development Finance Corp (DFC).
14. As the threshold for non-financial amendments is typically lower than the threshold for financial amendments, bondholders that agree to an exchange can also amend the terms of the old bond, requiring a simple majority to make them less attractive, and in some cases, less liquid than the new exchanged instruments. Changes can include the waiver of immunity, submission to foreign jurisdiction, listing requirements, deletion of the *pari passu* clause, removal of the acceleration remedy, or repeal of one or more events of default. Ecuador (2000) was the first case to use exit consents in sovereign debt restructurings.
15. In NML v. Argentina, NML used discovery orders to trace Argentina's global asset flows and tried to enforce judgments by targeting entities it argued were controlled by the Argentine state. The case set an important precedent in granting broad discovery rights to creditors under the US Foreign Sovereign Immunities Act (FSIA).
16. As of yet, CACs are only a feature of bonds, not loans. Bilateral loans (both commercial and official), syndicated loans, and sub-sovereign borrowings generally do not include CACs. As a result, holdout creditors can still be a significant risk to successful debt restructurings.
17. In Crystallex v. Venezuela (PDVSA and CITGO Case), Crystallex, a Canadian mining firm, secured a $1.4B arbitration award after Venezuela expropriated its assets. To enforce the award, Crystallex targeted PDVSA, Venezuela's state oil company, and its US-based subsidiary, CITGO. Crystallex argued that PDVSA was Venezuela's alter ego due to its lack of independence and use for sovereign purposes. A Delaware court agreed, ruling that PDVSA was Venezuela's alter ego under US law, enabling potential seizure of CITGO shares.
18. Even if the SOE is 100% owned by the sovereign, the enterprise's legal entity tends to be separate from that of the sovereign. Any legal basis for piercing the corporate veil must demonstrate that the entity is an extension of the sovereign and carries out activities in place of the sovereign unit.
19. Other costs of default include a decline in international trade via tariff and nontariff barriers, a drying up of trade credit, and possible reductions in foreign direct investment.
20. A one standard deviation increase in investor losses is associated with a medium-term increase in the costs of borrowing by 120 basis points. Still the effect diminishes with time and can no longer be detected after seven years. See Cruces and Trebesch, "Sovereign Defaults."

REFERENCES

Brauer, Jane, Lucas Martin, and Merveille Paja. *Emerging Market Sovereign Defaults Primer – A Survival Guide*. GEMs FI Strategy Viewpoint. Bank of America Global Research, 2022.

Buchheit, Lee C. "The Legal Context." In *Sovereign Debt Restructuring and Debt Sustainability*, BIS Papers No. 72, 41–48. Basel: Bank for International Settlements, 2013.

Buchheit, Lee C., and Mitu Gulati. "Enforcing Comparable Treatment in Sovereign Debt Workouts." *Capital Markets Law Journal* 18, no. 1 (January 2023): 71–77.

Buchheit, Lee C., and Jeremiah S. Pam. "Uruguay's Innovations." *Journal of International Banking Law and Regulation* 19, no. 1 (2004): 28–31.

Buchheit, Lee C., Guillaume Chabert, Chanda DeLong, and Jeromin Zettelmeyer. *How to Restructure Sovereign Debt: Lessons from Four Decades*. Peterson Institute for International Economics Working Paper 19-8, 2019.

Cruces, Juan J., and Christoph Trebesch. "Sovereign Defaults: The Price of Haircuts." *American Economic Journal: Macroeconomics* 5, no. 3 (2013): 85–117.

Lalo, Eric. *Important Innovations in Sovereign Finance: The Arrival of Macro-Linked Bonds (MLBs) and Governance-Linked Bonds (GLBs)*. Rothschild & Co., 2024. https://www.rothschildandco.com (accessed 31 July 2025).

Lazard. *How to Make Sovereign Debt Restructurings More Effective: Hold Warring Parties to a Better Standard of "Comparability."* Policy Brief, 2022. https://www.lazard.com/media/c5bb0n11/lazard-policy-brief-on-comparability-of-treatment-may-2022.pdf (accessed 31 July 2025).

Martinez, Leonardo, Francisco Roch, Francisco Roldán, and Jeromin Zettelmeyer. *Sovereign Debt*. IMF Working Paper WP/22/122, 2022.

Sturzenegger, Frederico, and Jeromin Zettelmeyer. "Haircuts: Estimating Investor Losses in Sovereign Debt Restructurings, 1998–2005." *Journal of International Money and Finance* 27, no. 5 (2008): 780–805.

Waever, Simon. *Looking Back to Look Ahead: Distressed EM Sovereign Credit Strategy*. Morgan Stanley, 2022.

PART FIVE

Innovations and Future Trends

CHAPTER NINETEEN

Sustainable Investing

EMERGING SOCIAL trends and new challenges for humanity are reshaping the traditional goals of investment portfolios. A key development is a focus on sustainable investing (SI), which impacts how investors evaluate, access, and manage sovereign risk and returns.

At its simplest, SI incorporates a broad array of additional considerations into investment decisions while also generating financial returns. In practice, SI can take many different forms, ranging from the integration of environmental, social, and governance (ESG) risks into investment decisions, influencing issuers to take a more sustainable approach in their practices, and impact investing related to achieving measurable outcomes.

There are several considerations when investing using a sustainability approach. Sustainability criteria need to be clearly defined, and legal and regulatory requirements for SI investments require strict adherence. Credit analysis has to be extended to incorporate ESG factors not typically included in sovereign fundamental analysis. Securities issued under an SI label need to be verified and monitored. Portfolio risk analysis and performance metrics need to be extended to incorporate SI risks and specified sustainability targets.

This chapter delves into these topics and summarizes the main issues in managing portfolios with sustainability mandates. SI in the sovereign debt space is a relatively new field and is continually evolving. As the breadth and depth of the available data and frameworks expand, so too will the ability of portfolio managers to better tailor portfolio risks to SI outcomes and objectives.

The chapter starts with an overview of sustainable investment strategies and types of SI-labeled instruments. Next, the construction and management of SI portfolios and how they may differ from traditional sovereign debt portfolios are discussed. Following this is an overview of SI and ESG regulation and the various categories of SI funds. How sovereign issuers are assessed on ESG criteria is discussed next, with a particular focus on environmental risk analysis. The chapter closes with a review of sustainability frameworks for sovereign bonds and a list of resources for further information.

19.1 SUSTAINABLE INVESTMENT STRATEGIES

Sustainable investing is a broad concept that means different things to different people.[1] SI investment strategies include negative and positive screening, ESG integration, impact investing, thematic investing, and investment stewardship, to name a few. The choice among them is influenced by asset owners' sustainability objectives and local regulations, and is enhanced by the availability of data, ESG standards, and taxonomies.

The early days of values-based investing employed *negative screening* as the primary tool to limit the investable universe. This strategy excludes issuers or sectors that do not meet specific criteria based on the client's preferences, values, or ethics. These *exclusions* may prevent investing in sectors like the tobacco, fossil fuel, or weapons industries based on ethical or environmental considerations.

Meanwhile, *positive screening* focuses on issuers or sectors that advance specific sustainability goals. It includes filters for *best-in-class* issuers or leaders in ESG practices relative to their peers. Issuers leading in renewable energy adoption, social inclusion, or governance would align with this objective.

A second category is *ESG integration*. This refers to the systematic and explicit inclusion of *financially material* ESG factors into traditional financial analysis and investing. Environmental factors might encompass a focus on climate risk, social factors could include health and education indicators, and governance factors may examine corruption levels and policy effectiveness. The aim is to mitigate risks that could affect the financial performance of issuers or instruments.

Thematic investing focuses on issuers or sectors that align with specific sustainability themes, such as clean energy or gender equality. Examples include investing in green energy companies, female-owned businesses, or sustainable infrastructure projects.

Net-zero investing is a thematic investing strategy that focuses on directing investments toward issuers, projects, or funds committed to achieving *net-zero* carbon emissions by a specific date, typically 2050. The goal is to minimize the carbon footprint of an investment portfolio as much as possible. The implementation of this strategy involves investing in clean energy, sustainable infrastructure, carbon capture technologies, or sovereign entities with strong climate mitigation and environmental policies.

A fourth category is impact investing, which aims to achieve positive outcomes such as improving access to education, clean water, or affordable housing. The strategy requires defining, measuring, and reporting the impact or outcome of the investment. The investor must demonstrate intentionality to drive positive change and assess effectiveness in achieving ex post outcomes. As such, it is a more time- and data-intensive approach with a longer investment cycle than other SI strategies.

A fifth category is *engagement and investment stewardship*. This strategy utilizes bondholder power to influence issuer behavior through interactions with key decision-makers. In the sovereign space, engagement occurs through industry-wide investor forums involving the government, central bank, and key stakeholders. Engagement can also happen via the new issue process when governments meet with investors to raise financing from the market.

Engaging with sovereigns is more complex than interacting with corporations. Investors possess limited power compared with corporate shareholders. Specifically, since governments are sovereign entities that pursue multiple goals, with financing being just one small part.

The main tool investors can utilize to influence government action is by voicing their concerns to policymakers. In extreme cases, investors can publicly divest from sovereign issuers when government policies do not align with broader sustainability goals. For instance, in 2019, several asset managers divested from Brazilian sovereign bonds and selected corporate issuers due to concerns about the government's deforestation policies.

The investment strategies mentioned here are not mutually exclusive and are frequently combined. For instance, ESG integration is often paired with positive and/or negative screening. Impact investing usually occurs alongside engagement and stewardship. The introduction of these criteria into investing strategies requires portfolio managers to consider and evaluate sustainability-driven risk factors in addition to the traditional metrics for generating financial returns.

At the firm level, the asset management industry has taken different approaches to SI mandates. An account-by-account approach applies the client's chosen sustainability theme only to that specific client's portfolios. Other firms take a thematic approach and avoid investing in particular sectors or issuers across all client portfolios. There are also firmwide approaches where each manager applies their own SI strategy to manage client assets.

Note that SI strategies are distinct from corporate responsibility activities pursued by asset management firms. These are rated on a scale of 1–5 by the UN PRI for signatories that demonstrate leading practices within the responsible investment industry.

19.2 INSTRUMENTS

Sovereign bonds linked to sustainability factors have become increasingly popular as governments aim to finance sustainable projects and achieve their sustainability goals. They range from *Use of Proceeds (UoP)* instruments to *Sustainability-Linked* or *Key Performance Indicator (KPI)–Linked* instruments. Collectively, these securities are called SI or ESG-labeled instruments. We discuss their key features and provide guidelines for investors interested in these opportunities.

19.2.1 Types of SI-Labeled Instruments

UoP instruments finance specific sustainability-themed activities. One of the first types of UoP securities was green bonds, issued by corporates looking to fund sustainable and green projects.[2] In 2017, France issued the first sovereign green bond, using the proceeds to finance energy transition, sustainable infrastructure, and climate change mitigation.

Other UoP instruments include *social bonds* that fund projects with social outcomes, such as affordable housing, healthcare, and education. *Sustainability bonds* are a blend of green and social bonds. An example is the 2021 EU sustainability bond, which financed efforts to combat climate change, promote economic recovery, and foster social cohesion.

Closely related is the *SDG bond*, whose proceeds finance projects aligned with the UN Sustainable Development Goals (SDGs). In 2020, Mexico became the first country to issue a sovereign bond linked explicitly to the SDGs. The bond aimed to finance programs aligned with the SDGs, demonstrating Mexico's commitment to the 2030 Agenda and sustainable development.

A second category of SI instruments is *sustainability-linked bonds (SLBs)*, where the issuer's financial and sustainability performance is tied to specific targets or KPIs over a given timeframe. Unlike UoP bonds, the proceeds from SLBs are not earmarked. Instead, the bond's terms—such as the coupon rate, maturity, or callability—are connected to the achievement of ESG targets.

This type of issuance can be suitable for issuers with strong SI credentials who seek to advance their sustainability journey. Chile issued the first sovereign SLB in 2022, with the bond's interest rate linked to progress in achieving its national climate targets. The bond featured a step-up coupon and pays a higher rate if Chile fails to meet its emission reduction and renewable energy generation goals.

Aside from UoP and SLB bonds, a number of innovative instruments are emerging in the SI-labeled space. *Debt-for-nature* and *debt-for-impact* swaps restructure or refinance a portion of a country's external debt in exchange for commitments to environmental or social outcomes. In 2023, Ecuador executed a landmark $1.6 billion *Galápagos Swap*, redirecting resources toward the preservation of one of the most ecologically sensitive areas on the planet. Meanwhile, in 2024, the Bahamas executed a $120+ million debt-for-nature swap focused on marine conservation.

Other hybrids are *super bonds* that combine characteristics of UoP bonds (such as green bonds) with *KPI-linked mechanics* (from SLBs). These instruments offer greater flexibility while maintaining the integrity of UoP accountability. Similarly, *transition bonds* (like Japan's 2024 climate transition bonds) provide financing for countries with high emission profiles but credible decarbonization plans. New forms of resilience-linked sovereign bonds, such as *catastrophe bonds* and those with hurricane clauses, are also gaining traction among frontier and climate-vulnerable issuers.

SI instruments are identified and labeled according to their compliance with third-party standards. These include the Climate Bond Initiative (CBI) certification, one of the most recognized standards for green bonds. Also important are the International Capital Markets Association (ICMA) labels that define the framework for SI-labeled instruments through the Green, Social, Sustainability, and SLB bond frameworks. Marketable securities are further labeled in Bloomberg following Bloomberg's internal sustainability labeling, which may not always align with the classification of individual investors.

SI-labeled instruments may trade with lower liquidity and higher bid-offers than conventional sovereign bonds. This may reflect their scarcity of supply, which could change as the market grows and deepens. Buyers of SI bonds tend to have specific SI mandates or are constrained by mandatory SI guidelines. Consequently, they prefer buy-to-hold strategies, further reducing the liquidity of these instruments compared to conventional bonds.

There is no consistent difference in the issuance yield of SI-labeled bonds compared to conventional bonds. In some instances, there is a *greenium* where the SI bond is issued at a lower yield than the conventional curve; in others, there is a concession with SI bonds being less expensive. The final pricing ultimately depends on market conditions, issuer specifics, and instrument structure.

19.2.2 Investor Checklist

SI-labeled sovereign bonds require careful evaluation of their sustainability objectives and issuer credentials. This ensures proceeds are indeed used as listed and minimizes greenwashing risks. The latter refers to behaviors or activities intended to create the impression that an entity or project contributes more to sustainable activities than it does in practice.

There are several factors for investors to consider. Issuer credentials should be assessed, in particular, their track record and commitment to sustainability. Emphasis should be placed on the scope of sustainable policies, policy implementation, future policy actions, ESG targets, and any failures to meet prior commitments.

Particular attention must be placed on assessing greenwashing risks. Their activities must be holistically evaluated for controversies, regardless of the instrument, project type, or theme. For instance, sovereign green bond issuers should be evaluated not only on their record in managing climate risk but also on their approach to human rights, treatment of minorities, and adherence to other sustainability parameters.

Next, the instrument's alignment with international SI taxonomies, standards, and frameworks should be evaluated. Most sovereign SI instruments are issued per the ICMA's standards, such as the Green Bond Principles (GBP), Social Bonds Principles (SBP), or Sustainability Bond Guidelines. Other established international frameworks for sovereign issues include the United Nations Sustainable Development Goals (SDGs), the EU Taxonomy, the International Sustainability Standards Board (ISSB) Frameworks, and the Climate Bonds Initiative Taxonomy. These frameworks ensure transparency, consistency in reporting, and best practices in constructing SI instruments.

It is essential to check whether the use of proceeds is exclusively for SI-related projects and that these are clearly defined. The best practice is to ringfence 100% of the proceeds, as funds are fungible across expenditure items in most government budgets. If the proceeds are only partially reserved for SI activities, the terms and ratios used for them should be stated. Another aspect to assess is how much of the proceeds will be used for refinancing existing debt versus funding new ESG-related activities. This is essential to evaluate the *additionality* of the investment, which refers to the extent to which the investment generates additional ESG-related activity.

For SLBs, bond terms should clearly define how KPIs or performance targets are determined and outline the follow-up actions (such as increases in coupon rates) if those targets are not met. Attention should also focus on whether the targets are ambitious or overly lenient. Since the use of proceeds in SLBs is completely fungible for the issuer, it is essential to consider their sustainability objectives and national development plans for transitioning to an improving trajectory.

Many instruments have third-party verification or certification. These assess whether the listed projects financed by the bonds align with the stated SI objectives and impact goals. This type of independent verification provides another layer of credibility.

Investors should seek detailed, measurable, and outcome-based impact reports with progress updates throughout the life of the bond. In some instances, these reports are certified by third-party auditors, but the issuer often produces them. Additionally, it is crucial to have governance frameworks for fund allocation to ensure alignment with the country's sustainability frameworks.

These checks and balances are vital for sovereign debt investors. Most SI fixed-income instruments have limited legal enforceability if funds are misused or targets are unmet. This arises as ESG requirements are rarely explicitly coded in legal documentation.[3] Once a bondholder has parted with their money, there is little they can do to influence a sovereign's behavior. The exception is for SLBs, where instrument features may change (e.g., coupon adjustments based on KPI triggers) and are included in the instrument documentation. This makes adhering to the checklist and ensuring the issuer has a solid commitment to sustainability critical.

PRO TIP: *Be weary of greenwashing risks by carrying out rigorous internal checks and cross-checking with third-party assessments of SI-labeled instruments and their issuers.*

19.3 CONSTRUCTING AND MANAGING SI PORTFOLIOS

Constructing SI portfolios follows the same principles as traditional portfolios, with adjustments to balance the additional considerations of sustainability factors with the portfolio's financial goals. Client mandate requirements, the sustainability approach, and definitions of sustainability play a central role.

In most cases, the investable universe is adjusted to exclude sovereigns with poor sustainability practices. Benchmarks (if any) are tailored with sustainable investing considerations for the chosen asset class. Portfolio construction and instrument selection are designed to meet SI targets such as the share of green bonds, carbon footprint, or net-zero goals. Attention is paid to greenwashing, red flags, and risks of forced sales. Finally, traditional performance and monitoring metrics are supplemented with impact reporting and engagement with issuers.

We discuss these factors below, emphasizing the key differences from traditional sovereign portfolio management.

19.3.1 Client Objectives

Similar to traditional sovereign debt portfolios, the asset owner's requirements and mandate guidelines play a crucial role in SI-themed portfolios. The SI strategy they choose will significantly influence the type of portfolio that must be constructed. The asset owner's definition of success and their perspective on any trade-off between sustainability and financial objectives should be clearly articulated.

The methodology and analytical tools available to the asset manager for achieving these goals should be clearly communicated to the client. For instance, if an ESG integration strategy is selected, the framework for assessing materiality should be explicitly described. If a thematic approach is the focus, then the expected outcomes and impact measures should be reviewed. This ensures both parties are aligned on the objectives of the portfolio from the outset.

Key questions for the asset owner include:

- *Definition of sustainability:* Does the client see sustainable investment (SI) primarily as a risk management tool or as a catalyst for change? In this context, clearly outlining the client's objectives and their success criteria, as well as the asset manager's ability to meet these goals, is beneficial.
- *Financial returns versus SI:* What priorities exist for obtaining financial returns versus fulfilling sustainability objectives? If a decision is required, which should be prioritized? Current research on whether SI supports or hinders financial returns is still in its early stages; thus, concrete conclusions should be cautiously approached.[4] In this case, the investor must assess the client's position when a trade-off is involved.
- *Exclusions:* What criteria define the investable universe? Some asset owners create their own exclusion lists. Others depend on asset managers or benchmark providers to identify issuers or sectors for exclusion. It is crucial to address how the exclusions in the benchmark affect tracking error and how the investment manager intends to minimize the adverse impact on performance.
- *SI targets:* How does the client define SI performance? This could involve setting a goal for the portfolio's SI/ESG score, the proportion of SI-labeled instruments, or metrics based on outcomes like carbon footprint or decarbonization score. In the case of thematic investments, specific targets may be established.
- *Reporting and monitoring:* What are the client's expectations regarding reporting and monitoring? The frequency, depth, and scope require discussion. Certain funds explicitly outline impact reporting criteria. If the client expects issuer engagement, it is essential to address the nature, focus, and frequency.
- *Controversies and red flags:* Are there specific issuers or sectors to avoid? What steps should be taken if holdings encounter controversies or red flags? Will the client initiate directed forced sales? How will underperformance against the benchmark be addressed in these situations?
- *Sensitivities and other considerations:* What are the client's opinions on tracking error and off-benchmark allocations? Are there specific instruments that should be avoided? What additional factors should the investment manager bear in mind?

Being clear about the client's requirements and how the SI strategy differs from traditional strategies in the same asset class lays a solid foundation for constructing and managing SI portfolios effectively.

PRO TIP: *Be clear on how sustainable investment portfolios differ from your traditional portfolios and the sources of any differences in risk metrics and performance.*

19.3.2 SI Sovereign Indices

Like traditional portfolio construction, SI investment strategies can be passive or actively managed, typically relative to a benchmark. Various SI-themed benchmarks for sovereign debt have been developed to help investors systematically incorporate ESG factors into their investment portfolios. These benchmarks can be utilized as part of either a passive or active investment strategy and share similar logistical and construction parameters with the traditional financial benchmarks we reviewed in Chapter 10.

There are several sustainability-themed index providers for sovereign debt. Some providers have developed versions of their flagship indices, while others have concentrated on specific themes such as climate change, natural resource management, social ESG factors, ESG-labeled instruments, and the sustainable debt asset class.

- *ESG-inclusive benchmarks* include traditional sovereign bond indices with an ESG overlay. This is achieved by incorporating ESG factors into the selection or weighting of sovereign bonds. Examples include the MSCI ESG Sovereign Index and the FTSE Russell ESG Sovereign Bond Index Series.
- *Sustainable sovereign debt benchmarks* focus on sovereign debt investments that specifically meet sustainability criteria, including climate goals, social considerations, and governance practices. Examples include the Bloomberg MSCI Green Bond Index and the S&P Green Bond Index.
- *Exclusionary benchmarks* exclude sovereign bonds from countries or regions with poor ESG performance. This may consist of issuers with weak ESG practices, such as high carbon emissions or poor human rights records. Examples include the Barclays MSCI ESG Sovereign Exclusion Index and the Vigeo Eiris Sovereign Bond Index.
- *Thematic ESG sovereign bond benchmarks* monitor sovereign instruments that are aligned with specific sustainability or thematic goals, such as addressing climate change, promoting human rights, or supporting social development. Examples include the FTSE Climate ESG Sovereign Index and the MSCI Low Carbon Sovereign Bond Index.
- *Region or subgroup benchmarks:* There are also ESG-focused sovereign bond indices specifically for emerging market economies, which may face unique ESG risks compared to developed economies. These include the J.P. Morgan ESG Emerging Markets Bond Index Suite and the MSCI Emerging Market ESG Sovereign Index.

There are several distinct features of sustainability indices. The first is the integration of ESG ratings into traditional index construction. ESG ratings are utilized to define the investable universe and to reweight index constituents in comparison to non-ESG versions. Understanding the methodology of index ratings and how it may differ from the investor's own ratings is crucial for identifying alpha opportunities.

The benchmark may be tilted toward sustainability-linked sectors such as renewables and include SI-labeled instruments like green, social, and sustainable bonds. If the investable securities in this universe are limited, this may constrain the investor's ability to gain exposure and trade the portfolio.

SI indices often exclude countries that do not meet a minimum threshold of standards, such as a poor record on human rights or a high dependency on fossil fuels. Exclusions may also be based on ESG ratings; for example, the lowest quintile of issuers is often excluded. In some instances, the client may impose additional exclusions, making it important to assess the tracking error and performance impact.

Fourth, there may be a greater emphasis on controversies and red flags when determining exits from the index compared to traditional benchmarks. The index rules and timing of exits may be quicker than those for traditional indices. Meanwhile, the binary nature of categorization might lead to more forced sales than would otherwise occur.

The appropriate benchmark is the one that aligns with the client's sustainability investment strategy *and* preferred exclusions. As noted previously, client exclusions not also excluded by the benchmark can result in significant tracking error and performance drag. Client-directed forced sales due to controversies or sensitivities can further affect alpha. Choosing the right benchmark and communicating performance expectations clearly is, therefore, crucial.

PRO TIP: *Look ahead and forecast issuers that may be excluded from benchmarks for poor sustainability practices.*

19.3.3 SI/ESG Targets

SI portfolios often include specific sustainability targets along with the usual performance and risk objectives. Common targets may consist of achieving an average ESG rating for the portfolio that exceeds the benchmark; establishing target exposures for SI-labeled instruments as a percentage of the portfolio; ensuring the portfolio's carbon footprint is lower than the benchmark; and setting issuer engagement targets to encourage them on their sustainability journey.

More specialized targets include alignment with the Paris Agreement, ensuring that the portfolio invests in bonds issued by countries transitioning to a low-carbon economy and supporting climate resilience. There may also be net-zero targets involving exposure to issuers aligned with net-zero emissions by a specific date.[5]

Impact targets may be set for impact-oriented funds. Impact measurement has been standardized by the Global Impact Investing Network (GIIN), whose IRIS+ is a system for measuring, managing, and optimizing impact.

19.3.4 Reporting and SI Risks

SI portfolios often have additional reporting requirements. The first type relates to the requirements of the regulatory jurisdiction. The second depends on the SI investment strategy and the asset owner's requirements. They may take the form of ex ante flagging of potential controversies or exclusions, utilizing forecasting tools for SI performance. They may involve ex post assessment of the use of proceeds and impact targets. There may also be requirements to demonstrate how the asset manager is progressing on their own sustainability journey.

SI-focused investments can present unique risks, such as greenwashing and red flag controversies. The portfolio manager needs to stay informed about the portfolio holdings, as well as what the SI ecosystem (via data providers, benchmark providers, and others) and the market consider poor SI practices. The investor must also strictly adhere to regulatory and legal requirements regarding their fiduciary duty and SI-related activities. These requirements are evolving and are continually being reassessed, necessitating continual review and oversight.

19.4 ESG REGULATIONS

ESG regulations vary by region, and no single global standard has been established. Understanding and staying updated on rules and legal requirements is essential. More so, as sustainability-related regulations and frameworks are evolving at different paces across the world.

Sustainability-related regulations have three primary objectives: promoting ESG practices, enhancing transparency, and establishing specific ESG standards. Regulation of investors focuses on adherence to fiduciary responsibility in incorporating material SI risks.[6] Another aspect ensures that investors perform due diligence to prevent greenwashing or the misrepresentation of sustainability-linked activities in their investments.

The best approach for investors to avoid these risks is to (i) seek the guidance of ESG experts in assessing issuers, securities, and projects, (ii) involve compliance and legal experts to help interpret ESG regulations, (iii) use common sense and ask questions when evaluating issuers' claims on ESG, and (iv) err on the side of caution in cases of doubt.

ESG disclosures for financial products and firms aim to ensure that ESG-labeled financial products accurately reflect the role, influence, and impact of sustainability factors in investments. *Taxonomies* focus on establishing standard definitions and methodologies for defining SI activities and projects. *Regulation of issuers' ESG disclosures* seeks to improve the availability, quality, and comparability of the information investors use. *Oversight of vendors providing ESG data and ratings* emphasizes the transparency of methodologies, assumptions, and processes related to conflicts of interest.

19.5 ESG FUND CLASSIFICATIONS

Some jurisdictions have established classifications for ESG funds that reflect the regulatory and legal requirements for sustainable investing.

The European Union's SFDR (Sustainable Finance Disclosure Regulation) is one of the most comprehensive frameworks in the world for classifying ESG funds. It requires financial market participants and financial advisors to disclose how sustainability risks are integrated into their investment processes and to categorize funds based on their ESG objectives. There are three main categories.

Article 6 Funds do not promote ESG principles and are not explicitly focused on sustainability. These include traditional sovereign debt funds without an ESG strategy. Article 8 Funds (Light Green) promote environmental or social characteristics but do not prioritize sustainable investment as their main goal. Funds that integrate ESG into issuer or instrument selection fall under this category. Article 9 Funds (Dark Green) are explicitly designed to achieve positive environmental and/or social outcomes and must meet strict criteria. For example, a fund focused on clean energy, renewable projects, or SDG-aligned investments would fall into this category.

In the US, ESG fund classifications are less formalized compared to the EU but are evolving. The SEC has introduced guidance on ESG disclosures and is increasingly advocating for more precise definitions and reporting requirements for ESG investments.

MorningStar, a leading investment research firm, has developed its own approach to classifying ESG funds. General ESG investment funds have ESG as a central focus but do not concentrate on a specific theme or area of action. Sustainability-themed investment products target specific ESG themes such as climate action, resource security, human development, healthy ecosystems, and basic needs. MorningStar also applies ESG Commitment labels to funds, which range from low to medium to high, indicating the funds' commitment to integrating ESG into their investment processes. MorningStar's Impact Focus label tracks how funds measure and report on their ESG impact.

19.6 SOVEREIGN ESG ASSESSMENTS

To invest based on sustainability criteria, sovereign issuers need to be marked on their ESG performance. This is determined through ESG assessments that evaluate an issuer, bond, or project based on its sustainability objectives and performance. They are typically represented as a *score or rating* and a detailed analysis of qualitative and thematic variables. These assessments are often enhanced by *red flag screens* identifying violations of key sustainability standards. Investor *engagement* with sovereigns adds further context regarding policy trajectories, forward-looking perspectives, and governance dynamics.

ESG scores are composite metrics of a country's environmental, social, and governance performance. Ecological factors include climate change risks, climate policy and adaptation, and natural resource management. Social factors encompass social stability and cohesion, human rights and labor standards, and demographic trends. Governance factors cover political stability, the rule of law and legal framework, public sector efficiency, and fiscal management. Table 19.1 shows examples of variables under each E, S, and G pillar. These scores are often translated into ESG ratings, which are peer-ranking metrics used to compare issuers.

19.6.1 Data Sources and Vendors

There are various ESG data and analytical sources. Multilateral organizations such as the World Bank, the IMF, and the UN maintain comprehensive cross-country databases

TABLE 19.1 Select ESG Rating Indicators

	ESG Pillar					
	Environment		Social		Governance	
Sub-Pillar	***Climate change and environmental risks***	▪ Exposure to extreme weather events, natural disasters, and long-term climate change impacts	***Social stability and cohesion***	▪ Poverty rates and inequality metrics ▪ Infant mortality, life expectancy, and health indicators ▪ Access to primary schooling and education indicators	***Political stability***	▪ Political system, governance quality, and institutional strength
	Climate policy and adaption	▪ Commitment to global climate agreements, carbon emissions reduction goals, renewable energy targets ▪ Carbon emissions per capita ▪ Renewable energy capacity ▪ Energy efficiency	***Human rights and labor standards***	▪ Assessment of human rights including freedom of expression ▪ Labor rights ▪ Treatment of minority groups	***Corruption***	▪ Corruption Perception Index
	Natural resource management	▪ Quality of management, overexploitation of resources, unsustainable policies ▪ Deforestation rates ▪ Air quality	***Demographic trends***	▪ Population aging ▪ Migration and urbanization trends	***Rule of law and legal framework***	▪ Quality of legal framework and judicial independence ▪ Enforcement of property rights
					Public sector efficiency and fiscal management	▪ Responsible management of public debt ▪ Effective policy making ▪ Assessment of bureaucracy and red tape

on ESG indicators with historical time series. These sources are generally free (with some paid options) but may experience long delays in data releases.

Academics, think tanks, and NGOs also compile data on various sustainability topics. Examples include the ASCOR initiative, which provides climate policy alignment metrics; the IADB green bond portal for data on green labeled securities; the World Bank ESG portal for data on ESG projects; Transparency International, which collects data on corruption indicators; and Freedom House, which includes information on political rights and civil liberties.

Private ESG vendors include specialist providers like Verisk Maplecroft and Sustainalytics, which compile detailed metrics across ESG variables across a panel of countries. These are complemented by thematic vendors focusing on climate change, human rights, or corruption. Credit rating agencies—Moody's, S&P, and Fitch—have also integrated ESG assessments into their sovereign credit evaluations (see Chapter 5).

Variation in vendor methodologies and approaches leads to greater score dispersion in ESG ratings compared to traditional credit ratings. This requires a more detailed and cautious approach when interpreting ESG ratings, ensuring thorough assessments and a clear understanding of any red flags or controversies associated with them.

In practice, sovereign debt investors assess an issuer or project's sustainability practices using a combination of proprietary frameworks and vendor-supplied evaluations. This approach enables a more precise definition of sustainability and enhances alignment with client preferences.

19.6.2 ESG Ratings in Action

ESG ratings are a useful input in the credit selection process but have limitations. Aggregation biases due to using large sets of variables may exaggerate or downplay serious ESG risks and obscure the actual drivers of the ESG rating. Small methodological changes can significantly affect the ESG rating, raising questions about the consistency of scores. These drawbacks underscore the importance of incorporating in-depth contextual analysis of ESG information alongside quantitative metrics to come to a wholistic assessment of an issuer's ESG credentials.

ESG assessments offer a comprehensive view of a sovereign's alignment with sustainability goals. Unlike credit ratings, which evaluate default probabilities and potential losses, they lack a single interpretation. As a result, they don't translate easily into a quantifiable financial impact for a portfolio. However, specific indicators, such as climate change risk, can act as proxies for long-term credit trends. Therefore, they should be seen as complementary to, rather than replacements for, sovereign credit ratings.

Empirically there is a clear income bias in sovereign ESG assessments. Higher-income countries typically receive better ESG scores due to their level of development, policy frameworks, and institutional strength. Consequently, a best-in-class approach directs investment flows to high-income countries that have less need for additional financing. In contrast, a negative screening approach excludes nations that require improvements in their ESG credentials. Therefore, using ESG scores to allocate capital within a sustainability framework necessitates adjustments for income groups.

The complexities increase when examining climate change risks. Many countries affected by climate change are often not the primary contributors to global climate issues. Emissions frequently stem from the level of economic development, highlighting the debate over a *just transition.*[7] Similarly, emissions from less-developed exporting economies often originate from the production of goods consumed by consumers in developed countries. These factors further reinforce the importance of adjusting for income, using data to attribute each country's contribution accurately, and understanding their future policy paths.

Sovereign engagement can enhance ESG assessments and help meet client requirements for impact in sustainable investment mandates. It can clarify policy trajectories, planned reforms, and shifts in governance that quantitative metrics often miss. Additionally, engagement allows investors to influence issuer behavior toward more ambitious sustainability standards, particularly in emerging and frontier economies.

19.7 ENVIRONMENTAL RISK ANALYSIS

Environmental analysis, which includes climate, biodiversity, and other nature-related risks, is an increasingly important focus for sovereign ESG and credit analysis. It entails assessing ecological hazards as part of ESG sovereign analysis, modeling impacts on the macroeconomy and credit indicators, and accurately accounting for each country's contribution to carbon emissions and global environmental risks. While climate risk has historically been a primary concern due to the Paris Agreement, there is a growing emphasis on nature-related and biodiversity risks in this analysis with the establishment of the Kunming-Montreal Global Biodiversity Framework (GBF).

Climate risk assessments categorize *physical risks*, such as the effects on economic activity from floods, wildfires, or rising sea levels, and *transition risks*, which stem from the move to a low-carbon economy. Key focus areas include a country's vulnerability to these risks, the economic consequences for critical sectors or regions, government policy responses, mitigation and adaptation strategies, and overall resilience, including infrastructure and social protection programs.

In addition to ESG scores and assessments, there are several other tools for evaluating climate-related risks for sovereigns:

- *The Network for Greening the Financial System (NGFS)* scenarios assess the potential impact of different levels of policy action across various global warming pathways.
- *The Climate Change Exposure Index (CCEI)* evaluates climate resilience by analyzing a nation's geography, susceptibility to extreme weather events, and degree of development.
- *Rating agencies produce specialized country reports* on climate-related risks and their resilience to environmental changes.

- *The Climate Transparency Report* assesses the progress of G20 countries regarding carbon emissions reductions, featuring accounting data and an analysis of national climate policies.
- *The Carbon Action Tracker (CAT)* evaluates governments' climate performance and the alignment of countries' pledges and actions with climate targets (e.g., the 1.5 °C or 2 °C targets).
- *The Partnership for Carbon Accounting Financials (PCAF)* methodology enables investors to estimate the carbon footprint or emissions of sovereign bond portfolios. It allocates a country's emissions proportionally based on the bond's exposure and aggregates them at the portfolio level. This enables portfolio managers to compare their portfolios against benchmarks and establish targets for Paris alignment and net-zero emissions.

19.8 SUMMARY

Sustainable investing is a growing component of investing across fixed-income and other asset classes. This chapter reviewed various sustainable investing strategies and the newly emerging instruments used in sovereign debt portfolios. Sustainability standards and frameworks, which play an essential role in classifying SI instruments, were also described.

Portfolio construction in SI mandates differs in some aspects from traditional fixed-income mandates. The chapter emphasized the key elements to consider when aligning with the client's SI objectives. SI benchmarks, SI portfolio targets, and reporting requirements were also discussed.

SI or ESG regulation is moving rapidly and at varying speeds across the world. In this context, the main types of regulation and various ESG fund classifications were reviewed. The chapter closed with an overview of ESG sovereign analysis, data requirements, and resources for environmental risk assessment.

NOTES

1. See UN PRI, *Definitions for Responsible Investment Approaches*, and Citibank, *SI Primer Deck*, for further details.
2. Variants of green bonds are green sukuks (a Shariah-compliant version of green bonds, like Malaysia's 2017 green sukuk); and blue bonds, which focus on projects related to ocean and water conservation, like the Seychelles Blue Bond of 2018.
3. See Curtis, Gulati, and Weidemaier, "Green Bonds, Empty Promises."
4. Academic research suggests a positive link between ESG and a lower cost of sovereign debt, particularly the governance and social pillars. See UN PRI, *A Practical Guide to ESG Integration*, and J.P. Morgan Global ESG Research, *ESG First Principles*.
5. Net zero means that any carbon emissions produced by the issuer are either offset or counterbalanced by actions that remove an equivalent amount of carbon from the atmosphere. This can be through carbon capture, reforestation, or other nature-based solutions. See IIGCC, *Sovereign Bonds and Country Pathways; Target Setting and Implementation Guidance*; and *Making NDCs Investable*.

6. For example, the EU's Sustainable Finance Disclosure Regulation explicitly directs fiduciaries to incorporate ESG factors if they are financially material.
7. A just transition is defined as ensuring that no one is left behind or pushed behind in the transition to low-carbon and environmentally sustainable economies and societies.

REFERENCES

Citibank. *SI Primer Deck: Where SI Came From, What It Means and Where It's Going.* Citi Research, 2019.

Curtis, Quinn, Mitu Gulati, and Mark C. Weidemaier. "Green Bonds, Empty Promises." *North Carolina Law Review* 2023. Virginia Public Law and Legal Theory Research Paper No. 2023-14, Virginia Law and Economics Research Paper No. 2023-05, UNC Legal Studies Research Paper No. 4350209. Available at SSRN: https://ssrn.com/abstract=4350209 or http://dx.doi.org/10.2139/ssrn.4350209 (accessed 1 August 2025).

Institutional Investors Group on Climate Change (IIGCC). *Sovereign Bonds and Country Pathways: Towards Greater Integration of Sovereign Bonds into Net Zero Investment Strategies.* April 2024.

Institutional Investors Group on Climate Change (IIGCC). *Sovereign Bonds & Country Pathways: Target Setting and Implementation Guidance.* April 2024.

Institutional Investors Group on Climate Change (IIGCC). *Making NDCs Investable – The Investor Perspective.* June 2024.

J.P. Morgan Global ESG Research. *ESG First Principles: A Comprehensive Guide to ESG Strategies, Regulations, and Data.* 2022. www.jpmorganmarkets.com (accessed 1 August 2025).

UN PRI Sovereign Debt Advisory Committee. *A Practical Guide to ESG Integration in Sovereign Debt.* London: UN Principles for Responsible Investment, 2019. https://www.unpri.org/fixed-income/a-practical-guide-to-esg-integration-in-sovereign-debt/4781.article (accessed 1 August 2025).

UN PRI Sovereign Debt Advisory Committee. *ESG Engagement for Sovereign Debt Investors.* London: UN Principles for Responsible Investment, 2020. https://www.unpri.org/sovereign-debt/esg-engagement-for-sovereign-debt-investors/6687.article (accessed 1 August 2025).

UN PRI Sovereign Debt Advisory Committee. *Human Rights in Sovereign Debt: The Role of Investors.* London: UN Principles for Responsible Investment, 2022. https://www.unpri.org/sovereign-debt/human-rights-in-sovereign-debt-the-role-of-investors/9151.article (accessed 1 August 2025).

UN PRI. *Bringing ESG Factors into Sovereign Debt Indices.* Podcast transcript. London: UN Principles for Responsible Investment, 2022. https://www.unpri.org/the-pri-podcast/bringing-esg-factors-into-sovereign-debt-indices/10189.article (accessed 1 August 2025).

UN PRI. *Considering Climate Change in Sovereign Debt.* London: UN Principles for Responsible Investment, 2023. https://www.unpri.org/sovereign-debt/considering-climate-change-in-sovereign-debt/11894.article (accessed 1 August 2025).

UN PRI. *Definitions for Responsible Investment Approaches.* London: UN Principles for Responsible Investment, 2023. https://www.unpri.org/investment-tools/definitions-for-responsible-investment-approaches/11874.article (accessed 1 August 2025).

CHAPTER TWENTY

The Next Frontier: Digitization, AI, and Big Data

SOVEREIGN BOND markets are on the cusp of a major transformation. Advances in financial technology, debt structure design, market access platforms, and AI-powered analytics are changing the way sovereign debt is issued, traded, analyzed, and managed.

The adoption of blockchain technology is increasing transparency, efficiency, and security in debt issuance and trading. Digitization of markets and the use of advanced trading platforms are expanding market access and liquidity, especially in emerging markets. Innovations in bond design, such as sustainability-linked and catastrophe bonds, are providing new ways to align investor returns with policy goals and risk mitigation. The integration of machine learning and AI-driven risk models is improving the ability of portfolio managers to analyze complex macroeconomic signals and anticipate shifts in sovereign creditworthiness more accurately.

Together, these trends point to a more dynamic, data-driven future for sovereign debt investing—one that presents both opportunities and challenges for portfolio managers operating in a changing global landscape. This chapter delves into these innovations and their potential paths forward, examining the tools and capabilities portfolio managers will require to adapt to this shifting landscape.

20.1 BLOCKCHAIN AND DIGITIZATION

Breakthroughs in digitization and blockchain technology are changing the game for sovereign debt issuance, trading, and settlement. These advancements can boost transparency, efficiency, and investor access but also bring new regulatory, infrastructure, and technology adoption challenges. This section explores the changing landscape of digital sovereign bonds, blockchain's role in public debt markets, and what it means for portfolio managers.

20.1.1 Digitization of Sovereign Bond Markets

For a long time, issuing, trading, and settling sovereign bonds has been an involved, paper-heavy process. One major innovation at the end of the 20th century was dematerialization, which turned physical securities like share certificates into electronic format and stored them in digital accounts. Now, digitization and blockchain technology are further transforming these processes.

Digitization is the process of turning traditional, often paper-based, financial processes into digital formats. Digital platforms have made it easier for governments to issue sovereign bonds using electronic systems to sell bonds directly to investors. This streamlines the issuance process and reduces the need for intermediaries like primary dealers.

Platforms like the US Treasury's TreasuryDirect allow retail investors to buy bonds directly, bypassing traditional brokerages. This infrastructure is gradually being made available across the world in emerging and frontier markets. This democratization broadens the investor base, enhances liquidity in sovereign bond markets, and enables investors to access sovereign bonds from international markets more easily.

20.1.2 Blockchain Applications for Sovereign Bonds

Blockchain technology, a decentralized and immutable ledger system, is reshaping the infrastructure of sovereign bond markets. By using blockchain, *digital bonds* can be created and issued as tokenized assets, simplifying processes, speeding up settlement, and improving transparency in custody. Smart contracts can automate coupon payments and redemptions, reducing administrative costs and errors.

Governments and financial institutions are testing the potential of blockchain for issuing digital bonds. In 2018, the World Bank introduced Bond-i (Blockchain Operated New Debt Instrument), raising A$110 million on a private Ethereum-based platform.[1] This marked the world's first digital bond to be created, allocated, transferred, and managed throughout its life cycle using blockchain technology.

A notable benefit of blockchain and digital bond issuance is tokenization. This permits fractional ownership, enabling investors to purchase smaller denominations than traditional bonds, which often have high minimum investment thresholds. This democratizes access to sovereign bond markets, allowing retail investors and smaller institutions to participate, which could potentially increase market liquidity.

In 2020, the Bank of Thailand launched a blockchain-based platform for issuing digital savings bonds.[2] The bonds were tokenized, allowing fractional ownership as low as $30, and targeted retail investors through Krung Thai Bank's blockchain platform. Since then, the government has expanded blockchain infrastructure more broadly.

Blockchain-based bonds may be integrated with central bank digital currencies (CBDCs), allowing for smooth cross-border transactions and further reducing counterparty risk. In 2021, the European Investment Bank (EIB) issued a $100 million two-year digital bond on the Ethereum network blockchain.[3] The bond was settled using the central bank digital currency provided by the Banque de France. These innovations are monitored in the ICMA Tracker of New FinTech Applications in Bond Markets.[4]

For portfolio managers, blockchain-based bonds offer enhanced transparency. Every transaction—issuance, transfer, or redemption—is recorded on the blockchain, creating an auditable trail. This minimizes the risk of fraud and ensures adherence to regulatory requirements, such as anti-money laundering (AML) and know-your-customer (KYC) rules.

Blockchain facilitates faster settlement and reduces counterparty risk. Traditional bond settlement processes, often performed through clearinghouses, can take days (T + 2 or longer). Blockchain allows for near-instantaneous settlement (T + 0) by removing intermediaries. Portfolio managers access liquidity through faster settlement, which is vital in volatile markets. Moreover, blockchain's decentralized nature minimizes dependence on centralized clearinghouses, reducing systemic risk.

However, operational challenges exist, such as the need to adopt new technology, uncertain regulations, and cybersecurity threats. To make the most of digital and blockchain tools, asset managers need to invest in technology training and infrastructure. Smaller firms with limited resources may struggle, placing them at a competitive disadvantage.

The regulatory landscape for blockchain bonds and tokenized assets is rapidly evolving. Portfolio managers must navigate diverse issues such as the classification of tokenized assets under securities laws and also stay informed about new and changing regulations like the EU's Markets in Crypto-Assets (MiCA) framework and the US's GENIUS Act to ensure compliance.

Security and risk management are also key concerns. Although blockchain is inherently secure, digital platforms remain vulnerable to cyber threats. To safeguard client assets and data, managers need to implement strong cybersecurity measures.

Blockchain's transparency and immutability improve risk management by offering a clear record of transactions. However, portfolio managers must tackle new risks, such as vulnerabilities in smart contracts or the possibility of disruptions to blockchain networks. Furthermore, the volatility of tokenized assets, particularly in emerging markets, demands close monitoring.

The adoption of digitization and blockchain in sovereign bond investing is still in its early stages, but the trajectory is clear. To keep up, portfolio managers must adapt to this new paradigm by building expertise in digital and blockchain technologies. Those who successfully incorporate these tools into their workflows will gain a competitive edge, with lower costs, faster execution, and greater transparency. However, they must also navigate the challenges of regulatory compliance and technological complexity to fully benefit from these opportunities.

PRO TIP: *Set up notifications on ICMAs Tracker to keep abreast of new digital bonds and structures.*

20.2 INNOVATIONS IN DEBT STRUCTURES

There have been several innovations in sovereign bond design. These include the issuance of tokenized and digital bonds, the growth of sustainable-labeled instruments, increased use of catastrophe and state-contingent structures, and renewed interest in blended finance and credit enhancement.

20.2.1 Tokenized and Digital Sovereign Bonds

Tokenized digital sovereign bonds are a game-changer in sovereign debt markets. They offer real-time settlement (T + 0), smart contract-enabled coupons, fractional ownership, and programmable access. These features can boost operational efficiency and attract new investors, but they also create new risks tied to platform security, custody, and regulation.

For portfolio managers, the key takeaway is to prepare for hybrid custody infrastructure, evaluate on-chain and off-chain pricing and credit analytics, and stay on top of changing regulatory frameworks for tokenized securities.

20.2.2 Sustainable Investing Bonds

The rise of sustainable investing has spurred the growth of green and sustainable sovereign bonds, as discussed in Chapter 19. These instruments finance projects that address climate change, social development initiatives such as health and education, and various ESG-themed activities. These bonds appeal to sustainability-focused investors, thereby expanding the investor base for sovereign debt.

These bonds are set up as *Use of Proceeds* bonds, *KPI-linked* instruments, or super bonds that blend elements of both. In the future, sustainable-labeled bonds might include performance-based metrics, such as carbon reduction targets, verified by blockchain or IoT (Internet of Things) sensors. This would boost accountability and attract impact-driven investors.

For portfolio managers, the key to sustainable investing is to integrate sovereign-level sustainability and climate performance analytics, impact modeling, and real-time verification metrics for the indicators driving these instruments.

20.2.3 State-Contingent Debt Instruments

State-contingent debt instruments (SCDIs) are also gaining traction. Climate-vulnerable countries are issuing catastrophe bonds and including hurricane clauses in bond contracts. These features provide temporary relief from debt service following extreme events or economic shocks. In doing so, they transfer some of the risk to investors and give countries temporary and automatic debt relief.

Barbados's 2019 restructured sovereign bond includes a catastrophe clause that lets the government defer debt service payments for up to two years if a natural disaster, like a hurricane, triggers a qualifying insurance payout. This clause, the first of its kind in a sovereign Eurobond, has since become a model for climate-resilient debt instruments in vulnerable countries.

Similarly, St. Vincent and the Grenadines and Grenada have added natural disaster clauses to their debt agreements. The emergence of these instruments means that risk modeling tools must consider climate tail risk, parametric triggers, and expected coupon variation under stochastic catastrophe models.

These are closely related to new variations of value recovery instruments (VRIs). Traditionally, VRIs have been tied to GDP or commodities like oil. In recent restructuring efforts, VRIs have been refined to adjust debt repayments based on economic performance and the adoption of governance targets.

In Sri Lanka's 2024 debt restructuring, Macro-Linked Bonds (MLBs) and Governance-Linked Bonds (GLBs) were introduced. The MLBs adjust payments based on GDP thresholds, providing symmetric upside and downside adjustments to align with economic outcomes. The main difference from traditional GDP warrants is the symmetric adjustment, giving relief if outcomes are worse than expected. Meanwhile, the GLBs reduce interest rates by 75 basis points if Sri Lanka meets governance targets, such as government revenue-to-GDP ratios and fiscal transparency, by 2028.

It is expected that these innovations in VRIs will remain a component of sovereign debt restructurings in the future.

20.2.4 Blended Finance and Credit Enhancement

Blended finance and credit enhancement have seen renewed interest after a decline in the 2000s following the success of the Brady Plan. To attract private capital for climate action and development finance in emerging markets, multilateral development banks and development finance institutions are now offering partial guarantees, insurance wraps, and subordinated capital tranches.

These enhancements can partly mitigate the risks associated with investing in frontier markets. Their benefits must be weighed against a careful evaluation of how the guarantees are activated and whether the pricing of these instruments remains attractive after accounting for the credit uplift.

20.3 TECHNOLOGICAL TRANSFORMATION OF MARKET ACCESS AND TRADING

Advances in technology, including the use of digital trading platforms and electronic trading, are transforming market access and trading.

The digitization of trading platforms—such as Bloomberg ET, MarketAxess, and MTS—is reducing friction in price discovery and secondary market trading of sovereign debt (see Chapter 9). The main benefits include tighter bid-ask spreads, greater transparency, automated RFQ execution and trade analytics, and enhanced liquidity monitoring tools.

Portfolio managers can access live market data, execute trades instantly, and monitor bond yields precisely. Digital repositories store bond data, like coupon rates and credit ratings, in accessible formats for quicker portfolio rebalancing. For example, managers can use digital dashboards to visualize yield curves or stress-test portfolios against interest rate changes for proactive decision-making.

Decentralized finance (DeFi) platforms, which are built on blockchain, may eventually shake up traditional sovereign bond markets by allowing peer-to-peer trading and lending. DeFi protocols could enable investors to lend directly to governments or trade tokenized bonds without intermediaries, cutting costs and expanding market access. However, portfolio managers will need to navigate DeFi's regulatory uncertainty and security risks, including vulnerabilities in smart contracts.

20.4 UTILIZATION OF MACHINE LEARNING AND AI-BASED RISK MODELS

As data availability and computational power have grown, portfolio managers are increasingly turning to machine learning (ML) and artificial intelligence (AI) to enhance sovereign bond investing. This section introduces the application of big data and ML techniques for sovereign credit analysis, including the use of alternative data sources, predictive models for credit events, and country-specific risk scoring. It also examines how AI-driven tools are being applied to bond selection and relative value strategies, enabling more dynamic and data-rich assessments of pricing, liquidity, and spread risk. These innovations are reshaping how investors monitor risk, allocate capital, and generate alpha in sovereign bond markets.

20.4.1 Leveraging Big Data for Macro and Sovereign Credit Analysis

Big data, marked by its huge volume, fast velocity, and diverse variety, is transforming how portfolio managers assess macroeconomic trends and sovereign credit risks. By tapping into massive datasets and cutting-edge analytics, big data allows for more in-depth and quicker insights into economic conditions and sovereign bond performance. The techniques draw from various sources, including economic indicators, social media, satellite images, and transactional data.

Typically, traditional macroeconomic indicators like GDP or inflation come out with a delay. Big data provides real-time alternatives, such as credit card transactions or online retail sales, which quickly show consumer spending trends. For instance, economists can use real-time data to gauge the impact of a central bank rate hike on consumer behavior or mortgage financing within a few days, rather than waiting for monthly data to be released. This allows for faster analysis of how policy changes affect the macroeconomy and markets.

Using alternative data sources, like satellite imagery, can offer new insights into economic activity. Data on port traffic or agricultural output can help forecast growth, trade, and sovereign credit risk. For example, a decline in port activity in an emerging market might indicate an economic slowdown, prompting portfolio managers to make interest rate, yield curve, or currency trades. Similarly, web traffic and job postings can provide more detailed information on employment trends, which can enhance macroeconomic analysis.

Big data allows for sentiment analysis on social media, providing real-time insights into public opinion and political stability. By examining posts and trends, sovereign analysts can assess the likelihood of changes in governance or social unrest that could affect markets and bond yields. For instance, a surge in anti-government sentiment in a country might indicate higher credit risk and the potential for wider sovereign credit spreads.

Big data also facilitates the development of predictive models that evaluate sovereign credit risk by using thousands of variables, such as debt-to-GDP ratios, foreign exchange reserves, and geopolitical events. When combined with machine learning algorithms, these models can identify patterns in changes in credit ratings and historical defaults, enhancing the accuracy of credit risk assessments.

20.4.2 AI Tools and Analytics

Artificial intelligence technologies, including machine learning, natural language processing, and predictive analytics, are transforming how institutional investors assess and manage their sovereign bond portfolios.

Machine learning models can quickly forecast changes in the yield curve by examining past data and key economic factors, like inflation, GDP growth, and central bank policies. For instance, a machine learning model might predict market trends based on forecasted data inputs, allowing portfolio managers to adjust positions. It could also spot patterns in yield spreads between developed and emerging market bonds, allowing managers to fine-tune their portfolio allocations.

Natural Language Processing (NLP) tools analyze news articles, central bank statements, and social media to gauge market sentiment. For instance, NLP can extract sentiment from a central bank governor's speech to predict policy changes that may affect bond yields. Portfolio managers can use these insights to anticipate market movements and adjust their strategies accordingly.

Predictive analytics assist portfolio managers in evaluating sovereign credit risk by modeling scenarios rooted in macroeconomic indicators and geopolitical events. For instance, AI models can simulate the effects of a sovereign default or currency devaluation on bond portfolios, allowing managers to hedge risks effectively.

Together, these tools empower portfolio managers to proactively make investment decisions, conduct enhanced sovereign credit and macroeconomic assessments, and better optimize portfolio holdings.

In the future, AI could enable real-time portfolio rebalancing by automatically adjusting bond allocations based on market signals. Portfolio managers must adopt AI platforms and develop expertise in interpreting model outputs to leverage these capabilities effectively.

While these opportunities exist, they also come with challenges. Adopting AI and digital tools demands a significant investment in infrastructure and training, which may be tough for smaller firms to match. Investors can be overwhelmed by data overload, needing advanced tools to sift through and analyze the relevant information. Since AI models depend on high-quality data, using incorrect or biased data can result in flawed predictions, affecting investment results. Utilizing alternative data, such as consumer spending or social media, also raises concerns about privacy.

More broadly, asset managers must ensure that digital and AI tools comply with regulations such as the EU's Markets in Financial Instruments Directive (MiFID II). This particularly relates to data privacy and transparency, per the General Data Protection Regulation (GDPR).

20.5 IMPLICATIONS FOR PORTFOLIO MANAGERS

The innovations in sovereign debt instruments and investing have profound implications for portfolio managers, reshaping their trading and execution infrastructure, investment strategies, operations, and risk management practices.

As sovereign debt investing evolves, portfolio managers will require a set of specialized tools to navigate the future. These tools include platforms like Ethereum and Hyperledger, which can manage tokenized bonds and facilitate secure issuance, trading, and settlement. To ensure smooth operations, portfolio managers must integrate these blockchain platforms with their existing systems.

To leverage AI and ML analytics, platforms such as Bloomberg or proprietary AI models are necessary. These tools are used for yield curve prediction, credit risk assessment, and portfolio optimization and should facilitate real-time data integration and scenario analysis.

ESG analytics software and tools are also needed to assess the impact of green, social, and sustainability-linked bonds and their compliance with sustainability standards and frameworks for effective monitoring of sustainable investments.

Finally, enhanced cybersecurity frameworks should be implemented to protect digital bond transactions and AI-driven portfolios from cyberattacks, ensuring data integrity and client trust. Additionally, there should be increased regulatory and compliance oversight for tokenized and digital assets.

20.6 SUMMARY

This chapter examined the future of sovereign debt investing through the lens of technological advancement and structural innovation. It explored how blockchain and digitization are transforming sovereign debt issuance, settlement, and transparency, while innovations in sovereign debt structures, such as sustainability-linked bonds and state-contingent debt, are redefining risk-sharing.

The rise of digital platforms and e-trading is expanding market access, improving liquidity, and reducing transaction costs, particularly in emerging and frontier markets. We are at the initial stages of this transformation, which is proceeding rapidly. Meanwhile, the adoption of machine learning and AI-driven risk models is enhancing sovereign credit analysis by enabling faster, more nuanced interpretation of complex data.

Together, these developments are reshaping the tools, strategies, and responsibilities of portfolio managers, requiring them to adapt to a more data-centric, real-time investment environment while opening up new and diverse markets for investing.

NOTES

1. World Bank, *World Bank Prices First Global Blockchain Bond*, 2018.
2. IBM, *Bank of Thailand Launches World's First Government Savings Bond*, 2020; and https://www.bot.or.th/content/dam/bot/documents/en/news-and-media/news-pdf/2020/n5963e.pdf (accessed 22 August 2025).
3. European Investment Bank, *EIB Issues Its First Ever Digital Bond*, 2021.
4. https://www.icmagroup.org/fintech-and-digitalisation/fintech-resources/tracker-of-new-fintech-applications-in-bond-markets (accessed 22 August 2025).

REFERENCES

European Investment Bank. *EIB Issues Its First Ever Digital Bond on a Public Blockchain*. Luxembourg: EIB Group, April 2021. https://www.eib.org/en/investor-relations/press/all/fi-2021-19-eib-first-digital-bond-on-public-blockchain? (accessed 1 August 2025).

IBM. *Bank of Thailand Launches World's First Government Savings Bond on IBM Blockchain Technology*. October 5, 2020. https://newsroom.ibm.com/2020-10-05-Bank-of-Thailand-Launches-Worlds-First-Government-Savings-Bond-on-IBM-Blockchain-Technology (accessed 1 August 2025).

World Bank. *World Bank Prices First Global Blockchain Bond, Raising A$110 Million*. Press release, August 23, 2018. https://www.worldbank.org/en/news/press-release/2018/08/23/world-bank-prices-first-global-blockchain-bond-raising-a110-million (accessed 1 August 2025).

Acknowledgments

This book is the result of many conversations, debates, and insights generously shared by investment professionals, researchers, and policymakers across the sovereign debt and investment communities. The focus of these efforts has been on improving understanding of sovereign debt markets and managing risk more effectively.

I am particularly thankful to Lee Buchheit, Joyce Chang, Pramol Dhawan, Emmanuel Roman, and Jeromin Zettelmeyer for their thoughtful feedback and guidance at critical stages. Tony Crescenzi offered early encouragement for the initial idea and provided crucial guidance on navigating the publishing industry. A special thanks to Judith Newlin, who believed in the initial concept and saw it through to completion.

I am also grateful to Monia Bianco, Amer Biset, Jane Brauer, Richard Burdekin, Sarah Carlson, Guillaume Chabert, Richard Clarida, Damon Clark, Luis Costa, Michael Davidson, Giovanni Dell'Ariccia, Aitor Erce, Tom Fallon, Mark Flanagan, Jan Friederich, Rex Ghosh, Jonny Goulden, Mitu Gulati, Sean Hagan, David Hauner, Gloria Kim, Frank Laurent, Fernando Llosado, Gregory Makoff, Samy Muaddi, Jonathan Munro, Lucas Martin, Samuel Mary, Jens Nystedt, Carmen Nuzzo, Luis Oganes, Ed Parker, Kumaran Ram, Valentina Ramírez, Carmen Reinhart, Shelly Shetty, Michael Story, Joseph Stiglitz, Murat Ulgen, Simon Waever, and Mark Weidemaier for their contributions.

Finally, I would like to thank the editorial and publishing team at Wiley Finance for their guidance, patience, and professionalism throughout this process. Any errors or oversights are mine alone.

About the Author

Dr. Lupin Rahman is a leading expert in sovereign debt and emerging market economics, with over two decades of experience in global financial markets. She has held senior positions in asset management, international financial institutions, and policy advisory roles, combining deep analytical insight with hands-on experience in sovereign bond portfolio management. Her work spans emerging markets, macroeconomic research, debt sustainability analysis, crisis resolution, and sustainable investing, making her uniquely placed to guide readers through the complexities of sovereign bond investing.

Educated at the London School of Economics, Dr. Rahman holds a PhD in Economics. As the Head of Emerging Markets Sovereign Credit and a member of the ESG Leadership team at PIMCO, Dr. Rahman drove innovative strategies in sovereign debt investing, leveraging her deep understanding of economic policy and market dynamics. At the International Monetary Fund and the World Bank Group, she shaped global debt sustainability frameworks and advised on sovereign borrowing strategies. Her writing reflects a balance of academic rigor and practitioner relevance, offering readers a thoughtful and practical perspective on sovereign debt markets. With a long-standing commitment to knowledge sharing and mentoring, this book is a culmination of years of professional insight, aiming to support the next generation of portfolio managers and policymakers alike.

Index

Note: Page numbers in *italics* and **bold** refers to figures and tables respectively.